Social Influence
Processes and Prevention

SOCIAL PSYCHOLOGICAL APPLICATIONS TO SOCIAL ISSUES

Published under the auspices of the
Society for the Psychological Study of Social Issues

Volume 1   SOCIAL INFLUENCE PROCESSES AND PREVENTION
Edited by John Edwards, R. Scott Tindale,
Linda Heath, and Emil J. Posavac

A Continuation Order Plan is available for this series. A continuation order will bring delivery of each new volume immediately upon publication. Volumes are billed only upon actual shipment. For further information please contact the publisher.

Social Influence Processes and Prevention

Edited by

John Edwards, R. Scott Tindale,
Linda Heath, and Emil J. Posavac
Loyola University of Chicago
Chicago, Illinois

A project of the faculty and students
in the Applied Social Psychology Graduate Program
at Loyola University of Chicago
published under the auspices of the
Society for the Psychological Study of Social Issues

Plenum Press • New York and London

mc

Library of Congress Cataloging-in-Publication Data

Social influence processes and prevention / edited by John Edwards ...
[et al.].
       p.   cm. -- (Social psychological applications to social issues
; v. 1)
   "A project of the faculty and students in the Applied Social
Psychology Graduate Program at Loyola University of Chicago and
published under the auspices of the Society for the Psychological
Study of Social Issues."
   Includes bibliographical references.
   ISBN 0-306-43293-5
   1. Deviant behavior--Prevention. 2. Health promotion. 3. Social
pressure.   I. Edwards, John (John David) II. Society for the
Psychological Study of Social Issues. III. Series.
HM291.S58837 1990
362'.0424--dc20   89-23236
                                                                CIP

© 1990 Plenum Press, New York
A Division of Plenum Publishing Corporation
233 Spring Street, New York, N.Y. 10013

Printed in the United States of America

7—24—91

Contributors

Elliot Aronson, Department of Psychology, Stevenson College, University of California, Santa Cruz, California 95064

Andrew S. Baum, School of Medicine, Uniformed Services University of the Health Sciences, Bethesda, Maryland 20814

Constance L. Cappas, Department of Psychology, Bowling Green State University, Bowling Green, Ohio 43403

Eric F. Dubow, Department of Psychology, Bowling Green State University, Bowling Green, Ohio 43403

John Edwards, Department of Psychology, Loyola University of Chicago, Chicago, Illinois 60626

Richard I. Evans, Department of Psychology, University of Houston, Houston, Texas 77204

Joan E. Finegan, Centre for Administrative and Information Studies, University of Western Ontario, London, Ontario, Canada N6A 5C2

Jeffrey D. Fisher, Department of Psychology, University of Connecticut, Storrs, Connecticut 06260-1020

William A. Fisher, Department of Psychology and Department of Obstetrics and Gynecology, The University of Western Ontario, London, Ontario, Canada N6A 5C2

Cynthia Fleck-Kandath, School of Medicine, Uniformed Services University of the Health Sciences, Bethesda, Maryland 20814

E. Scott Geller, Department of Psychology, Virginia Polytechnic Institute and State University, Blacksburg, Virginia 24061

Marti Hope Gonzales, Department of Psychology, University of Minnesota, Minneapolis, Minnesota 55455

Linda Heath, Department of Psychology, Loyola University of Chicago, Chicago, Illinois 60626

James Jaccard, Department of Psychology, State University of New York at Albany, Albany, New York 12222

Barbara Loken, Department of Marketing, Carlson School of Management, University of Minnesota, Minneapolis, Minnesota 55455

Stephen J. Misovich, Department of Psychology, University of Connecticut, Storrs, Connecticut 06260-1020

Maurice B. Mittelmark, Bowman-Gray School of Medicine, Wake Forest University, Winston-Salem, North Carolina 27103

Sarah E. A. Nesselhof-Kendall, School of Medicine, Uniformed Services University of the Health Sciences, Bethesda, Maryland 20814

Michael S. Pallak, American Biodyne Research Corp., South San Francisco, California 94080

Bettye E. Raines, Department of Psychology, University of Houston, Houston, Texas 77204

Dennis P. Rosenbaum, Center for Research in Law and Justice and Department of Criminal Justice, University of Illinois at Chicago, Chicago, Illinois 60680

Clive Seligman, Department of Psychology, The University of Western Ontario, London, Ontario, Canada N6A 5C2

Althea Smith, Visions Incorporated, 68 Park Avenue, Cambridge, Massachusetts 02138

Janet Swim, Department of Psychology, The Pennsylvania State University, University Park, Pennsylvania 16802

Robert Turrisi, Department of Psychology, State University of New York at Albany, Albany, New York 12222

Contributors

Choi K. Wan, Department of Psychology, State University of New York at Albany, Albany, New York 12222

Carol Silvia Weisse, Department of Psychology, Union College, Schenectady, New York 12308

Preface

The field of social psychology traditionally has been defined, wholly or in part, as the scientific study of social influence. Although comprising diverse specialized topics of inquiry, social psychology maintains at its core the investigation of how an individual's thoughts, feelings, and actions are influenced by other people. It is fitting, therefore, that this inaugural volume in a series on social psychological processes and social issues features this central process of social influence as its main theme.

Throughout its nearly 100-year history as a discipline, social psychology has been both a basic and an applied science, although the relative emphasis accorded to these two interrelated functions has varied over time. For about the past 20 years, the "applied side" of social psychology has received increased attention. As reflected in the chapters of this book, the applied orientation has resulted in an expanded range of topics, subject populations, settings, and research methods employed by social psychologists. What has remained constant, though, is the guidance provided by a body of theory, data, and principles about social psychological processes that are regarded as fundamental. It is assumed that these processes are "basic" in the sense of being relevant to many specific phenomena and practical problems. At the same time, it is expected that attempted applications to different topics will not only reveal the generalizability of these fundamental processes but will also suggest modifications in our understanding of them. In the present case, this book is intended to help identify possible solutions to social problems through applying knowledge about social influence processes and to advance general knowledge about the processes themselves.

Aside from testing and expanding the limits of basic psychological processes as they apply to current social problems, another aspect of applied social psychology entails the design and evaluation of interventions intended to ameliorate or even prevent such problems. Accordingly, another theme and purpose of this book is to demonstrate how social change strategies derived from theories and basic research on social influence may be effective in retarding the growth of social problems at some stage in their development. At least to the extent that problems originate from human experience and behavior, it is reasonable to work for prevention by humanely attempting to influence how people think, feel, and act.

This book begins with a brief chapter presenting two frameworks for applying social psychological processes to social issues generally, and for conceptualizing the myriad forms of social influence as variants of one fundamental process. These frameworks are intended to place the chapters of this book into the larger contexts of a broad-scale research agenda for applied social psychology, and of an integrative synthesis of social influence components and strategies. The other chapters present, in a personalized way, what the authors have learned and thought about the practical utility and policy implications of preventing selected social problems by social influence.

In broad terms the substantive content of these chapters concerns attitudes and behaviors related to personal well-being and/or the well-being of other people and society as a whole. Chapters 2, 3, and 4 present a variety of social-influence-based approaches to preventing the spread of AIDS and related issues, including other sexually transmissible diseases and teenage pregnancy. Chapter 5 also deals with unwanted pregnancy and other health matters, such as alcohol abuse and drunk driving. Chapters 6 and 7 consider the abuse of other harmful substances, especially tobacco, as well as healthy diet and regular exercise, which are the targets of health-promotion programs.

Chapter 8 introduces methods for overcoming negative intergroup relations in the form of prejudice, discrimination, and racism. Chapter 9 focuses on the antisocial behavior of aggression and how media effects on aggressiveness can be mitigated. Chapter 10 discusses media and other influences on the mutual relationship between fear of crime and crime-preventive activities. Chapter 11 features an applied behavior analysis of driver safety with an emphasis on discouraging drunk driving and encouraging the use of seat belts. Chapters 12 and 13 present models for conserving the natural resources of water and energy. The concluding chapter provides direction to social psychologists for placing their ideas, talents, and research activities into the stream of public policy making.

The faculty and students of Loyola University's Applied Social Psychology Program are pleased to have the opportunity to work with the Society for the Psychological Study of Social Issues and with Plenum Publishing Corporation in preparing this first volume in a series on social psychological processes and social issues. We hope this book on social influence applied to preventing social problems will be useful to students and researchers in social psychology, and to practitioners in any social problem realm, by providing models of truly applied science.

Acknowledgments

This volume on the basic processes of social influence applied toward understanding and preventing social problems is the product of the combined efforts of several organizations and many individuals. It is the first of a planned series on applications of social psychological processes to social issues involving the collaboration of SPSSI, Plenum Press, and Loyola University of Chicago's graduate program in applied social psychology.

We wish to thank the officers and publication committee of SPSSI, particularly Jeffrey Rubin and Louise Kidder, for giving us the opportunity to edit this series and for their efforts and support in bringing the present collection of chapters into print. We also thank the editorial and production staffs of Plenum Press, especially Eliot Werner, for their interest and assistance in this project.

Our appreciation for their contributions at several stages in creating this book is extended to our colleague Dr. Fred Bryant, and to many students in our graduate program. Those students who most actively participated in such phases as researching and recommending possible topics and authors, and writing reviews of initial drafts, include Jill Carmody, Helen Hirschfeld, Claudia Lampman, Todd Miller, John Molcan, John Petraitis, Elizabeth Sanders, Leslie Scott, Susan Sheffey, Jim Sinacore, Jerry Vasilias, and, especially, Denise Archambault.

We gratefully acknowledge the 26 members of our Editorial Advisory Board for their support of this project generally, for their replies to our survey and other solicitations of advice about potential themes and authors, and for their careful and helpful reviews of chapter drafts. Special mention for their assistance should be made of board members Sharon Brehm, Bob Cialdini, Chris Dunkel-Schetter, Ron Fisher, Susan Green, Stuart Oskamp, Mike Pallak, Linda Perloff, and Carol Werner.

Finally and most significantly, we thank the 27 authors for their efforts, which transformed our idealistic plans for this volume into reality. Everyone who is concerned with the psychological study of social issues rightly owes them gratitude, not simply for writing these chapters but moreso for the important theoretical, empirical, and practical advancements made by their work.

JOHN EDWARDS
R. SCOTT TINDALE
LINDA HEATH
EMIL J. POSAVAC

Contents

5. Implications of Behavioral Decision Theory and Social Marketing for Designing Social Action Programs 103

James Jaccard, Robert Turrisi, and Choi K. Wan

6. Applying a Social Psychological Model across Health Promotion Interventions: Cigarettes to Smokeless Tobacco 143

Richard I. Evans and Bettye E. Raines

7. Heart Health Program: Applying Social Influence Processes in a Large-Scale Community Health Promotion Program 159

Barbara Loken, Janet Swim, and Maurice B. Mittelmark

8. Social Influence and Antiprejudice Training Programs 183

Althea Smith

12. A Two-Factor Model of Energy and Water Conservation 279

Clive Seligman and Joan E. Finegan

13. Alternative Social Influence Processes Applied to Energy Conservation 301

Elliot Aronson and Marti Hope Gonzales

14. Public Policy and Applied Social Psychology: Bridging the Gap ... 327

Michael S. Pallak

1

Frameworks for Applying Social Psychological Processes to Social Issues

John Edwards

This volume is the first of a planned series on applications of fundamental social psychological processes to social problems. As such it is part of a much larger effort by the Society for the Psychological Study of Social Issues to sponsor the publication of works that address the causes, nature, and possible solutions to societal concerns. Other aspects of this effort include SPSSI's programs at professional conferences, the *Journal of Social Issues,* dozens of books on special topics such as international relations and racism, and the *Applied Social Psychology Annual* series that was initially edited by Leonard Bickman and concluded under the editorship of Stuart Oskamp. In effect, the present volume represents a continuation of the latter series but with a different focus owing to a change in publishers and editors. While most of the publications sponsored by SPSSI have emphasized a single social issue, usually discussed from the standpoint of diverse theoretical and empirical traditions, this volume takes the complementary approach of considering diverse social issues within the framework of theory and research on the single but broadly defined process of social influence. The complementarity of these alternative ways of presenting applied social science can be seen by taking a perspective that combines both general social processes and social issues.

A Social Psychological Perspective on Applied Research: The Process/Problem Matrix

When considering what is "applied" about applied social psychology, several aspects come readily to mind, such as the central purpose of the work, the

John Edwards • Department of Psychology, Loyola University of Chicago, Chicago, Illinois 60626.

setting in which it is conducted, the intended audience for its product, and the way that theories are used for guidance (Edwards, 1981). For me, the most salient of these is the distinctive type of theoretical perspective from which a problem is viewed. It is not so much the substantive area of concern (e.g., education, criminal justice, health care, prejudice) or the methodology (e.g., surveys, quasiexperiments) that set social psychologists apart from other social scientists, but a unique set of theoretical assumptions, concepts, propositions, and principles along with a body of related research findings. Collectively, these afford a rather distinct way of looking at processes that occur within and between people. These processes are fundamental in the sense of being potentially relevant to many types of individual, group, organizational, and social problems. Thus, the starting point for the applied researcher, regardless of the nature of the particular question at hand, is a theoretical conceptualization of the problem based on relevant psychological process or processes.

According to this way of thinking, social psychology can be defined by a matrix with one dimension consisting of substantive topic areas and the other consisting of theoretical perspectives on fundamental social psychological concepts and processes. An example of such a matrix is shown in Figure 1. The set of topic areas comprising the columns is obviously not exhaustive. Likewise, the social psychological terms comprising the matrix rows, which resemble the chapter headings of a traditional social psychological textbook, are intended to be suggestive. Arbitrary and incomplete though it is, Figure 1 illustrates a way of organizing the domain and agenda of applying social processes to social issues.

As portrayed by this matrix, much of the literature in applied social psychology consists of works built with a "column" theme. There are several advantages of this approach, such as offering a reasonably comprehensive account of a given social issue. But the "row" theme adopted in the present volume may have some advantages of its own. First, it can draw attention to the social processes and various theories about them that constitute the uniqueness of a social psychological perspective. Second, sóme cross-fertilization may occur by juxtaposing applications of a general process to several specific problems. Third, the row approach can contribute to the development of theoretical perspectives by revealing their strengths and weaknesses when applied to different topics. If these potential advantages are realized, then students of basic research and theory may achieve new insight into the practical value of knowing about fundamental social processes, and activists in diverse social problem areas may acquire new ideas about the origins of, and possible strategies for preventing, those problems. At least these were our hopes in assembling a book on attempts at prevention based on processes of social influence.

Social Influence as a Collection of Processes

Among the processes in Figure 1, the type that has perhaps the longest history of study and still maintains immense popularity among social psychologists

Substantive topic areas

Social psychological concepts and processes	Educa-tion	Law and justice	Health care	Work life	Environ-ment	Discrim-ination
Social cognition, e.g., attribution, heuristics, self-concept						
Social learning, e.g., modeling, verbal conditioning						
Social motivation, e.g., achievement, approval, consistency						
Social influence, e.g., persuasion, conformity, leadership						
Communication, e.g., language, nonverbal messages, proxemics						
Interpersonal actions, e.g., helping, liking, aggression						
Intragroup relations, e.g., coalition formation, polarization						
Intergroup relations, e.g., conflict, bargaining, cooperation						

Figure 1. A matrix conceptualization of applied social psychology.

(cf. Zanna, Olson, & Herman, 1987) is social influence. In fact, some mainstream textbooks define the field of social psychology as largely the study of how people influence and are influenced by others. As should be expected of a topic that has garnered such long-standing prominence, the study of social influence has taken many directions leading to the identification of many facets of this broad process. We have, then, a wealth of influence processes referred to as education, persuasion, imitation, induced counterattitudinal action, conformity, compliance, conditioning, leadership, and obedience. Furthermore, each of these processes can be subdivided into even more specific forms. Compliance, for example, includes numerous varieties graphically designated as low-balling, and the foot-in-the-door technique, among others (Cialdini, 1985). That these are alternative forms of social influence generally is suggested by their several common components, including an influencer, a strategy, a mechanism by which the strategy is expected to work, a target person or collective, and a reaction by the target. A framework summarizing these components for several social influence types along with suggestive elements of each is shown in Table 1.

These forms of influence are neither exhaustive (see Falbo, 1977, for another typology) nor mutually exclusive. For instance, the line separating education from persuasion is not sharply drawn in practice. Moreover, the examples listed for strategies, mechanisms, and other components merely hint at the richness of ideas generated by theory and research on each influence type. Most notably, the column of responses refers only to those intended by the influencer while omitting the perhaps more frequent alternatives of no change, reactance, passive resistance, and so forth.

These limitations notwithstanding, Table 1 suggests several important points. First, social influence requires two parties who in many cases are engaged in a dynamic system of mutual effects. An influencer sets out to produce some change in the target, but the target may affect the other's choice of strategy (Rule & Bisanz, 1987). Second, a particular influence form may set in motion any number of mechanisms that account for the target's response. To cite one case, a persuasion campaign implemented via the mass media may include elements of learning information, accepting arguments, imitating a model, seeking consistency, and feeling rewarded. Third, intervention programs designed to ameliorate or prevent social problems frequently employ a combination of strategies to accomplish an integrated series of purposes. In a comprehensive effort (see, for example, Loken, Swim, and Mittelmark, this volume) various media may be used to draw attention to, and educate some community about, a problem. Captive groups in schools, hospitals, churches, businesses, and community organizations may be used for applying peer pressure, role-playing exercises, and other means for altering attitudes and intentions; and features of the physical environment may be manipulated to encourage desired and discourage undesired behaviors. Finally, it must be recognized that social influences are involved not just in planned attempts to prevent problems but also presumably in their orgination and perpetuation. If a problem such as racial discrimination has its origins in such influences as stereotypic media images, peer group support, and social reward structures, then the logical basis for prevention would be to change those images, supports, and rewards as sources of influence.

To summarize these derivations from Table 1, social influence comprises many overlapping forms, strategies, and mediators that are often employed in combination by an influencer with the aim of changing the knowledge, beliefs, attitudes, and behavior of a nonpassive target person. How these forms of influence have been or might be employed in prevention programs can be seen by previewing their place in the chapters that follow.

Education. Some sort of education is recommended by most of the present authors, either as a means for informing general audiences about a problem or for

Table 1. Forms and Components of Selected Social Influence Processes

Influence type	Influencer	Strategy	Mechanisms	Target	Response
Education	Teacher, media campaign	Give information	Learn, recall skill, knowledge	Students, mass audiences	Use knowledge and skills
Persuasion	Social advocates	Arouse emotions, provide arguments	Process arguments, mindless agreement	Message recipient	Attitude change
Imitation	Role model	Perform actions	Observe, encode, rehearse	Observer	Imitate actions
Induced counter-attitudinal action	Cajoler	Subtle coaxing, role-play	Self-persuasion, reduce dissonance	Actor	Seek consistency with action
Conformity	Group majority	Express judgment	Social comparison, being accepted	Group minority	Overt agreement
Compliance	Requester	Series of requests	Commitment, being consistent	Consenter	Yield to request
Conditioning	Trainer	Control stimuli, schedule rewards	Need reduction, habit formation	Learner	Change rate of behavior
Leadership	Group leader	State goals, show consideration	Accept relative status	Follower	Carry out instructions
Obedience	Power figure	Give orders	Resign personal responsibility	Servant	Submit to demands

training specific people in skills required to cope with or prevent the problem. The chapters by Geller, by Loken et al., and by Rosenbaum and Heath are among those reporting how television and radio announcements, pamphlets, billboards, films, and other mass media are used to raise public consciousness. Relatedly, some of these and other authors (e.g., Dubow and Cappas, W. Fisher) call for changes in the images and models conveyed through mass media to dispel misinformation. However, several chapters (e.g., by Weisse et al.) note that while ignorance is one probable cause of social problems, merely providing knowledge is inadequate for effecting behavior change. Beyond providing more correct information, additional educational strategies for training people in skills needed for change are discussed by many of our authors, including Dubow and Cappas, Evans and Raines, Loken et al., Seligman and Finegan, and, in particular, Smith.

Persuasion. Virtually all of the present chapters discuss one or more aspects of persuasion strategies leading to changes in attitudes and, occasionally, in behaviors. Some (e.g., Aronson and Gonzales, Jaccard et al., and Loken et al.) draw upon the communication/persuasion model pioneered by Hovland and associates. This approach deals with the characteristics of influence sources, message content, communication media, and message recipients. Of these, one that plays a central role in several chapters here (e.g., Fisher and Misovich, Rosenbaum and Heath, Weisse et al.) is the fear-arousing content of a message. The assumptions are that fear (or some other emotion) helps attract attention to issues, and that the incentives associated with fear reduction can be gained by accepting the advocated attitude. However, too much fear arousal can engender resistance, and, as discussed in detail by Rosenbaum and Heath, new attitudes and actions that should reduce fears may instead make them worse.

Another attitude model frequently applied in these chapters (e.g, Evans and Raines, Loken et al., Seligman and Finegan) is the Fishbein/Ajzen theory of reasoned action. According to this approach, behavioral intentions are determined by attitudes toward a specific act and perceived social norms. This theory, as well as the aforementioned communication model and its derivatives, such as the cognitive response and elaboration likelihood theories developed by Petty and Cacioppo and their associates, emphasizes systematic information processing as the basis of attitudes and action. As noted in several chapters here (e.g., Dubow and Cappas, Evans and Raines), this processing may include counterarguing a message and thus a failure of the intended impact. Furthermore, it is known that persuasion need not involve thoughtful processing of facts and arguments, but can result from rather mindless acceptance of conclusions based on simple rules or heuristics such as ''experts should be believed'' (Chaiken, 1987). Although some reference to the power of message acceptance rules and cues that set them off is made in the following chapters (e.g., the advice from Aronson and Gonzales that information be presented vividly), these shortcut routes to persuasion have yet to be widely applied in prevention campaigns.

Imitation. Social learning was portrayed in Figure 1 as a distinct process, but it is also a significant form of social influence. As argued most convincingly in the chapter by Dubow and Cappas, if the ability and inspiration to perform undesirable behavior can be acquired by observing role models, then the same should hold for more desired actions. Dubow and Cappas, among others (e.g., Aronson and Gonzales, Evans and Raines, Geller, Weisse *et al.*), discuss how the effectiveness of this strategy depends on many factors, such as the characteristics of models and the consequences of their behavior, as well as the target person's sense of efficacy about imitating the modeled action. Related to imitation is the process of social diffusion described by several authors (e.g., Aronson and Gonzales, Fisher and Misovich, Loken *et al.*). Diffusion occurs when local "opinion leaders" are used as models of positive behavior and attitudes within their social network.

Induced Counterattitudinal Behavior. The strategy of subtly cajoling people to engage in actions contrary to their attitudes or habitual practices is not only integral to conditioning processes discussed later but is also derived from theories about cognitive dissonance and self-persuasion. Several chapters here illustrate the effectiveness of this technique. For example, Fisher describes a series of role-playing exercises beginning with a "fantasy walk-through" and leading to practice of the new skills in real-life situations, Evans and Raines review their work wherein people rehearse tactics for resisting peer pressure, and Smith reports on a training program including a number of simulations such as taking the role of another person. As explained in the chapter by Geller and elsewhere, it is important that the inducements for behavior (whether counterattitudinal or not) be minimally sufficient and that there be public commitment to the new action in order for it to yield long-term, intrinsically based attitude and behavior changes.

Conformity. This form of influence occurs generally in group settings when a numerical minority, despite internal reservations, accedes to the norm manifested by the majority. Several chapters (e.g., by Fisher and Misovich, Loken *et al.*, Weisse *et al.*) discuss how both the normative (outwardly going along with the group to avoid rejection) and the informational (inwardly accepting group norms that seem correct) aspects of conformity can be applied in prevention programs. The concept of a reference group (i.e., one used as a basis for social comparison whether a person is a member or not) is used by several authors (e.g., Aronson and Gonzales, Dubow and Cappas, Fisher and Misovich) to indicate that acceptance of group norms does not necessarily require actual group interaction. In a related sense, as Seligman and Finegan report, one's perception of social norms can be strongly predictive of preventive actions in some problem domains. The perceptions are probably most salient when in the physical presence of a reference group. The effectiveness of such situations is known to vary with many factors, such as the size, unanimity, and attractiveness of the majority, how active or passive is the pressure applied, and so forth. Although many of these factors cannot be controlled outside the laboratory, they play a role in determining how naturally occurring groups such as peer networks (see Evans and Raines) and community organizations (see Loken *et al.*, Rosenbaum and Heath) can be employed in spreading social-issue-relevant information, attitudes, and behavior.

Compliance. Simply asking people to change their ways appears to be a rarely used strategy in prevention efforts. Perhaps change agents do not expect it would work. Another deterrent may be that some specific compliance tactics (e.g., the foot-in-the-door technique mentioned by Aronson and Gonzales) are considered as deceptive. Other methods, such as coaxing commitment to new behaviors (see the chapters by Aronson and Gonzales and by Geller), may be more palatable. No doubt the issue of manipulativeness applies not just to compliance but to all forms of social influence in some degree. With that in mind, further studying the body of compliance principles (Cialdini, 1985) may yield new methods for prevention programs that are ethically acceptable.

Conditioning. As presented in this book most thoroughly by Geller, many effective social influence devices have been drawn from the behavioristic tradition. Some of these include controlling features of the physical environment to facilitate desired and inhibit undesired actions (see Dubow and Cappas, Geller, Jaccard *et al.*), increasing the degree and likelihood of penalties or other disincentives for excessive actions (see Geller), giving informative feedback to encourage self-regulation (see Aronson and Gonzales, Geller, Loken *et al.*, Seligman and Finegan), and offering incentives ranging from cost savings to individual rewards to having a chance to win a lottery (see Geller, Loken *et al.*). Other important contributions of the applied behavioral analysis approach to social influence are its emphasis on rigorous evaluation of intervention impacts on baseline behavior rates, and a growing number of methods for transferring control from external to internal sources.

Leadership. It is now commonly accepted among social scientists that leadership refers not merely to holding a high status position but to functions and actions performed by any number of group members that influence others. As noted in several chapters (e.g., by Dubow and Cappas, Evans and Raines, Smith, and Weisse *et al.*), those who naturally fill a leader role (e.g., parents, teachers), and others who emerge (e.g., in peer networks, neighborhood clubs) as leaders are key figures in mobilizing behavior change on the large scale. Social scientists are among those who can fulfill leadership functions in social problem prevention. In his chapter on social policy, Pallak urges social scientists first to become familiar with how policies are made and then to use leadership qualities such as expertise to influence policy makers.

Obedience. None of our authors advocates the exertion of power to force people into behaving in new and "better" ways. More so than any other type of influence, obedience may seem irrelevant on practical and moral grounds to a discussion of preventing problems in a free society. However, as suggested in several of these chapters, our self-imposed laws are expected to be obeyed, and new policies, legislation, and judicial decisions are intended to effect behavior change. Furthermore, it is most likely that giving and submission to orders occur frequently in situations of clear status differential, as, for example, when parents make demands of their children. Although obedience strategies are contrary to the standards of social scientists and activists, their inclusion here in the kit of influence tools serves as a reminder that the feasibility and effectiveness of an influence process depends upon many aspects of the sociocultural context.

We have been guided through the foregoing preview of chapter contents by the social influence "row" of Figure 1 as expanded in Table 1. The columns of Figure 1 present an array of substantive social issues and problems. A brief preview of how these are addressed in this volume is needed to complete our two-dimensional framework.

Varieties of Social Issues

Not all of the problem areas identified in the columns of Figure 1 could be included in this volume. Applications of social influence processes to preventing problems in work life, education, and other areas would require a two-volume set. Even so, a relatively broad range of issues is covered in these chapters in ways no doubt applicable to the omitted problem domains.

Considered foremost here are several issues related to health practices and disease. Of these, the one perhaps at the apex of national consciousness now and for the foreseeable future is AIDS. The chapters by Weisse *et al.*, by J. Fisher and Misovich, and by W. Fisher discuss the nature, incidence, transmission, preventive strategies, and other aspects of this tragic condition. Related to AIDS because of one primary mode of its spread is contraception. Further implications of unprotected sexual behavior, such as the spread of other diseases and unwanted pregnancies, are discussed by W. Fisher and by Jaccard *et al.*

The abuse of substances including drugs, alcohol, and tobacco contributes to many health problems. The chapters by Weisse *et al.*, by J. Fisher and Misovich, and by W. Fisher describe how the forms of drug abuse involving injections have an impact on the contagion of AIDS and other diseases. Among the problems associated with excessive alcohol consumption is drunk driving, as discussed in the chapters by Jaccard *et al.* and by Geller. The use of tobacco, whether smoked or smokeless, as a risk factor in heart disease and other killers is discussed by Evans and Raines and by Loken *et al.* The latter authors also consider other practices related to heart health, such as exercise and nutrition.

Several chapters deal in varying degrees with prejudicial attitudes and discriminatory behavior—for example, the stigma attached to people with AIDS, targets of crime, unwed teenage mothers, and other victims. Most directly relevant to this type of social problem is the chapter by Smith, which discusses prejudice against women and racial minorities.

Issues of law, crime, and aggressiveness are tightly interrelated as discussed in a number of the chapters. The previously mentioned chapters concerned with illicit substance abuse are part of this theme. Geller's chapter deals not only with drunk driving but also with legal and other aspects of increasing the use of seat belts. The chapter by Dubow and Cappas describes how aggressive, antisocial behaviors can be stimulated by exposure to certain television programs. Considering another aspect of this issue, Rosenbaum and Heath describe the role of mass media and other influences on crime prevention and the fear of crime.

The final social issue incorporated in this volume is the conservation of resources, especially water and energy, as discussed in the chapters by Aronson and Gonzales and by Seligman and Finegan. Arguably, all of these chapters, including Pallak's closing discussion on public policy, deal in some respects with the conservation of our most valuable natural resource, which, of course, is people.

Some Lessons and Directions

Although perhaps more appropriate for the end than for the beginning of a book, a number of general observations about the status of applying social influence processes to preventing social problems warrant discussion at this point. To borrow part of a phrase from Winston Churchill, considering some lessons learned along with possible future directions will bring us to the end of the beginning. First, since prevention is a theme throughout this book, it must be acknowledged that efforts toward preventing a problem can be made at many stages, ranging from before it gets started to when it has become a full-blown crisis. Unfortunately, most problems do not draw much attention until reaching the later stages. One consequence of this fact, as discussed most fully in the chapters by J. Fisher and Misovich, W. Fisher, and Weisse *et al.,* is that prevention efforts usually must begin by overcoming barriers established by the gratifying aspects of the *status quo* and the reluctance to embrace the untried ways. Accordingly, the effectiveness of social influence processes can be expected to vary with the developmental stage of a problem.

A second lesson is that each of the general forms of social influence, such as education, persuasion, and imitation, is applicable across social problems. However, further study is needed to determine if more specific approaches thus far applied to only one or a few problem fields can be generalized. For example, what would happen if the concepts of the health beliefs model discussed by Fisher and Misovich and by Loken *et al.* were transplanted into attempts at preventing prejudice, crime, or other problems? Or, what would happen if the behavioral analysis approaches presented by Geller and by Jaccard *et al.* were transplanted into problem areas other than the ones discussed by those authors? Even if direct transplantation fails, there remains hope that cross-fertilization will yield a crop of new hybrid forms of social-influence-based prevention programs.

A third general observation is that a careful analysis of the outcomes one is attempting to influence can also affect the choice of a prevention strategy. One example of outcome analysis is whether one is trying to dissuade people from continuing an existing practice, to persuade them to adopt a new one, or both. As Geller, among others, has shown, some interventions are more effective for persuading than for dissuading. Another instance of analyzing outcomes concerns whether the desired result entails a one-time-only versus continual action. The papers by Rosenbaum and Heath and by Seligman and Finegan illustrate the value of this distinction. Finally, Jaccard *et al.* discuss criteria and methods for determining in advance not only what positive outcomes to seek but also the negative ones to avoid.

A fourth lesson is that many scientist/practitioners of social influence represented in this book (e.g., Aronson and Gonzales, Evans and Raines, Jaccard *et al.*, Weiss *et al.*) have explicitly incorporated individual difference variables into their work. These variables include demographic characteristics, various personality traits, and numerous concepts related to cognitive structures and processes. As several of our authors have noted, the daunting implication of person–situation interactions is that prevention programs should be tailor-made for each type of person and ultimately, therefore, for every targeted individual.

The fifth note sounded here resonates with Eagly's (1987) commentary on the cognitive emphasis characterizing social influence research of the 1980s. The notion that people are rational information processors whose actions follow predictably from their knowledge and attitudes is gradually being assimilated into less simplified conceptualizations of social influence. The most personally convincing evidence of the limitations of a solely cognitive model of social influence comes from a series of studies at Loyola (Archambault & Edwards, 1989; Edwards & Archambault, 1988; Edwards, Pingitore, Torpy, & Archambault, 1989) showing no relationship between people's knowledge about an issue and their attitudes, experiences, and behavior intentions. Other authors in this volume (e.g., Weisse *et al.*) have reached the same conclusion that knowledge may be a necessary but not sufficient basis for attitudes and actions. Thus, more complex models are developing (cf. Sherman, 1987) that represent not only knowledge processing but also shortcut decision rules, affective/motivational stirrings, and other intrapersonal and interpersonal mediators of social influence.

Questions about the Ethics of Defining Social Problems

To bring this beginning to an end, some concluding comments seem appropriate about how social problems are defined. In their elegant discussion of this question, Seidman and Rappaport (1986) argue that "the definition of a social problem is time, place and context bound'' (p. 1). According to these authors, the specific aspects of these defining characteristics as they apply to the current American scene are (1) *individualism,* i.e., individuals (as opposed to economic and political systems) are responsible for their own problems; (2) *single standards,* i.e., victim-blaming is part of a larger process that labels as deviant those who fail to comply with norms; (3) *pragmatism,* i.e., we convert psychological considerations into monetary and other tangible values; (4) *generalization from extreme examples,* i.e., committing the fallacy of exaggerating certain problems based on atypical but sensational events; (5) *problemization,* i.e., regarding minor difficulties as major perils, thereby overextending our coping resources; and (6) *uniform standards,* i.e., applying the same cure to everyone regardless of suitability or individual needs.

These aspects of how social problems are defined raise many ethical questions that we all must answer for ourselves. Such questions can be asked in relation to the forms and components of social influence processes discussed here. In what sense and for whom does some pattern of attitude and behavior constitute a "problem"? Which form or forms of social influence are most appropriate for the problem and the target persons of concern to the problem solver? Who are the problem solvers or influencers and what values and motivations underlie their attempts to change others? What specific influence strategies are used, on what basis are they selected, and do they sacrifice human dignity for cost-effectiveness? Who has been chosen as the target of influence? Are they only the socially defined "deviants," or instead are they the producers and decision makers who are positioned to have great impact on both the causes and solutions to social problems? Finally, what are the moral obligations for the social scientist/practitioner when, perhaps out of a need for at least the illusion of control (Langer, 1975), the targets of social influence respond with resistance? It is hoped that these questions afford yet another framework for contemplating the following chapters on the applications of social influence processes to preventing social problems.

References

Archambault, D., & Edwards, J. (1989, May). *Relations among AIDS-related knowledge, experience, attitudes and risk behavior.* Paper presented at the meeting of the Midwestern Psychological Association, Chicago, IL.

Chaiken, S. (1987). The heuristic model of persuasion. In M. Zanna, J. Olson, & C. P. Herman (Eds.), *Social influence: The Ontario symposium* (Vol. 5, pp. 3–39). Hillsdale, NJ: Erlbaum.

Cialdini, R. B. (1985). *Influence: Science and practice.* Glenview, IL: Scott, Foresman.

Eagly, A. H. (1987). Social influence research: New approaches to enduring issues. In M. Zanna, J. Olson, & C. P. Herman (Eds.), *Social influence: The Ontario symposium* (Vol. 5, pp. 271–285).

Edwards, J. (1981). *The use of theory in applied social research.* Paper presented at the XVIII Interamerican Congress of Psychology, Santo Domingo, Dominican Republic.

Edwards, J., & Archambault, D. (1988, April). *"Valent" versus neutral knowledge as correlates of health attitudes, behaviors, and intentions.* Paper presented at the meeting of the Midwestern Psychological Association, Chicago, IL.

Edwards, J., Pingitore, R., Torpy, E., & Archambault, D. (1989, May). *Relationships among knowledge, experiences and attitudes toward elderly persons.* Paper presented at the meeting of the Midwestern Psychological Association, Chicago, IL.

Falbo, T. (1977). Multidimensional scaling of power strategies. *Journal of Personality and Social Psychology, 35,* 537–547.

Langer, E. J. (1975). The illusion of control. *Journal of Personality and Social Psychology, 32,* 311–328.

Rule, B. G., & Bisanz, G. L. (1987). Goals and strategies of persuasion: A cognitive schema for understanding social events. In M. Zanna, J. Olson, & C. P. Herman (Eds.), *Social influence: The Ontario symposium* (Vol. 5, pp. 185–206). Hillsdale, NJ: Erlbaum.

Seidman, E., & Rappaport, J. (Eds.). (1986). *Redefining social problems.* New York: Plenum Press.

Sherman, S. J. (1987). Cognitive processes in the formation, change and expression of attitudes. In M. Zanna, J. Olson, & C. P. Herman (Eds.), *Social influence: The Ontario symposium* (Vol. 5, pp. 75–106). Hillsdale, NJ: Erlbaum.

Zanna, M., Olson, J., & Herman, C. P. (Eds.). (1987). *Social influence: The Ontario symposium* (Vol. 5). Hillsdale, NJ: Erlbaum.

2

Psychosocial Aspects of AIDS Prevention among Heterosexuals

Carol Silvia Weisse, Sarah E. A. Nesselhof-Kendall, Cynthia Fleck-Kandath, and Andrew Baum

Acquired immunodeficiency syndrome (AIDS) is a frightening disease that has captured the attention of the world during the current decade. It is controversial, partly because of the groups within which it initially was spread, and it is deadly. Moreover, there is no cure for AIDS once someone has it and no vaccine to prevent people from being infected by the AIDS virus. Consequently, other methods must be used to curb its spread and prevent healthy people from infection. We know that the disease is spread primarily from sexual contact or exposure to contaminated blood; casual contact does not appear to spread the disease, but sexual intercourse with individuals who have been infected or exchange of bodily fluids are the major routes of transmission. Behavior change directed at minimizing these risks hold the greatest promise of preventing the spread of AIDS and controlling the epidemic.

In this chapter, we will describe AIDS, related complexes, and the nature of the disease's assault on the immune system. Ways in which the AIDS virus is spread will be discussed, and the complications of becoming infected and/or ill will be considered because these factors may actually inhibit attempts to curb transmission of the virus. For example, some of the most important barriers to effective prevention are related to the nature of the disease—it is asymptomatic until it has progressed to advanced stages, it provides no "notice" when infection occurs, and it is sexually transmitted. Basic research in social psychology that is

Carol Silvia Weisse • Department of Psychology, Union College, Schenectady, New York 12308   **Sarah E. A. Nesselhof-Kendall, Cynthia Fleck-Kandath, and Andrew Baum** • School of Medicine, Uniformed Services University of the Health Sciences, Bethesda, Maryland 20814.

pertinent to these issues will be discussed, as will lessons learned from research on contraception and prevention of other sexually transmitted diseases.

In preventing the spread of AIDS, there are at least two basic groups on which one may focus. First, there are those who are already infected with the AIDS virus. These people are the carriers of the virus and are an important target for preventive efforts. Second, there are those who are disease-free, who have not been infected by the virus, who are either at high risk for infection by virtue of sexual habits, drug use, or other behavioral variables, or who are at low risk because of "safe" behavioral predispositions. Since discovery of the disease, efforts at prevention have been targeted mostly at high-risk people who are not yet infected. In this chapter, we will focus on a group that may be a risk but has not received so much attention—adolescents and young adults who are at risk because they are becoming sexually active and have a poor record of behavior that might protect them from infection. In discussing this, we will consider research on other groups and evaluate possible interventions that may be derived from what is known about persuasion, social influence, and behavior change.

What Is AIDS?

Recognized in 1981, AIDS is a severely debilitating immunodeficiency that predisposes the host organism to various opportunistic diseases and cancers (Jawetz, Melnich, & Adelberg, 1987). It is fatal: At least half of those Americans diagnosed with AIDS have died, between 20 and 30% who test positive for the virus's antibodies will contract AIDS within the next 5 years, and at least 1.5 million Americans are currently thought to carry the AIDS virus. By 1991, 179,000 deaths will be attributed to the disease (Koop, 1986). Approximately one-third of all cases reported are from New York City and San Francisco, and in New York it is the leading cause of death for all men between the ages of 20 and 40 (Centers for Disease Control, 1987c).

As suggested by its name, AIDS attacks the immune system and renders it less able to protect infected persons from infection by other pathogens. The immune system is extremely complex and consists of a wide variety of cells and organs. At the center of this system are lymphocytes—white blood cells that carry out many functions. Of particular importance are one type of lympyhocyte, called helper T cells, which provide stimulatory messages and growth factors that serve to promote effective and efficient immune responses during infection. The AIDS virus, originally called HTLV-III but renamed HIV (human immunodeficiency virus), is cytotoxic for the T4 helper cell. By attacking these immune cells, the virus makes them less able to provide critical "help" to other cells, leading to a powerful compromise of immunocompetence.

The term *AIDS* actually refers to the end stage of a disease process of variable length, triggered by infection with the AIDS-causing HIV. The virus may be communicated from those who are already infected to others by way of exchange of bodily fluids—blood, semen, vaginal secretions, and so on. Once in the body, it invades host cells and either becomes dormant or proceeds to replicate and expand very slowly. This latency period is variable and may be affected by a variety of factors. However, infection can be detected during this stage by the presence of antibodies to the HIV that have been produced by the body, and may be transmitted during this stage as well. As the virus becomes active, it has strong immunosuppressive effects; the virus may infect the central nervous system, and it begins to be manifest in clinical symptoms. Depending on the symptoms evident, the degree of immunosuppression, and the onset of other illnesses, the seropositive person (an individual who evidences presence of the HIV by showing antibodies but who does not necessarily exhibit symptoms) progresses through several disease stages before reaching the final phase of the disease—AIDS.

For this reason, it is probably best to refer to the entire disease process as HIV disease. There are reasons to believe that dysfunction appears prior to diagnosis of AIDS, and it is misleading to refer to healthy HIV positives as having AIDS. Despite recent evidence of the inevitability of AIDS once the virus has infected one's body (Lui, Darrow, & Rutherford, 1988) it is possible that some may not develop AIDS symptoms or may progress very slowly toward that end.

Clinical manifestations of AIDS and its related conditions vary with the stage of the disease and present some obstacles to successful prevention. Among those who are infected with the virus, there may be few if any signs or symptoms that might alert one to its presence. The disease may progress to a stage known as AIDS-related complex (ARC). Symptom onset ranges between 6 months and 5 years, and includes tiredness, weight loss, diarrhea, loss of appetite, and night sweats (DeVita, Hellman, & Rosenberg, 1985). AIDS is similar to ARC but includes a diagnosed opportunistic infection or other disease indicative of a progressive immunosuppression. Opportunistic diseases are caused by organisms that normally bring no harm to people with intact immune systems. Among the most common for AIDS victims are pneumocystis carinii pneumonia, a parasitic lung infection with symptoms similar to other forms of pneumonia, and Kaposi's sarcoma, a malignant, metastasizing cancer of the soft tissue.

In addition to predisposing its host to opportunistic infections, the AIDS virus infects the central nervous system (e.g., Navia, Cho, Petito, & Price, 1986a; Stoler, Eskin, Benn, Angerer, & Angerer, 1986) as well as the macrophage/monocyte population within the brain (Gabzuda et al., 1986; Gartner, Markovitz, Markovitz, Betts, & Popovic, 1986). This can lead to a syndrome known as AIDS dementia. The AIDS dementia complex is defined as a "disabling cognitive and/or motor dysfunction" (Centers for Disease Control, 1987c). It is associated with poor concentration, loss of memory, and motor slowing, progressing finally to mutism, paraplesia and incontinence (Navia, Jordan, & Price, 1986b). One study has shown that 40% of AIDS patients develop neurological symptoms, 73% of AIDS patients show central nervous system disease upon autopsy, and 10% of AIDS and ARC patients show neurological complications up to 1 year before the actual AIDS diagnosis (Wolcott, 1986).

Anxiety syndromes are also very common in AIDS and ARC patients, as well as HIV positive patients (Forstein, 1984). Guilt, isolation, ostracism, and a fear of death have also been observed among AIDS patients (Wolcott, 1986). These symptoms may be caused by variables associated with HIV disease rather than by the disease itself. For example, fear of infection or stigmatization may cause people to withdraw from HIV positive individuals, causing loss of social support and withdrawal by the victim as well. Regardless of their origin, however, early neurological and psychological complications add additional obstacles to prevention interventions: Poor memory may make recommendations about behavior changes hard to remember, while the psychological symptoms—such as depression—may also interfere with education and motivation to change behaviors. Unfortunately, more is known about the symptoms and epidemiology of AIDS than about its treatment. *There is no cure, and there is no vaccine,* making behavioral change the most important route of preventing the spread of disease.[1]

Preventing Transmission

Because there are no current cures or biomedical technologies that can be applied to stop the HIV epidemic, attention has turned to preventing spread of the infection. The HIV has been isolated in several bodily fluids, including blood, semen, vaginal secretions, saliva, tears, breast milk, cerebrospinal fluid, amniotic fluid, and urine (Centers for Disease Control, 1987b). However, HIV transmission has been linked only with blood, semen, vaginal secretions, and possibly breast milk (Centers for Disease Control, 1987b). Current research has shown that direct contact with infected body fluid is the only mode of transmission for HIV. Skin or mucous membrane exposure rarely results in subsequent HIV infection, unless there are open wounds, sores, or other means for contracting a viral infection (Centers for Disease Control, 1987a). To prevent further spread of AIDS and HIV, individuals must take the necessary precautions to guard against contact with body fluids from any individual, not just those known to have AIDS or carry the virus. Among the precautions that have been taken are screening of donated blood and increased monitoring of those handling blood products. Prevention efforts have focused on the promotion of safer drug use (i.e., use of clean needles), as well as the use of condoms and changes in sexual behaviors. These behavior

---

[1] Clinical trials for a vaccine began in the fall of 1987, but even if the vaccine proves effective, widespread use will no be possible until the late 1990s (Barnes, 1987). There are several drug treatments for the disease being tested. Two antiviral drugs—AL-721 (which combines gamma interferon with tumor necrosis factor) and dideoxycytidine—are now in clinical trials to determine both toxicity and correct dosage (Barnes, 1987). One drug—Zidovudine—(brand name: Retrovir; formerly called AZT, or azidothymidine) is the only antiviral AIDS drug approved by the FDA (World Health Organization, 1987). Zidovudine inhibits the replication of retroviruses, as the drug is incorporated into the viral DNA as a chain terminator (WHO, 1987). Use of Zidovudine has been shown to increase the number of circulating T4 cells and to have a virostatic effect: Patients on the drug have shown weight gains and an increase in general well-being (WHO, 1987).

changes—often called "safer sex"—are probably the most important means for reducing transmission of HIV. Abstaining from sexual activity, reducing the number of sexual partners, use of condoms during intercourse, and engaging in mutual monogamous sexual relationships with a seronegative partner are specific ways of reducing risk of transmission.

Risk Groups

Are there people who are more likely to be infected and who, therefore, need more attention? It is true that different groups of people, by virtue of sexual behaviors, drug use, or medical status, have different levels of risk for HIV infection. According to the *Surgeon General's Report* (Koop, 1986), 70% of reported AIDS cases in this country are male homosexuals and bisexuals, and 25% are intravenous drug users. The remaining 5% is divided among people who have had blood transfusions (e.g., in surgery), hemophiliacs, and others. Because of this distribution of cases, prevention efforts have been primarily directed at homosexual men and IV drug users. However, the fact that culturally distinct groups have historically been of greatest risk for infection may have lulled those not in these groups into a potentially dangerous sense of invulnerability. The truth is that nearly everyone is at risk. Heterosexual transmission has been shown to occur from males to females (Padian *et al.*, 1987; Piot *et al.*, 1984; Redfield *et al.*, 1985) and from females to males (Fischl *et al.*, 1987; Redfield *et al.*, 1985). While the high percentage of AIDS cases in homosexual men was the early focus of the media, attention is now slowly being shifted to other populations, including drug users, adolescents, women, and minorities.

Statistics show an alarming increase in the number of IV drug abusers with AIDS and HIV infection (MacDonald, 1986). This population is of importance for several reasons. Research suggests that the frequency of unprotected sex is greater among drug users than among those who do not use drugs (Martin, 1987), and those under the influence of psychoactive substances may be less likely to use clean needles, thereby increasing the chances of the infection spreading among members of the drug-using community. Further, drug users may be heterosexual and may have sex with drug-free people, providing a path of transmission of AIDS into the heterosexual population.

Several groups that have not yet been hit hard by HIV disease may be at risk for reasons that may not be clear to them. Teenagers often experiment with their developing sexuality, yet they often neglect to use effective contraception and practice safer sex because of a heightened sense of invulnerability. Teenagers are often not taught enough about sexually transmitted diseases, including AIDS, and are not very knowledgeable in safer sex practices, especially the use of condoms. Issues pertinent to adolescents and AIDS will be discussed in depth later in this chapter.

Women are also at risk, and recent data suggest that cases of AIDS among women are increasing. Of 97 women who were sexual partners of HIV-positive men, 23% tested positive for HIV, with the number of sexual contacts positively associated with HIV infection (Padian *et al.*, 1987). While surveys show that the major route of HIV transmission for women is through IV drug abuse, heterosexual contact with an infected person is the second largest contributor (Guinan & Hardy, 1987a). In April 1987, there were 2,388 reported cases of women with AIDS, only 7% of all AIDS cases, but 26% of heterosexual AIDS cases in the United States (Guinan & Hardy, 1987b).

Minorities also appear to be at risk for AIDS. A majority of women with AIDS are minority group members (Guinan & Hardy, 1987b). Another example of the overrepresentation of minorities in the AIDS epidemic is found by looking at the United States Army. Between October 1985 and December 1986, five times as many black as white civilian applicants, and three times more Hispanic than white applicants tested positive for HIV (Centers for Disease Control, 1987c). Often with less access to health care, minorities present a problem in HIV treatment and detection, as well as in prevention interventions. The focus of such interventions should be geared toward specific groups and should consider the different cultural values, languages, and social norms of the groups being targeted.

Barriers to Preventing HIV Infection

There are many factors that appear to hinder prevention efforts directed at AIDS. The asymptomatic nature of HIV infection and the reluctance of many people to test for infection means that there are probably thousands of people capable of spreading the disease who do not know it. The complications associated with ARC and AIDS, particularly those affecting judgment, memory, and mood, present a challenge to those working with patients to prevent them from spreading the disease. The historical context of the epidemic, in which distinct subcultures have been those at greatest risk, may have contributed to feelings of invulnerability among those not in these groups, and to a reluctance to engage in safer behaviors. The coincidence of the illness with drug use may also hinder prevention efforts, and the nature of the primary route of transmission—sexual behavior—makes prevention even more difficult. The remainder of the chapter deals with ways of overcoming these barriers to effective prevention, considering social psychological research that may be relevant, as well as research on prevention of sexually transmitted diseases and promotion of contraception as sources of information for this effort. Finally, we will discuss what is known about present prevention efforts and how we may refine AIDS prevention interventions to increase their effectiveness.

Adolescents and AIDS

Adolescents represent a potential high-risk group for several reasons: They often exhibit feelings of invulnerability to health threats, are not very knowledgeable about AIDS, and are becoming sexually active and may be characterized by risky behaviors. Studies have shown that teenagers are poor contraceptors and that they display little responsibility for their health (Radius, Dielman, Becker, Rosenstock, & Horvath, 1980; Zelnik & Shah, 1983). Furthermore, adolescents often feel invulnerable to disease and appear to have little knowledge about AIDS or other sexually transmitted diseases (DiClemente, Zorn, & Temoshok, 1986; Hunger, 1976; Price, Desmond, & Kukulka, 1985; Yacenda, 1974). If explorations of newly found sexual desires are accompanied by experimentation with drugs or alcohol, problems with safer-sex practices may be compounded. Thus, one can argue that adolescents be considered a high-risk group because they are becoming sexually active, are unaware of or do not follow safer-sex precautions, and may not be responsive to efforts to protect their health and well-being. However, because their attitudes about sexuality are in early developmental stages, it may be possible to achieve effective long-term behavior change by helping them form appropriate beliefs about safer sex and AIDS.

On the average, young men and women report sexual intercourse to occur for the first time between the ages of 13 and 17 (Smith, Nenney, Weinman, & Mumford, 1982; Zabin, Hardy, Smith, & Hirsch, 1986; Zelnik & Shah, 1983). During their first sexual encounter, less than half report use of contraception (Zelnik & Shah, 1983), and even fewer may be regular contraception users. When contraception is used, the methods chosen may not help protect against AIDS; the most popular form of contraception in this age group is the use of birth control pills, particularly among blacks (Zelnick & Shah, 1983). The incidence of pregnancy among 11- to 19-year-olds is approximately 20% (Zabin *et al.*, 1986).

One reason for poor use of contraception among adolescents is that they are not very knowledgeable about birth control and even less knowledgeable about AIDS and other sexually transmitted diseases (Hunger, 1976; Price *et al.*, 1985; Yacenda, 1974). Many young adults do not know what precautions are needed to prevent transmission of AIDS, and nearly 10% are unaware that heterosexual transmission is possible (Strunin & Hingson, 1987). Recent surveys of high school students in areas where AIDS has been most prevalent suggest that many teenagers do know about AIDS. For example, DiClemente *et al.* (1987) found that 9 in 10 high school students in San Francisco who were studied knew that AIDS was transmitted by sexual intercourse. Variability in knowledge about AIDS was also found: Many respondents believed that AIDS could be spread by touching, kissing, or other casual contact. Men at risk report changing certain behaviors owing to fear of AIDS (McKusick, Wiley, *et al.*, 1985), but many adolescents do not. Strunin and Hingson (1987) surveyed 16- to 19-year-olds, and while 70% were sexually active, only 15% of those that were sexually active changed their behaviors because of their concern about AIDS. Of these adolescents reporting behavior changes due to fear of AIDS, only 20% did so effectively.

In addition to lacking knowledge about AIDS, contraception, and STD prevention, adolescents possess attitudes and beliefs of invulnerability that make them a difficult group to educate or warn about less safe sexual practices. More than half of adolescents report they are not concerned about their own health, and few accept responsibility for their health (Radius *et al.*, 1980). Age may be an important factor in feelings of invulnerability. Among inner-city children and adolescents, perceived vulnerability to venereal diseases increases with age (Gochman & Saucier, 1982). Further, because of their youth and inexperience, adolescents may not understand the relationship between risk of pregnancy and frequency of coitus. For example, Smith *et al.* (1982) found that 74% of teenage women who were not using birth control reported that they did not want to become pregnant. Furthermore, while 92% knew where to obtain birth control, only 11% used it. Similarly, many high school students surveyed in San Francisco reported that they were less likely to get AIDS than were most people and did not believe their risk of infection was high (DiClemente *et al.*, 1987).

Developmentally, some adolescents may not be ready or able to make important decisions regarding the consequences of their sexuality. Nadelson, Notman, and Gillon (1980) found that on the average approximately 20% of pregnant women reported having used contraception; therefore, either they were not using contraception regularly or they were using it ineffectively. Almost one-third (28%) of these women felt that they did not need contraception, believing that pregnancy would never happen to them. This denial of the need for contraception suggests that some adolescents may not be mature enough or comfortable enough with their decision to have sex to make rational decisions concerning birth control. Adolescents may also lack the decision-making and communicative skills that are critical for practicing safer sex. Some may be afraid of asking their partners to wear condoms or lack the assertiveness needed for regular and effective condom use. Teenagers may fail to use condoms because they "get caught in the heat of the moment," while others may simply feel too awkward or embarrassed about their use.

Social Psychological Approaches to Preventing AIDS

Social psychology has traditionally included the study of a number of basic processes and applications that are relevant to the prevention of AIDS. The spread of AIDS may be prevented by behavior change that reduces or eliminates the risk of infection for those people not already ill or carrying the AIDS virus. A number of recommendations for minimizing or eliminating this risk of infection have been suggested, including reduction of the number of sex partners, use of condoms, abstinence from sex, maintenance of monogamous relationships, use of clean needles by intravenous drug users, and stockpiling one's own blood prior to surgery in which transfusion may be necessary. Research on attitude change and persuasion, resistance to peer pressure, modeling, and naive theories of illness is pertinent to the implementation of campaigns designed to achieve these and other prevention goals.

Attitude Change and Risk Prevention

Attitudes toward health and disease are powerful determinants of both health-promoting and health-risk behaviors. Attitude formation is influenced by many factors: socioeconomic, institutional, family and peer influences, the mass media, and personal experience (McGuire, 1964). Once an attitude about a particular object or situation has been formed, it is resistant, although not invulnerable, to change. Social psychologists have been instrumental in identifying factors that influence attitude change and in manipulating these factors to determine when and how attitudes can be altered.

An important step in the study of AIDS prevention is the clarification of prevailing attitudes toward the risk-avoidant behaviors that are necessary for the prevention of further spread. Interventions subsequently focusing on the formation of positive and the elimination of negative attitudes toward disease prevention may provide a defense against the disease. For our purposes, attitudes may be defined as predispositions to behave in certain ways toward specific situations, objects, or people (Zimbardo, Ebbesen, & Maslach, 1977). Attitudes have three components: affect, cognition, and behavior. Affective aspects of an attitude consist of the emotional evaluation of, or liking for, the stimulus, while cognitive constructs reflect beliefs and knowledge. Behavioral tendencies and responses to the stimulus are also viewed as crucial (Zimbardo et al., 1977).

This three-dimensional definition of attitude implies that any attempt at long-term health behavior change must address each of the three components in order to be effective. It is possible for an intervention to be successful in changing an individual's affective response toward an object but to have no real effect on behavior. Likewise, if a change in behavior is observed (which is often used as a measure of success in an intervention program), but no concurrent changes in affect or belief are noted, observed behavior change may be transient and unstable. For example, in AIDS prevention, we may, through various techniques, induce someone to use a condom on one occasion, but if that person views condom use as unpleasant or unnatural, it is conceivable that use of condoms, for this person, will be less likely to develop into a habitual behavior than for someone who both uses condoms and has more fully accepted their use.

Changing an individual's emotions or cognitions about an object or behavior can be a consequence of change in the behavior itself. When individuals engage in a behavior that is not consistent with their feelings about that behavior (e.g., a person refuses sex with a potential partner even though he or she is extremely attracted to the person and would like to have sex), a state of cognitive dissonance could ensue in which affect and/or cognitions do not match behavior (Festinger, 1954, 1957). According to dissonance theory, the individual is then motivated to reduce this state of dissonance. Reduction of this tension can be achieved by changing behavior so that it is consistent with affect (e.g., having sex with the partner), changing affect so that it matches behavior (e.g., believing that the partner was not that desirable after all), or by changing cognitions so that they match behavior (e.g., "I'd like to have sex with him/her but it's not worth the risk of contracting a disease").

Thus, an intervention resulting in initial behavior change may then be followed by affective and/or cognitive changes. However, change in behavior not followed by affective-cognitive change might result in only a transient adoption of risk-avoidant behavior, or could work against efforts to reduce risky behavior. If someone engages in unprotected sex, the behavior, which is now irrevocable, may be inconsistent with prevailing beliefs about AIDS. In this case, the behavior cannot be altered so beliefs and attitudes about AIDS may be changed, possibly leading to further risk taking.

Group Pressure

Another approach to changing behavior and beliefs focuses on pressures toward uniformity within a group, or one's need to conform (Lewin, 1947). The desire to behave in a manner similar to one's reference group is a powerful motivator of health-promotive and risk-avoidant behavior. The lone smoker in a group of non-smokers, or the solitary couch potato in a circle of hard-core joggers, is under considerable pressure to alter his or her behavior in concordance with group norms or to leave the group. Similarly, a sexually nonactive teen wishing to fit in with a group of friends who are all sexually active may feel tremendous pressure to conform. These pressures may be particularly severe for adolescents, and many prevention programs that advise teens to "say no" and provide some defense against these pressures have been described (e.g., Evans, Smith, & Raines, 1984). Yet interventions on behalf of postponing sexual activity may be met with equally potent pressures emanating from friends to conform to the behavioral standards of the group. Although this paints a dim portrait of success for intervention programs aimed at altering risky but normative behaviors, it conversely raises expectations that a program successful in positively changing attitudes of the majority (or of the imitated) will be successful in changing the affect and behavior of many more. Similarly, interventions that portray safe practices as the "mainstream" or normative state may be effective.

Mass media campaigns for health promotion are illustrative of this notion. Although most campaigns are, by themselves, largely ineffective in persuading a particular individual to drop a certain risk behavior, they appear to have a cumulative effect over time. A shift in the cultural climate may take place, resulting in fewer persons adopting the risk behavior initially noted (Taylor, 1986). An example of this is seen in the current status of cigarette smoking in this country.

Antismoking campaigns alone are unlikely to have persuaded individual smokers to quit, yet they have gradually produced a marked change in public opinion toward smoking and smokers, which is likely to prevent many from initiating the habit. It is also likely that growing pressure in many groups have led some smokers to quit.

Fear Appeals

Many believe that fear can motivate people to change a particular behavior. If they fear that an act will lead to severe consequences, or if they fear that failure to change behavior will change their health, compliance with recommendations may be enhanced. Fear is a powerful motivator, but research has shown that the level of fear does not necessarily relate to behavior change (Janis & Feshbach, 1953; Leventhal, 1970). Janis and Feshbach (1953) described this relationship as curvilinear; moderate fear appeals seem effective in inducing behavioral change, but low fear appeals may be ignored, and high fear appeals may be so frightening that they paralyze the individual into inactivity (Leventhal, 1970). This finding presents a special problem with regard to AIDS prevention. High fear arousal is attendant with the disease and its poor prognosis, possibly leading to "behavioral paralysis" with regard to risk avoidance. Individuals may be so frightened that they ignore information about AIDS and deny their own risk of infection. This may account for otherwise puzzling behavior, such as sexual promiscuity in diagnosed seropositive individuals or in those not infected but who are at high risk for infection. To combat this, emphasis might be placed on gradually decreasing this fear, possibly focusing on the steps that can be taken to reduce the likelihood that HIV + persons will progress to ARC and AIDS, or on the effectiveness of risk-avoidant behaviors. In addition, providing information about general risk-avoidant behavior to elementary school-age children, who may not yet be fully cognizant of the disease and its outcome, may lead to adoption of such behaviors before the "high fear message" has an opportunity to become salient and interfere.

Education

Many of the principles we have considered so far relate to the affective aspects of attitude change. However, a number of issues pertaining to beliefs and knowledge are also relevant. Informational appeals aimed at increasing health behavior change are widely used. This is based, in part, on the belief that the greater one's knowledge of health risks associated with certain behaviors, the greater will be the likelihood that the individual will avoid these behaviors; the case of the cigarette smoker who knows that smoking is bad for one's health, yet continues to smoke, is but one example of the lack of congruence between knowledge and behavior. Increasing information about health risks is a necessary but insufficient step toward reducing risk behavior.

If nothing else, informational appeals alert people to risks they might otherwise not know about. Research has been conducted on the efficacy of informational appeals on changing behavior, and at least three major components of these appeals have been identified: (1) the source (communicator), (2) the message, and (3) the receiver (Hovland, Janis, & Kelley, 1953). Within each of these components, a number of factors have been delineated that affect the success of an appeal. An exhaustive discussion of these is beyond the scope of this chapter. We will instead briefly discuss some of these variables with greatest relevance to health behavior change and AIDS prevention.

A number of variables that affect the persuasiveness of attitude change attempts have been identified. Attractiveness, similarity, credibility, and trustworthiness are all important source characteristics (Berscheid & Walster, 1978; Dion & Stein, 1978). Similarly, how the message is delivered—whether conclusions are drawn explicitly or left to be inferred, whether the message is highly divergent from that held by the audience, or whether opposing arguments are presented or only one side is aired—may affect persuasion. Finally, the "influencibility" of the audience and its initial information level may be important in determining how effective a persuasive attempt is.

Persuasive impact increases when the source is seen as knowledgeable about the topic, of high intelligence, of high social status, or of high prestige (Hovland & Weiss, 1951). The source must also appear trustworthy (e.g, sincere, not intent on persuasion, without underlying motives for desiring a particular outcome). Arguing against one's own best interest is an effective means of eliciting trust and a feeling of sincerity (Walster, Aronson, & Abrahams, 1966). Scientists, doctors, and others in the medical field enjoy a high degree of credibility. But a highly scientific message may not be readily understood by laypersons and is thus less likely to be heeded.

Evidence also suggests that explicitly drawn conclusions are more useful in generating attitude change than are conclusions left to the audience to derive (Evans, Rozelle, Noblitt, & Williams, 1975). Attempts to change attitudes about risky behaviors might be better advised to draw specific conclusions, such as "avoid having more than one sex partner," rather than simply providing information about rates of transmission and allowing people to draw their own conclusions. At the same time, messages that are highly discrepant from the needs or prevailing attitudes of the audience may not be as effective as moderately discrepant appeals. In a sexually active target group, asking for complete abstinence from sex may be less successful in achieving change ethan suggesting reduction of the number of partners or recommending that people be more selective in choice of sexual partners. Finally, the influencibility of the target audience is important. The notion of influencibility has been an elusive one, but if target groups are motivated to attend to an appeal, are strongly driven to conform to the norms of a particular group, or are at a developmental stage where attitudes are in flux, messages may be more effective.

Attitude change does not necessarily cause behavior change, nor do changes in behavior necessarily reflect or require attitude change. In implementing health intervention programs, it is important to know not only that a change in health behavior/attitude has occurred but, more importantly, *why* it has occurred, what *components* of attitudes were responsible for the change, and what manipulations were responsible, in turn, for the component changes. Models of health behavior that integrate attitude change theory appear better able to account for the reasons behind health behavior change, thus making findings based upon them potentially reproducible and more useful.

Health Beliefs

The Health Belief Model (Rosenstock, 1974) predicts the practice of health behaviors on the basis of beliefs about a particular health threat and about the likelihood that a health behavior will lead to a reduction in threat. Belief in a particular health threat is determined by general health values (how much people are concerned about their health), beliefs about personal susceptibility and vulnerability to an illness (how likely people feel they are to contract a disease), and beliefs about the severity and consequences of the illness. Belief in the efficacy of a health behavior in reducing risk is further affected by beliefs that the benefits of performing the behavior will outweigh the costs of performance. This model has been used effectively to predict health behavior change including breast self-examination (Calnan & Moss, 1984), preventive dental care (Kegeles, 1963), and weight loss behavior (Becker, Maiman, Kierscht, Haefner, & Drachman, 1977).

Use of the Health Belief Model in AIDS risk prevention calls for consideration of issues specific both to AIDS prevention and to components of the model. For example, issues of vulnerability to AIDS will be very different, depending upon which risk group is being addressed. For gay men, perception of vulnerability to AIDS is likely to be high, leading to a possible increase in adoption of risk-avoidant behaviors. Adolescents, however, may perceive their susceptibility to AIDS as very low and may be more resistant to risk-reduction efforts It is essential that intervention efforts be tailored toward specific groups at risk for AIDS.

A second component of this model that deserves some attention with regard to AIDS is the cost/benefit factor of risk-reducing behavior. Although the benefits of a behavior such as condom use are clearly high (reduction in risk of HIV exposure, VD contraction, and unplanned pregnancy), they may seem far less compelling than the immediate cost of engaging in this behavior (e.g., embarrassment in obtaining condoms or at having to ask a partner to cooperate, reduced sexual pleasure, interrupted spontaneity).

Social Learning Theory

Social learning theory (Bandura, 1977a, 1977b) posits that behavior is predicted both by perceptions of self-efficacy toward an action (the belief in one's ability to perform a specific action) and the outcome efficacy of that action (the belief that successfully performing an action will result in a specific outcome). Self-efficacy information is derived from performance accomplishments, vicarious experience, verbal persuasion, and physiological arousal (low arousal while performing is interpreted as lack of anxiety and thus good performance). Through the increase of self-efficacy and outcome efficacy toward a behavior, the probability of performance of that behavior will be increased. Increasing self-efficacy may be crucial for successful AIDS prevention since it appears to be in increasing compliance with many health regimens (e.g., Marlatt, 1982). For example, role playing is a method whereby performance accomplishments can be "practiced" through rehearsal of situations in which risk-reductive behavior can be used. By successfully "saying no" or insisting on safer sex in a role-play situation, a person may gain a semblance of performance accomplishment with a resulting increase in self-efficacy. Models who tell or show how they performed a particular action may also be effective in increasing efficacy. Particularly effective are models who verbalize their own fears or concerns about performing a behavior (e.g., "I thought that it I asked my lover to use a condom he would look elsewhere for sex") but who ultimately perform successfully.

Naive Theories of Illness

One final socially derived cognitive factor that cuts across all of the health behavior models we have discussed is the perception of the causes, outcomes, and treatment effects of a particular disease. People derive and use "commonsense" models of diseases and disease processes (e.g., Leventhal, Nerenz, & Steele, 1984). This may be particularly important for AIDS because the combination of a frighteningly lethal outcome, its association with controversial risk groups, and its sometimes uncertain etiology has resulted in a plethora of misinformation. A misinformed public is a threat, not simply because they may foster prejudice toward various risk groups but because they will act according to their beliefs about cause, progression, and cure of AIDS. For example, it is clear that many persons still consider AIDS to be a disease of hemophiliacs, gays, and IV drug users. Many believe that because they do not fall into these categories, they are not at risk for the disease and thus are free to practice what better-informed persons would consider risky behaviors. There may also be a "trade-off" effect based on causal beliefs. For example, the widespread advocacy of condom use as a means of preventing AIDS may lead persons into falsely believing that if they use condoms they eliminate all risk of AIDS and are free to engage in promiscuous and casual sex. Another naive AIDS belief, held by many heterosexuals, is that "they can tell" if someone "is that sort of person" (i.e., bisexual, promiscuous, or in a high-risk group) and thus eliminate risk through some intuitive sixth sense. Dissemination of accurate information about AIDS will eliminate, in part, naive ideas about causation and spread, and may subsequently affect behavior itself.

Thus far we have considered general implications of research on social behavior and attitudes for the prevention of AIDS. We have also noted, however, that interventions may be most effective if they target specific groups, particularly if these groups are resistent. The next section focuses on the special needs of adolescents and the problems teenagers pose for AIDS prevention interventions. There are few studies examining adolescents and AIDS; therefore, we will draw from studies investigating teenage pregnancy and contraception. In addition, we will consider studies that examine the spread and control of sexually transmitted diseases. The information that we have from these studies may help formulate intervention and prevention techniques that are most appropriate for adolescents.

Prevention Efforts and Adolescents

Aside from avoiding contaminated needles, one can guard against AIDS the same as one guards against any other sexually transmitted disease: (1) avoiding sexual exposure to infected sexual partners and/or (2) placing a barrier between infectious and susceptible membranes. In the case of AIDS, avoiding sexual encounters with infected partners is difficult because carriers of the virus often remain asymptomatic for several years. Because sexually active teenagers have no way of knowing whether their partners are infected, they must either abstain from sexual intercourse, use a condom, or engage in safer practices such as those noted earlier. To suggest that all adolescents abstain from sex is unrealistic and may lead to reactance or to feelings of guilt about sex. This may have undesired effects, either by increasing sexual activity or by increasing unprotected sex, since guilt does not necessarily discourage having sex but may deter use of contraception (Kastner, 1984). The most useful approach to preventing the spread of AIDS in teenagers, then, is to advise caution and to encourage condom use for those who decide to have intercourse.

Interventions aimed at encouraging contraceptive use provide useful information for promoting safer sex practices such as condom use among teenagers. While teenagers are overall poor contraceptors, some studies have identified factors that predict better contraceptive behaviors. One factor of particular importance is the relationship a teenager has with his or her parents. In a study of teenage women, Kastner (1984) found parent communication, knowledge about methods of contraception, and permissiveness of home environment to be predictors of regular contraceptive use. Boyfriend support was also found to be predictive of contraceptive use in these young women. There was no relationship between parent communication or contraceptive knowledge and sexual experiences. These results suggest that while parent communication and contraceptive knowledge do not encourage sexual activity, they are related to regular use of contraception when young women do become sexually active.

Gispert, Brinich, Wheeler, and Krieger (1984) reported similar findings about the importance of parent–child relations in predicting adolescent contraceptive behavior. In this study, regular contraceptive use was associated with a positive mother–daughter relationship and with the presence of a father in the home. Both of these studies examining predictors of contraceptive behaviors suggest that AIDS prevention campaigns may profit through parental participation. Encouraging parents to discuss AIDS and safer sex practices with their children may help to increase knowledge and persuade children to adopt safer sex practices. Parents who openly communicate with their children may be able to encourage condom use. Parents do, however, need to be reassured with evidence that "sex talks" with their children will not increase the likelihood of their children engaging in sexual activities, but will increase the chances of safer sex when their child does decide to do so.

Education may also be an effective tool in prevention efforts with adolescents. There is some evidence that knowledge is related to greater use of contraceptives (Eaton, 1979). Young people with sex education are no more likely to have sex but are less likely to become pregnant (Zelnik & Kim, 1982); therefore, education could potentially increase the frequency of safer sex among those who are having sex and not necessarily encourage sexual activity among students. Unfortunately, while young people are often denied knowledge about sex before puberty, they are expected to know how to behave appropriately in order to avoid disease and pregnancy (Darrow & Pauli, 1984).

Providing information in school classes or at home may be necessary but is clearly not sufficient to ensure that safer sex practices will be adopted. How it is disseminated may also be important. As discussed earlier, scare tactics may not be effective in changing behavior. Perceived seriousness of venereal disease (VD), for example, does not correlate with the likelihood of taking preventive measures (Simon & Das, 1984). Information about the effectiveness of preventive behavior may be more useful. Rogers and Mewborn (1976) studied fear appeals and attitude change about VD in college students and found that unless they understand the efficacy of coping responses, individuals may resist recommendations of a communicator. Increases in the noxiousness of messages about VD facilitated attitude change only when the recommended coping response was described as highly effective. To increase the likelihood that people will adopt safer sex practices, it may be necessary to highlight the effectiveness of these practices for the prevention of AIDS.

Other effective means for increasing knowledge about AIDS transmission might include peer teaching in the classroom. Jordheim (1975) found peer teaching to be more effective than traditional instruction for altering knowledge and attitudes about VD. Outside of the classroom, more anonymous and nonthreatening sources of correct information should be available. The most common concerns of callers to the national VD hotline were related to confidentiality, fear, and anxiety (Knox, Mandel, & Lazorowicz, 1981). AIDS hotline services may also provide an effective educational approach because of the nonthreatening anonymity offered callers.

Interventions should also be directed toward helping adolescents to develop interpersonal skills and to deal with peer pressures. Research on initiation of cigarette smoking in adolescents has clearly established the importance of peer pressure in the performance of high-risk behavior (Evans *et al.*, 1984), and learning to deal with these social influences is critical for carrying out effective interventions to encourage safer sex practices. Communicative skills that reflect assertiveness and persuasion are critical for encouraging condom use, particularly in resistant or manipulative partners. Prevention programs for adolescents should also include methods for helping them develop these skills. More regular contraception and better attitudes toward family planning were found in students who completed a cognitive and behavioral group training program (Schinke, Blythe, & Gilchrist, 1981). Students in the program gained knowledge along with problem-solving skills and persuasive patterns of interpersonal communication. Other programs designed to heighten motivation to participate in health promotion programs (e.g, Lund, Kegeles, & Weisenberg, 1977) and encourage assertiveness have incorporated reinforcement and role playing (Hagenhoff, Lowe, Hovell, & Rugg, 1987). Solomon and DeJong (1986) used soap-opera-style videos to encourage high-risk men to use condoms and women to be assertive in requesting their partner's use of condoms.

In addition to programs that motivate and assist adolescents in developing stronger interpersonal skills, programs should be designed to address problems associated with substance use. Alcohol and drugs may increase the likelihood of having sex while at the same time decreasing the chances that safer sex practices will be carried out. In a study of Australian military troops, Hart (1974) found the influence of alcohol to be a major reason for failure to use condoms. Pemberton *et al.* (1972) found that 71% of male VD patients and 29% of female VD patients reported using alcohol before intercourse with the infected partner. Among homosexual men, use of alcohol, marijuana, and poppers is positively associated with less safe sex practices (Stall, McKusick, Wiley, Coates, & Ostrow, 1986). These studies show that alcohol and other drugs are powerful forces against safer sex practices and, therefore, may increase a person's risk of contracting AIDS. Experimentation with alcohol and other drugs often begins during adolescence; naive adolescents have difficulty estimating the effects of these substances and may become easily intoxicated. This places a number of teenagers at risk for abandoning safer sex practices. Interventions need to be designed to assist adolescents in dealing with sex in drug- and alcohol-related situations. Teenagers must be taught to plan ahead for sex before alcohol or drug use begins, and to limit their use of these substances.

The problems associated with modifying sexual behavior among adolescents are many and are partially due to the unique development stage defined by adolescence. We have discussed these issues in detail for two reasons. First, we are concerned that heterosexual adolescents may be a high-risk group for AIDS infection owing to their increasing sexual activity and apparent perceptions of invulnerability and lack of concern about their health. Second, many of the barriers to effective behavior change among adolescents are social ones, and they may require different approaches than are needed to induce safer behavior by the general population. Consequently, we have discussed several specific strategies that may prove effective in overcoming these obstacles and in reducing teenagers' risk of coming in contact with the HIV. A number of more general issues are also relevant, including those associated with general promotion of condom use.

Conclusions

With all that has happened and with all the information and publicity about AIDS that has reached the general public through the media, one would expect that some behavior change has already occurred. To some extent, this is true. A number of informational campaigns about AIDS have been initiated, some targeting specific groups, such as homosexuals or minorities, and others directed more toward the general public. Results are mixed and incomplete because many of these campaigns have not been evaluated. However, data suggest that some behavior change has occurred among members of high-risk groups, raising hopes that interventions with adolescents may be effective. In one study, marked decreases in sexual activity associated with HIV transmission were noted among homosexual physicians and college students as the AIDS epidemic grew, and these changes in behavior were associated with perceived risk for developing AIDS (Klein *et al.*, 1987). Another study reported decreases in sexual activity and increases in condom use among gay men in New York City after learning about AIDS (Martin, 1987).

Not all findings are this clear or positive, however. For example, a study in San Francisco examined sexual activity among gay men in 1983 (McKusick, Horstmann, & Coates, 1985). Among men involved in stable relationships with one other, or "unattached" men who did not frequent gay bathhouses, major reductions in frequency of sexual contacts were observed, but among men who used bathhouses, these changes were negligible. Knowledge about AIDS was relatively high among these men but was not related to reported behavior change.

Other studies suggest that informational campaigns alone will be inconsistent at best in preventing risky behavior (e.g. Temoshok, Sweet, & Zich, 1987). An educational campaign in the United Kingdom, for example, produced some increases in knowledge about AIDS but had no effect on attitudes or intentions regarding behavior (Sherr, 1987). In another study, knowledge about AIDS in a sample of gay men has not related to reported behavior change (Joseph *et al.*, 1987). Surveys of IV drug users indicate that they knew about AIDS and that sharing needles increased one's risk of infection, but that many had not changed their behavior to reduce this risk (Friedman *et al.*, 1987). Increased use of sterile needles has been reported in a number of studies, and there is some reason for optimism regarding the prospects for further change among current users (DesJarlais & Friedman, 1987).

Evidence suggests that condoms provide good protection against the transmission of AIDS between sexual partners. The AIDS virus cannot penetrate an intact condom (Conant, Hardy, Sernatinger, Spicer, & Levy, 1986), and there is a lack of seroconversion among sexual partners of AIDS patients when condoms are used (Fischl *et al.*, 1987). Condoms can be purchased over the counter and do not require a medical examination or ingestion of a pill, yet condoms are not usually preferred as a means of contraception. The most common complaints about condoms voiced by men are that they interfere with sex and reduce pleasure (Darrow, 1974). Women do not react as negatively to the use of condoms but appear to feel they are the man's responsibility (Nadelson *et al.*, 1980). These biases are partially responsible for the fact that condoms are not a more widespread method of contraception in the United States.

A number of methods for increasing condom use have been proposed on the basis of these biases against their use. Ways that condoms may enhance intercourse have been described. For example, condoms can promote pleasure and prolong sexual experiences by sustaining erection (Felman, 1979; Hatcher, 1978). Solomon and DeJong (1986) use videotapes to show how condom use can be erotic. The videotapes provide viewers with the message that condoms are not troublesome to use and that it is acceptable to encourage sex partners to use them. More information should be made available on the sensitivity of these products and of how condom use can be incorporated as a sensual part of foreplay (Harvey, 1972). While people are often afraid to suggest to their partner that they wear a condom, role playing may help to overcome these fears and plan persuasive discussions. Grieco (1987) offers a number of ways to encourage manipulative or defensive partners to use condoms. The effectiveness of these suggested coercive techniques has not, however, been evaluated.

Increasing the availability of condoms may also increase their use. The majority of VD patients, most of whom are not regular condom users, report that they would use free condoms if they were made available (Felman & Santora, 1981). One study has shown that condom use increases when they are made available at no charge. Arnold and Cogswell (1971) report nearly a threefold increase in the use of condoms following distribution of 18,000 condoms in 13 weeks. Free condoms were made available in places that adolescent males were known to frequent (barbershops, pool halls, and grocery stores). Similar projects could include places where women go (e.g., beauty parlors, clothing stores, and health clubs) to encourage both men and women to carry condoms and to use them more frequently. More open and imaginative methods of condom distribution may help to encourage their use.

Though prevention through promotion of safer sex practices independent of AIDS appears to be a promising approach, the fact that risk perceptions may still be unrealistic among many groups suggests that the need to widely distribute information about AIDS and how it is spread is clear (e.g. Bauman & Siegel, 1987). Though it may not be enough to educate, lack of information may lead to risky behavior. In a study in an area where the incidence of HIV infection was low, nearly three-quarters of homosexuals who were interviewed reported engaging in high-risk sexual activities, while only 13% reported use of condoms (Jones *et al.*,

1987). As with adolescents, the low rate of HIV infection may be associated with low perceptions of risk, leading to adoption of fewer safer practices.

These findings, as well as the issues that we have already discussed, suggest a multilevel plan for prevention of AIDS through alteration of high-risk behaviors. Informational campaigns appear to be important but clearly should be supplemented by other interventions that focus on social pressures, attitude formation, and other psychosocial variables associated with risky behavior. The use of models who are clearly aware of behavior change that reduces risk of HIV infection and who engage in safer sex practices is also important, and we have begun to see messages about AIDS and condom use written into the scripts of popular television shows. Targeting attitudes and variables that are not related to AIDS transmission but may be crucial in the decision to engage in high-risk behaviors also appears to be needed. Changing perceptions of vulnerability and risk, teaching social skills that help people deal with pressure to engage in high-risk behaviors, and assessing that people have accurate knowledge of AIDS, contraception, and how the disease is spread also emerge as priorities for prevention efforts.

Finally, the fact that AIDS is beginning to spread far beyond previously identified high-risk groups suggests the need to target both those who already have been infected and those not associated with these groups. Of particular concern are those who are most sexually active or who are relatively naive about sex, as well as women and minorities, who appear to show either more severe manifestations of the disease or a higher overall prevalence than the general population. While efforts to educate and support those in high-risk groups must continue, our efforts to prevent the spread of AIDS must also take a broader approach, targeting many subpopulations in society and providing information and skills that will help everyone minimize the risk of infection.

ACKNOWLEDGEMENT. The opinions or assertions contained herein are the private ones of the authors and are not to be construed as official or reflecting the views of the Department of Defense or the Uniformed Services University of the Health Sciences.

References

Arnold, C. B., & Cogswell, B. E. (1971). A condom distribution program for adolescents: The findings of a feasibility study. *American Journal of Public Health, 61,* 739–750.

Bandura, A. (1977a). *Social learning theory.* Englewood Cliffs, NJ: Prentice-Hall.

Bandura, A. (1977b). Self efficacy: Toward a unifying theory of behavioral change. *Psychological Review, 84,* 191–215.

Barnes, D. (1987). Meeting on AIDS drugs turns into open forum. *Science, 237,* 1287–88.

Bauman, L., & Siegel, K. (1987). Misperception among gay men of the risk for AIDS associated with their sexual behavior. *Journal of Applied Social Psychology, 17,* 329–350.

Becker, M. H., Maiman, L., Kierscht, J., Haefner, D., & Drachman, R. (1977). The health belief model and dietary compliance: A field experiment. *Journal of Health and Social Behavior, 18,* 348–366.

Berscheid, E., & Walster, E. H. (1978). *Interpersonal attraction* (2nd ed.). Reading, MA: Addison-Wesley.

Calnan, M. W., & Moss, S. (1984). The health belief model and compliance with education given at a class in breast self-examination. *Journal of Health and Social Behavior, 25,* 198–210.

Centers for Disease Control. (1987a). Update: Human immunodeficiency virus infection in health-care workers exposed to blood of infected patients. *Morbidity and Mortality Weekly Reports, 36,* 285–289.

Centers for Disease Control. (1987b). Recommendations for prevention of HIV transmission in health-care settings. *Morbidity and Morality Weekly Reports, 36,* 1S–18S.

Centers for Disease Control. (1987c). Revision of the CDC surveillance case definition for acquired immunodeficiency syndrome. *Morbidity and Mortality Weekly Reports, 36,* 1S–13S.

Conant, M., Hardy, D., Sernatinger, J., Spicer, D., & Levy, J. A. (1986). Condoms prevent transmission of AIDS-associated retrovirus. *Journal of the American Medical Association, 255,* 1706.

Darrow, W. W. (1974). Attitudes toward condom use and the acceptance of veneral disease prophylactics. In M. H. Redford, G. W. Duncan, & D. J. Prager (Eds.), *The condom: Increasing utilization in the United States* (pp. 173–185). San Francisco: San Francisco Press.

Darrow, W. W., & Pauli, M. L. (1984). Health behavior and sexually transmitted diseases. In K. K. Holmes, P. Mardh, P. F. Sparling, & P. J. Wiesner (Eds.), *Sexually transmitted diseases* (pp. 65–73). New York: McGraw-Hill.

DesJarlais, D., & Friedman, S. (1987). Target groups for preventing AIDS among intravenous drug users. *Journal of Applied Social Psychology, 17,* 251–268.

DeVita, V., Hellman, S., & Rosenberg, S. (Eds.). (1985). *AIDS: Etiology, diagnosis, treatment, and prevention.* New York: J. B. Lippincott.

DiClemente, R. J., Zorn, J., & Temoshok, L. (1986). Adolescents and AIDS: A survey of knowledge, attitudes, and beliefs about AIDS in San Francisco. *American Journal of Public Health, 76,* 1443–1445.

DiClemente, R. J., Zorn, J., & Temoshok, L. (1987). The association of gender, ethnicity, and length of residence in the bay area to adolescents' knowledge and attitudes about acquired immunodeficiency syndrome. *Journal of Applied Social Psychology, 17,* 216–236.

Dion, K. K., & Stein, S. (1978). Physical attractiveness and interpersonal influence. *Journal of Experimental Social Psychology, 14,* 97–108.

Eaton, L. F. (1979). The relationship of unwanted teenage pregnancy to sex knowledge, attitudes toward birth control, acceptance of one's sexuality, parental acceptance, risk taking, and age. *Dissertation Abstracts International, 40,* 2477A. (University Microfilms No. 7925140)

Evans, R. I., Rozelle, R., Noblitt, R., & Willians, D. L. (1975). Explicit and implicit persuasive communication over time to initiate and maintain behavior change: A new perspective utilizing a real-life dental hygiene program. *Journal of Applied Social Psychology, 5,* 150–156.

Evans, R. I., Smith, C. K., & Raines, B. E. (1984). Deterring cigarette smoking in adolescents: A psychosocial-behavioral analysis of an intervention strategy. In A. Baum, S. Taylor, & J. E. Singer (Eds.), *Handbook of psychology and health* (Vol. 4, pp 301–318). Hillsdale, NJ: Erlbaum.

Felman, Y. M. (1979). A plea for the condom, especially for teenagers. *Journal of the American Medical Association, 241,* 2517–2518.

Felman, Y. M., & Santora, F. J. (1981). The use of condoms by VD clinic patients. *Cutis, 27,* 330–336.

Festinger, L. (1954). A theory of social comparison processes. *Human Relations, 7,* 117–140.

Festinger, L. (1957). *A theory of cognitive dissonance.* Stanford: Stanford University Press.

Fischl, M. A., Dickinson, G. M., Scott, G. B., Klimas, N., Fletcher, M. A., & Parks, W. (1987). Evaluation of heterosexual partners, children, and household contacts of adults with AIDS. *Journal of the American Medical Association, 257,* 640–644.

Forstein, M. (1984). The psychosocial impact of the acquired immunodeficiency syndrome. *Seminars in Oncology, 11,* 77–82.

Friedman, S., DesJarlais, D., Sotheran, J., Garber, J., Cohen, H., & Smith, D. (1987). AIDS and self-organization among intravenous drug users. *International Journal of Addictions, 22,* 201–220.

Gabzuda, D. H., Ho, D. D., delaMonte, S., Hirsch, M. S., Rota, T. R., & Sobel, R. A. (1986). Immunohistochemical identification of HTLV-III antigen in brains of patients with AIDS. *Annals of Neurology, 20,* 289–295.

Gartner, S., Markovitz, P., Markovitz, D., Betts, R., & Popovic, M. (1986). Virus isolation from and identification of HTLV-III/LAV-producings cells in brain tissue from a patient with AIDS. *Journal of the American Medical Association, 256,* 2365.

Gispert, M., Brinich, P., Wheeler, K., & Krieger, L. (1984). Predictors of repeat pregnancies among low-income adolescents. *Hospital and Community Psychiatry, 35*(7), 719–723.

Gochman, D. S., & Saucier, J. (1982). Perceived vulnerability in children and adolescents. *Health Education Quarterly, 9,* 142–155.

Grieco, A. (1987). Cutting the risks for STDs. *Medical Aspects of Human Sexuality, March,* 70–84.

Guinan, M., & Hardy, A. (1987a). Epidemiology of AIDS in women in the United States—1981 through 1986. *Journal of the American Medical Association, 257,* 2039–2042.

Guinan, M., & Hardy, A. (1987b). Women and AIDS: The future is grim. *Journal of the American Women's Medical Association, 42,* 157–158.

Hagenhoff, C., Lowe, A., Hovell, M. F., & Rugg, D. (1987). Prevention of the teenage pregnancy epidemic: A social learning theory approach. *Education and Treatment of Children, 10*(1), 67–83.

Hart, G. (1974). Factors influencing venereal infections in a war environment. *British Journal of Venereal Diseases, 50,* 68.

Harvey, P. D. (1972). Condoms: A new look. *Family Planning Perspectives, 4,* 27–30.

Hatcher, R. A. (1978). Reasons to recommend the condom. *Medical Aspects of Human Sexuality, 12,* 91.

Hovland, C. I., Janis, I. L., & Kelley, H. H. (1953). *Communication and persuasion.* New Haven: Yale.

Hovland, C. I., & Weiss, W. (1951). The influence of source credibility on communication effectiveness. *Public Opinion Quarterly, 15,* 635–650.

Hunger, K. F. H. (1976). Education at school about sexually transmitted diseases. *British Journal of Venereal Diseases, 52,* 100–101.

Janis, I. L., & Feshbach, S. (1953). Effects of fear-arousing communications. *Journal of Abnormal and Social Psychology, 48,* 78–92.

Jawetz, E., Melnich, J., & Adelberg, E. (1987). *Review of medical microbiology.* San Francisco: Appleton & Lange.

Jones, C., Waskin, H., Gerety, B., Skipper, B., Huli, H., & Mertz, G. (1987). Persistence of high-risk sexual activity among heterosexual men in area of low incidence of the acquired immunodeficiency syndrome. *Sexually Transmitted Diseases, 14,* 72–82.

Jordheim, A. E. (1975). A comparison of the effects of peer teaching and traditional instruction in venereal disease education with criterion measures of knowledge, attitudes, and behavioral intentions. *Dissertation Abstracts International, 35* 5970B–5971B. (University Microfilm No. 75–13, 895).

Joseph, J., Montgomery, S., Emmons, C., Kessler, R., Ostrov, D., Wortman, C., O'Brien, K., Eller, M., & Eshleman, S. (1987). Magnitude and determinants of behavioral risk reduction: Longitudinal analysis of a cohort at risk for AIDS. *Psychology and Health, 1,* 73–95.

Kastner, L. S. (1984). Ecological factors for predicting adolescent contraceptive use: Implications for intervention. *Journal of Adolescent Health Care, 5*(2), 79–86.

Kegeles, S. (1963). Why people seek dental care: A test of a conceptual formulation. *Journal of Health and Human Behavior, 4,* 166–173.

Klein, D., Sullivan, G., Wolcott, D., Landsverk, J., Namir, S., & Fawzy, F. (1987). Changes in AIDS risk behaviors among homosexual male physicians and university students. *American Journal of Psychiatry, 144,* 742–747.

Knox, S. R., Mandel, B., & Lazorowicz, R. (1981). Profile of callers to the VD National Hotline. *Sexually Transmitted Diseases, 8*(4), 245–254.

Koop, C. E. (1986). *Surgeon general's report on acquired immune deficiency syndrome* (DHHS Publication). Washington, DC: U.S. Government Printing Office.

Leventhal, H. (1970). Findings and theory in the study of fear communications. In L. Berkowitz (Ed.), *Advances in experimental social psychology* (Vol 5). New York: Academic Press.

Leventhal, H., Nerenz, D. R., & Steele, D. J. (1984). Illness representations and coping with health threats. In A. Baum, S. E. Taylor, & J. E. Singer (Eds.), *Handbook of psychology and health, Vol. IV: Social psychological aspects of health* (pp. 219–252). Hillsdale, NJ: Erlbaum.

Lewin, K. (1947). Group decision and social change. In T. Newcomb & E. Hartley (Eds.), *Readings in social psychology.* New York: Holt, Rinehart & Winston.

Lui, K., Darrow, W., & Rutherford, G. (1988). A model-based estimate of the mean incubation period for AIDS in homosexual men. *Science, 240,* 1333–1335.

Lund, A. K., Kegeles, S. S., & Weisenberg, K. (1977). Motivational techniques for increasing acceptance of preventive health measures. *Medical Care, 15*(8), 678–692.

MacDonald, I. (1986). Coolfast report: A PHS plan for prevention and control of AIDS and the AIDS virus. *Public Health Reports, 101* 341–48.

Marlatt, G. A. (1982). Relapse prevention: A self-control program for the treatment of addictive behaviors. In R. B. Stuart (Ed.), *Adherence, compliance, and generalization in behavioral medicine.* New York: Brunner/Mazel.

Martin, J. (1987). The impact of AIDS on gay male sexual patterns in New York City. *American Journal of Public Health, 77,* 578–81.

McGuire, W. J. (1964). Inducing resistance to persuasion: Some contemporary approaches. In L. Berkowitz (Ed.), *Advances in experimental social psychology* (Vol. 1). New York: Academic Press.

McKusick, L., Horstmann, W., & Coates, T. (1985). AIDS and sexual behavior reported by gay men in San Francisco. *American Journal of Public Health, 75,* 493–496.

McKusick, L., Wiley, J. A., Coates, T. J., Stall, R., Saika, G., Morin, S., Charles, K., Horstman, W., & Conant, M. A. (1985). Reported changes in the sexual behavior of men at risk for AIDS, San Francisco, 1982–84—the AIDS behavioral research project. *Public Health Reports, 100,* 622–629.

Nadelson, C. C., Notman, M. T., & Gillon, J. W. (1980). Sexual knowledge and attitudes of adolescent: Relationship to contraceptive use. *Obstetrics and Gynecology, 55*(3), 340–345.

Navia, B., Cho, E., Petito, C., & Price, R. (1986a). The AIDS dementia complex: II. Neuropathology. *Annals of Neurology, 19,* 525–535.

Navia, B., Jordan, B., & Price, R. (1986b). The AIDS dementia complex: I. Clinical features. *Annals of Neurology, 19,* 517–524.

Padian, N., Marquis, L., Francis, D., Anderson, R., Rutherford, G., O'Malley, P., & Winkelstein, W. (1987). Male to female transmission of human immunodeficiency virus. *Journal of the American Medical Association, 258,* 788–790.

Pemberton, J., McCann, J. S., Mahony, J. P. H., MacKenzie, G., Dougan, H., & May, I. (1972). Socio-medical characteristics of patients attending a V.D. clinic and the circumstances of infections. *British Journal of Venereal Diseases, 48,* 391–396.

Piot, P., Taelman, H., Minlangu, K. B., Mbendi, N., Ndangi, K., Kalambayi, K., Bridts, C., Quinn, T. C., Feinsod, F. M., Wobin, O., Mazeo, P., Stevens, W., Mitchell, S., & McCormick, J. B. (1984). Acquired immunodeficiency syndrome in a heterosexual population in Zaire. *Lancet, 2,* 65–69.

Price, J. H., Desmond, S., & Kukulka, G. (1985). High school students' perceptions and misperceptions of AIDS. *Journal of School Health, 55*(3), 107–109.

Radius, S. M., Dielman, T. E., Becker, M. H., Rosenstock, I. M., & Horvath, W. J. (1980). Adolescent perspectives on health and illness. *Adolescence, 15,* 375–384.

Redfield, R. R., Markham, P. D., Salahuddin, M. S., Wright, D. C., Sarngadharan, M. G., & Gallo, R. C. (1985). Heterosexually acquired HTLV-III/LAV disease AIDS-related complex and AIDS:

Epidemiological evidence for female to male transmission. *Journal of the American Medical Association, 254,* 2094–2096.

Rogers, R., & Mewborn, C. (1976). Fear appeals and attitude change. Effects of a threat's noxiousness, probability of occurrence, and the efficacy of coping responses. *Journal of Personality and Social Psychology, 34,* 54–61.

Rosenstock, I. M. (1974). The health belief model and preventive health behavior. *Health Education Monographs, 2,* 354–386.

Schinke, S. P., Blythe, B. J., & Gilchrist, L. D. (1981). Cognitive-behavioral prevention of adolescent pregnancy. *Journal of Counseling Psychology, 28*(5), 451–454.

Sherr, L. (1987). An evaluation of the UK government health education campaign. *Psychology and Health, 1,* 61–72.

Simon, K. J., & Das, A. (1984). An application of the health belief model toward educational diagnosis for VD education. *Health Education Quarterly, 11*(4), 403–418.

Smith, P. B., Nenney, S. W., Weinman, M. L., & Mumford, D. M. (1982). Factors affecting perception of pregnancy risk in the adolescent. *Journal of Youth and Adolescence, 11*(3), 207–215.

Solomon, M. Z., & DeJong, W. (1986). Recent sexually transmitted disease prevention efforts and their implications for AIDS health education. *Health Education Quarterly, 13,* 301–316.

Stall, R., McKusick, L., Wiley, J., Coates, T., & Ostrow, D. (1986). Alcohol and drug use during sexual activity and compliance with safe sex guidelines for AIDS: The AIDS behavioral research project. *Health Education Quarterly, 13,* 359–371.

Stoler, M., Eskin, T., Benn, S., Angerer, R., & Angerer, L. (1986). Human T-cell lymphotropic virus type III infection of the central nervous system. *Journal of the American Medical Association, 256,* 2360.

Strunin, L., & Hingson, R. (1987). Acquired immunodeficiency syndrome and adolescents: Knowledge, beliefs, attitudes, and behaviors. *Pediatrics, 79*(5), 825–828.

Taylor, S. E. (1986). *Health psychology.* New York: Random House.

Temoshok, L., Sweet, D., & Zich, J. (1987). A three-city comparison of the public's knowledge and attitudes about AIDS. *Psychology and Health, 1,* 43–60.

Walster, E., Aronson, E., & Abrahams, D. (1966). On increasing the persuasiveness of a low prestige communicator. *Journal of Experimental Social Psychology, 2,* 325–342.

Wolcott, (1986). Psychological aspects of acquired immune deficiency syndrome and the primary care physician. *Annals of Allergy, 57,* 95–102.

World Health Organization. (1987). Progress in the development and use of antiviral drugs and interferon. *Report of a WHO Scientific Group.* Geneva: Author.

Yacenda, J. S. (1974). Knowledge and attitudes of college students about venereal disease and its prevention. *Health Services Reports, 89*(2), 170–176.

Zabin, L. S., Hardy, J. B., Smith, E. A., & Hirsch, M. B. (1986). Substance use and its relation to sexual activity among inner-city adolescents. *Journal of Adolescent Health Care, 7*(5), 320–321.

Zelnik, M., & Kim, Y. J. (1982). Sex education and its association with teenage sexual activity, pregnancy and contraceptive use. *Family Planning Perspectives, 14*(3), 117–126.

Zelnik, M., & Shah, F. K. (1983). First intercourse among young Americans. *Family Planning Perspectives, 15*(2), 64–70.

Zimbardo, P. G., Ebbesen, E. B., & Maslach, C. (1977). Influencing attitudes and changing behavior (pp. 20–21). Reading, MA: Addison-Wesley.

3

Social Influence and AIDS-Preventive Behavior

Jeffrey D. Fisher and Stephen J. Misovich

The AIDS epidemic has thus far resulted in 97,258 cases of AIDS and claimed 57,094 lives (*CDC Weekly Surveillance Report,* July 31, 1989), and projections indicate that there will be a total of 270,000 AIDS cases by 1991 (National Academy of Sciences, 1986). In addition, there are probably 1.5 million HIV-positive individuals in the United States, each of whom can transmit the virus (National Academy of Sciences, 1986). Unless a cure for AIDS is found, a large percentage of these individuals will eventually die as a result of AIDS.

In the absence of a cure or vaccine for AIDS, the only means of controlling the epidemic involves behavior change, which has traditionally been the domain of psychologists. Although only a small share of the available resources for fighting AIDS has been directed toward changing behavior, at present this appears to be the only viable way to stem the toll of the disease. Ultimately, it is human behavior that communicates the AIDS virus, and ultimately, it is human behavior that must be changed.

An approach to behavior change that has long captured the attention of social psychologists is the use of social influence. Broadly defined, social influence involves the study of both direct and indirect ways in which people can affect each other. Historically, this work has included research in such areas as attitude formation and change, conformity, compliance, obedience, modeling, social comparison, and group norms. In many circumstances, social influence techniques have significant effects on behavior (e.g., Petty & Cacioppo, 1981). While social

Jeffrey D. Fisher and Stephen J. Misovich • Department of Psychology, University of Connecticut, Storrs, Connecticut 06269–1020.

influence may be brought to bear to lower AIDS risk or to increase AIDS-preventive behavior (APB), it should also be noted that it may be partly responsible for present high levels of AIDS-risk behavior and low levels of prevention.

To date, little research has been devoted to elucidating social influence processes which contribute to AIDS risk, or which could elicit higher rates of AIDS-preventive behavior. In the past several years, our research team at the University of Connecticut has been concerned with psychosocial aspects of the AIDS epidemic, and some of our research is germane to social influence. Specifically, we have studied what types of AIDS-relevant social influence individuals are most likely to seek out and accept, and what types they consider to be most reliable and credible. We have also considered how social influence may affect AIDS risk-taking, AIDS prevention, AIDS knowledge and fear. Our work has considered the effects of various sources of social influence, including the consequences of media exposure and relevant others' attitudes, on AIDS-risk behavior and prevention. In addition, the studies have focused on the interrelationships between AIDS fear, knowledge, risk behavior, and preventive efforts. For example, we have been interested in whether increasing levels of AIDS fear are associated with greater efforts at prevention.

In this chapter we present some of the empirical data we have gathered relevant to social influence and AIDS, and highlight some of our other findings as well. To conduct our empirical studies, we had subjects fill out a rather extensive questionnaire battery. We have collected data in three populations: heterosexual college students who completed the questionnaire as part of a psychology course requirement, gay and bisexual men recruited from a Hartford, Connecticut, gay men's group that was paid for its participation, and medical personnel (primarily nurses) who work at local hospitals and who were paid for completing the questionnaire. The instrument itself varied slightly in content from group to group, but each version contained items measuring the following: fear of AIDS, attitudes toward AIDS prevention, knowledge of AIDS, evaluation and use of various sources of AIDS information, questions related to the practice of safer and unsafe sexual behavior, and several personality scales.

Each of the populations we studied—heterosexual college students, gay and bisexual men, and medical personnel—is of interest in the current AIDS crisis, and each may be affected by social influence. Heterosexual college students, a group known to be sexually active and to use contraceptive techniques irregularly, may constitute a major AIDS-risk group in the future (Fisher & Misovich, 1988). Social influence processes may be partially responsible for their current levels of risk and may also be used to lessen them (J. D. Fisher, 1988). Gay and bisexual men may engage in high-risk behaviors associated with their life-style, and social influence processes may be both a part of the cause of the risk and a component in efforts directed toward lowering it. Finally, medical personnel, unless they take appropriate precautions, may be at risk owing to exposure to patients who either have or can transmit AIDS. In addition to their use of precautions, how willingly and with how much care and concern they treat people with AIDS may be affected by social influence.

Chapter Organization

The major focus of this chapter will be to examine the potential impact of social influence on AIDS prevention. In organizing our discussion, we first highlight several potent *sources of social influence* that may have an impact on people's AIDS-relevant attitudes and behavior—including experts, the media, and social network influence. With respect to AIDS, we indicate people's perceptions of, and preferences for, these different sources of social influence. We then discuss some social psychological *processes* by which social influence may affect people's levels of AIDS risk, prevention, knowledge, and fear. These include processes associated with group norms and conformity pressures, among others. Our review will be selective, focusing on those that have been of greatest interest to us in our research and thinking. We then turn to *individual differences in exposure to social influence* to address the question "What types of people are most and least likely to seek out or accept information about AIDS?" Fourth, we discuss some *effects* of exposure to social influence concerning AIDS. Our data suggest when and for whom particular sources of social influence are apt to have positive effects and indicate some interventions that might be beneficial. Finally, we mention some additional applications of our work.

Sources of Social Influence

For the last 4 or 5 years, information about AIDS has been emanating from nearly every source imaginable. Newspapers and news magazines rarely print an issue that does not contain at least one article about AIDS; professional journals report AIDS information as it relates to a particular occupation; organizations have been formed with the intent of propagating AIDS information or reducing AIDS fear; and people sometimes discuss AIDS with their physicians, sexual partners, friends, and family. With so many sources of social influence regarding AIDS (e.g., the media, expert sources, friends, and social networks), which do different groups of people tend to seek out, and how highly do they evaluate them? We first consider this question and then a related issue: What factors lead to people's rejection of social influence concerning AIDS?

Use and Evaluation of Social Influence Sources

Since the mechanisms of AIDS transmission are biological in nature, it could be expected that source expertise would play an important role in whom one would look to for AIDS information. However, several factors may conflict with this tendency. From the perspective of the literature on help-seeking, people tend to shy away from sources of help (information from experts, in this case) that are threatening to them (Fisher, Nadler, & Whitcher-Alagna, 1982; Nadler & Fisher, 1988). For example, on several occasions a number of experts have come to the University of Connecticut to give lectures to students on AIDS and AIDS prevention. Although there are approximately 500 seats in the auditorium, each time few were filled. For students, going to such a lecture may have involved the threatening possibility that others could label them as gay, an IV drug user, bisexual, or sexually promiscuous. Since attending a public forum on AIDS may be threatening for many, sources of expert social influence that can be consumed privately, without such "side effects" (e.g., pamphlets, television shows), may often be more effective in reaching large numbers of people.

There are other moderators of reliance on experts for AIDS information. These include the availability of expert sources, one's level of resources for accessing experts, one's typical patterns of seeking information about the unknown (e.g., calling "mom and dad" vs. seeking expert advice), and a mistrust of certain experts (Gross & McMullin, 1984). Concerning the latter, for drug users, seeking AIDS information from some experts may be perceived as tantamount to "turning oneself in"—to be avoided at all costs. Others (e.g., gay men) may be concerned that medical experts and the public health "establishment" are biased, or even prejudiced, against them. This may lead them to seek sources of information they believe are more objective or sympathetic to their situation (e.g., information from gay-oriented health professionals). In general, research indicates that people are unlikely to rely on sources for help or information whose credibility they doubt (Fisher et al., 1982).

How do our data accord with these assertions? While there is certainly anecdotal evidence of gay concern about bias in the medical and public health establishments, Table 1 reveals that for gay men, health care professionals constituted the source of social influence ranked first in terms of overall information received. It should be noted, however, that the questionnaire did not distinguish between receiving information from health care professionals oriented toward gays and other health care professionals. Thus, it cannot be determined whether or not there is a decided preference for obtaining AIDS information from gay-oriented health professionals. The second most commonly utilized source of information was mainstream newspapers, and gay newspapers were a close third.

When gay subjects were asked to rank the sources of information in terms of their reliability and validity, an interesting pattern emerged. Health care professionals were ranked first, gay newspapers second, and pamphlets third; mainstream newspapers received a much lower rank. This suggests that mainstream newspapers are relied on but not preferred, and that gay newspapers and other sources of social influence (e.g., pamphlets)—if made available and relevant to AIDS issues—could be highly utilized. Additional evidence that gay men do not perceive the press, the electronic media, and perhaps heterosexual people in general as particularly reliable sources of AIDS information is provided in Table 2.

While gay men have a high interest in the topic of AIDS, according to our data heterosexual college students as a group are relatively unconcerned and uninvolved in the AIDS situation. In general they do not tend to actively seek out information on their own (Fisher & Misovich, 1988). While there are many possible reasons for these findings, one is that for a young population experimenting

Table 1. Sources of AIDS Information Rated Most Frequently Used and Most Reliable and Valuable

Source of AIDS information	Percent of individuals in each group who ranked each source below as their *primary* source of information			Percent of individuals in each group who ranked each source below as the most *reliable and valuable* source	
	Gays	Nurses	Students	Gays	Nurses
Radio/TV	10%	6%	48%	9%	3%
Magazines	10	15	20	3	7
Newspapers	19	13	26	5	3
Gay newspapers	17	—	—	19	—
Friends	3	2	—	2	0
Health care professionals	24	—	—	51	—
Pamphlets	7	2	—	12	2
Professional journals	—*	43	—	—	56
Nurse epidemiologist	—	14	—	—	24
In-services at work	—	17	—	—	12
Other	8	7	6	—	—

*A dashed line indicates that this source was not among the choices given to this group.

Table 2. Perception of Subjects Regarding How the Press and TV, and Heterosexuals in General Have Reacted to the AIDS Issue

	Gays	Nurses	Students
Response of each group to the question "How do you think the press and TV have treated the AIDS issue?"			
Overreacted	20%	24%	9%
Reacted appropriately	42	63	69
Not taken the issue seriously enough	38	13	22
Response of each group to the question "How have most heterosexual people reacted to the AIDS issue?"			
Overreacted	35%	52%	22%
Reacted appropriately	33	20	24
Not taken the issue seriously enough	62	28	44

with sex, the admission of a serious risk from AIDS is too threatening (perhaps because of dissonance), so it is denied. Rather than actively seeking information, such individuals will probably utilize that which is most easily accessible, when they rely on it at all. Indeed, our results indicate that most heterosexual students use the more readily available sources, namely, television and the press (Table 1), and seem to be quite pleased with the way they have treated the AIDS issue (Table 2). Given this pattern of media utilization and satisfaction, it would appear that further informational attempts along these lines would be well received by heterosexual individuals in the late teens and early 20s.

In contrast, health care workers, who are generally quite interested in AIDS and who feel they are already knowledgeable, preferred specialized, high-expertise sources. Professional journals were ranked the most frequently used and most reliable source of information by respondents, and in-services at work were the second most highly ranked. We found that nurses rated the information that could be provided by the nurse epidemiologist as highly credible, although they had received relatively little information from this individual; this suggests that highlighting his or her role could be useful (Table 1). The majority of nurses in the sample believed that the press and television had reacted appropriately, generally giving medium-to-high rankings to these sources, but thought that the heterosexual public in general had overreacted to the AIDS situation (Table 2).

Overall, it appears that people interested and concerned with the issue of AIDS (e.g., gay men and health professionals) prefer to seek information from sources which are authoritative, which are articulated to their particular needs and concerns, and which they believe take AIDS seriously. Those who are less interested in AIDS issues (e.g., students) probably rely on the most readily available sources of social influence.

Factors Associated with Rejection of AIDS-Relevant Social Influence

Several factors may lead to the rejection of AIDS-relevant social influence attempts. As suggested above, people engaged in activities that they do not desire to change or feel they cannot change may avoid information that highlights the risk of their current behaviors and recommends changing them. This may include heterosexual college students and gay men enmeshed in high-risk life-styles, and health care workers whose job requires frequent contact with people with AIDS. For these individuals, information about the dangers of AIDS may cause dissonance. In addition, individuals with negative attitudes toward particular AIDS-related issues (e.g., gay men with negative attitudes toward AIDS prevention, health care workers with negative attitudes toward people with AIDS) may also find that much media-based information is inconsistent with their beliefs and behaviors. Again, this could cause dissonance. Thus, the latter groups may avoid AIDS information, especially social influence attempts aimed at changing their attitudes or behaviors.

We have collected data relevant to the above hypotheses. Subjects were asked to indicate their response to the question "I tend to turn off or tune out news reports about AIDS" on a 7-point Likert-type scale, with 1 indicating "always" and 7 "never." We observed that health care workers who felt more negatively toward gay and IV-drug-using AIDS patients were more likely to report "tuning out" or actively avoiding AIDS information, compared with those who felt more positively toward such patients. The same relationship existed between general attitudes toward AIDS patients and information seeking: Health care workers who felt negatively toward AIDS patients read fewer articles and saw fewer television programs about AIDS ($r = .30$, $p < .02$; $r = .32$, $p < .01$, respectively). With the gay sample, our data suggest that people who have negative feelings toward APBs typically do not seek out information about AIDS. Respondents who felt that AIDS-preventive behaviors were not efficacious were more apt to report "tuning out" information about AIDS ($r = .25$, $p < .055$), and those who thought condoms reduced the enjoyability of sex "tuned out" AIDS information ($r = .30$, $p < .01$), as did individuals with negative affect toward APBs in general ($r = .24$, $p < .07$).

The general trend that seems to be emerging is that individuals whose AIDS-relevant beliefs or behaviors are inconsistent with those portrayed by the media may avoid media-based sources of social influence. People who do not want to change their behavior or feel they cannot do so also avoid AIDS information. Unfortunately, the latter groups of individuals are probably those most in need of attending to such messages. Since our research is correlational, however, it is also possible to interpret the above findings as suggesting that seeking AIDS information is associated with more favorable attitudes and behaviors.

Another determinant of avoidance of AIDS information is the perception of manipulative intent in its source. To the extent that people believe social influence involves manipulative intent, they will resist it (Petty & Cacioppo, 1979). For example, if someone feels that AIDS-risk information is being presented to impose morality rather than to increase their personal safety, they may resist it due to suspicion of the communicator's intent or to a sense of reactance (Brehm, 1966). Thus, students who view AIDS communications as scare tactics to reduce their sexual activity may reject them, and gays who perceive safer sex information as designed to make their life-style more palatable to the heterosexual majority may react against it. In addition, health care workers may be suspicious of hospital administrators' attempts to reduce their concerns about incurring AIDS from patients. They could view such communications as intended to make them willing to work under dangerous conditions. This contention receives support from our data indicating that 38% of health care workers believed hospital administrators had not taken the AIDS issue seriously enough. Given the above, the efficacy of such messages may be in doubt. Overall, it seems that the source of AIDS information may be very important. Unless the communicator is trusted by the recipient of the social influence attempt, manipulative intent may be assumed and the message discounted.

Another reason why individuals may resist information about AIDS derives from inoculation theory (McGuire, 1969). This theory suggests that when people hear arguments that contradict their own beliefs and such arguments are refuted soon afterward, they may become "inoculated" against similar persuasive appeals in the future. It is possible that in the early stages of the AIDS epidemic, some gays could have been exposed to hysterical arguments emanating from nongay sources against homosexual sexual activity. If at that point they generated their own counterarguments against the reliability of these assaults, such beliefs could have carried over to the present time, when the information being presented by nongay sources is hopefully more unbiased. In effect, they may have "inoculated" themselves against some reliable forms of information about AIDS-risk behaviors.

Finally, whether gay men accept or reject social influence from other gays and gay organizations depends on several factors. The AIDS situation may have one of two conflicting effects on gays' identifying and affiliating with other gays, and thus accepting gay network social influence. On the one hand, concern about AIDS may lead gay men to join gay networks and to associate with gay organizations to obtain AIDS information and deal with their anxiety. They may also affiliate more with other gays out of feelings of identification and social responsibility. On the other hand, the fear of prejudice and discrimination against gays occasioned by AIDS, and even the fear of AIDS (gay men in our sample reported concern about making new gay acquaintances because of AIDS), may lead to rejection of gay individuals, networks, and organizations and their social influence. This may be especially true among gays who are ambivalent about their own homosexuality. These individuals, who would remain aloof from the gay community under ordinary circumstances, can be expected to maintain an even greater distance during the AIDS crisis. In fact, AIDS and its secondary effects (e.g., fear of becoming ill, concern about prejudice and discrimination) may be making some of these people even more uncomfortable with their gay orientation.

Social Influence Processes, AIDS-Risk Behavior, and Prevention

Below, we draw on social psychological research and theory to highlight and explain some social influence processes that are a major source of people's willingness or unwillingness to engage in AIDS prevention *and* a potential key to behavior change resulting in a lessening of AIDS risk. We focus first on reference-group-based social influence processes. Reference groups consist of individuals a person likes, identifies with, and associates with. Two types of social influence may emanate from such groups: *normative social influence* (involving various forms of group-based social pressure, such as pressure to conform) and *informational social influence* (general information as well as specific information about others' beliefs, behaviors, and outcomes) (Deutsch & Gerard, 1955). While informational social influence can occur through interactions with one's reference group, it may also emanate from other sources (e.g., the media). Following our coverage of reference-group-based normative and informational social influence, we discuss informational social influence that derives from other sources.

Reference-Group-Based Normative Social Influence

The Effect of Reference Group Norms, Values, and Beliefs

Reference group norms, values, and beliefs may have a potent effect on members' attitudes and behaviors (e.g., Newcomb, 1943). That group norms affect people's behavioral choices regarding prevention has been documented by Fishbein and Ajzen (1975). In that research, the attitudes of significant others toward a particular preventive act (e.g., using contraceptives) were an important determinant of the individual's own behavior. With respect to AIDS, relevant group norms may involve, for example, using or not using condoms during intercourse, engaging in other safer or risky sexual practices, and sharing or not sharing IV needles. These may increase or decrease transmission of the AIDS virus.

Depending on situational conditions, then, groups can exert considerable pressure on individuals to avoid APBs, or to use them. A major reason why group pressure can be so powerful in moderating behavior is people's motivation to be liked by others, which often requires them to be *like* others, i.e., to avoid appearing deviant (Byrne, 1971; Nadler & Fisher, 1988). Frequently the mere anticipation of being rejected for engaging in network-inconsistent behaviors is sufficient for one to avoid them. This suggests that if individuals could be convinced that their use of APB would not compromise others' liking for them, AIDS prevention could be increased. For example, we have found that while college students are very hesitant to initiate discussion about APBs, they would not object—and might even appreciate—their partner bringing up the topic (Fisher & Misovich, 1988). A social influence campaign emphasizing this fact might reduce people's fear of being disliked for engaging in presex discussion of APBs, and it could increase discussion of safer sex.

A related reason why people adhere to group norms and espouse group values is that they fear sanctions for nonconformity. If the typical script for intercourse is to have it without a presex discussion regarding protection against sexually transmitted diseases (STDs), people will fear sanctions for failing to conform to this script. Interviews with students suggested that they found it "easier to have [unprotected] sex than to discuss STD prevention." Both males and females feared rejection by their sex partner (i.e., sanctions) if they failed to conform to group norms and brought up the topic of AIDS prevention. In some minority groups with relatively high rates of HIV infection, cultural norms make it very difficult for partners to discuss sexual matters (Morales, 1987), much less AIDS prevention. Such discussion might be considered inappropriate and could lead to sanctions. Similarly, in the gay community the vestiges of "free sex" norms from the 1970s and early 1980s (Hirsch & Enlow, 1984) may make it difficult for some men to discuss safer sex, and in certain segments of the IV-drug-using community, social norms for sharing the "works" may make it difficult to discuss or initiate safer injection practices (DesJarlais, Friedman, & Strug, 1986).

In addition to specific norms that affect relatively circumscribed behaviors, general group norms and values may affect risk-taking behavior more generally. For example, appearing to be concerned about AIDS or engaging in APB may be inconsistent with "machismo" values in some racial and ethnic groups (e.g., Vaz-quez-Nuttall, Avila-Vivas, & Morales-Barreto, 1984). Other norms may be associated with one's age. It is normative for people in their teens and early 20s to feel invulnerable, i.e., to believe they are impervious to negative events (Kreipe, 1985). Further, research findings indicate that people often view risk as a value and do not want to appear less risky than their peers (e.g., exhibit neurotic over-concern) (Levinger & Schneider, 1969; Wallach & Wing, 1968). Taken together, such normative values may have significant effects on risk-taking behavior in young people. They imply that lack of AIDS prevention should be widespread in this age group (for evidence to that effect, see Fisher & Misovich, 1988) and that individuals may be very reluctant to appear more concerned than their peers. Exhibiting concern would not conform to the predominant values that individuals are invincible, risk-taking admirable, and neurotic overconcern a negative trait.

Such prevailing norms could cause difficulties for the individual who attempts to institute AIDS-preventive behavior in a group where APBs are viewed negatively. Classic research on groups indicates that "opinion deviates" may be the recipients of sanctioning communications from the group in order to maintain uniformity of opinion (Schachter, 1951). Recent theoretical work suggests that when people attempt to make volitional behavior changes that violate group norms, social influence at the group level often plays a regressive role (Nadler & Fisher, 1988). Reference groups typically have a vested interest in the *status quo* and frequently exert negative forms of social influence (e.g., sanctions) when change is involved (Fisher & Goff, 1986; Nadler & Fisher, 1988). They may resist change and exert prohibitions on those attempting it. Possible reasons for this include the fact that change which is inconsistent with the group's values may threaten the perceived veracity of group beliefs, the way the group views itself, the correctness of the behavior, or even the relations between group members (Nadler & Fisher, 1988).

Nadler and Fisher suggest that for volitional change to be accepted by one's reference group, it must be *consistent* with group norms. For example, if group norms favor casual sex, behavioral changes in that direction will be supported and encouraged, while changes toward a more conservative approach to sex will be resisted. This implies that until AIDS prevention constitutes a normative behavior or at least a valued ideal in reference groups, normative social influence may inhibit rather than facilitate APB. Various scenarios could cause AIDS prevention to be viewed as more consistent with network values. For example, one could imagine that attitudes toward and social support for using condoms would be very different in networks of college men where a member had become HIV positive or developed AIDS than in a network where this had not occurred. In the former case APB would probably become consistent with network values, as it has in social networks of many gay men. Otherwise, the network may be much more interested in preserving the status quo than in encouraging changes which question group values and practices.

Once APB becomes consistent with group values or norms, social influence may be expected to favor it. Groups can provide an important measure of social support for changes they advocate (Nadler & Fisher, 1988). Self-help groups for alcoholics and gamblers are evidence of this. In segments of the gay community where norms support APB, group social influence may help members to display it, and there may even be sanctions against those who do not. Overall, an important means of increasing APB would be to make it consistent, rather than inconsistent, with group norms. If this could be done though societal attempts at social influence (e.g., through the media, local educational interventions), social influence at the group level might be expected to reinforce APB (J. D. Fisher, 1988).

In groups where APBs are inconsistent with group values, attempts must be made to help individuals to initiate and maintain changes in spite of regressive social influence. Research suggests that when reference group values are antagonistic to desired changes, individuals may be more successful at initiating and maintaining new behaviors if they become part of a secondary reference group supportive of the changes they are contemplating (Fisher, Goff, Nadler, & Chinsky, 1988). For example, alcoholics with a family history of alcoholism will fare better if they join a secondary group like Alcoholics Anonymous instead of attempting to initiate and maintain change solely within their primary network. In the case of AIDS, informal informational or social groups composed of concerned individuals committed to APB would offer more support than society at large for those who want to change their behavior to prevent AIDS.

The social influence literature suggests other group-level factors that may determine the ease with which one can resist conformity pressure and initiate behaviors inconsistent with group norms. For example, individuals with small reference groups that are anti-APB may be more able to resist conformity pressures than those with larger groups (Tanford & Penrod, 1984). Similarly, the less cohesive the group, the easier it is to resist group social influence (Forsyth, 1983). If group opinion is not unanimous (e.g., if at least one other group member favors APB), pressures to conform are reduced (Allen & Levine, 1971; Morris & Miller, 1972). In addition, if one perceives the group's opinion as evolving to be closer to one's own, pressures to conform are progressively lessened (Campbell, Tesser, & Fairey, 1986). Taken together, the above findings suggest that individuals with smaller, less cohesive social networks that have attitudes toward APBs that are becoming more positive will have an easier time initiating and maintaining APBs than those enmeshed in other types of networks that sanction against AIDS prevention.

Social Influence and Feelings of Social Responsibility

In addition to imposing sanctions on network-inconsistent behaviors and supporting changes consistent with group norms, social influence exerted by groups can affect APB in other ways. Especially in times of distress, group membership in and of itself can engender feelings of cohesion with, and social responsibility for, other group members. Such feelings, based merely on one's connection with the group, may represent true belonging, caring, and concern, or yet another type of conformity to group norms (e.g., responding to group pressure to exhibit feelings of social responsibility). The former is exemplified when groups band together in times of crisis (e.g., Jews supporting Israel when it is under attack). Similarly, elements of the gay community have coalesced during the AIDS crisis; there has been a tremendous outpouring of social responsibility among gay men. It is argued that such feelings could be a significant contributing factor in those studies that have observed increased APB in gays (e.g., Martin, 1987). Unfortunately, gays who do not feel part of the gay community are less subject to this type of influence, and have been found to engage in lower levels of APB (Fisher & Misovich, 1987). Social influence techniques designed to elicit feelings of belonging, group cohesion, and social responsibility in unaffiliated gays and in other groups affected by AIDS (e.g., certain minorities) may result in greater self-help efforts at the group level, and increased APB at the individual level.

Reference-Group-Based Informational Social Influence

In addition to normative social influence, reference groups may also convey informational social influence. Since they contain valid sources of information (e.g., about the attitudes, behaviors, or outcomes of relevant others), reference groups may have a significant impact on members' attitudes and actions. Typically, people attend to information from reference groups because they have a general motivation to be right or to know the facts, i.e., what is true or correct (Deutsch & Gerard, 1955).

Social Comparison, Perceptual Biases, and Perceived Vulnerability

One type of information that people may acquire from similar others is perceptions of vulnerability to negative outcomes, including the likelihood of contracting AIDS. On the basis of social comparison (Festinger, 1954) as well as objective data, information on the base rate of negative events in a population may affect members' relative levels of perceived vulnerability and fear. For example, gay men feel more vulnerable to AIDS than nurses, who feel more vulnerable than heterosexual college students (Fisher, Misovich, & Kean, 1987).

Although the relative perceived vulnerabilities found *between* populations do reflect differences in objective risk, we have observed an interesting perceptual bias. Within any specific population, individuals tend to feel that they, themselves, are less vulnerable to AIDS than others. For example, gay subjects thought *other* gays were more likely to contract AIDS than they were (Fisher *et al.*, 1987). This illusion of relative invulnerability has been found in additional domains—for example, college women's perceptions of the likelihood that they would be mugged, burglarized, have a car stolen, or develop cancer (Janoff-Bulman, Madden, &

Timko, 1980). To protect themselves from concern about threatening negative events, people may assume they are less vulnerable owing to some perceived dissimilarity (e.g., a risk factor in others not characteristic of them). Unfortunately, the perception that "it will happen to someone else" may be an important determinant of low APB rates, since low perceived vulnerability has been related to poor preventive health behavior (Janz & Becker, 1984).

This suggests that information that individuals are *not* less vulnerable to AIDS than others in their population may be an effective means of increasing APB. When asked what it would take to get them to engage in APB, college students we have interviewed stated, "A close friend who contracted AIDS." In effect, they indicated that information that they are as vulnerable as similar others (cf. Perloff & Fetzer, 1986) would constitute a source of social influence that would elicit APB. Such a heightened sense of vulnerability due to negative outcomes of close others has occurred for many gay men and may be in part responsible for behavior change. To the extent that AIDS is seen by people as occurring among others like them, they may use the "representativeness heuristic" (Tversky & Kahneman, 1974) and conclude that they are susceptible to AIDS (see Weinstein, 1980, for a discussion of related issues).

Unfortunately, the illusion of relative invulnerability may be difficult to counteract. One way to accomplish this may be to present objective statistical evidence that one *is* as vulnerable as similar others, though Snyder (1978) found that even providing actuarial data did not completely dispel this bias. Nevertheless, such information might help negate the argument that others are more vulnerable to AIDS.

When an exemplary member of a population or someone famous or privileged, such as a political leader or a movie star, contracts AIDS and publicizes it, this too could work to dispel perceived invulnerability, in that people's stereotypes of who incurs AIDS might change. They may decide that they themselves fit into a category of people who may become exposed. Similarly, the illusion of invulnerability may be attenuated when large numbers of group members contract AIDS, such as has occurred in the gay population. If the heterosexual community contracts AIDS in significant numbers and/or important members of the community contract it, this may have an impact on the illusion of relative invulnerability and motivate behavior change. Clearly, the outcomes of relevant others may represent important sources of informational social influence that could effect changes in APB.

Informational Social Influence from Other Sources

Up to now our discussion of informational social influence has focused primarily on *indirect* sources of information—on how people extract data from the outcomes, attitudes, or behaviors of their reference group, broadly defined. The information one acquires is not designed to change his or her attitudes or behaviors, though change may result from its acquisition. In contrast, much informational social influence comes from direct communications specifically designed to provide information to people while simultaneously persuading them (e.g., media campaigns to increase APB). Here, the issue of the efficacy of various social influence strategies becomes important. Two major determinants of efficacy are whether such communications are one- or two-sided, and the level of fear they elicit. We will review each of these in turn.

One- Versus Two-Sided Communications

Informational communications aimed at increasing APB may present one or both sides of relevant issues (cf. Hovland, Lumsdaine, & Sheffield, 1949). Research suggests that two-sided communications, which deal with the pros and cons of the position being advocated, are more effective when (a) the population in question is somewhat knowledgeable about the issue and its costs and benefits, and/or (b) the target group is initially opposed to the position being advocated.

If a message is aimed at persuading people to use condoms on each instance of sexual contact with a person whose HIV status is unknown, a two-sided approach emphasizing the costs and benefits of condoms may be most efficacious. Our research indicates that most individuals are knowledgeable about condoms and aware that their use entails both costs and benefits, and condoms are not universally well liked. Acknowledging that they are somewhat uncomfortable and can interrupt spontaneity, but that aside from abstention they are the only way to prevent exposure to AIDS, might not only appear more credible but be more persuasive. Because two-sided communications are more resistant to counterpersuasion (cf. Lumsdaine & Janis, 1953; Petty & Cacioppo, 1981), they may also inoculate people against inevitable counterarguments by peers and even sex partners—e.g., the old saw that "wearing condoms is like taking a shower with boots on."

The two-sided approach seems appropriate in other APB contexts as well. By now, most people know there is a great deal of complexity to the issue of AIDS prevention and at least a degree of uncertainty about whether recommended preventive measures will, in fact, work. People need to hear this complexity echoed in social influence attempts. Anecdotal evidence suggests that nurses react negatively to one-sided messages from administrators which suggest that employing a particular set of APBs will leave them risk-free. Similarly, the educated public now knows that there is no such thing as completely safe sex or totally risk-free interactions with people with AIDS, so one-sided messages emphasizing the "complete safety" of certain acts may be viewed with suspicion.

In this regard, the recent switch to acknowledging degrees of relative risk in all sexual behaviors (e.g., the notion of "safer" rather than safe sex) and a degree of risk for medical personnel in all contacts with AIDS patients may constitute two-sided communications, which will be viewed as more credible and which may ultimately be more effective. The same is true of messages aimed at parents whose children attend schools with others who have AIDS or who are HIV positive. Anecdotal evidence suggests that physicians are more successful in convincing parents of their children's safety while attending school with children with AIDS if they acknowledge a degree of risk but suggest that it is relatively safer than other common activities in which the children engage (e.g., crossing the street).

Levels of Fear

In addition to whether it is one- or two-sided, the level of fear elicited by a message may be an important determinant of its efficacy in increasing prevention (Janis & Feshbach, 1953; Leventhal, 1971). It has been suggested that high fear appeals may be more effective than low fear appeals when (1) the condition described is unpleasant, (2) the individual believes that the event in question will really occur, and (3) the recommended action (e.g., APB) appears to be effective (Maddux & Rogers, 1983; Rogers, 1975). It is clear that these three elements will not be at levels opportune for high fear appeals under all circumstances. Concerning the first element, AIDS *is* universally perceived to be unpleasant. In terms of the second, the likelihood of someone believing that AIDS will strike them may vary depending, in part, on the risk factors they have incurred. Regarding the third, the perceived efficacy of APB will probably vary as a joint function of one's belief in the effectiveness of condoms, nonoxynol -9, and other methods for preventing AIDS, and his or her feelings of personal efficacy in taking the recommended action (cf. Maddux & Rogers, 1983).

In effect, while the perceived unpleasantness of AIDS is universal, the extent to which people believe they are vulnerable to AIDS, and the level of efficacy they associate with AIDS prevention will vary across individuals. High fear appeals may be more effective for those who believe AIDS to be unpleasant, feel vulnerable to it, and perceive APBs to be efficacious. For other individuals, high fear communications may actually be *less* effective than low fear appeals. High fear interventions that include an element designed to make people believe that AIDS really can strike them, as well as a communication that APBs are effective, should have a more positive impact than interventions not including these two elements.

Some of our data speak to parts of this issue. They suggest that the interaction of people's level of fear of AIDS and their perceived efficacy of APBs is predictive of AIDS prevention. We have consistently found that the interaction of variables associated with fear and variables associated with efficacy reveals that individuals low on both dimensions are much less apt to use APBs than those who fall in the other fear × efficacy quadrants. It may be important to direct social influence attempts to the former group, since in some cases they engage in APB only about one-third as often as the others. One possibility would be to attempt to increase both fear and perceived efficacy of APBs in these individuals to levels where they are associated with prevention.

Individual Differences, Exposure to Social Influence, and AIDS Prevention

In this section we report our findings on the relationship between individual difference variables and factors related to AIDS prevention. We discuss the effect of individual differences in acceptance of being gay, health locus of control, repression-sensitization, and sensation seeking.

Acceptance of Being Gay

We have found that for gay men, a major individual difference predictor of both exposure to social influence and the practice of APB is the extent to which one is comfortable with being gay. Since no measure of this construct existed, we created our own 8-item scale measuring subjects' feelings about their sexual orientation. Included are items measuring subjects' affective response to their homosexuality, their satisfaction with their sexual orientation, and their comfort with homosexuality as a life-style. Interitem correlations produced an alpha of .69.

Acceptance of being gay predicted the extent to which gay men were "engaged" in a social network of gay individuals ($r = .38$, $p < .001$). (The engagement variable reflects how much one considers himself a member of a gay social network, his duration of membership, the extent to which he can discuss his concerns about AIDS with others in the network, and his satisfaction with the discussion.) Thus, it appears that acceptance of being gay is associated with greater levels of reference-group-based normative and informational social influence regarding AIDS. Acceptance of being gay is also correlated positively with exposure to AIDS-relevant social influence via the media ($r = .36$, $p < .005$), and negatively with the likelihood of "tuning out" information about AIDS ($r = .27$, $p < .03$). Perhaps as a result of its association with exposure to higher levels of normative and informational social influence, acceptance of being gay is related to greater knowledge about AIDS ($r = .42$, $p < .001$), to greater perceived efficacy of APBs ($r = .64$, $p < .001$), and to less affective fear of AIDS ($r = .22$, $p < .09$).

Finally, acceptance of being gay is correlated with the performance of APBs. Again, this is assumed to be due to its association with pro-APB normative and informational social influence. Specifically, acceptance of being gay is correlated with greater self-reports of control of sexual impulses (e.g., less endorsement of items such as "when I'm sexually aroused, I tend to throw caution to the wind") ($r = .40$, $p < .001$), with more safer sex behaviors ($r = .32$, $p < .01$), and with a greater intention to perform safer sex behaviors in the future ($r = .30$, $p < .01$).

All of the above suggest that social influence attempts directed toward increasing acceptance of being gay in gay men may have dramatically favorable results. They may lead to greater membership in gay social networks, increased exposure to constructive forms of social influence, and, ultimately, to more APB. Unfortunately, however, societal values, if anything, may be moving toward making gay men *less* comfortable with their sexual orientation. Our data imply that such a trend could have very negative effects. This is also consistent with Nadler and Fisher's work on help-seeking, which suggests that acceptance of one's condition is an important determinant of seeking help or support from others. Until this occurs, seeking support is highly self-threatening and may be avoided (Fisher et al., 1988; Nadler, Sheinberg, & Jaffe, 1981).

Health Locus of Control

In addition to acceptance of being gay, health locus of control (Wallston, Wallston, Kaplan, & Maides, 1976), was expected to correlate with exposure to social influence regarding AIDS. However, this personality construct, which reflects whether an individual expects contingencies between health behavior and outcomes (internal locus of control) or not (external locus of control), was not associated with subjects' actual exposure to informational communications (e.g., from the media) regarding AIDS. Neither was it related to exposure to informational or normative social influence from engagement in a gay social network. Nevertheless, in gay men health internality was related to greater levels of AIDS knowledge ($r = .39$, $p < .002$), to less affective fear ($r = .32$, $p < .001$), to greater perceived efficacy of APBs ($r = .28$, $p < .02$), and to higher levels of safer sex behavior ($r = .25$, $p < .05$). It also predicted greater intention to perform safer sex in the future ($r = .35$, $p < .005$), higher sexual impulse control ($r = .25$, $p < .05$), and a more favorable attitude toward safer sex in general ($r = .26$, $p < .05$). Similar results occurred with nurses. Health internals exhibited more knowledge ($r = .34$, $p < .007$) and more on-the-job APBs ($r = .25$, $p < .04$) and were more likely to "overdo" safety precautions ($r = .27$, $p < .04$). This suggests that internals may be at considerably less risk for AIDS than health externals, and that social influence attempts need to be directed at health externals in order to increase knowledge and the practice of APBs. Perhaps messages stressing the contingencies between practicing APBs and favorable health outcomes could help overcome externals' inherent tendency to view the two as noncontingent.

Repression-Sensitization

The construct of repression-sensitization, as developed by Byrne (1964), deals in part with a person's tendency to avoid or accept threatening information. Repressors tend to deal with threatening information through denial or avoidance, while sensitizers focus on threatening information and ruminate about it. One implication of the notion of avoiding or focusing on threatening information is that repressors may block out AIDS-relevant communications and may be unlikely to seek our fear-inducing AIDS information. Sensitizers, on the other hand, may be apt to attend to fear-inducing information but may respond to it by feeling more afraid than repressors.

In addressing the above predictions, our research found no significant relations between repression-sensitization scores and seeking out or avoiding normative or informational social influence about AIDS, regardless of its source. On the other hand, we observed strong evidence that for all of the groups studied, sensitizers reported higher levels of AIDS fear than repressors. Among nurses, repression-sensitization correlated positively with a measure of affective fear ($r = .48$, $p < .0001$). Nurses who were sensitizers were also significantly more afraid of incurring AIDS ($r = .32$, $p < .01$), reported more AIDS anxiety at work ($r = .28$, $p < .02$), and reported being more distracted at work because of AIDS concerns than did repressors ($r = .35$, $p < .004$). Similar results were obtained in the student sample and in the sample of gay men.

Overall, this suggests that it may be important to deal with sensitizers' high fear levels, perhaps through some sort of social influence technique. One possibility involves interventions focusing on particular types of information. Our research with nurses implies that the *type* of information one is exposed to about AIDS may affect levels of fear. Information may be categorized as fear-inducing (e.g., AIDS has spread to some health care workers) or fear-reducing (e.g., it is very rare to contract AIDS from a needle-stick injury). We have found that the internalization of fear-reducing knowledge is negatively correlated with fear of AIDS at work ($r = .22$, $p < .08$) and the desire to avoid AIDS patients ($r = .27$, $p < .03$), which suggests that social influence techniques that propagate fear-reducing information may be effective in lowering fear.

In addition to being more fearful, sensitizers tend to pay closer attention to threatening information, and to spend more time thinking about it than repressors. Because what constitutes safe sex practices and on-the-job AIDS prevention have been somewhat ambiguous (e.g., behaviors labeled "safe sex" 2 years ago are now described as "safer" sex activities), it seems likely that sensitizers would be more apt to have concluded that what constitutes appropriate APB is somewhat unclear. They would be more aware of the evolving uncertainty, more concerned about it, and more apt to feel that APBs are less effective. Repressors would be expected to have ignored the dangers of AIDS, and to have paid less attention to the uncertainty about what constitutes effective APB.

As expected, our data indicate that sensitizers feel less confident than repressors about the efficacy of AIDS-preventive behaviors. In our sample of nurses, sensitizers felt that health care workers were at a greater risk of incurring AIDS at work than did repressors ($r = .25$, $p < .05$). Sensitizers were also more likely to indicate that hospital administrators had not taken the issue of AIDS seriously enough ($r = .30$, $p < .01$). In the gay sample, sensitizers scored lower than repressors on a scale of APB efficacy ($r = .23$, $p < .07$), indicating a belief that AIDS-preventive behaviors were less useful. They also felt more negative affect toward APBs ($r = .28$, $p < .03$) and reported being less capable of controlling their sexual impulses ($r = .26$, $p < .05$). In addition, sensitizers felt they knew less about AIDS than other people ($r = .35$, $p < .005$), and a trend indicated that they actually did know less than repressors ($r = .21$, $p < .09$).

Overall, it would appear that sensitizers are much more frightened about AIDS than repressors, and are more likely to believe that AIDS-preventive behaviors, in one's personal life or the workplace, are ineffective. Sensitizers may also be less able to control their sexual impulses sufficiently to interrupt the sexual sequence of events and use APBs. The finding that repressors believe they know more than others, and may actually know more than sensitizers, is interesting given repressors' reported tendency to avoid frightening information. However, *because* of their lower fear levels, repressors may be more able to attend to the rational information being presented, while sensitizers may be so overwhelmed by fear that they cannot learn basic facts about AIDS. Our research suggests that fear-inducing information will not be effective with sensitizers, and that other social influence techniques may need to be developed for them. Such communications should present necessary information without frightening sensitizers and should focus on the efficacy of APBs in preventing AIDS.

Sensation Seeking

The sensation-seeking scale, as developed by Zuckerman (1979), measures an individual's tendency to prefer exciting, novel stimuli. High sensation-seekers prefer such stimuli (including experimentation with drugs and sex with many partners), while low sensation-seekers avoid them. Thus, it could be expected that high sensation-seekers would be at considerably higher risk for AIDS, a hypothesis that was confirmed in our research. Among gays ($r = .30$, $p < .01$) and college undergraduates ($r = .25$, $p < .005$), sensation seeking correlated positively with one's number of sexual partners, though this finding did not hold for nurses. With undergraduates, sensation seeking also correlated positively with the number of sexual encounters one had had with others with whom he or she was only slightly acquainted ($r = .22$, $p < .01$).

Since high sensation-seekers have been found to be less concerned with the consequences of their behaviors (Zuckerman, 1979), it could be expected that they would show less fear of AIDS. For example, nurses who were high sensation-seekers should be less concerned that treating AIDS patients would have negative consequences for them. This was observed in our data: High sensation-seeking nurses reported less AIDS anxiety ($r = .28$, $p < .02$) and less AIDS fear both in the workplace ($r = .32$, $p < .01$) and in their personal lives ($r = .28$, $p < .02$) than low sensation-seekers. They also reported more positive affect toward AIDS patients ($r = .29$, $p < .02$), were less apt to "overdo" APBs ($r = .26$, $p < .04$), and were less interested in reading pamphlets about AIDS ($r = .27$, $p < .03$). While sensation seeking predicted fear and associated behaviors in nurses, it was unrelated to fear of AIDS among gays and students. The reason for the inconsistent relationship between sensation seeking and fear in the three research populations is unclear.

Overall, it appears that high sensation-seekers probably do constitute a high-risk group for AIDS, owing to their greater number of sexual partners and generally low level of concern about incurring the disease. This group would probably respond favorably to very explicit, detailed information about AIDS-preventive behaviors, if it were presented in an interesting manner. Since sensation-seekers seem to be more interested in sexual activity, they would be likely to enjoy seeing movies that explicitly depict safe sex practices. Social influence could be exerted on this group by making movies with safer sexual activities more available. For health care workers, it is possible that high sensation-seekers would be interested in movies that showed the emotional benefits of working with people with AIDS, and might respond favorably to graphically presented examples of on-the-job safety.

Possible Effects of Exposure to Social Influence

In this section we report the results of our research on the effects of informational and normative social influence on people's AIDS knowledge, fear, and prevention. Since our research is correlational in nature, it can only suggest some possible effects of exposure to informational and normative social influence. As with any correlational work, there remains the possibility of reverse causality, and even the possibility of a third variable causing the relationship between the first two. Nevertheless, our data may be viewed as both suggestive and informative. To conclude the section, we apply the health belief model (Rosenstock, 1966) and other, related models of health behavior to systematically examine the effects of social influence on AIDS prevention.

Informational Social Influence and AIDS Prevention

Informational social influence from one's social network predicts increased knowledge about AIDS, which is correlated with APB. Specifically, one's extent of engagement with a gay social network (which should be associated with increased informational social influence) correlated positively with greater perceived knowledge about AIDS ($r = .29$, $p < .02$) and predicted a trend toward greater actual knowledge ($r = .20$, $p < .12$). Knowledge, in turn, correlated with present levels of safe sex behavior ($r = .24$, $p < .03$). This pattern of effects is viewed as reflecting the impact of social influence from the network, though we do not have direct evidence of this.

Informational social influence from the media also affected both knowledge and prevention. Among gay men, exposure to media-based information about AIDS was associated with greater perceived ($r = .30$, $p < .02$) and actual AIDS knowledge ($r = .22$, $p < .09$), greater perceived efficacy of AIDS-preventive behavior ($r = .24$, $p < .06$), and greater levels of sexual impulse control ($r = .30$, $p < .02$). People with low levels of media exposure are especially apt to perceive APBs as nonefficacious, and to have low sexual impulse control. Exposure to media information is also correlated with higher levels of condom use ($r = .27$, $p < .03$) and with a trend toward greater intentions to engage in future AIDS-preventive behavior ($r = .25$, $p < .057$).

In addition, increased knowledge (a result of information seeking) is associated with greater perceived efficacy of APB ($r = .37$, $p < .001$), more positive affect toward APB ($r = .49$, $p < .001$), and greater impulse control ($r = .28$, $p < .03$). All of this suggests that exposure to information about AIDS (e.g., from the social network and the media) leads to favorable outcomes. However, the correlational nature of our work makes it unclear whether informational social influence elicits these outcomes, whether those with more favorable attitudes toward APB are simply better informed, or whether some third variable is responsible for the relationship.

Informational social influence can also affect one's level of fear of AIDS, which in turn may be related to prevention. (As discussed earlier, the fear communication literature suggests conditions under which fear promotes prevention.) In assessing the fear–prevention relationship, we first measured people's levels of fear of AIDS, which are probably a function of objective risk factors, exposure to fearful communications, and personality characteristics. We then related fear to prevention. While in an experimental setting the fear–prevention relationship can be assessed unambiguously, in the "real world" studying the relation between people's fear of AIDS and their preventive efforts is more complex, since fear is multiply caused. Although it is possible for fear to lead to prevention, it is also possible for lack of prevention to elicit fear.

Our data indicate that among gay men, various measures of fear are related to prevention. There are relationships between one's perceived susceptibility to AIDS and present levels of safer sex behavior ($r = .24$, $p < .06$), and between the perceived susceptibility of close others to AIDS and present levels of safer sex ($r = .34$, $p < .008$). When a global measure of fear was created that included perceived susceptibility of self and others plus an affective fear component, there were marginal correlations between fear and present levels of safer sex ($r = .23$, $p < .07$), and between fear and two measures of present preventive behavior ($r = .23$, $p < .08$; $r = .26$, $p < .04$, respectively). If various other measures of fear included in our research are considered, along with other measures of prevention, it is clear that there is a consistent pattern of increasing fear being related to increased prevention. However, the observed relations would probably be stronger if in addition to fear causing prevention, lack of prevention did not also cause fear. Nevertheless, perceptions of AIDS as dangerous do seem to be associated with APB.

Normative Social Influence and AIDS Prevention

In addition to informational social influence, normative social influence may have an impact on AIDS prevention. For gay men, normative social influence resulting from group membership may affect feelings of social responsibility, be associated with sanctions for failing to change behavior, and elicit social support for change. Thus, membership in a social network may lead to the feeling that one is a part of the AIDS crisis and in part responsible for its solution, and to support for efforts at AIDS prevention and sanctions for failing to use APBs. The above reasoning suggests that social influence from one's network may result in increased APB among gay men. Outside the gay population, where there is a lower incidence of AIDS and where group values have not changed, normative social influence would work, if anything, to lessen APB (J. D. Fisher, 1988).

What do our data have to say about the effect of belonging to a social network of gay men? Overall, they corroborate much of the above reasoning. Men who were more highly engaged in a gay social network reported greater sexual impulse control ($r = .34$, $p < .01$), increased belief in the efficacy of APBs ($r = .50$, $p < .0001$), and higher levels of APB, both in the present ($r = .44$, $p < .001$) and intended for the future ($r = .43$, $p < .001$). In effect, social influence from the network may elicit feelings of social responsibility and social support for AIDS-prevention efforts. Gay men who do not belong to a gay social network, who (as we mentioned earlier) may also be less accepting of their homosexuality, are not exposed to such social influence and thus may lack important sources of information and support. Thus, nondisclosed gays may be at a relative disadvantage due to the lack of social influence from other gays.

Social Influence, Prevention, and the Health Belief Model

Another, perhaps more systematic, way to consider the effects of various sources of social influence on APB is through the elements of the health belief model (HBM). The HBM (cf. Rosenstock, 1966, 1974) has been widely used to conceptualize the conditions under which people engage in prevention activities, and may be applied to the case of AIDS-preventive behavior. Briefly, the model consists of several sequential phases that one must pass through in order to engage in prevention. Each of the phases can be affected by sources of informational and normative social influence.

The first phase, readiness to act, is assumed to be a function of perceived severity of, and susceptibility to, the disease. The second, costs and benefits of compliance, involves the individual's perceptions of relevant costs and benefits of a particular preventive behavior. The third phase, cues to action, may consist of either internal or external stimuli that direct the individual to preventive action. People engage in prevention when they are convinced of the severity of, and their susceptibility to, a disease, when they perceive that the costs of prevention are outweighed by the benefits, and when they have experienced either internal or external cues to action. Social influence can affect whether or not each of these "hurdles" is overcome.

Past research has generally tested the relationship between individual components of the HBM and preventive behavior (e.g., the relation between perceived vulnerability and prevention), rather than the entire sequential process posited by the model. Some of this work has supported the components of the model as useful for predicting health behavior (Becker et al., 1979). Our research included variables which could be considered good indicators of certain health belief model dimensions and which may be affected by social influence.

Correlations were computed between each of these indices and AIDS-preventive behavior. They revealed that an index of perceived severity correlated marginally both with current preventive behaviors ($r = .23$, $p < .07$) and with the intention to perform more APBs in the future ($r = .24$, $p < .06$). Indices of perceived susceptibility correlated marginally with present levels of safer sex ($r = .24$, $p < .07$) and current amount of APB ($r = .22$, $p < .08$). In addition, perceived efficacy of APB (an index of the perceived benefits of compliance) correlated with present levels of safer sex ($r = .28$, $p < .03$), with abstaining from risky practices ($r = .22$, $p < .08$), and with the intention to perform more safer behaviors ($r = .32$, $p < .01$) and more APBs in the future ($r = .38$, $p < .002$). Finally, cues to action (e.g., contact with HIV-positive people) correlated with indices of AIDS-preventive behavior ($r = .33$, $p < .01$).

In addition to the health belief model, several other investigators have attempted to predict the conditions under which preventive behavior should occur (Emmons et al., 1986; Joseph et al., 1987; Ostrow, 1986). Taken together, they suggest that the following factors may help predict APB: knowledge of the disease, perceptions of vulnerability or risk of incurring AIDS, beliefs about the efficacy of health care and the efficacy of APBs, difficulties in sexual impulse control, belief in biomedical technology to provide a cure for AIDS, gay network affiliation, perceived social norms supportive of behavior change, and demographic characteristics.

In our sample of gay men, knowledge correlated with present levels of safer sex behavior ($r = .28$, $p < .03$) but not with a measure of abstaining from risky practices. Similarly, perceived vulnerability to AIDS correlated with current levels of safer sex behaviors ($r = .24$, $p < .03$) but not with abstaining from risky ones. While we do not have a measure of perceived efficacy of health care, we do have an index of perceived efficacy of APBs. As noted above, this correlated with multiple indicators of APB. In addition, sexual impulse control correlated with current levels of safer sex behavior ($r = .26$, $p < .05$), with avoiding unsafe practices ($r = .37$, $p < .004$), and with future levels of safer sex behavior ($r = .28$, $p < .03$). Belief in biomedical technology (finding a vaccine or a cure in the immediate future) was not correlated with APBs. While we did not have an adequate measure of perceived social norms supportive of behavior change, engagement in a social network was correlated with multiple measures of APB, as previously discussed. Finally, there was little demographic variation in the gay sample to correlate with APB, and we had no measure of the accessibility of health care. Overall, then, our data support many of the elements hypothesized by others to affect prevention, and correspond fairly closely to data collected on the effect of these factors by Emmons et al. (1986). However, in contrast to Emmons et al., in our sample perceived efficacy of APB tended to be a stronger predictor of actual APB than knowledge.

Applications

Applications Suggested by the Data

Our data suggest a number of applications, many of which have already been noted. However, since they are correlational, the limitations on what one can extrapolate should be kept in mind. One implication that follows from our research is that there may be particular individuals who engage in risky behaviors who could benefit from carefully articulated social influence attempts to increase APB. The data suggest that homosexuals who do not accept being gay, externals, sensation-seekers, and sensitizers all show high-risk characteristics in one or more domains that need to be addressed. In addition, gay men with low sexual impulse control would seem to be at high risk. Different strategies would probably have to be used in each case, and some could be quite effective. For example, social influence techniques as well as societal changes that would increase acceptance of being gay could yield dramatic increases in gay social network membership and in APBs among some nondisclosed gays and others who do not accept their homosexuality. At the very least, care should be taken at the societal level not to institutionalize repressive practices that would make gay individuals less comfortable with their orientation.

Our data also provide evidence that both informational and normative forms of social influence may be effective in increasing knowledge, moderating fear, and encouraging APB. One's exposure to various media sources, one's level of knowledge, and the extent to which one is enmeshed in a gay social network are all associated with higher levels of APB. Thus, each of these types of social influence should be encouraged and strengthened. In addition, higher levels of fear and perceived vulnerability may increase APB, except perhaps under certain conditions noted earlier. And since the perceived efficacy of APBs seems to be an important predictor of practicing safer sex and avoiding unsafe sex, communications that stress efficacy would seem to be warranted, though claims that are too strong would probably be viewed as noncredible.

Other Possible Interventions

Other possibilities abound concerning the use of social influence techniques to deal with the AIDS crisis. Much of our discussion thus far has focused on the powerful (too often regressive) social influence that the network may exert on its individual members. However, it should be kept in mind that while the majority can exert strong influence on the minority, under appropriate conditions the reverse can occur as well (e.g., Moscovici & Faucheux, 1972). Research suggests that members of the minority are most likely to influence majority behavior when (1) they are consistent in their views over time, (2) they are not rigid or dogmatic in upholding their views, and (3) they are similar to the majority except in the particular position they are advocating (Baron & Byrne, 1987).

One way to incorporate the above criteria into an intervention to encourage APB within social groups involves the use of pro-APB peers to influence others. We have trained undergraduate fraternity and sorority members who are pro-APB to give AIDS-prevention workshops to fraternities and sororities on campus. Those who run the workshops are consistent in their views, are neither rigid nor dogmatic, and are similar to the majority aside from their pro-APB stance. Anecdotal evidence suggests that the workshops were quite successful, and empirical research will be performed to test this assertion in the future. Past research suggests the usefulness of similar others in occasioning attitude change (Berscheid, 1966), and this has been shown as well in the domain of prevention (Dembrowsky, Lasater, & Ramirez, 1978).

At the individual level, and unfavorable group norms regarding APB notwithstanding, any person in a sexual relationship can demand that his or her partner comply with a request to use a condom. We simply have to persuade people to make such demands. The problem is in supporting the individual in requesting compliance in the face of norms wherein APB is not part of the expected script. Nevertheless, requests for compliance frequently elicit the desired result (Bushman, 1984). For the partner faced with the potential loss of a pleasurable sexual experience, the benefits of compliance may often outweigh the costs. Reinforcement theories suggest that the sexual pleasure associated with compliance may make it more likely in the future.

Creating Favorable Attitudes toward APBs

Other approaches to increasing APBs involve forming more favorable attitudes toward them in the first place, changing unfavorable attitudes so they are more positive, and, once positive attitudes are in place, ensuring the consistency between attitudes and behavior. We will discuss each of these in turn.

How are negative attitudes toward APB formed? In addition to the sources of informational and normative social influence discussed earlier, other processes are involved in the formation of unfavorable attitudes toward APBs. First, people may actually have negative experiences while using them. Sex may be less enjoyable, their partner may react negatively, etc. Alternatively, they may avoid APBs because they expect them to elicit a negative reaction from their partner. Ideally, it will be possible for social influence attempts to convince people that, compared with contracting AIDS, these are minor inconveniences to be endured. It might also be stated that a partner who does not support another in engaging in APB is not a worthy partner.

The literature on applying the reinforcement-affect model of attraction to the domain of contraception (e.g., Byrne, 1983; W. A. Fisher, 1983) suggests another source of negative attitudes toward APBs. People who have negative affect toward sexual matters in general, which is conditioned through socialization experiences (e.g., parents who won't talk about sex), also tend to have negative feelings toward specific preventive behaviors. They fail to use condoms, do not engage in presex discussion about STDs, and tend to justify their lack of prevention with statements that such techniques are not efficacious. Since the root of their negative attitudes toward APBs is discomfort with sex, a prerequisite for increasing preventive behavior may be to elicit greater comfort in dealing with such matters. The more open societal attitude toward sex occasioned by the AIDS crisis and the better sex education it may spawn might possibly help to make young people, at least, sufficiently comfortable in dealing with sex to discuss and engage in APBs.

Another issue concerns when and for whom informational and normative social influence will be most important in eliciting more positive attitudes toward APB. Research should be done to assess the relative contribution of the Aact (i.e., one's own attitudes) and SN (i.e., attitudes of significant others) components of Fishbein's model (Fishbein & Ajzen, 1975) in the context of AIDS prevention. Is it relatively more important to change an individual's attitudes, to change the values of his or her reference group, or both, to effect an increase in APB? Recently, Ajzen (Ajzen & Timko, 1986) has suggested that a third factor, control, may be important as well. Our data indicate that those who feel they have no control over APB (e.g., insufficient control over sexual impulses to use it) may need to develop either more actual control or more confidence in their ability to exert control in order to succeed at APB.

Once attitudes toward APB are more favorable, how does one ensure that people's behavior corresponds to such attitudes? The attitude-behavior literature is fraught with examples of attitude-behavior inconsistencies. Nevertheless, there are ways to help ensure a consistency between attitudes and behavior. Research suggests that the more a particular attitude is "accessible" to a person, the more likely it is to affect behavior (Powell & Fazio, 1984). Cues in the environment can help make attitudes accessible, and attitudes that are expressed often or formed on the basis of direct experience are more accessible (Fazio & Zanna, 1981). Thus, signs, reminders, APB discussions, and the like could be expected to increase the practice of APB in those with favorable attitudes.

Another way to increase attitude-behavior consistency is to moderate the consumption of alcohol or the use of drugs. Research suggests that alcohol helps people ignore inconsistencies between their attitudes and behavior (Steele, Southwick, & Critchlow, 1981). Even if one is attitudinally positive toward the use of APBs, being under the influence of alcohol or drugs can help people avoid acting in an attitude-consistent manner, or avoid attending to and rectifying any attitude-behavior inconsistency at a particular moment.

Increasing Information Seeking

Another type of intervention to increase the use of APBs involves helping people to seek the information they need regarding AIDS. Our data suggest that information seeking is associated with beneficial outcomes, but theoretical and empirical work indicates that when it is threatening to seek help (e.g., information), people will refrain (Fisher et al., 1982). According to Fisher et al., anything that lessens the threat of seeking information should lead to increased efforts in that regard. We suggested earlier that public information forums may not be effective at disseminating information because attendance could be threatening, and that alternatives that do not involve such threat (e.g., electronic media, pamphlets) may be preferred. Other factors (e.g., allowing information to be obtained anonymously, lowering the costs of seeking it in any way possible, minimizing the stigma of seeking help for AIDS-related issues) may be effective in lowering threat and increasing information seeking, which may ultimately result in more APB.

The Effect of Cognitive Dissonance

Some types of social influence attempts may arouse cognitive dissonance (Festinger, 1957) in an individual. Since dissonance is an aversive psychological state, people may be apt to resist such communications and certainly won't seek them out. For those who smoke, messages on the relationship between smoking and cancer are aversive. Each smoker has his or her own way of discounting such information in order to avoid the dissonance it elicits. The same is probably true of messages about AIDS-risk factors for those who have already incurred AIDS risk or believe they must incur it in the future, especially if they feel little can be done to avoid future risk. Accepting such messages could create dissonance between the two cognitions "I engage(d) in AIDS-risk behaviors" and "AIDS can kill me."

Instead of permitting such individuals the option of discounting the dissonance-producing message altogether, some way could be found to allow them to experience the dissonance-arousing cognitions but to lower the resultant dissonance to tolerable levels. In effect, it could be beneficial to take part of the "sting" out of dissonance so it occurs at a level that prompts thoughtful consideration rather than discounting of information. People could then resolve dissonance through attitude or behavior change rather than denial. To some extent, presenting information about AIDS risk that highlights the hindsight–foresight distinction (Janoff-Bulman, Madden, & Timko, 1984) could be useful in this regard. For individuals with past risk exposure, such messages could indicate that the individuals may have enacted earlier behaviors without full knowledge of the threat AIDS poses, that they are probably still AIDS-free, but that they *are* responsible for performing APB in the future. Rather than inducing denial or discounting, such information may encourage the resolution of dissonance aroused by past risk behaviors in the direction of future AIDS prevention.

Dissonance may also be used to increase levels of APB in other ways. It is suggested that perhaps it might be effective to have individuals (e.g., students) who do not use APBs engage in counterattitudinal advocacy by attempting to persuade others to use APBs. If the communicators and communicatees are peers, this paradigm may be especially efficacious at inducing behavior change (Berscheid, 1966). Creating larger groups of individuals and structuring them so that pro-APB norms emerge may be another effective device for changing group members' behavior. Since constructed groups seem to evidence a "shift toward conservatism" following a discussion of matters associated with health risk (Fraser, 1971; Myers & Bishop, 1970), such a method may be both practical and effective.

Avoiding Other "Pitfalls" When Engaging in Social Influence Attempts

At the level of large-scale interventions involving the use of social influence to increase APB, several other things should be kept in mind. One is that attempts should be made to avoid psychological reactance (Brehm, 1966) in recipients of influence attempts. Reactance is an unpleasant psychological state brought on by a perceived loss of important freedoms, which motivates the individual to restore lost freedoms. When attempts at social influence are perceived as coercive, they may elicit reactance and go unheeded—in fact the recipient may be motivated to do exactly the opposite of what the other desires. Given that APBs represent a loss of important freedoms to begin with, it is especially important for communicators to avoid approaches that exacerbate freedom loss. (It is even possible that some of the lack of APB we are seeing today may be a reaction to the *overall* lack of freedom generated by AIDS.) Avoiding reactance is especially important in younger populations and perhaps in gay men, who may view society as not respecting their freedom sufficiently to begin with.

Another pitfall involves the need to avoid training a form of "learned helplessness" through attempts at social influence. Communications that suggest that almost anything (e.g., deep kissing, sharing toothbrushes) can cause AIDS may not only elicit reactance but may also lead to learned helplessness (Seligman, 1975). Some might simply come to the conclusion that they could "get AIDS from anything," so why try to prevent it? In effect, we are predicting that if more and more behaviors are restricted, less and less APB may result. Perhaps scaling behaviors as to their relative risk and highlighting the fact that AIDS is, overall, "hard to get" could lead to more effective attempts at social influence.

Special Characteristics of the Problem

Learned helplessness can occur in other ways as well. In fact, it may be endemic to the AIDS problem in certain contexts. Some segments of the population (e.g., gay men with a history of high-risk exposure) may believe they have incurred sufficiently high risk in the past that future AIDS prevention would have no benefit. If they are going to get AIDS, they are already "doomed," so why engage in APB? Others may feel that because they have incurred high levels of past risk and still have *not* contracted AIDS, they are invincible. This may be especially true of those who have tested HIV negative in spite of a history of risk exposure. Since the people with the most risk behaviors probably get tested, training them that there is no contingency between their actions and their health outcomes (which could occur if they find out they are HIV negative) is especially dangerous. Low-SES individuals whose life has trained them not to expect contingencies may also fail to appreciate the relationship between APB and favorable health outcomes. Overall, then, in many situations there may have been internalized a lack of contingency between APB and health outcome that must be overcome. Somehow these individuals need to come to believe that APB can make a difference.

A final characteristic of AIDS that makes APBs difficult to foster is the fact that AIDS involves a distant, future negative event with only some probability of occurring, which requires immediate sacrifices. (Making sacrifices under such conditions is not even as appealing as sacrificing now to receive a future reward, since here, sacrifices are only to avoid a possible punishment.) Such a set of contingencies is similar in some ways to "social trap" situations in which people must incur immediate costs (e.g., conserve energy now) in order to avoid negative consequences (e.g., a possible energy shortage) in the future. Unfortunately, research has observed that it is difficult to influence people to sacrifice in the present to avoid possible future negative outcomes (Fisher, Bell, & Baum, 1984; Hardin, 1968; Platt, 1973). However, in order to combat AIDS, social influence researchers will have to find an effective way to encourage people to do just that!

ACKNOWLEDGMENTS. This research has been supported by Grant No. 1171-0215-660 from the University of Connecticut Research Foundation, by a grant-in-aid from SPSSI, and by Grant No. 410-87-1333 from the Social Sciences and Humanities Research Council of Canada.

References

Ajzen, I., & Timko, C. (1986). Correspondence between health attitudes and behavior. *Basic and Applied Social Psychology, 7,* 259–276.

Allen, V. L., & Levine, J. M. (1971). Social support and conformity: The role of independent assessment of reality. *Journal of Experimental Social Psychology, 4,* 48–58.

Baron, R. A. & Byrne, D. (1987). *Social psychology: Understanding human interaction.* Boston: Allyn & Bacon.

Becker, M. H., Maiman, L. A., Kirscht, J. P., Haefner, D. P., Drachmon, R. H., & Taylor, D. W. (1979). Patient perceptions and compliance: Recent studies of the health belief model. In R. B. Haynes, D. W. Taylor, & D. L. Sackett (Eds.), *Compliance in health care.* Baltimore: Johns Hopkins University Press.

Berscheid, E. (1966). Opinion change and communicator-communicatee similarity and dissimilarity. *Journal of Personality and Social Psychology, 4,* 670–680.

Brehm, J. W. (1966). *A theory of psychological reactance.* New York: Academic Press.

Bushman, B. J (1984). Perceived symbols of authority and their influence on compliance. *Journal of Applied Social Psychology, 14,* 501–508.

Byrne, D. (1964). Repression-sensitization as a dimension of personality. In B. A. Maher (Ed.), *Progress in experimental personality research* (Vol. 1). New York: Academic Press.

Byrne, D. (1971). *The attraction paradigm.* New York: Academic Press.

Byrne, D. (1983). Sex without contraception. In D. Byrne & W. A. Fisher (Eds.), *Adolescents, sex and contraception.* Hillside, NJ: Erlbaum.

Campbell, J. D., Tesser, A., & Fairey, P. J. (1986). Conformity and attention to the stimulus: Some temporal and contextual dynamics. *Journal of Personality and Social Psychology, 51,* 315–324.

Dembrowski, T. M., Lasater, T. M., & Ramirez, A. (1978). Communicator similarity, fear arousing communications, and compliance with health care recommendations. *Journal of Applied Social Psychology, 8,* 254–269.

DesJarlais, D. C., Friedman, S. R., & Strug, D. (1986). AIDS and needle sharing within the IV-drug use subculture. In D. A. Feldman & T. M. Johnson (Eds.), *The social dimensions of AIDS: Method and theory.* New York: Praeger.

Deutsch, M., & Gerard, H. B. (1955). A study of normative and informational social influences on individual judgment. *Journal of Abnormal and Social Psychology, 51,* 629–636.

Emmons, C. A., Joseph, J. G., Kessler, R. C., Wortman, L. B., Montgomery, S. B., & Ostrow, D. G. (1986). Psychosocial predictors of reported behavior change in homosexual men at risk for AIDS. *Health Education Quarterly, 13*(4), 331–345.

Fazio, R. H., & Zanna, M. P. (1981). Direct experience and attitude-behavior consistency. In L. Berkowitz (Ed.), *Advances in experimental social psychology* (Vol. 14). New York: Academic Press.

Festinger, L. (1954). A theory of social comparison processes. *Human Relations, 1,* 117–140.

Festinger, L. (1957). *A theory of cognitive dissonance.* Evanston, IL: Row, Peterson.

Fishbein, M., & Ajzen, I. (1975). *Belief, attitude, intention, and behavior: An introduction to theory and research.* Reading, MA: Addison-Wesley.

Fisher, J. D. (1988). Possible effects of reference group-based social influence on AIDS-risk behavior and AIDS-prevention. *American Psychologist, 43,* 914–920.

Fisher, J. D., Bell, P., & Baum, A. (1984). *Environmental psychology* (2nd ed.). New York: Holt, Rinehart & Winston.

Fisher, J. D., & Goff, B. A. (1986, July). *Social support, life events, and change: Blood may be thicker than water, but is it always better?* Paper presented at the International Conference on Personal Relationships, Herzalia, Israel.

Fisher, J. D., Goff, B. A., Nadler, A., & Chinsky, J. (1988). Social psychological differences in help-seeking and support from peers. In B. M. Gottlieb (Ed.), *Marshaling social support: Formats, processes, and effects.* Beverly Hills, CA: Sage.

Fisher, J. D., & Misovich, S. J. (1987). *Technical report on undergraduate AIDS-preventive behavior, AIDS-knowledge, and fear of AIDS.* Unpublished manuscript, University of Connecticut.

Fisher, J. D., & Misovich, S. J. (1988). *Fear of AIDS, AIDS-knowledge, and AIDS-preventive behavior.* Unpublished manuscript, University of Connecticut.

Fisher, J. D., Misovich, S. J., & Kean, K. (1987). *Fear of AIDS, AIDS-knowledge, and AIDS-preventive behavior among college students, gay men, and medical personnel.* Unpublished manuscript, University of Connecticut.

Fisher, J. D., Nadler, A., & Whitcher-Alagna, S. J. (1982). Recipient reactions to aid. *Psychological Bulletin, 91,* 27–54.

Fisher, W. A. (1983). Emotional barriers to contraception. In D. Byrne & W. A. Fisher (Eds.), *Adolescents, sex, and contraception.* Hillsdale NJ: Erlbaum.

Forsyth, D. R. (1983). *An introduction to group dynamics.* Pacific Grove. CA: Brooks-Cole.

Fraser, C. (1971). Group risk taking and group polarization. *European Journal of Psychology, 1,* 493–510.

Gross, A. E., & McMullin, P. A. (1984). Models of the help-seeking process. In B. M. DePaulo, A. Nadler, & J. D. Fisher (Eds.), *New directions in helping* (Vol. 2). New York: Academic Press.

Hardin, G. (1968). The tragedy of the commons. *Science, 162,* 1243–1248.

Hirsch, D. A., & Enlow, R. W. (1984). The effects of acquired immune deficiency syndrome on gay lifestyle and the gay individual. *New York Academy of Sciences Annals, 437,* 273–282.

Hovland, C., Lumsdaine, A., & Sheffield, F. (1949). *Studies in social psychology in World War II, 3. Experiments on mass communication* (pp. 201–227). Princeton, NJ: Princeton University Press.

Janis, I. L., & Feshbach, S. (1953). Effects of fear arousing communications. *Journal of Abnormal and Social Psychology, 48,* 78–92.

Janoff-Bulman, R., Madden, M., & Timko, C. (1980). *The illusion of invulnerability.* Unpublished manuscript, University of Massachusetts.

Janoff-Bulman, R., Madden, M., & Timko, C. (1984). Victims' reactions to aid: The role of perceived vulnerability. In A. Nadler, J. D. Fisher, & B. M. DePaulo (Eds.), *New directions in helping* (Vol. 3). New York: Academic Press.

Janz, N. K. & Becker, M. H. (1984). The health-belief model: A decade later. *Health Education Quarterly, 11,* 1–47.

Joseph, J. G., Montgomery, S. B., Emmons, C. A., Kessler, R. C., Ostrow, D. G., Wortman,

C. B., O'Brien, K., Eller, M., & Eshleman, S. (1987). Magnitude and determinants of behavior risk reduction: Longitudinal analysis of a cohort at risk for AIDS. *Psychology and Health*, 73–96.

Kreipe, R. E. (1985). Normal adolescent development: Helping teenagers cope with change. *New York State Journal of Medicine, 5*, 214–217.

Leventhal, H. (1971). Fear appeals and persuasion: The differentiation of a motivational construct. *American Journal of Public Health, 61*, 1208–1224.

Levinger, G., & Schneider, D. (1969). A test of the risk-as-a-value hypothesis. *Journal of Personality and Social Psychology, 11*, 165–169.

Lumsdaine, A. A., & Janis, I. L. (1953) Resistance to counterpropagation produced by a one-sided versus a two-sided propaganda presentation. *Public Opinion Quarterly, 17*, 311–318.

Maddux, J. E., & Rogers, R. W. (1983). Protection, motivation and self-efficacy: A revised theory of fear appeals and attitude change. *Journal of Experimental Social Psychology, 19*, 469–479.

Martin, J. L. (1987). The impact of AIDS on gay male sexual behavior in New York City. *American Journal of Public Health, 77*, 1–4.

McGuire, W. J. (1969). The nature of attitudes and attitude change. In G. Lindzey & E. Aronson (Eds.), *Handbook of social psychology* (Vol. 3). Reading, MA: Addison-Wesley.

Morales, E. S. (1987). From the director: AIDS and ethnic minority research. *Multicultural Inquiry and Research on AIDS, 1*, 2.

Morris, W. N., & Miller, R. S. (1972). The effects of consensus-breaking and consensus-preempting partners on reduction of conformity. *Journal of Personality and Social Psychology, II*, 215–223.

Moscovici, S., & Faucheux, C. (1972). Social influence, conforming bias, and the study of active minorities. In L. Berkowitz (Ed.), *Advances in experimental social psychology* (Vol. 6, pp. 149–202). New York: Academic Press.

Myers, D. G., & Bishop, G. D. (1970). Discussion effects on radical attitudes. *Science, 169*, 778–789.

Nadler, A., & Fisher, J. D. (1988). *Personal change in an interpersonal perspective.* Unpublished manuscript, Tel-Aviv University.

Nadler, A., Sheinberg, O., & Jaffe, Y. (1981). Seeking help from the wheelchair. In C. Spielberger & I. Sarason (Eds.), *Stress and anxiety* (Vol. 8). Washington, DC: Hemisphere.

National Academy of Sciences. (1986). *Confronting AIDS: Directions for public health, health care, and research.* Washington, DC: National Academy Press.

Newcomb, T. M. (1943). *Personality and social change.* New York: Dryden Press.

Ostrow, F. H. (Ed.). (1986). *Biobehavioral control of AIDS.* New York: Irvington Press.

Perloff, L. S., & Fetzer, B. K. (1986). Self-other judgments and perceived vulnerability to victimization. *Journal of Personality and Social Psychology, 50*, 502–510.

Petty, R. E., & Cacioppo, J. T. (1979). Effects of forewarning of persuasive intent and involvement on cognitive responses and persuasion. *Personality and Social Psychology Bulletin, 5*, 173–176.

Petty, R. E., & Cacioppo, J. T. (1981). *Attitudes and persuasion: Classic and contemporary approaches.* Dubuque, IA: William C. Brown.

Platt, J. (1973). Social traps. *American Psychologist, 28*, 641–651.

Powell, M. C., & Fazio, R. M. (1984). Attitude accessibility as a function of repeated attitudinal expression. *Personality and Social Psychology Bulletin, 10*, 139–148.

Rogers, R. W. (1975). A protection motivation theory of fear appeals and attitude change. *Journal of Psychology, 91*, 93–114.

Rosenstock, I. M. (1966). Why people use health services. *Milbark Memorial Fund Quarterly, 44*, 94–127.

Rosenstock, I. M. (1974). The health belief model and preventive health behavior. *Health Education Monographs, 2*, 354–386.

Schachter, S. (1951). Deviation, rejection, and communication. *Journal of Abnormal and Social Psychology, 46*, 190–207.

Seligman, M. E. P. (1975). *Helplessness: On depression, development, and death.* San Francisco: Freeman.

Snyder, C. R. (1978). The "illusion" of uniqueness. *Journal of Humanistic Psychology, 19*, 33–41.

Steele, C. M., Southwick, L. L., & Critchlow, B. (1981). Dissonance and alcohol: Drinking your troubles away. *Journal of Personality and Social Psychology, 41*, 831–846.

Tanford, S., & Penrod, S. (1984). Social influence model: A formal integration of research on majority and minority influence processes. *Psychological Bulletin, 95*, 189–225.

Tversky, A., & Kahneman, D. (1974). Judgment under uncertainty: Heuristics and biases. *Science, 195*, 1124–1131.

Vazquez-Nuttall, E., Avila-Vivas, Z., & Morales-Barreto, G. (1984). Working with Latin American families. *Family Therapy Collections, 9*, 74–90.

Wallach, M., & Wing, C. (1968). Is risk a value? *Journal of Personality and Social Psychology, 9*, 101–106.

Wallston, B. S., Wallston, K. A., Kaplan, G. D., & Maides, S. A. (1976). Development and validation of the Health Locus of Control (HCC) Scale. *Journal of Consulting and Clinical Psychology, 46*, 580–585.

Weinstein, N. D. (1980). Unrealistic optimism about susceptibility to health problems. *Journal of Behavioral Medicine, 5*, 441–460.

Zuckerman, M. (1979). *Sensation seeking: Beyond the optional level of arousal*. Hillsdale, NJ: Erlbaum.

4

Understanding and Preventing Teenage Pregnancy and Sexually Transmitted Disease/AIDS

William A. Fisher

Most American teenagers have sexual intercourse, but most do not reliably use contraception or exercise precautions against sexually transmitted disease (STD). The predictable result of this pattern of behavior is a very high level of teenage pregnancy and infection with STD, accompanied by equally predictable sequelae, such as abortion, teenage parenthood, and welfare dependence (in the case of adolescent pregnancy), and sterility, lifelong infectiousness, and even death (in the case of adolescent STD infection). This chapter describes the problems of teenage pregnancy and STD, presents a model for understanding why teenagers expose themselves to these risks, and closes with discussion of a theory-based intervention to reduce adolescent pregnancy and STD infection.

The Problem: Adolescent Pregnancy and Exposure to Sexually Transmitted Diseases Including AIDS

Adolescent Pregnancy

According to a variety of sources, most Americans have premarital sexual intercourse while they are still in their teens (Coles & Stokes, 1985; Hofferth, Kahn, & Baldwin, 1987; Zelnik & Kantner, 1977, 1980), but the majority of

William A. Fisher • Department of Psychology and Department of Obstetrics and Gynecology, The University of Western Ontario, London, Ontario, Canada N6A 5C2.

these sexually active teenagers do not always use reliable methods of contraception (Coles & Stokes, 1985; Zelnik & Kantner, 1977, 1980). It may be estimated that some 30% of sexually active American adolescents become pregnant during their teenage years (Coles & Stokes, 1985; Zelnik & Kantner, 1980), and that there are more than 600,000 unintended pregnancies to single female teenagers in the United States in a given year (Alan Guttmacher Institute, 1981). Younger teens and those who are in less committed relationships are especially unlikely to use contraception, and thus unintended pregnancies often occur in situations where partner support for dealing with the pregnancy is minimal (Cvetkovitch & Grote, 1983; Fisher, et al., 1979; Gross & Bellew-Smith, 1983; Zabin, Kantner, & Zelnik, 1979).

American teenagers have the distinction of having a higher pregnancy rate than do teenagers in most other developed countries (Alan Guttmacher Institute, 1981; Jones et al., 1985; Westoff, Calot, & Foster, 1983). While there are black–white differences in adolescent sexual and contraceptive behavior (black teens report somewhat more premarital intercourse, somewhat less contraceptive use, and somewhat more pregnancies), these differences in many cases seem to be diminishing across time (Hofferth et al., 1987; Zelnik & Kantner, 1980), and they may in any event be of less significance than is popularly imagined. American teenagers—black and white—each have pregnancy rates that are far in excess of those in Canada, England, France, the Netherlands, or Sweden (Jones et al., 1985).

Unintended adolescent pregnancies in the United States result in live births to teenage mothers (in some 49% of the cases), abortions (in some 37% of the cases), and miscarriages or stillbirths (in some 14% of the cases; estimates based on Zelnik & Kantner, 1980; see also Alan Guttmacher Institute, 1981). Adolescent pregnancies are more likely to be carried to term by black mothers (71.4%) than by white mothers (38.6%; Zelnik & Kantner, 1980), and overall, births to teenage women may account for up to 26% of all first births in the United States (Moore & Werthheimer, 1984). For those teenagers who carry their pregnancy to term, the vast majority keep their baby rather than place it for adoption, and most unwed teenage mothers do not marry the father of their baby (Alan Guttmacher Institute, 1981). Adolescent childbearing carries with it increased risk of maternal and fetal health complications, especially for young teens (Alan Guttmacher Institute, 1981), high levels of high school dropout and welfare dependence for teenage mothers (Moore & Wertheimer, 1984; Mott & Marsiglio, 1985), a high likelihood of marital dissolution for teen mothers who are wed (Alan Guttmacher Institute, 1981), and, possibly, an increased likelihood of child abuse (Bolton, 1980). In terms of some of the more easily quantified costs—and ignoring much unquantifiable human misery—it has been estimated that the cost of welfare to teenage mothers and children in the United States was $16.65 billion in 1985 alone (Burt, 1986). In a more hopeful vein, Furstenberg, Brooks-Gunn, & Morgan (1987) have discussed paths to more positive outcomes for teenage mothers, and Nuckolls, Cassel, and Kaplan (1972) and Zuckerman, Walker, Frank, Chase, and Hamburg (1984) have discussed the critical role of social support in averting some of the negative outcomes of teenage parenthood.

To summarize, then, data from multiple sources indicate that American adolescents are relatively likely to be sexually active but are relatively unlikely to use contraception during their teenage years. This results in hundreds of thousands of unintended pregnancies and associated abortions, adolescent parenting, truncated educations, welfare dependence, and the like, which constitute social problems of the first rank for the United States.

Adolescent Exposure to Sexually Transmitted Disease

STD infections, such as gonorrhea, chlamydia, and herpes, are occurring at epidemic levels in the United States today (Faro, 1983; Hyde, 1986; Masters, Johnson, & Kolodny, 1985), and adolescents are frequent victims of STD infection (Bell & Holmes, 1984; Kroger & Wiesner, 1981; Shafer et al., 1984). Moreover, today's adolescents have to deal with the threat of AIDS. There are more than 94,000 diagnosed AIDS cases in the United States as of this writing (Federal Centre for AIDS, 1989), and while few of these AIDS cases are adolescents, this should not be taken as comforting news. The incubation period of the AIDS virus is quite long (Rees, 1987), the virus is readily heterosexually transmissible (Fischl et al., 1987; Guinan & Hardy, 1987; Padian, 1987), and it is present in the general population at an alarmingly high level (Burke et al., 1987; Masters, Johnson, & Kolodny, 1988; Tempelis et al., 1987). Therefore, it seems entirely possible that heterosexually active adolescents are currently infecting one another with AIDS and that this will result in a sharp increase in symptomatic AIDS cases in this group some years down the line.

The serious consequences of STD to adolescents include lifelong infection and infectiousness (herpes and AIDS), pelvic inflammatory disease and sterility (chlamydia and gonorrhea), and the likelihood of death (AIDS), among other negative outcomes. What then are adolescents and others doing to reduce their risk of STD? On the one hand, the mass media have suggested that the sexual revolution may be ending and that young people may soon return to conservative sexual practices (Time, 1987; U.S. News and World Report, 1987). On the other hand, empirical research consistently indicates that many heterosexuals, and indeed many members of so-called high-risk groups, continue to engage in very high levels of unsafe sexual practices, undeterred by fear of STD (Bauman & Siegel, 1987; Joseph et al., 1987; Kegeles, Adler, & Irwin, 1988; Kelly, St. Lawrence, Brasfield, & Hood, 1988; Martin, 1987; McKusick, Horstman, & Coates, 1985; Smiley et al., 1988).

The degree to which young Americans continue to practice unsafe sex was recently demonstrated in research by Jeffrey Fisher and Steven Misovich (1987). These investigators surveyed the sexual behavior of 122 young, primarily heterosexual male and female undergraduates. Approximately 68% of these young people were coitally active; of those who were, 49% had intercourse with more than one partner during the preceding year, 18% had intercourse with persons with whom they were only slightly acquainted, 7.4% had sex with persons who were known to be promiscuous, and 2.5% had sex with persons who were known to be bisexual. Moreover, among coitally active students, 96% reported that they had not decreased their number of unsafe sexual practices during the past year, 80% had not limited their number of sexual partners to reduce risk of STD, 77% did not always use condoms, and 76% had never discussed STD with potential sex partners. Distressingly, 95% of the students in this survey chose *not* to keep an AIDS information sheet that was presented as part of the research debriefing (see also Baldwin & Baldwin, 1988, for further evidence of low levels of STD-preventive behavior among young Americans).

It is worth noting that the undergraduates in the Fisher and Misovich sample thought they were at low risk of ever being infected with AIDS (on average, they reported a 13% probability of ever being infected), but it is not necessarily the case that low perceived risk "causes" failure to act preventively. Research by Joseph *et al.* (1987) recently demonstrated virtually *no* relationship of perceived risk and preventive practices in a sample of gay males, and research by Bauman and Siegel (1987) has demonstrated that perceived risk of AIDS may vastly underestimate objectively assessed levels of risk.

In summary, then, STDs are widespread in the population and adolescents are often affected by such infections and their long-term negative effects. Despite the crisis atmosphere engendered by AIDS, recent data show that heterosexual young persons continue to engage in high levels of behaviors that put them at risk of contracting STDs. The present costs of STD infection to teenagers and to society are great, and the possibility that teenagers are at present infecting one another with the AIDS virus is a major and worrisome long-term concern.

Adolescent Pregnancy and Exposure to STD: Overlapping Behavioral Problems

It is important to realize that adolescent pregnancy and exposure to STD are problems with similar behavioral causes and similar possibilities for behavioral prevention. On the causal side, present patterns of adolescent sexual behavior (including multiple sexual partners, lack of presex discussion of prevention, and lack of contraceptive and condom use) elevate risk of both unintended pregnancy and STD. On the prevention side, behaviors such as sexual limit setting, presex discussion of prevention, and consistent contraceptive and condom use could reduce both pregnancy and STD.

Despite the overlap between behaviors that influence teenage pregnancy and STD, adolescents and health care providers often act as if these phenomena were unconnected. Adolescent contraceptive use, for example, follows a regular pattern of development from the use of no method (bad for pregnancy prevention, bad for

STD prevention), to the use of condoms (good for pregnancy prevention, good for STD prevention), to the use of oral contraception (good for pregnancy prevention, useless for STD prevention; Zelnik & Kantner, 1977). Thus, the "better" teens get at contraception, the 'worse" they get at STD prevention. By the same token, health care providers still seem much more committed to adolescent pregnancy prevention than to prevention of both adolescent pregnancy and STD. For example, each time a sexually active young woman is prescribed oral contraceptives but not counseled about condoms, she is put definitively at risk insofar as she is sexually active, unconcerned about pregnancy, and undefended from STD. It is clear that in the 1980s and beyond, both adolescents and health care providers must regard pregnancy and STD prevention as linked phenomena with reciprocal effects. The following discussion deals with how we may understand and reduce both adolescent pregnancy and STD simultaneously.

Understanding the Problem: Why Do Adolescents Risk Unplanned Pregnancy and Sexually Transmitted Disease?

Adolescents' tendency to risk unplanned pregnancy and STD may be explained, in part, by two fundamental facts (Byrne, 1983). First, there are *structural barriers* to adolescent pregnancy and STD prevention: To avoid pregnancy and STD, teens must perform complex and difficult sequences of behavior that are rarely explicitly taught and that are often socially disapproved. Second, there are internal, *psychological barriers* to pregnancy and STD prevention: Teens have been socialized with feelings, thoughts, and fantasies that promote sexual activity but inhibit performance of pregnancy- and STD-preventive behaviors. The following discussion deals with both structural and psychological barriers to adolescent pregnancy and STD prevention.

Structural Barriers to Pregnancy and STD Prevention

It is critical to understand that pregnancy and STD prevention requires adolescents to perform an objectively difficult and complex series of acts (see Byrne, 1983, for a discussion of this issue upon which the present work draws). Behavioral scripts to guide pregnancy and STD prevention are rarely if ever taught to teens, the behavioral acts involved are often disapproved of socially, and pregnancy- and STD-preventive behaviors have immediate costs but only distant and uncertain payoffs for teens. *Not* engaging in pregnancy- and STD-preventive behavior, in contrast, requires no learning, has immediate sexual payoffs and few immediate costs, but may in the long run be immensely costly for teens. Let us now examine the sequences of behaviors that are involved in three strategies for preventing teenage pregnancy and STD: sexual limit setting, contraceptive use, and the practice of safer sex.

The Sexual Limit-Setting Sequence

One pattern of behavior that is effective in eliminating risk of pregnancy and in reducing risk of STD is to set and observe limits on one's sexual activity such that intercourse does not occur. The sexual limit-setting sequence involves a number of behavioral steps which must be learned, practiced, and enacted, and which provide for both sexual intimacy and pregnancy and STD prevention.

The initial step in the sexual limit-setting sequence involves *self-acceptance of one's own sexuality*. It is necessary for an adolescent to admit the fact that he or she is a sexual being with the potential for future sexual activity before limit-setting or other preventive strategies even become an issue. Because social norms still stress that it is improper for teenagers to be sexually active, acknowledging sexual desire requires teens to admit that they are contemplating violation of an important social rule. For this reason, teens may understandably be reluctant to regard themselves as sexual beings with the need to plan preventive strategies regarding pregnancy and STD. Adolescents who cannot acknowledge their own sexuality obviously will be unlikely to plan for prevention.

A second step in the limit-setting sequence involves *making an advance decision that sexual limits are in one's own best interests*. It would be very helpful if teens were taught to think through what level of physical intimacy is best for them, in terms of their own values and priorities, and in advance of sexual situations that may involve high levels of arousal, alcohol, isolation from others, and like factors that may make decision making and limit setting more difficult. Teenagers who cannot recognize signs that sexual intimacy is upcoming and that decisions must be made will not be in a strong position to set preventive sexual limits.

A third step in the limit-setting sequence requires that the teenager *learn easy-to-translate-into-behavior information about how to set sexual limits*. Necessary information includes instruction on how conception takes place, how STDs are transmitted, how to bring up, negotiate, and observe sexual limits with a partner, and what pleasurable, nonintercourse behaviors are available. Explicit, scriptlike information concerning how adolescents may bring up, negotiate, and observe sexual limits, or concerning nonintercourse sexual options, is rarely available to teenagers today. Adolescents who lack such enabling information are clearly not in a strong position to practice preventive limit-setting strategies.

A fourth step in the limit-setting sequence is actually to *bring up and negotiate sexual limits with a partner*. Teenagers must be able to initiate discussion of sexual limits with their partners and to negotiate mutually agreed upon limits with them. This process requires, among other things, that adolescents think through why they find sexual limits to be beneficial and what the extent of these limits might be, and it also requires negotiating skills to come to agreement with a partner whose initial position may be distant from the teenager's own. Moreover, it will sometimes be the case that partners will fail to agree on mutually acceptable limits, and dealing with this outcome will require still additional skills, ranging from the ability to recognize and leave an unrewarding relationship, to skills for continuing a rewarding relationship on a platonic basis until agreement on desired level of sexual intimacy is reached.

A fifth step in the limit-setting sequence involves the *consistent observance of agreed-upon limits*. It is clear that temptations to go beyond agreed-upon sexual limits will occur from time to time in an adolescent relationship, and teenagers need to acquire skills to help them maintain the sexual limits they have decided upon. Such practices as reinforcing oneself and one's partner for observing limits, avoiding compromising situations, having agreed upon signals for sexual disengagement, and tactics for dealing with efforts by one partner to subvert the other's limits may facilitate the maintenance of sexual limits that have been judged beneficial by an adolescent.

A final step in the sexual limit-setting sequence involves *deciding when to move on to greater—but protected—sexual intimacy*. The sexual limit-setting strategy is for many teens part of a developmental progression that begins with relatively severe limits on sexual expression and eventually moves to a point where intercourse becomes acceptable and desired. It is believed that sexual limit setting short of intercourse is in the self-interest of younger teens who cannot deal effectively with intense relationships or with the intracacies of pregnancy and STD prevention. It is also clear, however, that many older teens can deal responsibly with these issues and will wish to abandon the limit-setting strategy for a pattern of behavior that includes sexual intercourse along with pregnancy and STD prevention, and such older teens will need to know how to make this transition planfully. At a minimum, such teenagers will have to be able to consider in advance whether sexual intercourse is now in their best interest, and then they will have to enact the sequences of contraceptive and safer sexual behavior that are described in the following sections.

The Contraceptive Behavior Sequence

Coitally active adolescents may avoid unintended pregnancy by appropriate use of contraception. Contraception—like limit setting—involves performance of a fairly complex sequence of sex-related behaviors.

The initial stage of the contraceptive behavior sequence is for the teenager to *accept his or her sexuality and to make an advance decision about the desirability of intercourse and the necessity for contraception*. Teenagers who are unwilling or unable to accept their own sexuality and to make such advance decisions are not likely to make any preparations for the possibility of intercourse.

A subsequent step in the contraceptive behavior sequence involves *learning relevant information about conception and contraception*. Once the possibility of intercourse has been acknowledged, the teenager needs to seek out practical information about how conception occurs and how it may be avoided. Sex education often makes explicit exactly how conception occurs, and often omits entirely mention of how to discuss, obtain, or use methods for preventing conception (see, for example, A. R. Allgeier, 1983; Yarber & McCabe, 1981, 1984). Without a base of knowledge regarding contraception that is easy to translate into behavior, pregnancy prevention will be difficult.

After self-admission of sexual activity and learning relevant information, it is necessary for a teenager to engage in *presex discussion and negotiation of contraception with a partner*. At a minimum, teenagers must be able to initiate discussion of contraception and to negotiate who will be responsible for it.

After contraceptive precautions have been agreed upon, at least one partner must *publicly acquire a method of contraception*. Most methods of contraception must be acquired in semipublic settings (e.g., a clinic or a pharmacy) that require the virtual announcement of one's sexual activity to other individuals (e.g., receptionists, nurses, physicians). While self-acknowledging one's sexual intentions, seeking relevant information, and presex discussion of contraception may be difficult, the public acquisition of a method of contraception may be most difficult of all (Fisher *et al.*, 1979; Fisher, Byrne, & White, 1983; Fisher, Fisher, & Byrne, 1977).

Assuming that contraception has been acquired, adolescents need to *consistently and correctly use the method of contraception they have chosen*. Consistency of contraceptive use might mean using a condom or inserting a diaphragm prior to each instance of intercourse, taking a daily pill, or like compliance to a contraceptive regime. Consistent contraceptive use may be relatively easy in certain cases (e.g., long-term relationships in which there is predictability of need and partner support) and relatively more difficult in others (e.g., just beginning or just ending relationships in which there is little predictability or support for consistent use; Fisher *et al.*, 1979; Foreit & Foreit, 1978; Gross & Bellew-Smith, 1983). What is critical to note is that pregnancy prevention requires highly consistent behavior that may depend on teens' ability to reinforce their own and their partners' contraceptive practices.

A final stage that will occasionally be part of the contraceptive behavior sequence involves *deciding to shift to a limit-setting or abstinent strategy*. For a variety of reasons, adolescents may decide to cease using contraception and to opt instead for a limit-setting strategy or abstinence. Teens need to be aware that if they find they dislike contraceptively protected intercourse—because of contraceptive side effects, lack of sensual pleasure in intercourse, relationship changes, or whatever—they are free to adopt alternative preventive practices such as sexual limit setting. Skills that are required for enacting such a shift could involve the capacity to reflect on the advantageous and disadvantageous personal consequences of one's present sexual practices, and discussion and negotiation skills to alter the sexual and contraceptive practices in a two-person relationship.

The Safer Sexual Behavior Sequence

Whether an adolescent chooses to reduce pregnancy risk by setting sexual limits or by using contraception, an adolescent today must also enact a series of safer sexual behaviors to avoid STD infection.

As was the case with sexual limit setting and contraception, *self-admission of sexual activity* is the first step in the safer sexual behavior sequence. Until a teenager acknowledges his or her own sexual desires, there will be no reason to decide upon or to plan for safer sexual expression.

Once sexual activity has been acknowledged and safer sex decided upon, the adolescent must acquire *relevant information about safer sex practices.* At a minimum, a teenager must learn information that is current and that can readily be translated into STD-preventive, safer sex practices, and the adolescent must be aware of how to update his or her preventive information on a regular basis. At present, our society seems unwilling to provide teens with behaviorally relevant information that would permit them to practice sex more safely—preferring instead to single-mindedly encourage abstinence—and therefore society continues to place teens at clear risk of STD and AIDS infection.

After relevant safer sex information has been learned, the adolescent must engage in *presex discussion and negotiation of safer sex limits with a partner.* Skills involved at this stage of the safer sex sequence involve the ability to bring up the topic of STD prevention *prior* to beginning sexual intimacy, the ability to persuade a partner about the mutual desirability of safer sex limits, and the ability to terminate or otherwise modify a relationship in which safer sex limits cannot be agreed upon.

Once safer sex limits have been negotiated, the adolescent and his or her partner must *consistently observe safer sex behavior practices.* Adolescents may engage in a hierarchy of more-to-less safe sexual practices, ranging from mutual body rubs and masturbation (''outercourse'') to vaginal intercourse with condoms and nonoxynol-9 spermicide, and adolescents must avoid impulsive unsafe sex practices (e.g., experimenting with unprotected anal intercourse). As was the case with the sexual limit-setting sequence, avoiding compromising situations, agreed-upon signals for sexual disengagement, skills for avoiding partners' attempts to subvert safer sex limits, and tactics for self- and partner reinforcement may help teenagers practice safer sex consistently.

A final stage in the safer sex sequence involves *recognition of circumstances under which safer sex is no longer necessary.* Under certain conditions (e.g., after an appropriate waiting period and HIV testing, and within agreed-upon monogamy) the practice of safer sex is not as critical and may be relegated to the history of the relationship.

Summary: Structural Barriers to Preventive Behavior

For clarity of exposition, I have discussed separately the behavioral sequences that are involved in sexual limit setting, contraceptive use, and safer sexual practices. There are important similarities, however, that are common across these means of preventing pregnancy and STD. Each of the preventive strategies begins with adolescents' self-admission of their sexuality, and each involves the active decision to engage in prevention, acquisition of relevant information, discussion and negotiation regarding the preventive strategy, and actually practicing

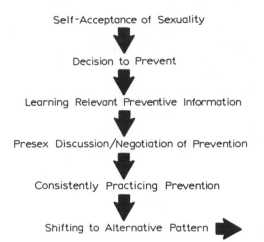

Self-Acceptance of Sexuality

Decision to Prevent

Learning Relevant Preventive Information

Presex Discussion/Negotiation of Prevention

Consistently Practicing Prevention

Shifting to Alternative Pattern

Figure 1. Common elements in behavioral sequences for sexual limit setting, contraception, and STD prevention.

preventive behaviors consistently. Each of the preventive strategies also includes a point at which one may legitimately abandon the strategy and shift to another pattern. These common elements in pregnancy and STD prevention are presented in Figure 1.

Just as there are many common behaviors in the sexual limit-setting, contraception, and safer sex sequences, there are many common difficulties as well. First, it must be emphasized that we simply do not teach teens explicit behavioral scripts concerning how they may set sexual limits, use contraception, or engage in safer sex. Second, it must be emphasized that even if teens do manage to piece together the elements of any of the three sequences, it is inherently difficult to perform such behaviors as anticipating sexual intimacy, persuading a partner to behave in a certain way, and consistently practicing prevention. As if these problems were not enough, it appears that adolescents also possess significant internal, psychological barriers to performing these sex-related preventive behaviors, a topic to which discussion now turns.

Psychological Barriers to Pregnancy and STD Prevention

According to a recently proposed theory, the Sexual Behavior Sequence, adolescents' feelings, thoughts, and fantasies about sex determine their sexual behavior (Byrne, 1977, 1983; Fisher, 1986). It is believed that, at present, many adolescents have sex-related feelings, thoughts, and fantasies which encourage sexual activity but which at the same time discourage pregnancy and STD prevention. The role of these internal barriers to pregnancy- and STD-preventive behavior is described in the discussion that follows.

Emotional Barriers to Pregnancy and STD Prevention

Adolescents possess generalized and stable emotional responses to sexuality that have implications for pregnancy and STD prevention (Byrne, 1983; Fisher *et al.*, 1983; Fisher, Byrne, White, & Kelley, 1988). Adolescents may be erotophobic (mostly negative in their feelings about sex), erotophilic (mostly positive in their feelings about sex), or anywhere in between these emotional extremes. With respect to pregnancy and STD prevention, it is proposed that highly erotophobic teens should be too uncomfortable to have intercourse and will not be in great need of pregnancy and STD prevention; highly erotophilic teens should be comfortable enough both to have intercourse and to plan for and practice prevention. Moderately erotophobic teenagers, in the present view, are at greatest risk of pregnancy and STD: Such individuals may be just comfortable enough about sex to engage in intercourse, but they may be far too uncomfortable about sex to admit their sexual desires and preventive needs in advance, to learn about sexual limit setting, contraception, and STD prevention, to discuss these issues with a partner, or ultimately to practice prevention consistently (Byrne, 1983; Fisher *et al.*, 1983; Fisher, Byrne, *et al.*, 1988).

Research over the past decade has examined the relation of young people's erotophobia–erotophilia and their likelihood of engaging in pregnancy- and STD-preventive behavior. Findings that illustrate how erotophobic and erotophilic emotions may inhibit or facilitate sex-related prevention are reviewed next.

The initial stage of each of the preventive behavior sequences, it will be recalled, involves self-admission by the adolescent that he or she may soon be sexually active and may therefore need to comtemplate preventive behavior. In the present view, erotophobic adolescents' negative feelings about sex should make it difficult for them to admit their future sexual intentions and preventive needs, while erotophilic adolescents' positive feelings about sex might actually make them eager to anticipate upcoming sexual activity. Fisher (1978) examined this relationship by assessing young men's erotophobia–erotophilia and their intentions to have sexual intercourse during the coming month. Results showed that erotophobic young men (51.55% of whom expected to have sex) were less likely to anticipate having intercourse than were erotophilic young men (77.30% of whom expected to have sex). When questioned about their actual sexual behavior a month later, moreover, it emerged that erotophobic young men had underestimated their likelihood of intercourse and as a result sometimes had intercourse that was not only unexpected but also contraceptively unprotected. Erotophilic men, for their part, were unlikely to have unexpected, or unprotected, intercourse. These results suggest, then, that erotophobic adolescents may find it difficult to acknowledge their future sexual intentions and related preventive needs in advance.

A second phase of the preventive behavior sequences involves learning relevant information about sex-related prevention. According to the present view, erotophobic adolescents' negative feelings about sex should make it difficult for them to seek out and retain information about sex-related prevention, while erotophilic adolescents' more positive feelings about sex should facilitate such learning. To test this hypothesis, Fisher *et al.* (1983) divided students in a human sexuality class into those who were relatively erotophobic and those who were relatively erotophilic, and then the students' marks on a sexuality midterm exam were compared. Erotophobic students' average mark (71.16%) was nearly a full letter grade lower than erotophilic students' average mark (78.80%) on the midterm exam. To the extent that such research may be generalized, it would seem that erotophobic adolescents may find it difficult to learn what they need to know about sex-related prevention, while erotophilic adolescents may find it easier to seek out and master such critical material (see also Fisher, Grenier, *et al.,* 1988; Goldfarb, Gerrard, Gibbons, & Plante, 1988).

A third stage of the preventive behavior sequences involves presex discussion, by adolescent couples, of sexual plans and preventive needs. According to the present theory, erotophobic adolescents should find it difficult to engage in such presex discussion of sex-related prevention, while erotophilic adolescents should find it less aversive. To examine the link between young people's erotophobia–erotophilia and their comfort with such presex discussion, Fisher, Miller, Byrne, and White (1981) created a laboratory analogue of sexual communication. Erotophobic and erotophilic students were brought into the lab and were asked to read a prepared speech on either a sexual or a neutral topic into a video camera (ostensibly for later presentation to an audience), and the students' reactions to communicating the sexual or the neutral messages were assessed. Results demonstrated that erotophobic (versus erotophilic) young men and women had significantly more negative affective reactions while communicating and expected significantly more negative reactions from recipients of the sexual communication. These findings suggest that erotophobic adolescents may have a difficult time engaging in critical presex discussion about sex-related prevention.

An additional phase of some of the preventive behavior sequences involves more or less public preventive behaviors, such as buying condoms in a pharmacy or visiting a clinic for contraceptive prescription or STD or HIV testing. Erotophobic adolescents should find it more difficult to engage in such public sex-related preventive behaviors than would erotophilic adolescents. Fisher *et al.* (1979; see also Fisher *et al.,* 1983) have studied the relation of erotophobia–erotophilia and public performance of sex-related preventive behavior. These investigators assessed the erotophobia–erotophilia of sexually active college women who were inconsistent users of contraception; some had never visited the campus contraception clinic, while the others had just gone public to acquire needed contraception at this clinic. As expected, results showed that the women who did not make a needed visit to the contraception clinic were significantly more erotophobic than were the women who did visit the clinic. To the extent that one can generalize from these findings, it would appear that erotophobia may inhibit performance of public sex-related preventive acts that are involved in pregnancy and STD prevention.

The final stage of the preventive behavior sequences that has been studied involves the consistent practice of sex-related preventive acts such as limit setting, contraceptive use, or safer sexual behavior. In the present view, erotophobic (compared with erotophilic) adolescents ought to be inconsistent in their performance of these sex-related preventive acts, because they seem to be less likely to engage in each of the behaviors that lead up to them. To examine the proposed link between erotophobia–erotophilia and consistency of sex-related preventive behavior, Fisher *et al.* (1979) compared the erotophobia–erotophilia of college women who were consistent contraceptors, inconsistent contraceptors, or sexually inactive. Results showed that the consistent contraceptors were highly erotophilic; these women were apparently comfortable enough with sex both to participate in sexual behavior and to prepare for it, in terms of critical contraceptive behaviors, in advance. The inconsistent contraceptors were moderately erotophobic; they seem to have been just comfortable enough to have intercourse, but too uncomfortable to plan for it by engaging in contraceptive behaviors in advance. The sexually inactive women were highly erotophobic; they were apparently too uncomfortable about sex to have intercourse, but they were in no jeopardy of pregnancy and therefore did not need to engage in any prerequisite preventive behaviors. Related findings (Fisher, 1984) have also determined that erotophobic (versus erotophilic) men are less consistent users of condoms.

It is worth noting that erotophobia inhibits sex-related prevention not only among adolescents but among educators and health care providers as well. For example, Yarber and McCabe (1981, 1984) surveyed a large number of practicing high school health educators with respect to their erotophobia–erotophilia, professional qualifications, experience, and whether or not they taught about contraception. Findings demonstrated that erotophobia–erotophilia was the strongest predictor of whether practicing health educators taught their students useful information about contraception. Erotophobic high school health educators thought that it was less important to teach adolescents practical information about where to obtain and how to use contraception, and they were less likely actually to teach their students such crucial material. In a related vein, Fisher and his colleagues (Fisher, Grenier, *et al.*, 1988) have demonstrated that erotophobic medical students know less about sexuality, systematically avoid instruction in this area, and do not benefit from certain kinds of sex education even when they receive it, compared with erotophilic medical students.

Overall, these results illustrate that erotophobia may act as an internal psychological barrier to adolescents' practice of pregnancy- and STD-preventive behavior. Moreover, health care providers' erotophobia may serve as a psychological barrier to their learning or service provision in these same critical areas.

Cognitive Barriers to Preventive Behavior

According to the Sexual Behavior Sequence, adolescents' cognitions play an important role in determining their sexual behavior and sex-related preventive practices. It is necessary to consider both adolescents' level of cognitive maturity and the contents of their cognitions about sex as factors that may inhibit or facilitate preventive behavior.

With respect to adolescents' level of cognitive maturity, research has examined factors such as age and general level of planfulness as determinants of sex-related preventive behavior. Concerning age, Cvetkovich and Grote (1983) report an extremely strong correlation between teenage girls' age of first intercourse and their degree of contraceptive protection at this time. Among girls who had first intercourse between ages 13 and 15, only 17% were contraceptively protected; among girls who had first intercourse between ages 17 and 18, 55% were protected. This finding was interpreted as indicating that younger girls' self-concepts do not include an image of self as sexually active and consequently contraceptive precautions are not undertaken. For older teens, self-concept includes acceptance of self as sexually active and contraceptive precautions thus occur more readily. Concerning adolescent planfulness and ability to adopt a future time perspective, Oskamp and Mindick (1983), among others, have reported consistent links between teenagers' abilities to plan for future events and their level of contraceptive protection. Thus, factors associated with level of cognitive maturity (e.g., breadth of self-concept, ability to plan for a future time) seem to be linked with adolescents' likelihood of engaging in sex-related preventive activity.

With respect to the content of adolescents' cognitions about sexuality, a number of concerns may be raised. First, adolescents may have wildly *inaccurate information* about conception, contraception, limit setting, and STD (see A. R. Allgeier, 1983; E. R. Allgeier, 1983; Morrison, 1985; Oskamp & Mindick, 1983; Zelnik & Kantner, 1979). For example, Morrison (1985) reviewed eight surveys of adolescents' knowledge of the fertile period in the menstrual cycle and found that fewer than half of all teens were accurately informed about this subject. Adolescents who possess inaccurate or incomplete information regarding sex-related prevention cannot be expected to engage in such behavior effectively.

Second, adolescents may have *irrelevant information* in the sense that what they know does not constitute a precise script about how they may actually enact limit-setting, contraceptive, or STD-preventive behavior in their own social milieu (A. R. Allgeier, 1983; Fisher, 1983, 1985). Adolescents may be knowledgeable about the fallopian tubes, about each of the side effects of oral contraceptives, and about each of the trimesters of pregnancy, but such information is irrelevant in the immediate sense to adolescents' practice of preventive behavior. The fact that much sex education consists of information that is irrelevant to the performance of preventive behavior may account for sex education's less-than-perfect record in producing meaningful increases in such behavior (see, for example, A. R. Allgeier, 1983; Kirby, 1984; Marsiglio & Mott, 1986).

Third, adolescents may possess *antiprevention beliefs* and may act in accord with these beliefs (E. R. Allgeier, 1983; Fisher, 1983, 1984). For example, adolescents may believe that contraceptive protection is unnecessary because they are too young to get pregnant, or they may believe that contraception is difficult or illegal to obtain or has unacceptable side effects. In addition to such specific beliefs, adolescents may have systems of beliefs ranging from religious ideology to external locus of control that work against sex-related preventive behaviors. It seems likely that there is a range of specific beliefs (e.g., "My partner will leave me if I set limits," "Only gays get AIDS") and belief systems ("My religion forbids me to be premaritally sexually active; how can I plan for sin?") that may be antithetical to adolescent sexual limit-setting, contraceptive, and STD-preventive behavior.

Fourth, there is a considerable amount of *frightening and/or dangerous information* about sex to which teenagers are regularly exposed. Media coverage of herpes, AIDS, epidemic levels of teen pregnancy, rape, and sexual abuse is frightening and may reinforce adolescent erotophobia in a way that deters teens from planning dispassionately their sexual activity. Media coverage of the "fact" that AIDS is running rampant in the heterosexual community (Masters *et al.*, 1988) or of the "fact" that women cannot get AIDS (*Cosmopolitan*, 1988) is dangerous in the sense that it sows either unjustified fear or false reassurance in relation to sex-related prevention.

Fifth, teenagers appear to possess many socially validated *prosex beliefs.* Teenagers may accurately perceive that many or most of their friends are sexually active, they may accurately observe that teenage media models are sexually active and sexually nondiscriminating, and they may have appropriately absorbed social scripts for dating and heterosexual involvement. Prosex cognitions, unbalanced by proprevention beliefs, likely account for much of the variance in patterns of unprotected sexual activity.

Sixth, there are a number of *pronatalist beliefs* that encourage and support pregnancy and childbearing even among teenagers. E. R. Allgeier (1983) has pointed out that teens may believe that the arrival of a baby is always an exciting and blessed event, that pregnancy is the most important thing a woman can achieve, that pregnancy is a solution to all their problems, and like beliefs that would tend to make pregnancy acceptable or actually to encourage it. Social support for such beliefs may emanate from popular music ("Having My Baby"), from supportive media coverage of movie stars who become single mothers, and from the attention that teen mothers may receive from their peer social circles.

In summary, then, it appears that cognitive factors may contribute to the incidence of unprotected adolescent sexual activity. Adolescents may not have self-schema that include the self as sexually active and in need of prevention, they may have a limited future time perspective, and their cognitions with respect to pregnancy and STD prevention may be inaccurate, irrelevant, frightening, dangerous, prosex, pronatalist, or frankly antiprevention. The existence of such cognitive obstacles to prevention makes adolescents' low levels of sexual limit-setting, contraceptive, and STD-preventive behavior somewhat more understandable.

Fantasy Barriers to Prevention

According to the Sexual Behavior Sequence, externally and internally produced images may affect adolescent sexual behavior and sex-related preventive practices. It is clear that adolescents are exposed to an unending stream of media imagery that prescribes the normativeness and desirability of early, frequent, consequence-free sexual encounters. There is some imagery to suggest that preventive behavior will have a negative outcome (e.g., in the motion pictures *Summer of*

'42 and *Goodbye Columbus,* contraceptive acquisition is punished), and little imagery that endorses sexual limit-setting or contraceptive and STD-preventive behavior. The procontraception scenes in *Saturday Night Fever*—in which John Travolta rejected sexual relations with a contraceptively unprepared partner—are a rare example of the modeling of sex-related prevention. In the wake of the AIDS epidemic, proprevention imagery seems to be increasing, but it is still vastly less frequent than is prosex imagery that lacks any preventive theme.

Adolescents' internal sexual fantasies, like those of the media, much more often involve sexual activity than sex-related prevention. Perper and Weis (1987), for example, found that young women could imagine detailed seduction fantasies concerning how to achieve sexual intimacy with a desired partner. These imagined strategies included the use of environmental signals (e.g., dress, music, and other cues), verbal strategies (e.g., sexy talk), nonverbal strategies (e.g., eye contact), and the like. Although the young women could imagine sexual limit-setting strategies, not a single young woman's seduction fantasy involved contraception or STD prevention. It has also been found that adolescents may imagine that health care providers will react negatively to requests for contraception (Fisher *et al.,* 1979) and that young men imagine that presex discussion of prevention will result in botched sexual encounters (Gross & Bellew-Smith, 1983). Thus, it appears that both externally and internally generated imagery encourages adolescent sexual activity, even as such imagery does not include—or actively discourages—adolescent performance of sex-related preventive acts.

Structural and Psychological Barriers to Preventive Behavior: An Integration

Sexual limit setting, contraception, and STD prevention require that adolescents execute complex and inherently difficult sequences of behavior that are not explicitly taught and that are disapproved of by society. Moreover, many adolescents are too emotionally ambivalent about sex to plan for or to practice prevention, they often are mis- or uninformed about the need for, and nature of, prevention, and they often have prosex but antiprevention fantasies. It is proposed that the combination of structurally difficult preventive behavior, together with internal, psychological barriers to performing such behavior, accounts for a major portion of adolescents' failure to engage in sexual limit setting, contraceptive use, and STD prevention. In the following section, discussion will focus on interventions to deal with the structural difficulties of sex-related preventive behavior and the internal psychological barriers to practicing such behavior.

Solving the Problem: Reducing Adolescent Pregnancy and Exposure to Sexually Transmitted Disease

Conceptual Foundations for Change

The present analysis makes it clear that interventions to promote sex-related preventive behavior will have to achieve two goals. First, it is necessary to train adolescents to perform relatively complex sequences of acts that are involved in sexual limit-setting, contraceptive, and STD-preventive behavior. Second, it is necessary to relax existing emotional, cognitive, and fantasy barriers to performing these behaviors, and to replace them with feelings, thoughts, and fantasies that motivate sex-related prevention. The conceptual basis of such interventions is discussed next.

Changing Emotions

Research has suggested that adolescents' ambivalent feelings about sex may inhibit performance of each of the behaviors that is involved in sexual limit setting, contraceptive use, and STD prevention. It follows that interventions might seek to relax existing anxieties about each critical preventive behavior and to instate in their stead positive feelings about sex-related preventive acts. (Alternatively, it would theoretically be possible to intervene to increase erotophobia to the point where sexual behavior did not occur and prevention was unnecessary, but for many practical and value-related reasons this possibility will not be pursued.)

With respect to reducing negative emotional responses to preventive behavior, two strategies—based on Wolpe's (1958) systematic desensitization procedures—are suggested. First, adolescents may participate in a *fantasy walk-through* of the sexual limit-setting, contraceptive use, and STD-prevention sequences. The fantasy walk-through procedure involves exposing teens to imagery of persons much like themselves who perform the preventive behavior sequences successfully. This could involve, for example, reading stories, viewing a videotape, or listening to a discussion that depicts a young couple more or less happily executing each phase of the relevant preventive sequence. By observing social comparison others who enact sex-related preventive behaviors with no negative· and some positive consequences, the fantasy walk-through should reduce expectancies that prevention will be difficult and should reduce negative emotional responses to each of the preventive behaviors. Second, once the fantasy walk-through has been completed, an *in vivo walk-through* of at least some critical preventive behaviors may be accomplished to further reduce anxieties. For example, teenagers may role-play with fellow students, bringing up and negotiating sexual limits, contraception, and safer sex; they may take a field trip to the local birth control center or have a representative of such a center visit class; they may visit a pharmacy, observe which nonprescription contraceptives are on sale, and talk to the pharmacist. Actual walk-throughs of critical preventive behaviors should further reduce adolescents' anxieties about one day performing similar behaviors themselves.

While desensitization procedures should reduce teens' negative feelings about sex-related prevention, it will still be necessary to instate positive feelings about these behaviors. It is suggested that counterconditioning techniques—involving the association of preventive acts with rewarding outcomes—may produce positive feelings about preventive behavior and may motivate teens to perform such acts. For example, each of the steps in the sexual limit-setting, contraceptive use, and STD-prevention sequences could be taught with humor, could be depicted as communicating love and concern for a partner, could be associated with sexual arousal, and could be described as increasing chances for success in securing sexual partners, depending upon the circumstances. The association of preventive behaviors with positive emotions such as mirth, sexual arousal, and interpersonal warmth should encourage teens actually to practice these behaviors. Recently, for example, there has been experimental demonstration that the association of sexual arousal with condom use resulted in improvement of both men's and women's attitudes toward condoms (Tanner & Pollock, 1988).

Changing Cognitions

With respect to changing cognitions that are pertinent to sex-related preventive behavior, three basic tasks must be accomplished. First, it is necessary to deal with the cognitively immature teenager whose sexual behavior is more advanced than his or her cognitive abilities. Second, it is necessary to teach teens relevant, scriptlike, easy-to-translate-into-behavior information concerning performance of sex-related preventive behaviors. Third, it is necessary to identify and clarify adolescent beliefs and belief systems that would tend to work against performance of sex-related preventive behaviors.

Regarding cognitive immaturity, interventions must be concerned with teens whose self-concepts do not include the fact that the teens are sexually active, and must deal with teens whose ability to consider and plan for future events is deficient. For teens who are sexually active but who do not view themselves as such—possibly because of the emotional cost of such an admission—interventions may seek to hold sexual behavior in check until the self-concept matures, and they may also seek to hasten the development of this more mature self-concept. To help hold sexual behavior in check, interventions that stress sexual limit-setting strategies may appeal to teens who do not see themselves as "sexually active," and limit setting may protect these teens until a more inclusive self-concept is developed. To hasten the development of self-concepts that include being sexually active (for teens who are), interventions may provide normative statistical information stressing that there is wide variability in the development of sexual behavior, that sizable numbers of young teens are coitally active even as numerous teens are not, and that teens who are sexually active can either acknowledge the fact and practice prevention, repress the fact and ultimately get into difficulty, or change their behavior to noncoital patterns with which they are more comfortable. For teens who are unable to perceive and plan for future events such as the need for limit setting, contraception, or STD prevention, it is necessary to stress the link between present behavior and important future outcomes. One very engaging method for linking present decisions and future outcomes is a computer game simulation of adolescent life recently authored by Cairns (1987). In this simulation, teens must make decisions about school, work, social life, sex, and the like, and then they must progress through the game and live with the consequences of their choices for all areas of their life. Such simulations may help extend teens' future time orientation to the point where they may cope more adaptively with sex-related prevention choices and weigh the future outcomes of these choices.

Concerning the provision of information, it is absolutely clear that teenagers require relevant, scriptlike information that informs them how they may execute each step of the preventive behavior sequences in their own social milieus. Such information may be provided visually (in forms such as videos), it may be written (in forms such as pamphlets), or it may be provided in both forms such that a well-done video serves initially to gain attention and inform, and the written material serves as a backup that can be stored and consulted when necessary. Whatever the delivery channel, the information that teens receive must inform them about how to engage in each critical step of the sexual limit-setting, contraceptive use, and STD-prevention sequences in their own social environment. The success of such a behavioral-scripting, skills-training approach has been demonstrated empirically (Kelly *et al.*, 1988; Schinke, 1984; Schinke, Blythe, & Gilchrist, 1981; see also discussion to follow of the successful application of these principles).

Concerning beliefs and belief systems that work against sex-related prevention, interventions must identify such beliefs, point out to teens the nature of these beliefs and their consequences, and attempt to persuade teens that either antiprevention beliefs or sexual behavior must change. It is recommended that research be conducted in groups that are targeted for intervention to determine the nature and incidence of antiprevention beliefs (see Ajzen & Fishbein, 1980, for a discussion of belief elicitation and attitude change research). As mentioned earlier, such beliefs vary widely and idiosyncratically, and include inaccurate information, frightening information, and frankly antiprevention information. Once clusters of such beliefs common to a group have been identified, they may become the target for values-clarification discussion (Fisher, 1983), which stresses the fact that a combination of antiprevention beliefs and continuing sexual behavior may have disastrous outcomes for teens, and that the beliefs and/or the behavior should probably change. For example, teens may reflect on the belief that contraception ruins the spontaneity of sex by considering how postcoital anxiety, abortion, pregnancy, or STD may ruin the spontaneity of life.

There is one caveat regarding belief change that must be mentioned. Occasionally, and tragically, adolescents' beliefs about the desirability of teenage childbearing represent accurate perceptions of a means for exiting a difficult environment. If a teenager is correct in believing that pregnancy would be desirable in his or her social situation, it is more necessary and more honest to try to change the social situation than it is to try to change only the propregnancy beliefs. For example, an adolescent may correctly believe that most of her friends will leave high school by age 16, will never be employed, and will then as a comparative "best bet" become single, welfare-dependent mothers. In such a case—and there are many—the needed interventions involve job training, housing renewal, and the like, not only sex education *per se*. One is even tempted to formulate a response competition model of adolescent pregnancy; ongoing responses (education, job plans) may increase the likelihood of preventive behavior that facilitates such responses.

Changing Imagery

At present, adolescents' have access to external images and internal fantasies that promote sex but do not promote prevention. Interventions must replace imagery of sex without prevention with imagery of sex with appropriate preventive behavior and with incentives for such behavior. For example, video media may be used to present models who are similar to viewers and who successfully perform each of the crucial preventive behaviors and achieve desired outcomes. Video presentations can also model prevention-free sexual behavior and its negative consequences, as well as efforts to sidetrack suggested preventive behaviors and successful negotiation strategies for adhering to prevention. Moreover, media literacy teaching to sensitize teens to the indiscriminate and consequence-free sexual messages they are seeing could blunt antiprevention effects of media as well. In this fashion, adolescents may come to imagine detailed guidelines for performing sex-related preventive acts, they may come to imagine the benefits of doing so, to see themselves as efficacious in sex-related prevention, and to imagine the costs of prevention-free sexual behavior.

Some Applied Concerns

Before interventions along the lines that have been discussed can be designed, a number of applied concerns must be dealt with. First, it is necessary to decide upon a setting for delivery of the intervention. Second, it is crucial to "yoke" interventions to existing community resources for supporting preventive behavior. Third, it is necessary to anticipate and prepare for political resistance to the introduction of sex-related interventions.

A Setting for Intervention

It is proposed that sex-related prevention interventions may most efficiently be delivered in school-based sex education settings, for a number of reasons.

First, public school is as nearly a universal experience as exists in our society. While supplementary means may be necessary to reach some teens, the vast majority are reachable in the school setting. Second, public school provides an opportunity for the early introduction and timely and continuous reinforcement of age-appropriate sex education material as it becomes relevant at succeeding developmental stages. Although the public schools are beleaguered, sex-related preventive education is viewed as so necessary and the schools are so potentially good a vehicle as to justify further claims on a system with already strained resources. Other settings for intervention, ranging from infusing soap operas and teen music and magazines with preventive messages, to use of the existing public health network to diffuse relevant information, may supplement basic reliance on continuous public school sex education (see also Fisher & Barak, 1989, for a discussion of antipornography education in school settings).

Yoking Interventions and Community Resources

It is critical to link interventions for sex-related prevention with existing community resources for the support of such behavior. Thus, for example, if a pro-contraception intervention were to take place, it would be essential to inform the targets of the intervention about easily accessible, user-friendly community resources for contraceptive acquisition. By the same token, it would be crucial to equip the targets of an STD prevention intervention with the information about where locally they can purchase condoms late at night, with the phone number of a hotline where they can get current STD information, the address and hours of an STD clinic, and like information. Research indicates that when sex-related prevention interventions are effectively backed up by community resources, the interventions may be quite successful (see, for example, the Zabin, Hirsch, Smith, Streett, & Hardy, 1986, report of the success of school-based sex education, yoked to accessible clinics, in reducing rates of urban teenage pregnancy). In contrast, even the most relevant sex-education information would be of little use, or would actually be frustrating, if there were no community resources available for acting on the preventive information that is provided. If supportive community resources are unavailable, improvements must be made in these resources in addition to improving sex education *per se*.

The Politics of Sex Education Intervention

It is clear that sex education interventions are as much matters of politics as they are matters of pedagogy or resources (Fisher, 1983). There are several potential political flashpoints that might be considered when introducing sex education interventions.

One very basic and politically sensitive issue involves the nature of the information to be conveyed in a sex education intervention. It is a truism that relevant and usable sex education may arouse great resistance, while irrelevant and unusable sex education arouses little resistance. Information that is relevant and usable by teens may be viewed by authority figures as helping teens to sin with impunity. In contrast, irrelevant and unusable information may be viewed by authorities as at least not facilitating disapproved behavior. A sterling example of such reactions occurred when the Canadian Public Health Association produced an exemplary series of AIDS-prevention commercials. The commercials that encouraged strict abstinence were immediately broadcast, while the commericals that suggested condom use have been the object of a continuing television boycott. It is critical to establish to authorities that sex education guides ongoing sexual behavior along more prudent lines, but does *not* encourage increased sexual activity (see, for example, Fisher, 1983; Zabin *et al.*, 1986).

A second political flashpoint involves institutional resistance to sex education. Often, institutional officials fear that changing the *status quo* would be politically costly. In such cases, it is necessary to emphasize that the *status quo* is currently quite unsafe for teens and that institutional inaction involves a strong public vote in favor of teen pregnancy, abortion, STD, infertility, and AIDS deaths.

A third political consideration involves the approach that interveners may make to the surrounding community. It is accepted wisdom among sex educators that it is necessary to seek broad community support from PTAs, newspapers, religious leaders, and the like, before introducing a sex education curriculum. It might be argued, however, that such activities are often viewed as permission-begging efforts by sex education forces that are not even persuaded of their own legitimacy. It might prove useful to approach the broader community in a way that will be perceived as informing the community that a legitimate and needed initiative will take place, rather than appearing to seek the community's permission for education that is so unimportant as to be optional.

Summary

It has been proposed that interventions to promote prevention of pregnancy and STD must change the way teens feel, think, and fantasize about preventive behavior. Moreover, it is necessary to deliver and reinforce continuously age-appropriate interventions, to yoke interventions to existing community resources, and to overcome potential political resistance to relevant interventions. In the next section of this chapter, an example of a pregnancy-prevention intervention that was designed along these conceptual lines will be described.

A Model Intervention: Preventing Pregnancy on a University Campus

The University of Western Ontario is a 20,000-student, publicly supported institution, located in London, Canada. During the late 1970s and early 1980s, the student pregnancy rate at the university was at a steady, relatively high level, and the Student Health Service decided to design and implement a pregnancy-prevention program that is based on the concepts discussed in this chapter. The pregnancy-prevention program is aimed at undergraduates—particularly younger undergraduates—and consists of three elements that were phased in during 1983 and 1984 and that have remained in place since that time. The three elements of the program include dormitory-based lectures, a pregnancy-prevention videotape, and a pregnancy-prevention booklet.

Pregnancy-Prevention Program Elements

Dormitory-Based Lectures. Since 1983, Student Health Service personnel have given pregnancy-prevention lectures to approximately one-third of all dormitory residents or about 1,000 students annually. The lectures are nonjudgmental, they legitimize both sexual limit setting and contraceptively protected sexual activity, they establish the approachability of campus health services, and they lay out behaviorally relevant information concerning how students may anticipate the need for contraception, how and where they may acquire it on campus, and how to use the various methods of contraception. The lectures also stimulate student discussion and questions, both in the lecture setting itself and in student-to-student and student-to-peer advisor discussions afterward. Because some 70% of dormitory residents are freshman, the dormitory-based lectures are an effective technique for reaching younger students who by virtue of youth, inexperience, and unpredictable sexual relationships may be highly vulnerable to unplanned pregnancy.

The Pregnancy-Prevention Videotape. A pregnancy prevention videotape— *Can We Talk?*—was produced in the summer of 1984 and is shown to well over 1500 students annually during the dormitory lectures described above, during annual health-promotion campaigns on campus, and as part of certain university courses. The videotape uses student actors to model a precise behavioral script concerning how to anticipate the need for contraception, how to discuss this with a partner, and where on campus and in the surrounding community one may acquire contraception in a nonjudgmental setting, and it stresses the need for consistent contraceptive use. The videotape opens with a young student couple agonizing over a possible pregnancy; they acknowledge in discussion their affection for each other, their desire to remain sexually active, and their need for contraception. After a negative pregnancy test, the couple seek counseling at the university's Student Health Service, where one of the staff physicians nonjudgmentally and humorously talks with the couple about contraception. The couple then visit a local drugstore, purchase needed contraceptives, and use them to prevent another pregnancy scare. The videotape also presents and debunks anticontraception beliefs on the part of some students. Throughout the film, both affection and humor are associated with the performance of the contraceptive behavior sequence.

The Pregnancy-Prevention Booklet. A pregnancy-prevention booklet—*Can We Talk? A Sexual Communication Guide for Students by Students*—was produced in the summer of 1984 (and has been updated since) and is distributed to each incoming first-year student and distributed at dormitory lectures, the campus health fair, and like activities, reaching some 5500 students annually. *Can We Talk?* was designed to function either independently of the videotape or as a print backup to it that students can refer to when needed. *Can We Talk?* explicitly lays out each phase of the contraceptive behavior sequence, and explains how to learn about contraception, how to discuss it with a partner, how to acquire it on campus or in the surrounding community, and how to use each method effectively. Sexual limit setting and engaging in orgasm-producing acts other than intercourse are also presented as legitimate and viable alternatives, and AIDS prevention is discussed as well. The pregnancy-prevention booklet uses humor and playfulness throughout, including user-friendly terminology and humorous drawings.

Resources Required for Intervention. The interventions described did not require enormous investments of time or money. The Student Health Service, as part of its service mandate, underwrites the dormitory lecture program. The pregnancy-prevention videotape and booklet were funded primarily by a Canadian government student summer employment grant of approximately $18,000. This funding was used to hire undergraduates who actually wrote the dialogue, acted in the video, and created the booklet with donated faculty advice. The result was material generated from the student point of view, which the target audience found accessible, legitimate, and relevant to their own needs.

Changing Students' Feelings, Thoughts, and Fantasies about Contraception

Changing Feelings. The interventions attempted to relax students' anxieties about each stage of the contraceptive behavior sequence and to replace such anxieties with more positive feelings about sex-related preventive behavior. For example, the dormitory lectures—which involve Student Health Service personnel who are accepting, nonjudgmental, and comfortable with sexuality—are intended to reduce students' anxieties about using existing services. The pregnancy-prevention video and booklet explicitly provide a fantasy walk through the entire contraceptive behavior sequence in which a student couple not only survive the process but actually respond to it with humor, affection, sexual arousal, and reassurance.

Changing Information. The lecture, video, and booklet each lay out a precise behavioral script for how students may execute the entire contraceptive behavior sequence in their own social environment. Information on how to set sexual limits and on AIDS prevention is also provided in these three delivery channels. This information is supplemented by information that debunks specific anticontraception beliefs, such as beliefs that campus clinic personnel are judgmental and that contraception is strictly a woman's problem. Students who participate in the intervention are thus exposed to behaviorally relevant preventive information and to information intended to immunize against common anticontraception beliefs.

Changing Fantasies. The interventions discussed herein were designed to create imagery guides for sex-related preventive behavior. For example, the video depicts a student couple performing each of the stages of the contraceptive behavior sequence in local settings that are familiar to students and in which they would have to enact preventive behaviors. The pregnancy-prevention booklet provides written descriptions of each stage of the contraceptive behavior sequence as well. These interventions aim to provide pregnancy-prevention imagery that may be internalized by students so that they can imagine just what they would need to do to enact the preventive behavior sequences.

Yoking the Intervention to Accessible Resources. Beyond altering students' feelings, thoughts, and fantasies in a procontraception direction, it is also necessary to make students aware of existing community resources to support contraceptive use and to create such resources where they do not yet exist. The interventions described here alerted students to the existence of nearby resources by modeling a visit to the Student Health Service for contraceptive counseling and prescription, and by modeling contraceptive purchasing at the drugstore nearest to campus. Moreover, it was judged that existing resources were inadequate in at least one respect. There was no convenient place on campus for students to buy condoms, which would be necessary if prescription contraception were not being used or if unexpected sexual opportunities arose. Hence, it was decided to install condom machines in the men's and women's washrooms opposite the student bar in the student center and in washrooms in student dormitories, and to model in the video the use of these machines. These machines now sell in the region of 1300 condoms annually in the men's washrooms and between 250 and 650 annually in the women's washrooms, and they are believed to be crucial elements in the pregnancy-prevention program.

The Proof Is in the Pregnancy Tests: Results of the Pregnancy-Prevention Program

In order to gain at least a crude idea about whether the pregnancy-prevention program has been successful, data on positive pregnancy tests at the university's Student Health Service have been collected over the years before and after introduction of the intervention. As can be seen in Table 1, there was a relatively steady rate of about 10 pregnancies per thousand female students from 1978–1979 through 1982–1983. In 1983–1984, the year the dormitory lectures were phased in, the student pregnancy rate dropped precipitously by 27.7% to only 7.3 pregnancies per thousand female students. In 1984–1985, when the video and booklet

Table 1. Unwanted Pregnancy Rates at the University of Western Ontario and Nationally before and after Pregnancy-Prevention Intervention

Academic year	Rate of positive pregnancy tests/ thousand women University of Western Ontario[a]	Percent change from preceding year	Abortion rate/thousand all Canadian women age 20–24[b]	Percent change from preceding year
1978–1979	9.4	—	17.3	—
1979–1980	10.2	+8.5%	18.1	+4.6%
1980–1981	10.7	+4.9%	18.2	+.6%
1981–1982	9.9	−7.5%	18.0	−1.1%
1982–1983	10.1	+2.0%	18.5	+2.8%
1983–1984[c]	7.3	−27.7%	17.4	−5.9%
1984–1985[d]	6.5	−11.0%	17.6	+1.2%
1985–1986	6.5	0.0%	17.4	−1.2%
1986–1987	6.6	+1.5%	—	—
1987–1988	6.5	−1.5%	—	—

[a] Data supplied by Student Health Services, University of Western Ontario.
[b] Data from Statistics Canada Yearbooks; data are available only through 1985–1986.
[c] Dormitory pregnancy prevention lecture intervention phased in.
[d] Video and booklet pregnancy prevention interventions phased in.

components were phased in as well, there was a further 11.0% drop in the pregnancy rate to 6.5 per thousand and this drop has been sustained through 1985–1986, 1986–1987, and 1987–1988.

To compare changes in pregnancy rates at the university with any possibly similar changes in the general population, where no systematic interventions occurred, abortion rate data from Canadian young women of similar ages are also presented in Table 1. Abortion rate data were chosen as a crude index of the incidence of unwanted pregnancy and were presumed to be comparable to the university positive pregnancy test data since nearly every positive pregnancy test at the university resulted in the termination of the pregnancy. As can be seen in Table 1, while there was a small decline in the national abortion rate in 1983–1984, there has been no large and sustained decline in the abortion rate in general among Canadian young women during the time of the intervention. Moreover, the interventions advertised the fact that the Student Health Service dealt nonjudgmentally with student pregnancy as well as with pregnancy prevention. This could actually have resulted in a greater proportion of pregnant women self-referring to the Student Health Service after the intervention, which could minimize the true pregnancy-prevention effects of the intervention and make the fairly dramatic effects depicted in Table 1 conservative estimates. At the same time, interpretation of effects of any uncontrolled intervention must be made cautiously, and alternate explanations of these changes are possible. What is needed it additional controlled and fine-grain research on such interventions, and this chapter will conclude with discussion of such needed future work.

An Agenda for Future Research and Intervention

Adolescents today remain at relatively great risk of unplanned pregnancy and STD infection. Initial conceptual and research attempts to understand these problems and interventions to reduce them have been promising, but it is clear that future research and interventions must still be pursued. The following are some suggestions for an agenda for future research and interventions in the area of sex-related preventive behavior.

First, it is suggested that future research adopt a micro-to-macro-level strategy for tracking effects of interventions. It would be useful to determine if interventions are affecting microlevel individual processes (e.g., feelings, thoughts, and images regarding prevention), and it would be useful to know whether such changes may in turn produce macrolevel behavioral outcomes (e.g., changed overt preventive behaviors). Research that maps out the effects of interventions on internal psychological processes and on external sex-related preventive behavior is very much needed.

Second, it is suggested that future micro- to macrolevel research be conducted separately with respect to the three different classes of sex-related preventive behavior. A more complete understanding of sex-related prevention will require knowledge about how interventions to promote sexual limit setting, contraception, and STD prevention affect related emotions, cognitions, imagery, and overt behavior. Once the separate processes are better understood, it should be possible to specify where common interventions are sufficient and where more specific interventions are required to increase particular preventive behaviors.

Third, large-scale and controlled field evaluations are needed of the effects of limit-setting, contraception, and STD-prevention interventions on affect, cognition, fantasy, and overt behavior. There are a number of promising outcome studies in the literature (e.g., Schinke, 1984; Zabin *et al.*, 1986), but controlled, true field experiments to describe the effects of interventions on the mediating variables (affect, cognition, and imagery) and outcomes (sexual limit setting, contraception, and safer sex practices) of interest here are still very much needed to verify to effectiveness of the proposed interventions in representative field settings. Teenage pregnancy and STD loom as important present and future social problems, and we can ill afford to ignore this research agenda.

ACKNOWLEDGMENTS. Preparation of this chapter was supporter by a grant (410-87-1333) from the Social Sciences and Humanities Research Council of Canada to the author. The author would like to thank Terry Pook for comments on an earlier draft of this chapter and Ardath Hill for supplying pregnancy test data.

References

Ajzen, I., & Fishbein, M. (1980). *Understanding attitudes and predicting social behavior.* Englewood Cliffs, NJ: Prentice-Hall.

Alan Guttmacher Institute. (1981). *Teenage pregnancy: The problem that hasn't gone away*. New York: Author.

Allgeier, E. R. (1983). Ideological barriers to contraception. In D. Byrne & W. A. Fisher (Eds.), *Adolescents, sex, and contraception* (pp. 171–205). Hillsdale, NJ: Erlbaum.

Allgeier, E. R. (1983). Barriers to contraception. In D. Byrne & W. A. Fisher (Eds.), *Adolescents, sex, and contraception* (pp. 171–205). Hillsdale, NJ: Erlbaum.

Baldwin, J. D., & Baldwin, J. I. (1988). Factors affecting AIDS-related sexual risk taking among college students. *Journal of Sex Research, 25*, 181–196.

Bauman, L. T., & Siegel, K. (1987). Misperception among gay men of the risk for AIDS associated with their sexual behavior. *Journal of Applied Social Psychology, 17*, 329–350.

Bell, T. A., & Holmes, K. K. (1984). Age-specific risks of syphilis, gonorrhea, and hospitalized pelvic inflamatory disease in sexually experienced U.S. women. *Sexually Transmitted Disease, 11*, 291–295.

Bolton, F. J., Jr. (1980). *The pregnant adolescent. Problems of premature parenthood*. Beverly Hills: Sage.

Burke, D. S., Brundage, J. F., Herbold, J. R., Berner, W., Gardner, L. I., Gunzenhauser, J. D., Voskovich, J., & Redfield, R. R. (1987). Human immunodeficiency virus infections among civilian applicants for United States military service, October 1985 to March 1986. *New England Journal of Medicine, 317*, 131–136.

Burt, M. R. (1986). Estimating the public costs of teenage childbearing. *Family Planning Perspectives, 18*, 221–226.

Byrne, D. (1977). Social psychology and the study of sexual behavior. *Personality and Social Psychology Bulletin, 1*, 3–30.

Byrne, D. (1983). Sex without contraception. In D. Byrne & W. A. Fisher (Eds.), *Adolescents, sex, and contraception* (pp. 3–31). Hillsdale, NJ: Erlbaum.

Byrne, D., & Fisher, W. A. (Eds.). (1983). *Adolescents, sex, and contraception*. Hillsdale, NJ: Erlbaum.

Cairns, K. (1987, September). *A computer assisted learning program for adolescent sex education*. Paper presented at the meeting of the Canadian Sex Research Forum, London, Ontario.

Coles, R., & Stokes, F. (1985). *Sex and the American teenager*. New York: Harper & Row.

Cosmopolitan (1988). A doctor tells why most women are safe from AIDS, January.

Cvetkovich, G., & Grote, B. (1983). Adolescent development and teenage fertility. In D. Byrne & W. A. Fisher (Eds.), *Adolescents, sex, and contraception* (pp. 108–123). Hillsdale, NJ: Erlbaum.

Faro, S. (1983). Sexually transmitted diseases. In R. W. Hale & J. A. Krieger (Eds.), *Gynecology. A concise textbook* (pp. 198–214). New York: Medical Examination Publishing Company.

Federal Centre for AIDS. (1989. June 5). *Surveillance update. AIDS in Canada*. Ottawa, Ontario: Author.

Fischl, M. A., Dickinson, G. M., Scott, G. B., Klimas, N., Fletcher, M. A., & Parks, W. (1987). Evaluation of heterosexual partners, children, and household contacts of adults with AIDS. *Journal of the American Medical Association, 257*, 640–644.

Fisher, J. D., & Misovich, S. J. (1987). *Technical report on undergraduate AIDS-preventive behavior, AIDS knowledge, and fear of AIDS*. Storrs, CT: University of Connecticut, Department of Psychology.

Fisher, W. A. (1978). *Affective, attitudinal, and normative determinants of contraceptive behavior among university men*. Unpublished doctoral dissertation, Purdue University.

Fisher, W. A. (1983). Adolescent contraception: Summary and recommendations. In D. Byrne & W. A. Fisher (Eds.), *Adolescents, sex, and contraception* (pp. 273–300). Hillsdale, NJ: Erlbaum.

Fisher, W. A. (1984). Predicting contraceptive behavior among university men: The roles of emotions and behavioral intentions. *Journal of Applied Social Psychology, 14*, 104–123.

Fisher, W. A. (1985). The psychology of adolescent contraceptive neglect: Theory, research, and proposed interventions. *Sex Education and Information Council of Canada Journal, 19*, 1–10.

Fisher, W. A. (1986). A psychological approach to human sexuality: The sexual behavior sequence.

In D. Byrne & K. Kelley (Eds.), *Alternative approaches to the study of sexual behavior* (pp. 131–171). Hillsdale, NJ: Erlbaum.

Fisher, W. A., & Barak, A. (1989). Sex education as a corrective: Immunizing against possible effects of pornography. In D. Zillmann & J. Bryant (Eds.), *Pornography: Research advances and policy considerations* (pp. 289–320). Hillsdale, NJ: Erlbaum.

Fisher, W. A., Byrne, D., Edmunds, M., Miller, C. T., Kelley, K., & White, L. A. (1979). Psychological and situation specific correlates of contraceptive behavior among university women. *Journal of Sex Research, 15,* 38–55.

Fisher, W. A., Byrne, D., & White, L. A. (1983). Emotional barriers to contraception. In D. Byrne & W. A. Fisher (Eds.), *Adolescents, sex, and contraception* (pp. 207–239). Hillsdale, NJ: Erlbaum.

Fisher, W. A., Byrne, D., White, L. A., & Kelley, K. (1988). Erotophobia–erotophilia as a dimension of personality. *Journal of Sex Research, 25,* 123–151.

Fisher, W. A., Fisher, J. D., & Byrne, D. (1977). Consumer reactions to contraception purchasing. *Personality and Social Psychology Bulletin, 3,* 293–296.

Fisher, W. A., Grenier, G., Watters, W. W., Lamont, J., Cohen, M., & Askwith, J. (1988). Students' attitudes towards sex, sexual knowledge, and willingness to treat sexual concerns. *Journal of Medical Education, 63,* 379–385.

Fisher, W. A., Miller, C. T., Byrne, D., & White, L. A. (1981). Talking dirty: Responses to communicating a sexual message as a function of situational and personality factors. *Basic and Applied Social Psychology, 1,* 115–126.

Foreit, K. G., & Foreit, J. R. (1978). Correlates of contraceptive behavior among unmarried U.S. college students. *Studies in Family Planning, 9,* 169–174.

Furstenberg, F. F., Jr., Brooks-Gunn, J., & Morgan, S. P. (1987). Adolescent mothers and their children in later life. *Family Planning Perspectives, 19,* 142–151.

Goldfarb, L., Gerrard, M., Gibbons, F. X., & Plante, T. (1988). Attitudes toward sex, arousal, and retention of contraceptive information. *Journal of Personality and Social Psychology, 65,* 634–641.

Gross, A. E., & Bellew-Smith, M. (1983). A social psychological approach to reducing pregnancy risk in adolescence. In D. Byrne & W. A. Fisher (Eds.), *Adolescents, sex, and contraception* (pp. 263–272). Hillsdale, NJ: Erlbaum.

Guinan, M. E., & Hardy, A. (1987). Epidemiology of AIDS in women in the United States 1981 through 1986. *Journal of the American Medical Association, 257,* 2039–2042.

Hofferth, S. L., Kahn, J. R., & Baldwin, W. (1987). Premarital sexual activity among U.S. teenage women over the past three decades. *Family Planning Perspectives, 19,* 46–53.

Hyde, J. S. (1986). *Understanding human sexuality* (3rd ed.). New York: McGraw-Hill.

Jones, E. G., Forrest, J. D., Goldman, N., Henshaw, S. K., Lincoln, R., Rosoff, J. I., Westoff, C. F., & Wulf, D. (1985). Teenage pregnancy in developed countries: Determinants and policy implications. *Family Planning Perspectives, 17,* 53–62.

Joseph, J. G., Montgomery, S. B., Emmons, C., Kirscht, J. P., Kessler, R. C., Ostrow, D. G., Wortman, C. B., O'Brien, K., Eller, M., & Eshleman, S. (1987). Perceived risk of AIDS: Assessing the behavioral and psychosocial consequences in a cohort of gay men. *Journal of Applied Social Psychology, 17,* 231–250.

Kegeles, S. M., Adler, N. E., & Irwin, C. E. (1988). Sexually active adolescents and condoms: Changes over one year in knowledge, attitude, and use. *American Journal of Public Health, 78,* 460–461.

Kelly, J. A., St. Lawrence, J. S., Brasfield, T. L., & Hood, H. V. (1988, July). *Group intervention to reduce AIDS risk behaviors in gay men: Applications of behavioral principles.* Paper presented at the Vermont Conference on the Primary Prevention of Psychopathology, Burlington, VT.

Kirby, D. (1984). *Sexuality education: An evaluation of programs and their effects.* Santa Cruz, CA: Network Publications.

Kroger, F., & Wiesner, P. J. (1981). STD education: Challenge for the 80s. *Journal of School Health,*
    April, 242–246.
Marsiglio, W., & Mott, F. L. (1986). The impact of sex education on sexual activity, contraceptive
    use and premarital pregnancy among American teenagers. *Family Planning Perspectives, 18,*
    151–162.
Martin, J. L. (1987). The impact of AIDS on gay male sexual behavior patterns in New York City.
    American Journal of Public Health, 77, 578–581.
Masters, W. H., Johnson, V. E., & Kolodny, R. C. (1985). *Human sexuality* (2nd ed.). Boston:
    Little, Brown.
Masters, W. H., Johnson, V. E., & Kolodny, R. C. (1988). *Crisis. Heterosexual behaviour in the*
    age of AIDS. New York: Group Press.
McKusick, L., Horstman, W., & Coates, T. J. (1985). AIDS and sexual behavior reported by gay
    men in San Francisco. *American Journal of Public Health, 75,* 493–496.
Moore, K. A., & Wertheimer, R. F. (1984). Teenage childbearing and welfare: Preventive and ame-
    liorative strategies. *Family Planning Perspectives, 16,* 285–289.
Morrison, D. M. (1985). Adolescent contraceptive behavior: A review. *Psychological Bulletin, 98,*
    535–568.
Mott, F. L., & Marsiglio, W. (1985). Early childbearing and completion of high school. *Family*
    Planning Perspectives, 17, 234–237.
Nuckolls, K. B., Cassel, J., & Kaplan, B. H. (1972). Psychosocial assets, life crisis, and the prog-
    nosis of pregnancy. *American Journal of Epidimiology, 95,* 431–441.
Oskamp, S., & Mindick, B. (1983). Personality and attitudinal barriers to contraception. In D. Byrne
    & W. A. Fisher (Eds.), *Adolescents, sex, and contraception* (pp. 76–107). Hillsdale, NJ: Erl-
    baum.
Padian, N. S. (1987). Heterosexual transmission of acquired immunodeficiency syndrome: Interna-
    tional perspectives and national projections. *Reviews of Infectious Diseases, 9,* 947–960.
Perper, T., & Weis, D. L. (1987). Proceptive and rejective strategies of U.S. and Canadian college
    women. *Journal of Sex Research, 23,* 455–480.
Rees, M. (1987). The sombre view of AIDS. *Nature, 326,* 343–345.
Schinke, S. P. (1984). Preventing teenage pregnancy. In M. Hersen, R. M. Eisler, & P. M. Miller
    (Eds.), *Progress in behavior modification* (Vol. 16) (pp. 31–64). Orlando, FL: Academic Press.
Schinke, S. P., Blythe, B. J., & Gilchrist, L. D. (1981). Cognitive-behavioral prevention of adoles-
    cent pregnancy. *Journal of Counseling Psychology, 28,* 451–454.
Shafer, M., Beck, S., Blain, B., Dole, P., Irwin, C., Sweet, R., & Schachter, J. (1984). Chlamydia
    trachomatis: Important relationships to race, contraception, lower genital tract infection, and Pa-
    panicolau smear. *Journal of Pediatrics, 104,* 141–146.
Smiley, M. L., White, G. C., Becherer, B., Macik, G. Matthews, T. J., Weinhold, K. J., McMillan,
    C., & Bolognesi, D. (1988). Transmission of human immunodeficiency virus to sexual partners
    of hemophiliacs. *American Journal of Hematology, 28,* 23–32.
Tanner, W. M., & Pollack, R. H. (1988). The effect of condom use and erotic instructions on attitudes
    towards condoms. *Journal of Sex Research, 25,* 537–541.
Tempelis, C. D., Shell, G., Hoffman, M., Benjamin, B. A., Chandler, A. & Francis, D. P. (1987).
    Human immunodeficiency virus infection in women in the San Francisco Bay area. *Journal of the*
    American Medical Association, 258, 474–475.
Time. (1987), The big chill. How heterosexuals are coping with AIDS, February 16, cover, pp. 56–
    59.
U.S. News and World Report. (1987). AIDS: At the dawn of fear, January 12, pp. 60–70.
Westoff, C. F. Calot, G., & Foster, A. D. (1983). Teenage fertility in developed nations. *Family*
    Planning Perspectives, 15, 105–109.
Wolpe, J. (1958). *Psychotherapy by reciprocal inhibition.* Stanford, CA: Stanford University Press.
Yarber, W. L., & McCabe, G. P. (1981). Teacher characteristics and the inclusion of sex education
    topics in grades 6–8 and 9–11. *Journal of School Health, 51,* 288–291.

Yarber, W. L., & McCabe, G. P. (1984). Importance of sex education topics: Correlates with teacher characteristics and inclusion of topics of instruction. *Health Education, 15,* 36–41.

Zabin, L. S., Hirsch, M. B., Smith, E. A., Streett, R., & Hardy, J. B. (1986). Evaluation of a pregnancy prevention program for urban teenagers. *Family Planning Perspectives, 18,* 119–126.

Zabin, L. S., Kantner, J. F., & Zelnik, M. (1979). The risk of adolescent pregnancy in the first months of intercourse. *Family Planning Perspectives, 13,* 215–222.

Zelnik, M., & Kantner, J. F. (1977). Sexual and contraceptive experience of young unmarried women in the United States, 1976 and 1971. *Family Planning Perspectives, 9,* 55–71.

Zelnik, M., & Kantner, J. F. (1979). Reasons for nonuse of contraception by sexually active women aged 15–19. *Family Planning Perspectives, 11,* 289–296.

Zelnik, M., & Kantner, J. F. (1980). Sexual activity, contraceptive use and pregnancy among metro-politan-area teenagers: 1971–1979. *Family Planning Perspectives, 12,* 230–232.

Zuckerman, B. S., Walker, D. K., Frank, D. A., Chase, C., & Hamburg, B. (1984). Adolescent pregnancy: Biobehavioral determinants of outcome. *Journal of Pediatrics, 105,* 857–863.

5

Implications of Behavioral Decision Theory and Social Marketing for Designing Social Action Programs

James Jaccard, Robert Turrisi, and Choi K. Wan

In recent years, there has been increased interest in applied research by social psychologists. Attempts have been made to identify significant social problems and then to address these problems by means of social interventions or social action programs. Psychological research and methodology has been used to guide the formulation of such programs. This chapter describes issues that we have confronted in the context of our own research programs on the prevention of unintended pregnancies and the prevention of drunk driving. Although we discuss many of these issues in general terms, we do not believe that they are applicable to all social action programs. Nor are they exhaustive of all the issues that must be addressed. Rather, they represent a cross section of some of the perspectives we have adopted when designing interventions to address two specific problems of social significance.

The general framework we use for designing social action programs consists of six basic activities: (1) specification of the social problem and delineation of program goals, (2) identification of the target population, (3) behavioral analysis, (4) isolation of behavioral determinants, (5) changing behavioral determinants, and (6) evaluation of the program. We will discuss each of these activities, in turn.

Specification of the Social Problem and Delineation of Program Goals

The planning and implementation of social action programs begins with the specification of program objectives. Such objectives can be viewed as intended

James Jaccard, Robert Turrisi, and Choi K. Wan • Department of Psychology, State University of New York at Albany, Albany, New York 12222.

consequences of the program. By definition, value judgments are placed on these consequences by program initiators—i.e., the consequences are viewed as desirable. Social action programs are frequently a response to a social problem. We define a problem as the failure to attain (or to make adequate progress toward) a goal, or the occurrence of an aversive end state. The more important the goal, and the further one is from attaining it, the more severe the problem. Similarly, the more important it is to avoid the negative end state, and the closer one is to having the end state occur, the more severe the problem. This definition of a problem makes explicit its value-laden character. What is considered to be desirable-undesirable and important-unimportant will differ across individuals. Similarly, judgments of how far we are from attaining a goal may differ. These latter judgments frequently can be explored empirically and evaluated on logical grounds. Judgments of goal importance can be evaluated by reference to a hierarchical system of values. But the fact remains, that value hierarchies can vary between groups, and discrepancies in value hierarchies must be addressed when designing social action programs.

Most discussions of social ethics by psychologists identify general questions that the social scientist should consider when planning an intervention. However, it is rare that writers will suggest an ethical system that can be applied to such an evaluation. Many social scientists do not offer such a system because they believe that ethical systems are culture- or group-specific. These scientists place an emphasis on discovering, through empirical means, the ethical system that characterizes the target population and then evaluating an intervention in light of this system. Other social scientists have offered ethical systems which they believe are near-universal and which the change agent can use as blueprint for evaluating any social action program. For example, Rokeach (1968) has described a set of 18 "terminal" values (i.e., desired end states, such as family security, freedom, equality, happiness) and 18 "instrumental" values (i.e., desired modes of conduct, such as independent, helpful, honest, polite) that he suggests characterize the range of possible values for a variety of people. This list of values may be useful in that it can suggest a set of concepts that the change agent should consider as *potential* sources of value conflict for the target population.

The description of program objectives can vary in terms of level of abstractness. In our research program on drunk driving, our major objective or goal is to reduce the incidence of drunk driving. This objective is a concrete one. We assume this is desirable because (a) it will reduce the number of automobile accidents, thereby saving the lives of many individuals; (b) it will conserve financial resources in terms of law enforcement, medical costs, insurance costs, etc. These resources can then be used for the attainment of other worthy goals; and (c) it will prevent suffering of relatives and friends of victims of drunk drivers. Thus, on a more abstract level, we appeal to three fundamental values (1) the maintenance of life, (2) the reduction of suffering, and (3) the conservation of finite, valuable resources.

When considered at abstract levels, values frequently conflict. Attaining some goals, by necessity, interferes with other goals or values. For drunk driving programs, values concerning freedom of choice are adversely affected—namely, the freedom to choose what one does (drink and drive). Social action programs usually involve trade-offs between values, and these trade-offs must be carefully considered. We have found that a heuristic device to help us clarify relevant values is the use of abstraction and concretization. This consists of trying to state concrete goals in abstract terms (as was illustrated with the drunk driving example above) and/or trying to state abstract goals in concrete terms. By thinking of the problem at several levels of abstraction, we find we are better able to identify points of conflict. The question then becomes one of striking an "optimum balance" between conflicting goals/values. For example, the abolition of alcohol as a way of eliminating drunk driving would infringe too much on one's freedom of choice.

Change agents are usually "outsiders" with their own set of values. In national programs, for example the government officials and social scientists who design programs are typically from a highly educated, affluent, established segment of society. The target populations are frequently poor, less educated, minorities or groups that are in a dependency relationship (e.g., poor health, addiction, criminals). The change agent must be cautious about the imposition of foreign values on a group of individuals. We try to minimize such problems by involving those affected by the intervention in the choice and exploration of program goals. Thus, we seek the reactions of individuals in the target population to the proposed interventions and carefully evaluate any reservations that they might have. We try to enact this assessment process throughout the course of the intervention, because the perceptions of those affected may change as they gain more experience with the intervention.

Given that many societies have segments with diverse and nonhomogeneous values, it may be possible in some cases to select target populations whose goals are compatible with those of the intervention to begin with. An example of this is our research program on birth control. The focus of this research is to help women who chose to use birth control to do so in a consistent and accurate fashion. We do not attempt to persuade the woman to use birth control. This is a decision that she has already made. Rather, we assist the woman in carrying out a behavior that she initiated on her own behalf.[1]

Value systems do not merely influence program goals and objectives. They influence all stages of the intervention process. Thus, the intervention strategy that one chooses (e.g., a persuasive strategy vs. a coercive strategy) will be influenced by one's values (balancing of freedom and social welfare), as will the decision to target an intervention on only a segment of the population (equal opportunity and accessibility versus pragmatism), and so on. Social ethics requires that extensive value analysis be conducted at all phases of intervention planning.

---

[1] Of course, there are individuals who believe that any action that is undertaken to facilitate the use of birth control is immoral and should not be the subject of a social action program.

Identification of Target Population

A second activity in the design of social action programs is the identification of the target population. Such identification may be self-evident by the nature of the program being developed, or it may be necessary to derive a set of criteria that establish relative priorities among possible target populations. Three criteria are frequently used to establish priorities. The first criterion is based on need or risk. For example, the initial problem of a health educator designing a cancer prevention program is to identify high-risk individuals whose preventive health action is lacking, delayed, or incomplete. It is these high-risk individuals who are of primary concern. The second criterion is based on the probability of program success. Two individuals might be of equal need, but the probability of altering their behavior might differ, given the nature of the social action program and the underlying determinants of their behavior. Given limited resources, the initiator may choose to focus efforts on individuals who are most likely to respond to the intervention. The third criterion is based on program costs. Practical constraints may limit whom the program can be directed at, even given equal need and equal probability of success. Application of this criterion typically involves a cost analysis of enacting the program on different populations, and choosing one or more populations that balance the components of need, probability of success, and program cost.

Generally speaking, there are two requirements of data that can be used to identify individuals who are at high risk. First, the data must allow the identification of these individuals early, before the adverse consequences of the behavior occur. Second, the data must be readily accessible and/or easily obtained. Once the data are obtained, different identification strategies can be developed, depending upon the nature of the data and the program. Two prediction strategies in common use are those based on actuarial prediction (e.g., Dawes, 1962; Sines, 1964, 1966) and those based on multiple regression procedures (e.g., Darlington, 1968; Kerlinger & Pedhazur, 1973). Because the latter strategy is most common in psychology, we will illustrate some of the issues that need to be confronted using an example from our research on contraceptive use.

Regression Approaches for Target Population Identification

Background Information

Although the fertility rate in the United States has exhibited a dramatic decline in the past 12 years (from approximately 2.3 in 1975 to approximately 1.75 in 1987), there has remained a substantial number of pregnancies that are unplanned. Current estimates are that almost 50% of pregnancies are not planned (Baldwin, 1987). The factors underlying the occurrence of unintended pregnancies are complex, but effective use of contraception is clearly an important factor in preventing unexpected pregnancies. For barrier methods of birth control, such as the diaphragm, effective use of contraception involves two components: (1) using the method consistently (i.e., each time that one has sexual intercourse) and (2) using the method accurately. For purposes of discussion, we will focus only on the former.

We have collected data from a representative sample of approximately 1200 women who use family planning clinics in the greater New York City metropolitan area. The sample was selected so as to focus on women who came to the clinic for purposes of obtaining either a diaphragm or birth control pills. The study was a four-wave panel design in which women were interviewed at 4-month intervals. At the initial interview, the women completed a wide range of interviews, designed to measure numerous social psychological variables, demographic variables, and contraceptive history/use. At each interview, a self-report measure of consistent contraceptive use over the previous 4 months was obtained. Scores on the measure could range from 0 to 6, with higher scores indicating greater consistency. Details of the measure and its validity are described in Jaccard, Helbig, Wan, Gutman, and Kritz (1987). Suffice it to say that the measure had predictive validity in that it was predictive of unintended pregnancy at later stages of the research project. One of the aims of our research was to isolate a prediction equation that could be used to predict, *a priori,* consistency of birth control use. Specifically, we attempted to isolate a prediction equation from variables measured at enrollment (time 1) that would allow family planning care providers to identify individuals who are "at risk" of using the diaphragm inconsistently during the approximately 8 months following that clinic visit.[2]

Three issues are discussed here that are relevant to this effort: (1) the reduction of the number of predictor variables, (2) the selection of a statistical criterion for defining weights, and (3) cross-validation of the prediction equation.

Reduction of the Number of Predictor Variables

At enrollment, measures had been obtained on literally hundreds of variables. This set had to be reduced to a manageable number. There are at least three ways one can effect such a reduction: First, one can identify predictors that are most relevant, given theory and past research, and eliminate those that are of questionable theoretical relevance. Second, one can eliminate measures that have low practical value (e.g., are time-consuming to administer, are demanding on the subject) and focus efforts on measures that are most feasible for clinical settings. Third, one can identify predictors on the basis of empirical considerations. This would require the identification of predictors which are not highly intercorrelated (thereby avoiding problems with multicollinearity and maximizing the multiple R) and which are reasonable predictive of the criterion variable. Skinner (1978) suggests performing a principal components analysis of the predictor variables (thereby identifying predictors that are highly correlated with each other but uncorrelated

---

[2] We characterize here only the results for diaphragm users.

with other predictors) and then regressing the criterion onto predictor scores defined on the basis of the principal components. This approach, however, requires that the correlation matrix on which the principal component analysis is based be stable and not subject to large amounts of sampling error. This was unrealistic in our situation, because the ratio of number of predictors to number of subjects was low, even after screening on theoretical and practical grounds. The goal should be to reduce the number of predictors so that one has at least 10 subjects for each predictor. One reduction principle would be to select only variables that have some minimal zero-order correlation with the criterion measure (e.g., corresponding to 5% explained variance). Dummy-coded qualitative variables can be evaluated relative to a minimum eta squared of .05 (see Weinberg & Darlington, 1976, for justification of this approach.) The above screen, coupled with those of theoretical relevance and practical utility, typically reduce the predictors to a manageable number.

When trying to isolate the best-fitting prediction equation, most researchers use some variant of stepwise regression. The set of variables isolated using the above strategy is subjected to a stepwise analysis, further reducing the number of predictors and isolating a prediction equation. This approach does not necessarily yield the best possible prediction equation. The alternative that we use is the "all-possible-regressions strategy" of McCabe (1975). This involves calculating every possible regression equation from all possible combinations of predictors and choosing the equation that is most predictive. Thus, the only way to ensure the isolation of the best-fitting equation is to literally compute every possible equation and evaluate each relative to the other. Of course, the evaluation process must consider the consequences of shrinkage and the practical gains of using expanded equations. For example, even though a five-predictor equation might yield a lower adjusted (for shrinkage) R than a six-predictor equation, one would probably prefer the five-predictor model, if the difference between the R's was only .01.

The all-possible-regression approach is not feasible when the number of predictors is large. However, BMDP has an effective algorithm that makes the approach viable for 30 or fewer predictors. When the number of predictors is greater than 30, then a stepwise approach is feasible. Stepwise regression is properly viewed as a computational shortcut for approximating the best-fitting prediction equation. It will never outperform the all-possible-regression approach, when the latter is feasible. All-possible-regressions also permits inclusion of qualitative variables (dummy-coded). Evaluating qualitative variables in the stepwise approach is problematic. Given the initial reduction strategy discussed above, the all-possible-regression approach generally should be feasible.

Methods for Defining Weights

Another important issue is the statistical method that should be used to derive the prediction equation. Traditionally, this has been accomplished using least squares multiple regression procedures. The advantage of least squares estimators is that they are unbiased. However, under certain conditions (e.g., small N relative to the number of predictors, multicollinearity), the estimates are subject to considerable sampling error and may perform quite poorly when applied to new samples. Statisticians recommend alternative estimators (e.g., ridge regression) for certain prediction situations, which are slightly biased, but which have considerably lower standard errors than their least squares counterparts. Monte Carlo studies have identified conditions where ridge estimators (Pruzek & Frederick, 1978), or variants of it, are superior to least squares estimators (Faden & Bobko, 1982; Morris, 1982).

Depending on the number of predictors that one ultimately focuses on, the degree of correlation between predictors, and the sample size for purposes of derivation, estimates should be based on either a least squares criterion, ridge criteria, or a unit weighting scheme (Wainer, 1978). Guidelines in this regard are provided by Pagel and Lunneberg (1985). Researchers should also be sensitive to the effects of outliers on the prediction equations, and introduce corrections if outliers are present (see Cook & Weisberg, 1983). An outlier is a score which exerts undue influence on the parameter estimates and which masks the trend of effects for the vast majority of the population.

Cross-Validation versus Statistical Estimation of Shrinkage

Another problem in the development of prediction equations is the fact that prediction equations are typically derived from a single sample of individuals. Regression analysis yields weighting coefficients that are optimal (in a least squares sense) only for that sample. When applied to another sample (of new clients), the degree of prediction will be adversely affected, since the weights may not be optimal for the new sample. This is referred to as shrinkage. The amount of shrinkage will be a function of the accuracy of prediction in the derivation sample (i.e, the size of the multiple R), the sample size in the derivation sample, and the number of predictor variables.

There have been two strategies for estimating the amount of shrinkage that is likely to occur. One approach is based on cross-validation and the other is based on the application of statistical corrections to a sample multiple correlation. The formulas that define the corrections have been shown to provide good estimates of shrinkage when the sample equation is applied to all possible random samples of the same N from the population of interest. There have been a number of Monte Carlo studies to evaluate different statistical correction formulas and to contrast them with cross-validation procedures. The results unequivocally demonstrate the superiority of the statistical approach and have isolated corrections that behave quite well (Campbell, 1967; Cotter & Raju, 1982; Herzberg, 1969; Huberty & Mourad, 1980). The cross-validation approach has been found to be limited, because parameter estimates are based on only half of the sample size. In general, it is preferable to use all of the available information to derive the prediction equation, and then estimate shrinkage using some form of statistical correction.

Results of Analysis

Using the above perspectives, we applied the three screening criteria and then used an all-possible-regressions approach for purposes of isolating relevant predictor variables. The initial analysis yielded a seven—predictor equation as being optimal. All equations with more than seven predictors failed to add more than 3% incremental explained variance relative to the seven-predictor equation. The multiple R for the seven-predictor equation was .73. In order to further evaluate the predictive utility of the equation, the various unstandardized regression weights and intercept term were used to generate a predicted score for each subject. The score was rounded to the nearest integer, and these scores were then compared with the observed consistency score (which ranged from 6 to 12 in our sample, because it was summed over two 4-month intervals). A pattern emerged such that when the equation predicted that a women would be quite inconsistent (i.e., score less than 10), the woman did, in fact, use the diaphragm inconsistently. In contrast, when the equation predicted that the woman would be a perfectly consistent user of the diaphragm (corresponding to a score of 12), the prediction was correct in approximately 85% of the cases. In short, the equation was useful in that if it predicted a woman would be quite inconsistent in her use of the diaphragm, the women was indeed inconsistent.

It is possible for a prediction equation with fewer predictors to yield a lower overall multiple R than the seven-term equation, but to yield roughly the same prediction pattern for the inconsistent users. We therefore compared prediction patterns for other equations and settled on a six-predictor model as being most appropriate. The six variables were perceptions of the partner's willingness to delay sex if the couple was unprepared, the perceived susceptibility to pregnancy, alcohol consumption, a friend having a negative experience with the diaphragm (e.g., an unwanted pregnancy), the woman's preference for casual as opposed to romantic sex, and the fear of becoming too old to have a (another) child.

A unit weighting scheme (Wainer, 1978) was also evaluated relative to the least squares estimators. This involved standardizing each predictor, adjusting the sign of the scores to take into account negative correlations, and then summing the scores to yield a predicted score. The prediction analysis was worse than the least squares estimators. In light of these results as well as an exploration of ridge estimators, we decided to retain the least squares estimators as our prediction weights.

Market Segmentation Approaches to Target Population Identification

Segmentation Strategies

Perspectives on the identification of target populations can also be gained from market segmentation research. According to this approach, target populations (e.g., drunk drivers, inconsistent users of birth control) are not homogeneous. For example, two individuals might be drunk drivers, but the motivations underlying each individuals's drunk driving behavior can be quite different. Market segmentation analysis involves subdividing target populations into homogeneous subsets and then adopting different intervention strategies for different segments (or focusing change efforts on only one segment). Everyday observation reveals numerous soda brands (e.g., regular, diet, caffeine-free) and car models (e.g., economy, family, luxury, sport) as evidence of marketing strategies directed toward different consumer segments. In essence, the matching of retail products to consumer preferences has evolved from theories and methods of market segmentation (e.g., Bearden, Teel, & Durand, 1978; Dickson & Ginter, 1987; Frank, Massy, & Wind, 1972; Green, 1977; Holbrook & Holloway, 1984; Scotton & Zallocco, 1980; Smith, 1956; Umesh, 1987; Wind, 1978; Wind & Silver, 1972).

A typical market segmentation strategy will first explore whether significant segments or subgroups exist in the population. A major issue at this juncture is the identification of variables on which homogeneity will be evaluated. This can be addressed either on the basis of strictly theoretical criteria (referred to as "*a priori* segmentation") or on the basis of conceptual/empirical criteria. A common empirical-based approach is one based on the statistical technique of cluster analysis. This can be illustrated in the context of research on drunk driving. Donovan and Marlatt (1982) hypothesized that chronic drunk drivers differ in terms of the psychosocial factors that underlie their drunk driving behavior. They administered a number of personality measures to a sample of drunk drivers, including such characteristics as assertiveness, depression, emotional adjustment, internality, externality, sensation seeking, assaultiveness, direct and indirect hostility, irritability, resentment, aggression, tension reduction, and inhibition. Scores on each scale were standardized to yield a common response metric for each variable. The similarity of scores across the variables for any two individuals was defined using a Euclidean distance score. This involves calculating the difference between a score on a variable for one individual with the score on the same variable for the second individual, squaring this difference, and then summing the squared differences across all variables. A summed score (called the "distance score") of zero indicates that the two individuals have identical scores across all variables. The larger the distance score, the more divergent are the responses between the two individuals. A distance score can be computed between all possible pairs of individuals. Given N individuals, this would yield an $N \times N$ symmetric matrix of distance scores. This matrix can be subjected to formal cluster analysis (see Dillon & Goldstein, 1981, for a description of this analytic technique) to identify clusters of individuals who have similar response patterns to other individuals within the cluster, but different response patterns from individuals in other clusters. Donovan and Marlatt (1982) found five subtypes of drunk drivers, using this approach. For example, one group was characterized by low levels of depression and sensation seeking, but high levels of assertiveness. Another group was identified as having high levels of depression and resentment, and low levels of emotional adjustment and assertiveness. These profiles suggest that different intervention strategies might be required for the different segments.

Factors other than motivational variables can be used as the basis of a segmentation analysis. For example, the media habits of drunk drivers might be assessed and a segmentation analysis performed using media-related variables. Such an analysis might indicate that the population is homogeneous in terms of exposure to certain types of media (e.g., drunk drivers may have preferences for certain types of television programs), or it may suggest that two or more segments exist. This, in turn, might influence the choice of a media strategy for conveying educational materials to drunk drivers.

Segmentation strategies also involve a cost-benefit analysis of the viability of intervention attempts on one or more segments of the population. Practical constraints, the probability of program success, and differential needs of the population might dictate a focus on only a few segments of the population.

Behavioral Analysis

Once the goals of the program have been developed and the target population specified, the identification of specific behaviors that need to be modified or instituted must be considered. Social action programs are exactly what the name implies—programs designed to influence social actions. To implement a social action program concerning ecology, for example, it is necessary to compile a list of specific behaviors (e.g., use of public transportation, ownership of only one automobile) that, if modified or initiated, would have an impact on our environment. It is of little value to increase ''ecological awareness'' in people if such awareness is not manifested in meaningful behaviors. As numerous researchers have noted (e.g., Cleary, 1972; Keyes, 1972; Krasner & Ullman, 1973; Rosenstock, 1974), in the final analysis our ultimate concern usually is with behavior (be it political behavior, health behavior, prejudicial behavior, fertility behavior, consumer behavior.)

The compilation of a set of specific behaviors to be modified raises a number of issues. First, it is critical that changing the behaviors will, in fact, lead to the intended consequences of the social action program. Often the relationship between the target behaviors and intended consequences is unclear. An example of this kind of relationship is a family planning program in India. The program was initiated to reduce the population growth rate of a given village. This was done by instituting an educational program on birth control. Given an analysis of the culture and norms of the village, the decision was made to try to increase the use of condoms as a method of birth control. After 2 years, the program was highly effective in that the use of condoms increased dramatically. A corresponding increase in the population growth rate, however, was also observed. Later analyses revealed that during the years prior to the program, the villagers had developed their own (sometimes unorthodox) methods of birth control that were quite effective. With the "success" of the condom program, these methods were essentially replaced by a less reliable form of birth control, with the result being an increase in accidental pregnancies. This problem could have been avoided if there had been greater attention to the nature of the relevant behaviors.

A second issue is that often the target behaviors will produce the intended consequences but will also result in unintended consequences. These consequences must be anticipated to the extent possible, and the ethical and practical ramifications of these unintended consequences considered.

Specification of relevant behaviors can vary in terms of the degree of abstraction. For example, the relevant behavior for our drunk driving research program is stopping people from drinking and driving. This statement of the target behavior, however, is of little utility. To be more concrete, we can focus on two sets of separate activities: (1) stopping people from driving (when they have had too much to drink) and (2) stopping people from drinking too much (when they might have to drive). Behavioral strategies that might characterize the former set of activities include using public transportation (e.g., buses or taxis), having a friend or "designated driver" drive instead, staying overnight instead of driving, or calling friends to have them drive you home. Behavioral strategies that might characterize the latter include pacing oneself when drinking, limiting the number of drinks one has in a given time period, and alternating the consumption of nonalcoholic beverages with alcoholic beverages.

The specification of behaviors in concrete terms is a core part of specifying alternative solutions to the social problem. It is not the entire part, because a solution is only a solution if people adopt the behavior and maintain it. The actual intervention is designed to accomplish this, and thus is also an integral part of the solution.

When evaluating potential behavioral targets, we have found it useful to draw upon the expertise of social scientists (e.g., other researchers studying the problem of drunk driving), practitioners in the field (e.g., counselors of alcoholics), as well as members of the target population (e.g., convicted drunk drivers, young drivers). One potentially useful methodology is that of focus groups, a common strategy used in marketing by consumer psychologists (see Boyd, Westfall, & Stand, 1986; Calder, 1977; Fern, 1982). Focus groups involve bringing together 6 to 12 individuals of a common background and having them generate possible solutions to the problem at hand in the context of group discussion. The group is generally led by a trained moderator (and hence is distinct from "brainstorming" strategies), who structures the discussion of the group. At present, there is some controversy as to whether focus groups are superior to nominal groups (i.e., individually interviewing 6–12 individuals and then pooling their responses, thereby eliminating group interaction; see Fern, 1982). It is evident, however, that consultation and pretesting with selected groups of relevant experts, practitioners, and target individuals can be illuminating in terms of behavioral analysis.

Isolating Behavioral Determinants

Another major activity in the design of social action programs is isolating factors that determine or influence the target behaviors. By understanding *why* people behave or fail to behave in certain ways, the social scientist is in a better position to enact changes that will influence behavior. Social psychology is replete with theories of human behavior. Some of these theories are domain-specific, whereas other theories are assumed to generalize across domains. In this section, we will discuss a framework that we have found to be useful for isolating behavioral determinants in a wide variety of situations involving social action programs.

Decision-Making Perspectives

Decisions to perform behaviors underlie much of human action. A person may make a decision about a birth control method to use, whether or not to perform preventive health behaviors, a political candidate to vote for, and so on. It follows that theories of decision making should prove useful in understanding why people behave as they do. Behavioral decisions can be classified into three types. *Impulsive* decisions are those that are determined by impulsive or emotional reactions, without reflection. *Routine* decisions concern familiar situations in which decisions are made with little reflection and in accordance with habits, customs, or moral/social rules. *Thoughtful* decisions are made after giving thought to such factors as the problem situation, the alternative courses of action available, and the probably consequences of each course of action. When making a decision in a familiar situation, the individual typically accepts the suggestion of impulse, habit, custom, or rule, without serious reflection. Most behavioral decisions in everyday life are of this character. However, when the decision is perceived as important, or when impulse, habit, or custom are questioned, then the individual will reflect on the matter, considering one or more courses of action.

Most decision theories are concerned with thoughtful behavioral decisions. One can further distinguish between two types of decision-making modes: active and passive. Active decision making refers to those times when the individual is actively reflecting on the problem or situation of interest (e.g., choosing a method of birth control). Passive decision making refers to the case where the decision is governed by the conclusions reached at some prior time, as a result of active decision making. Of primary interest to decision theorist are factors that an individual considers during the active decision-making state. These factors are of obvious interest when passive decision making is in effect, because passive decisions reflect conclusions drawn during active decision making.

There are at least eight types of activities that an individual can engage in during active decision making. Each of these activities may thus underlie the behavior of interest for the social action program. First is *problem recognition,* wherein an individual determines that a problem state exists and that a decision must be considered. Second is *goal identification*, in which the individual specifies, *a priori*, the purpose of the decision—i.e., the ideal outcome of the decision. In the context of contraceptive choice, this would involve specification of the ideal method of birth control. Third is *option generation/identification*, in which the individual thinks of potential alternative solutions to the problem at hand (e.g., different methods of birth control that are available). Fourth is *information search*, in which the individual seeks information, either about what additional options might be available or about properties of one or more of the options under consideration. Fifth is the *assessment of option information*, in which the individual considers the information he or she has about different decisions options. The term *information* is used in a general sense and refers to any consequence or concept subjectively associated with a given decision option. In considering the information about the different options, the individual forms a preference structure. Specifically, the individual forms an attitude toward performing each option. Given p decision options, the preference structure is a set of p attitudes. Consistent with Fishbein (1972) and most contemporary attitude theories, an attitude is defined as a general feeling of favorableness with respect to choosing the decision option. Sixth is the *choice process*, wherein one of the decision options is chosen for purposes of behavioral enactment. This choice will be some function of the preference structure. Seventh is *behavioral translation*, in which the individual translates the decision into overt behavior. Finally, *postdecision evaluation*, is the activity in which the individual reflects on the decision after the option has been enacted and evaluates the decision process in light of the outcomes that have resulted.

Not all of the above activities will necessarily be performed by the individual. Nor must they be performed in the sequence described. There is research in the social judgment and decision-making literature on each activity, and this research can be brought to bear when analyzing behavior. It is beyond the scope of the present chapter to highlight the many theories that apply to each decision activity. Some of the relevant research has been reviewed by Abelson and Levi (1985), Jaccard and Wood (1986), and Landesman and Jaccard (1987). However, we will briefly characterize a few relevant perspectives, using choice of a birth control method as an example. We will focus on the analysis of choice of a particular birth control method, given that one has decided to use birth control.

Problem Recognition. Problem recognition concerns whether the individual has anticipated that a decision about birth control is necessary *before* she is confronted with the possibility of sexual intercourse for the first time. Individuals are expected to vary in this "preparedness." Of interest are the factors that influence or facilitate problem recognition. A "problem" is defined as the failure to obtain a goal (or to make adequate progress toward that goal) or the occurrence (or anticipated occurrence) of a negative outcome (Landesman & Jaccard, 1987). In the case of a negative outcome (such an an unwanted pregnancy), individuals will be more likely to act on a problem if it is salient, if it is perceived as being important, and if one feels that something can be done to prevent it. Each of these factors is influenced by a multitude of variables, including exposure to certain types of information in school, discussions with parents and/or peers, or exposure to various mass media elements. In addition, certain individual difference variables will be relevant. For example, people who have external locus of control orientation (i.e., generalized beliefs that they have little control over what happens to them) will be less likely to recognize problems and move into an active decision-making mode to confront the problem.

Goal Identification. Goal identification focuses on what the individual perceives as the ideal option (e.g., method of birth control). This represents features of the birth control method that the individual wants to maximize (e.g., effective in preventing pregnancy, no health risks, convenient to use, partner approval). These features may differ in their subjective importance to the individual, and it is crucial to understand what factors are most important and why. Research has shown that individuals do not always make choices that are in accord with their stated values, and sometimes individuals are not even aware that they have failed to consider a feature that is important to them (e.g., Jaccard, 1981; Wiggins, 1972). Again, the relative importance of different features are expected to vary as a function of situational (e.g., social class) and individual difference (e.g., religiosity) variables.

Option Identification. Option identification refers to the specification of the different birth control methods that are available. Of interest is whether the individual is aware of all the available birth control methods, and if not, which methods the individual is unaware of. Factors influencing option identification are also important to isolate (e.g., the source from which the teen learned about the existence of a given method).

Information Search. Information search includes analysis of the individual's decision to actively seek out information about particular methods of birth control. One relevant set of variables focuses on who the individual seeks out and why some sources of information are preferred to others. For example, in the birth control area, Jaccard and Turrisi (1987) have identified 10 major referents that teens say they consult (e.g., mother, father, brother, sister, teacher, family planning clinic) and the dimensions on which the referents can vary with respect to the information-giving process (e.g., provides useful information, is difficult to talk to, respect my privacy, would get angry at me). These researchers used functional measurement methodology (Anderson, 1982; Jaccard & Becker, 1985) to isolate how these perceptions influence a teen's decision to seek out a given source for purposes of obtaining birth-control-related information. Also of interest in this regard is the vast literature on social support networks.

The decision to seek out information is also influenced by whether or not the individual perceives she is in need of information. Some individuals believe they are quite knowledgeable about birth control, when in fact they are not. Similarly, some individuals underestimate their knowledge of birth control methods. Thus, another set of relevant variables is the perceived knowledge of birth control relative to actual knowledge.

Assessment of Option Information. Given a wide array of information, individuals must combine the information and form preferences for different methods. Each method will have certain advantages and disadvantages, and the individual must trade off positive and negative features in forming her evaluations.

Jaccard and Wood (1986) recommend the use of a perceptual structure matrix for representing the information that an individual has about different methods of birth control. The columns of the matrix represent various birth control methods (e.g., pill, diaphragm) and the rows represent different informational dimensions on which the methods can differ (e.g., effectiveness, health risks, convenience in using). Each method is viewed by the individual as being more or less "good" or "bad" on a given dimension (e.g., the pill is good in terms of effectiveness, bad in terms of health risks, neutral in terms of convenience). The cells of the matrix represent the perceptions of the individual about a given method on a given dimension. Jaccard and Wood (1986) describe cluster-analytic approaches that can be used to identify methods of birth control that are perceived similarly across dimensions and to identify dimensions that covary in terms of their "standing" across different methods. For example, health risks and effectiveness may be perceived as being inversely related, whereas cost and effectiveness may be perceived as being positively related. Analysis of the perceptual structure matrix reveals what information individuals have about birth control vis-à-vis choosing a birth control method and indicates key relationships between perceptions. Jaccard and Becker (1985) and Jaccard and Wood (1986) describe how this approach differs from traditional expectancy-value formulations.

Jaccard (Jaccard & Becker, 1985; Jaccard & Wood, 1986) also has developed an approach for studying trade-off processes in the evaluation of birth control methods that is distinct from traditional expectancy-value formulations. The approach uses Anderson's (1981) information integration theory and functional measurement as a conceptual framework. In the Jaccard and Becker study, individuals were presented descriptions of hypothetical methods of birth control and asked to rate each method in terms of how favorable or unfavorable they would feel about using it. The descriptions were constructed so that different factors (e.g., effectiveness, health risks) were placed "in conflict," and individuals had to choose between them. The ratings were anlayzed using functional measurement methodology to isolate the trade-off processes individuals used, without ever making the individuals verbalize the process *per se*. Jaccard and Becker evaluated four general classes of trade-off rules based on decision theory and found support for a different weight-averaging process, which is counter to expectancy-value formulations. A useful feature of the Jaccard and Becker approach is the employment of external validity checks in the trade-off analysis.

The Choice Process. Given a set of preferences, the individual must choose one or more methods to use, based on those preferences. A common choice rule in the decision literature is that the individual will choose methods toward which the most positive attitude is held (Jaccard, 1981). This is referred to as the principle of optimization or maximization. The principle of maximization has fallen into descriptive disrepute in favor of satisficing rules (e.g., Janis & Mann, 1977; Mitchell, Rediker, & Beach, 1986; Simon, 1976). According to critics of optimization, decision makers are frequently faced with a large number of consequences and outcomes to consider at a given time. The time, effort, and cost required to gather information about the various outcomes precludes a careful search and appraisal of information when making a choice. Even when all relevant information is at hand, the amount of information to be processed may exceed the cognitive capabilities of the individual. The result is a choice that is not "optimal." Simon (1976) has suggested "satisficing" as an alternative way in which humans approach decision problems. According to this perspective, the individual chooses an option that is "good enough," or that meets a minimal set of requirements. Such a strategy, it is argued, can be effected with superficial information search and minimal cognitive effort. The person merely considers courses of action sequentially until he or she discovers on that is "good enough."

The idea that people do not "maximize" or "optimize" has led some theorists to characterize the decision making of individuals as irrational. However, Miller and Starr (1967) have pointed out that rationality is a relative concept. "The effect of . . . psychological (limitations) . . . is to cause people to act irrationally—but it should be noted that this is simply a matter of definition, rationality having been defined as maximization of economic utility" (p. 25). Jaccard (1981) and Jaccard and Wan (1987) have argued that individuals frequently optimize their choice vis-à-vis their attitudes toward options; that is, the individual always chooses the option toward which he or she feels most positive. According to these theorists, at any given time, the individual considers different courses of actions when confronted with a choice. Some of the behavioral options may be viewed positively by the individual while other behavioral options may be viewed negatively (including the option to search out other choice alternatives). On the basis of the information that is available, *at that time,* the individual forms an attitude toward each of the options and chooses the one with which he or she feels most favorable. Using an external criterion (such as maximized economic utility), the choice may indeed be a suboptimal one. But from the subjective perspective of the individual, the choice is the best one in the sense that he or she feels most favorable toward the chosen option, all things considered. Jaccard has presented several empirical demonstrations of the predictive power of a maximization rule using attitudinal concepts (e.g., Jaccard, 1981; Jaccard & Becker, 1985; Jaccard & Wan 1986, 1987). Further, Jaccard and Wan (1987) review difficulties with assessing "satisficing" versus optimizing strategies using traditional decision theory. For example, failures to find maximization can be criticized because (1) the studies focus on a set of consequences that may or may not correspond to the consequences that the individual is considering; (2) the studies assume a combinatorial rule, trade-off process, or integration strategy for perceptions of consequences that do not correspond to what the decision maker uses; and (3) the studies focus on concepts (subjective probability and utility) that are not considered by the individual when forming attitudes. The attitude construct is useful because it allows one to assess the perceived overall "utility" of options without recourse to such considerations (see Jaccard, 1981).

Behavioral Translation. Once a choice has been made, the individual must translate the choice into behavior. For example, if a teen decides to use the contraceptive sponge, she must then learn where she can acquire it, actually acquire it, learn how to use it, and then actually use it. There is a large literature on factors that influence the relationship between a person's decision to perform a behavior and actual behavioral performance (e.g., Ajzen & Fishbein, 1980; Davidson & Jaccard, 1979; Fishbein & Ajzen, 1975). Jaccard (1975) discusses the implications of factors such as the extent to which the behavior is dependent on other people or events, the extent to which the behavior requires memory of previous decisions or information, the individual's ability to perform the behavior, and habitual factors. For birth control decisions, it also is important to assess the individual's knowledge about how and where to acquire birth control, her perceived obstacles in enacting the behavior, how these obstacles are dealt with, and her perceptions of the "delivery system" in general. Research on innovation diffusion and adoption has much to offer in this context.

Postdecision Evaluation. Postdecision evaluation involves evaluating one's choice after the option has been enacted. This will frequently lead to a reassessment of the validity of one's initial information and, potentially, a change in the decision. Key variables for this activity include satisfaction with one's decision, identification of the sources of dissatisfaction, the willingness of the individual to change one's decision, and factors that influence such willingness to change.

Additional Variables. The above description of relevant variables for the eight activities of decision making has been primarily cognitive in focus. More global variables, such as personality variables, may also influence decision making. Such global variables are important and should also be included in an analysis of decision making. Landesman and Jaccard (1987) discuss four general classes of variables that can impinge on decision-making activities. The first is *personality-based orientations* and includes such constructs as locus of control, risk-taking propensity, impulsiveness, and conscientiousness. Jaccard and Dittus (1987) have conducted a review of the decision-making literature to identify personality orientations that influence each aspect of the decision-making process. The second class of global variables is *emotional and affective constructs,* which includes such concepts as life satisfaction, self-esteem, anxiety, and depression. Useful taxonomies of emotions have been presented by Daly, Lancee, and Polivy (1983) and Buck

(1985). The third class of variables concerns *intellectual and cognitive abilities* and includes both general intelligence and more specialized cognitive abilities (e.g., abstract versus concrete thinking) of the individual. The fourth class includes those variables that may generally be classified as *sociodemographic* in nature. They include age, sex, race, religion, socioeconomic status, school enrollment status, and formal instruction on sex. These variables may either directly affect the decision-making process or moderate the effect of cognitive, personality, and affective variables on decision making.

It is beyond the scope of this chapter to illustrate in detail the implications of each of the decision activities for the design of social action programs. Suffice it to say that we have found it useful to conduct a comprehensive analysis of behavior in light of each of the activities. In order to be more concrete, we will provide two illustrations. First, we will discuss one of the decision activities (behavioral translation) in some depth, illustrating how it affects the planning of a social action program. Second, we will discuss the framework more generally in terms of its implications for the analysis of drunk driving.

Behavioral Translation and the Analysis of Social Action Programs

As noted above, several factors influence whether or not a behavioral decision is translated into actual behavior. Six factors are discussed here.

Time Interval. One factor affecting the relation between a behavioral decision (BD) and behavior (B) is the time interval between the measurement of the decision and the observation of behavior. As the time interval between these two measures increases, the correlation between BD and B may be expected to decrease. If one wishes to predict whether an individual will obtain a birth control method at a given clinic at 2 p.m. on Wednesday, the most predictive measure would be one taken just before the 2 p.m. appointment. The earlier one obtains this measure of BD prior to the overt behavior, the lower the decision–behavior correspondence might be. Obviously, it is not the passage of time *per se* that influences the BD–B relation. Rather, some event must occur during the time period that either changes the decision or renders performance of the behavior impossible.

Exposure to New Information. A second factor affecting the BD–B relation is the exposure to new information after the measurement of the decision. During the time interval between measurement of the decision and the observation of behavior, the individual may be told that the birth control method is dangerous. Rather than obtain a harmful method, the person might change her or his decision and remain at home. For social action programs to be successful, they must address such information a person might receive that would change her or his decision.

Prior Events. A third factor influencing the strength of the decision–behavior relation is the number of behaviors or "steps" the individual must perform before the desired behavior can be performed. For example, in order to use birth control pills, a person must (1) learn where one can go to obtain birth control pills, (2) make an appointment with a doctor, (3) arrange transportation to the appointment site, (4) arrive at the doctor's office, (5) obtain a prescription from the doctor, (6) go to a pharmacy and obtain the prescription, and (7) use the pill. Different behaviors may require different numbers of steps leading to their performance. As the number of steps increases, the correspondence between BD and B might decrease. This will be true especially when performance of one or more of the steps is dependent on some other person or event. For example, a person might expect to ride a bus to a family planning clinic, but the bus might not arrive.

Memory. A fourth factor affecting the relationship between a decision and behavior is memory. A person may decide to go to a clinic to obtain a birth control method, but then later forget all about it. Social action programs can counter this variable with reminders.

Abilities. Another variable influencing the BD–B relation is abilities. A behavioral decision is nothing more than a decision to act. If the person does not have the ability to perform the action, the measured decision will not correspond with actual behavior. For example, a woman may decide to have a two-child family, but she may not know any birth-prevention techniques. Therefore, she will probably have more than two children.

Habit. A sixth factor affecting the decision–behavior relation is habit. A person may decide to perform a behavior but, by force of habit, perform an alternative one. For example, individuals may decide to stop smoking cigarettes, but find themselves unconsciously having the usual after-dinner cigarette.

To summarize, it can be argued that many behaviors of concern to social action programs are volitional and hence guided by one's behavioral decision. However, prediction of behavior from behavioral decisions may be reduced by a number of factors that must be taken into account to improve behavioral prediction. This is especially true when there is a long interval between measurement of the decision and observation of behavior, when performance of the behavior can only occur following some sequence of behaviors, and when these sequenced behaviors are dependent upon other people or events.

The preceding analysis has a number of implications for the design and implementation of social action programs. First, many social action programs are aimed at influencing people's beliefs and attitudes in hopes of persuading them to perform some behavior. The present analysis suggests that persuading people is not enough. A program may be completely successful in that it makes people decide to perform a given behavior, but unless people enact their decision, the program will be of little value. The preceding analysis suggests some of the factors that will influence whether or not people enact their decisions and identifies certain problems social action programmers should confront to design effective programs. Second, it may be that for many behaviors there is no need to persuade individuals to perform the behavior because they already intend to do so. In this case, there should be a shift in the focus of the program—that is, the program should direct itself toward helping people carry out their decisions rather than attempting to influence the decision. Finally, programs may sometimes be concerned with maintaining decisions over time rather than changing decisions. Thus, procedures for making "correct" behavioral decisions resistant to change might be the proper focus for many programs.

An example of the importance of the above considerations can be elaborated in the context of political campaigns. The program objective from the perspective of a campaign manager is to get the candidate elected. One of the relevant behaviors for accomplishing this is getting people to vote for the candidate (others might include donating money to the candidate, canvassing for the candidate). An analysis of the voting decision–voting behavior relationship indicates that this theoretical link is critical for political campaigns. One factor that can influence this relationship is the sequence of behavioral steps one must perform to enact behavioral criterion. In our present electoral system, a person must (1) learn where to register to vote, (2) arrange transportation to the registration office, (3) arrive at the registration office, (4) register to vote, (5) learn where to vote on election day, (6) arrange for transportation to the polls, (7) arrive at the polls, and (8) vote for the candidate. Not all of these steps are under the control of the individual, and failure to perform any one of them will render performance impossible. A person may have difficulty learning where to register to vote. Or one may arrange transportation with a friend, but the friend may fail to show up. Or one may simply forget the registration deadline. And so on.

Most political campaigns implicitly recognize that voting decisions will not always manifest themselves in voting behavior. Thus, emphasis is often placed on "registration drives" and, on election days, efforts to "get the vote out." These strategies can essentially be viewed as attempts not to change voting decisions or influence them but rather to ensure that the voting decisions are translated into voting behavior. Inherent within such strategies is the necessity to register and get to the polls only those individuals who will vote for the campaign's candidate.

An Analysis of Drunk Driving

A major issue facing researchers studying the topic of alcohol is the problem of drunk driving. Estimates suggest that between 30 and 50% of all fatal automobile crashes involve alcohol. Other reports have suggested an even greater role for alcohol in fatal traffic accidents. Deterrence through law enforcement as well as education and rehabilitation programs have been the major methods of attempting to confront the problem of drunk driving. Research has suggested that law enforcement alone is not an adequate solution because of the low probability of arrest. Therefore, considerable attention has been directed toward identifying factors that are associated with drunk driving in an effort to increase the effectiveness of treatment and education programs.

The conceptual framework that we use to study drunk driving is based, in large part, on decision theory as outlined above. The approach focuses on the case where individuals find themselves in a situation where they have been drinking and must decide whether to drive or not.

Driving Decisions and Attitudes

The first set of theoretical links in our framework are illustrated in Figure 1. The uppermost box represents drunk driving, i.e., the occurrence or nonoccurrence of driving at levels that exceed the legally mandated blood alcohol level (BAL). This behavior is influenced by an individual's decision to drive: If an individual decides not to drive, than drunk driving cannot occur (at least with respect to the individual in question). If the individual decides to drive, then drunk driving can occur (if the BAL exceeds legal limits). Although this link may seem psychologically trivial, it serves to formally recognize that an individual's decision to drive or not drive does not necessarily correspond to his or her driving behavior *per se.* For example, an individual may decide to drive, but the car won't start. Or a friend may physically prevent the individual from driving if the friend perceives that the individual is too intoxicated. Although a decision to drive will not always result in driving *per se,* it usually will. Thus, an understanding of cognitive factors that underlie this decision is important.

Jaccard (1981; Jaccard & Becker, 1985; Jaccard & Wan, 1986) has devel-

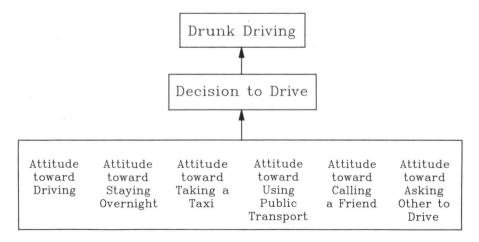

Figure 1. Theoretical link between drunk driving behavior, decision to drive, and attitudes toward behavioral alternatives.

oped and tested a decision framework in which an individual's choice among behavioral alternatives is said to be a function of his or her attitudes toward each of the various alternatives. An attitude is defined in a very restricted manner—namely, the extent to which the individual feels favorable or unfavorable toward choosing the alternative in question. For *n* different alternatives, there are *n* attitudes, and the set of *n* attitudes is referred to as a *preference structure*. On the basis of extensive empirical evidence (e.g., Jaccard, 1981; Jaccard & Becker, 1985), it is posited that an individual will typically choose that alternative toward which the most positive attitude is held.

In a driving situation where an individual is drinking, there are a number of behavioral alternatives that an individual can choose between. Some of these are illustrated in Figure 1. The alternatives listed are illustrative, not exhaustive. Of psychological interest are which alternatives are salient to an individual (i.e., which alternatives he or she thinks of), the determinants of alternative salience, and factors that influence the attitude toward each alternative. If individuals have a positive attitude toward driving, and negative attitudes toward the other alternatives, they will usually decide to drive. It is interesting to note that many of the educational efforts in the popular media are aimed at influencing the salience or attitudes of driving alternatives (e.g., "Have a friend drive you home—it may save your life") and/or the decision–behavior link (e.g., "Don't let a friend drive home drunk"). Thus, an important aspect of our framework is the specification and analysis of perceived (and actual) behavioral alternatives in the drunk driving situation.

Determinants of Attitudes

Factors that determine the extent to which an individual feels favorable or unfavorable toward a given behavioral alternative are complex. In the psychological literature, there are numerous theories that elucidate cognitive factors that influence, in part, attitudes towards behavioral alternatives (e.g., Anderson, 1981; Fishbein & Ajzen, 1975). A common theme throughout these theories is that attitudes are influenced by perceptions of the consequences (or advantages and disadvantages) of performing each behavioral alternative. Thus, for example, the attitude toward driving may be influenced by such cognitions as (1) the perceived probability that one will get in an accident and the perception of how negative it would be if that were to happen, (2) the perceived probability that one will be stopped by a policeman and the perception of how negative that would be if it were to happen, and so on (see Figure 2a). The attitude toward having a friend drive you home might be influenced by such perceptions as (1) how embarrassing it would be to have to ask your friend to drive you home, (2) the inconvenience that would ensue from having to retrieve your car at a later date, and so on. Of psychological interest are the cognitions that underlie each attitude and how these cognitions combine to yield a preference structure of a given form.

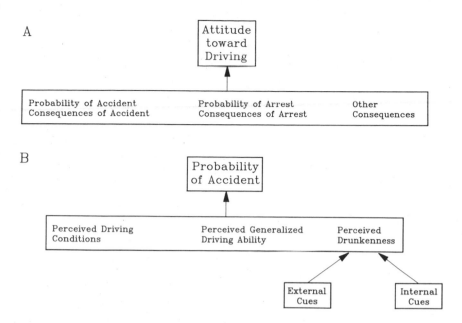

Figure 2. Higher-order cognitions and first-order cognitions for attitude toward driving and probability of arrest.

Determinants of Perceptions

Cognitions that directly influence an attitude are referred to as *first-order* cognitions. Higher-order cognitions are those that influence first-order cognitions. Figure 2 illustrates selected relevant higher-order cognitions for the first-order cognition concerning the probability of getting in an accident. For example, if one perceives the driving conditions as being favorable (e.g., well-lighted, dry roads on quiet city streets), if one perceives oneself as an excellent driver, and if one does not consider oneself very drunk, then the perceived probability of getting in an accident might be very small.

Note that in the above framework, judgments about how drunk one is in a given situation is a higher-order cognition that is fairly far removed from the ultimate criterion, drunk driving behavior (see Figure 2b). This suggests that such judgments will influence driving behavior in complex ways. For example, judgments of drunkenness should (but may not) influence the perceived probability that it is unsafe to drive (i.e., "I will get in an accident"). This perception of "unsafeness" will, in turn, influence how favorable or unfavorable the individual feels about driving. Only if the impact of this belief is such that the attitude toward driving becomes less favorable than the attitude toward other behavioral alternatives (e.g., taking a taxi home) will the individual decide not to drive. In short, the driving decision is multivariate in character and the impact of any given cognition or judgment can be understood only by examining the multiple variables that are operating. By the same token, an educational campaign that focuses on higher-order cognitions, such as teaching individuals to accurately understand how many drinks they can have and still be under the legal BAL, may be ineffective if the higher-order cognition doesn't manifest effects through first-order cognitions, attitudes, decisions, and, ultimately, behavior. Our research program has attempted to explore the implications of all the above for understanding drunk driving behavior.

Personality and Other Influences

The description of our framework thus far has been primarily cognitive in nature, as conceptualized by formal decision theory. It must be emphasized that we do not believe that individuals engage in active decision making (e.g., weighing of advantages and disadvantages of different behavioral alternatives) whenever they find themselves in a situation where they might have to drive after consuming alcohol. Such decisions surely are not so "rational." Rather, we believe that, over time, an individual forms general beliefs (cognitions) about the various behavioral alternatives in such situations (e.g., "Asking someone else to drive me home could be embarrassing"). These beliefs derive from past personal experiences, observing the experiences of others, exposure to various programs in the media, and so on. The totality of one's beliefs about a given behavioral alternative are "psychologically summarized" in the form of attitudes (i.e., general feelings of favorableness or unfavorableness about each alternative). In most everyday situations, the attitude toward driving is the most favorable one and the other behavioral alternatives will not even be salient. However, at any given time, something may happen that makes the individual question, or at least pause to think about, the decision to drive (e.g., a friend saying something, or a transitory feeling of lack of coordination). At this time, attitudes towards the other alternatives may quickly be reviewed and a choice made accordingly. Or, more active consideration of the cognitions underlying a given attitude may result.

From an educational perspective, it is important to understand the generalized cognitions and attitudes that may be present as well as the factors that "trigger" reflection on the decision to drive. In fact, one might argue that a purpose of educational efforts should be to make driving decisions *more* cognition—i.e., teach individuals to carefully consider a decision and the reasons (cognitions) underlying it.

Of interest is identifying the kinds of individuals and/or situations that are likely to invoke thoughtful decision strategies in drunk driving situations. There are numerous personality and individual difference variables that have been suggested in the literature that may be relevant. For example, locus of control has been implicated in drunk driving behavior (e.g., Donovan & Marlatt, 1982). If people feel that they have little control over what happens, then how drunk they think they are may not affect the perceived probability of getting in an accident ("It is out of my hands—fate will determine what happens"). The extent to which cognitions derive from basic dispositions such as locus of control or other personality variables could have implications for the design of education programs. Our research program is attempting to isolate such relationships.

The Case of Multiple-Act Criteria

Behavioral decision theory is useful for the analysis of performance of a specific behavior at a given time. However, frequently we are interested in studying multiple behaviors. For example, the consistent use of contraception can be conceptualized as a multiple-act criterion consisting of an aggregation of many individual actions over a period of time (e.g., 100 acts of intercourse over a period of a year). When the behavioral criterion of interest constitutes a multiple act, then additional perspectives beyond those discussed above must be brought to bear.

Several attitude theorists (e.g., Epstein, 1979; Fishbein & Ajzen, 1974; Jaccard, 1974) have argued that multiple-act criteria will best be predicted from general as opposed to specific variables. According to these theorists, both general attitudes and specific situational factors (e.g., the availability of birth control method, perceived timing of ovulation) will influence behavior in a given situation (e.g., contraceptive use in a specific sexual encounter). The impact of the general, more stable variables (such as the attitude toward avoiding pregnancy) will have a common influence across all situations. In contrast, the nature of the impact of situational variables (e.g., when an individual thinks the time of the month is "safe," she may be inclined not to use birth control, whereas when she perceives it as "not safe," she may be inclined to use birth control) will vary from occasion to occasion. When behavioral scores are aggregated across occasions (e.g., use–nonuse of birth control is aggregated occasions of sexual intercourse), the common influence of the general attitudes will be evident, whereas the more specific situational influences will cancel each other (thus representing error variance) and not reveal any systematic relationship with the overall score. As an illustration of this, Fishbein and Ajzen (1974) described to subjects a set of 100 behaviors dealing with matters of religion and asked them to indicate the behaviors they performed. A multiple-act criterion was obtained by summing dichotomous scores (1 = performed, 0 = not performed) over the 100 behaviors. Subjects also completed five traditional scales that measured the general attitude toward religion. Consistent with expectations, the attitude scales correlated highly with the multiple-act criterion, whereas there tended to be no systematic relationship with each of the 100 behaviors taken separately. Similar conclusions have been reached in more carefully controlled studies of aggregate prediction (e.g., Epstein, 1979). This line of research suggests that multiple-act criteria can be profitably studied with nonspecific, more general attitudinal variables whose influence is likely to operate across time and situations. These, and other general variables, are likely to interact to influence behavior and hence may be useful to study in the context of multiple-act criteria.

Changing Behavioral Determinants

The preceding section outlined approaches to the analysis of behavior that directs the social action programmer to those variables on which a change effort should focus. Once these variables have been isolated, procedures must be undertaken to change these behavioral determinants. In general, two types of strategies can be used: (1) environmental manipulation, in which structural features of the environment are altered so as to affect the behavioral alternatives that are available to the individual, and (2) persuasive communications, in which the psychological state (beliefs, attitudes, or decisions) of an individual is modified by exposure to information. We will first consider the strategy of persuasive communication.

Persuasive Communications

McGuire (1985) has suggested the use of an input/output model to conceptualize the complex process of attitude change via persuasive communications. Central to the notion of output variables (i.e., dependent variables) are the cognitive and behavioral acts that the audience must engage in for a communication to be successful. These include (a) being exposed to the communication, (b) attending to it, (c) maintaining interest, (d) comprehending the message, (e) cognating (e.g., accommodating or assimilating the message), (f) attitudinal acceptance, (g) retention of the attitude, (h) retrieval of the attitude at some later time, and then (i) incorporating it into decision making. The input or variables in the model that influence each of the above include source factors (e.g., credibility), message factors (e.g., appeal type), receiver factors (e.g., audience characteristics), and channel factors (e.g., media). Conceivably, each input variable could have a different effect on each of the output variables, and the joint influence of multiple input variables can be complex. There is a vast literature on this input/output framework and its implications for structuring persuasive efforts (see McGuire 1969, 1985 for reviews of this literature). We briefly highlight some major trends in this research, fully recognizing that our statements are general considerations that might not hold in any one particular persuasive situation.

Source Factors

Major categories of source factors include the concepts of expertise and trustworthiness. Expertise refers to knowledge, expert status, and familiarity with the topic. Trustworthiness refers to sincerity, honesty, and good intentions. A summary of studies examining the effects of variations in expertise indicate that, in most cases, higher levels of expertise are associated with higher levels of persuasion (e.g., Eagly, Wood, & Chaiken, 1978; Harmon & Coney, 1982; McGuire, 1985; but see Aronson, Willerman, & Floyd, 1966, for exceptions). Several factors contribute to the perception of source expertise. First, perceived source expertise tends to increase with general knowledge cues, such as education level, social status, and professional attainment (e.g., Hass, 1981). Second, it has been found that the more attractive the source, the more expert he or she is likely to be perceived to be (e.g., Dion & Stein, 1978; but see McGuire, 1983). Third, the more similar the source is perceived to be to the receiver, the more expert the source will be perceived to be (e.g., Stoneman & Brody, 1981). Fourth, there is a tendency to perceive males as being more expert than females (e.g., Broverman, Broverman, Vogel, Clarkson, & Rosenkrantz, 1972; see also Mayo & Henley, 1981). Fifth, the perception of expertise is adversely affected by the source taking a position on an issue that is highly discrepant from that of the receiver; moderate levels of discrepancy seem optimal (e.g., Insko, Murashima, & Saiyadain, 1966). Finally, nonverbal cues can affect perceptions of source expertise. These include (a) auditory cues (e.g., perceived source expertise is adversely affected by high pitch (Ekman & Friesen, 1974), long latencies in answering questions (Harrison, Hwalek, Raney, & Fritz, 1978), slowness of speech (Miller, Maruyama, Beaber, & Valone, 1976), signs of nervousness, and the use of very formal grammar); (b) kinetic cues (e.g., eye contact that is atypically low or atypically high adversely affects perceptions of expertise (Exline, 1972); and (c) dress and hair styles (e.g., Harris et al., 1983). Taken together, this body of literature suggests that perceptions of source expertise can be enhanced by presenting the relevant credentials of the source; using a source who is attractive, familiar with the topic, and similar to the target population; having the source speak at a slightly faster-than-average rate, taking a position that is only moderately discrepant from that of the audience; and having the source dress appropriately, make good eye contact with the audience, and exhibit few signs of nervousness. Research has also suggested that credibility cues have more impact when they are presented early in the persuasive context, prior to the presentation of message arguments (e.g., Ward & Mc-Ginnies, 1974).

Several studies have examined factors that influence perceptions of trustworthiness. One major determinant is the extent to which the source is perceived as having a vested interest in the position he or she is taking. In general, the less the perceived vested interest, the more trustworthy the source is perceived. For example, if a car salesman tells an individual that a particular car on his lot is not very good (hence, arguing against his vested interest), the customer will tend to perceive that salesman as being trustworthy. A second factor that influences trustworthiness is the social position of the source. Research suggests that scientific, medical, and academic groups are more trusted than military, police, and judicial groups, who, in turn, are more trusted than business and media leaders (e.g.,

Etzioni & Diprete, 1979). A third factor that influences perceived trustworthiness is the extent to which the source is liked. In general, we tend to trust people whom we like or with whom we become friendly. Liking of a source is influenced by numerous factors, including perceived similarity, attractiveness, and nonverbal cues (e.g., posturing—McGinley, LeFevre, & McGinley, 1975; eye contact and eye blinks—Cutrow, Parks, Lucas, & Thomas, 1972). Thus, trustworthiness can be increased by minimizing self-interests and engaging in activities that will foster liking and friendship.

Sources may also be more effective in persuasive situations if they are perceived as being powerful (McGuire, 1985). Factors that influence perceived power include perceptions of the source's control over reinforcements (e.g., Axelrod & Aspeche, 1982; Michener & Burt, 1975), the source's concern with compliance (e.g., Gaes & Tedeschi, 1978), and the source's ability to scrutinize compliance (e.g., Heilman, 1976).

Message Factors

Psychological research on message factors has focused on types of arguments and appeals, message style, inclusions and omissions from messages, the amount of message material, the ordering of message contents, and the extremity of the position urged. In terms of types of arguments, Reynolds and Burgoon (1983) have presented a typology of arguments used in persuasive messages, as have Capaldi (1979) and Perelman (1982). Studies on fear arousal suggest that negative appeals (e.g., fear) seem to have an immediate impact on attitudes; however, if they are too strong, they may result in rejection of the message (McGuire, 1968). On the other hand, positive appeals frequently result in longer retention and consistency of behavioral compliance (Beck, 1979). Studies examining style have indicated that a clear, moderately forceful presentation that also varies in speed will be influential (Eagly, 1974). Research from both the marketing and psychological literature have found that humor can be beneficial for attention and retention, as long as it is related to the persuasive position (e.g., Kaplan & Pascoe, 1977; Ogilvy & Raphaelson, 1982). Ordering studies have focused on opening with the strongest argument versus leading up to the best argument. Theoretically, a stronger argument may make weaker arguments more acceptable (e.g., linearity effects; see Anderson, 1981), or stronger arguments may be more acceptable following weaker arguments (e.g., foot-in-the-door/reciprocal concessions). Results are mixed, indicating that the two orders of presentation seem to be equally effective (e.g., McGuire, 1985). Finally, research findings are mixed concerning the optimal amount of information (e.g., Becker & Doolittle, 1975; Cook & Wadsworth, 1972). It appears that repetition in arguments may aid retention and attitude change, but they are inconsistent in affecting compliance.

Social action programmers have utilized a wide variety of message-based strategies when attempting to induce change. One common strategy used in underdeveloped countries is that of melding new concepts with existing folklore and knowledge systems. For example, Niehoff (1966, p. 108) describes this strategy in connection with the failure of a medical program in an African village. Villagers were completely unfamiliar with germ theories of disease and instead tended to attribute sickness to spirits. Attempts to explain the source of a common disease (caused by the tsetse fly of a nearby river) in terms of germ theory were unsuccessful. As an alternative strategy, the change agents might have suggested that the spirits were in the flies, thereby adapting a new idea to an old belief.

A second strategy has focused on attribution-based approaches. This approach emphasizes the manipulation of the individual's self-concept. For example, instead of presenting rational arguments about the disadvantages of drunk driving, the message might focus on such themes as "responsible people don't drive drunk" or "people who are concerned and sensitive to others won't drive drunk." Research has suggested that attributional approaches may be more effective than "rational," argument-based approaches for inducing long-term behavioral change (McGuire, 1985).

There also exists a large body of research on compliance-inducing strategies (see Cialdini, 1984). This includes evaluation of the utility of inducing small levels of compliance first, before requesting larger levels of commitment and effort, and the framing of compliance requests in such a way as to make them appear to involve relatively lower levels of effort and commitment.

Receiver Factors

Research with receiver factors has focused on examining individual differences in influenceability and compliance using demographic predictors (e.g., age, gender), personality predictors (e.g., self-esteem), and behavioral predictors (e.g., activity). Studies examining age indicate that influenceablity and conformity reach their maximum around 9 or 12, followed by a decrease inversely related to age increments (e.g., Ward & McGinnies, 1974). The majority of studies examining gender have indicated that females tend to be more influenceable (e.g., Eagly & Carli, 1981; McGuire, 1969). For example, females tend to be more swayed by reciprocity appeals (e.g., Fink *et al.,* 1975) and find conformity to be a positive virtue (e.g., Santee & Jackson, 1982). Research examining personality predictors has found that high chronic low self-esteem individuals are more easily influenced than their low chronic low self-esteem counterparts (e.g., Deaux, 1972). Intelligence has been found to be curvilinearly related to persuasive success, with moderately intelligent individuals exhibiting the greatest amount of attitude change. Finally, studies have found individuals who take an active role in the persuasive process (e.g., recitation or counterattitudinal advocacy) to be more easily influenced than passive individuals (e.g., Hovland, 1951; Wicklund & Brehm, 1976). Such audience factors might be taken into consideration when evaluating the probability of program success on different segments of the target population.

One of the most powerful predictors of persuasion in our research program has been the "persuasive mind-set" of the individual. We have found that individuals tend to approach discussions with others in either a "debate mind-set" or a "learning mind-set." In the debate mind-set, people feel they must defend their position or attitude, and consequently, they attempt to counterargue the arguments presented by the change agent. In the learning mind-set, people are oriented toward learning something new in the spirit of information exchange. Two individuals may be exposed to the identical persuasive message yet have different orientations in terms of the type of mind-set. Individuals in the "debate" mode will generally be unyielding and difficult to persuade. Individuals in the "learning" mode will be much more open to change, because they do not feel their beliefs are being attacked (rather they are being "explored" in a mutual learning environment). It is possible to structure persuasive appeals so as to induce a learning mind-set as opposed to a debate mind-set, and we have found that this has a dramatic effect on the effectiveness of the persuasive attempt.

Channel Factors

Channel factors refer to the medium used to convey a message. In terms of mass media, the major mechanisms of information transmission are newspapers, magazines, radios, television sets, and books. Newspapers reach about 140 million Americans each day (Hiebert, Ungurait, & Bohn, 1982; Standard Rates and Data Service, 1987). The average reader picks up a newspaper approximately 1.9 times a day and reads 1.2 different papers daily (Hiebert *et al.*, 1982). Statistics from the Newspaper Advertising Bureau (Bogart, 1980) indicate that readership is equally distributed among categories of gender, age (18 years old and upward), education, family income, race, and mobility. Magazines also are utilized by a substantial portion of the American population. Estimates suggest that 9 out of 10 adults read approximately seven magazines monthly (Sandage, Fryburger, & Rotzoll, 1979). Unlike newspapers however, most individuals do not read a magazine in a single sitting. The average magazine is read by 3.8 adults (*Magazine Newsletter of Research*, 1982). Thus, magazine advertisements have greater longevity relative to those found in newspapers. The average magazine reader is 34 years old, married, living in the suburbs, a high school graduate, and above average in family income (Hiebert et al., 1982). However, as evidenced by the large variety of topics in print, interests vary considerably. Magazines are an economical medium because of their predictable (i.e., homogeneous) readership.

In terms of radio, the average American household has approximately 5.7 radios (*Radio Facts*, 1981) and spends about 3 hours per day listening to the radio. This estimate is fairly consistent across categories of gender, age, education, income, and household size (*Radio Facts*, 1981). The major time blocks for reaching the largest audiences, ordered from best to worst, are the a.m. and p.m. drive times (e.g., 5:30 a.m.–10:00 a.m. and 3:00 p.m.—7:00 p.m.; largest audience and most heterogeneous), followed by weekend day (e.g., 10:00 a.m.–7:00 p.m.), evening (7:00 p.m.–12:00 midnight), and overnight (12:00 midnight–5:30 a.m.).

Research examining the extent of television viewing indicates that 98% of all homes in the United States have television (Kalter, 1987), the average number of television sets per household is approximately 2.4 (Poltrack, 1983), and the average family watches television between 6 and 7 hours per day (Kalter, 1987). The variety of programs on television is considerable. The top seven markets, based on Arbitron estimates of audience size, are New York City, Los Angeles, Chicago, Philadelphia, San Francisco, Boston, and Detroit (*TV and Cable Factbook,* 1986). The time slots based on estimates of audience size and composition ranging from best to worst are: 8:00 p.m. to 11:00 p.m. (e.g., large size, heterogeneous), 7:00 a.m. to 5:00 p.m. (e.g., moderate size, women and children's programming), weekend 7:00 a.m. to 5:00 p.m. (e.g., moderate size, children's shows, sports, religious), 5:00 p.m. to 8:00 p.m. and 11:00 p.m. to 1:00 a.m. (e.g., moderate size, news programming, variety, films). Research examining background characteristics indicates that females, 18 years of age and older, are the most common viewers, followed by males within the same age range, children ages 2 to 12, and teenagers (Poltrack, 1983). However, these rankings interact with program scheduling. On weekend mornings, children are the most common viewers, followed by men, women, and teenagers. On weekend afternoons, men are the most common viewers, followed by women, children, and teenagers. Finally, late at night, women are the most common viewers, followed by men, teenagers, and children (Poltrack, 1983).

Of course, there are media other than those discussed here through which a target audience can be reached. For example, part of our drunk driving research is aimed at developing educational materials that will be included in high school health textbooks. Dissemination of information in the context of our research on birth control is aimed at person-to-person interactions between staff members at family planning clinics and clients. For more widespread programs, person-to-person strategies usually focus on opinion leaders as the target population. The assumption is that changes in leaders will "filter through" to produce changes in followers. Issues of identifying opinion leaders and just who should convey the message to these opinion leaders has been the subject of considerable research. Materials can also be distributed through the mail as well as during special seminars and tutorials (e.g., as is the case with parent education programs about teen birth control use). Matching the medium to the message and the target audience is crucial when designing social action programs.

Environmental Manipulation

Environmental manipulation strategies involve the formal alteration of structural features of the environment so as to affect the behavioral alternatives that are available to the individual. The approach is well illustrated in the context of server intervention strategies as a way of combating drunk driving. The assumption is that drunk driving can be reduced if appropriate changes in the environment are made to discourage the access to alcohol of individuals who are likely to drive while drunk or to provide such individuals with alternatives to driving. Server intervention strategies for bars or taverns involve at least two levels. The first is the owner/manager level, in which the owner of a bar or tavern is encouraged to adopt policies that either discourage excessive consumption of alcohol or lower the probability that someone will drive while intoxicated. This would include such policies as the availability of nonalcoholic beverages, the club remaining open for 1 hour after bar sales stop, beer being sold in glasses or mugs as opposed to pitchers, elimination of ''happy hours,'' and providing free transportation home if a person is judged to be too intoxicated to drive. The second level is that of the server/bartender, in which the server is encouraged to estimate the intoxication level of a customer and intervene or refuse further service if the customer is assumed to be too drunk to drive (see Geller, this volume).

Additional environmental manipulation strategies for reducing the adverse consequences of drunk driving include law enforcement efforts, such as sobriety checks. Automobile manufacturers could reduce both the number and severity of drunk driving accidents by making automobiles more safe in general. This may result in reduced profits, but the social benefits outweigh the monetary gains. Better public transportation systems could also help provide individuals with more viable options to that of driving while drunk. Finally, improvements in roadway markings and visibility might also reduce the number of accidents due to drunk driving.

Both the environmental manipulation and persuasive communication intervention strategies are designed to affect one or more of the behavioral determinants underlying social problem. There has been considerable debate about which approach is more effective. It is our belief that neither approach is *a priori* superior to the other. Both have their strengths and limitations. The effectiveness of each will depend in large part on the parameters of the problem at hand. We are convinced, however, that both types of interventions must be guided by a strong theory of underlying behavioral determinants in order to be effective. Thus, both environmental manipulations and persuasive communications probably will have little effect if they are not responsive to the way in which the individual construes the target behavior. We have found the behavioral decision making framework described earlier to be most useful in conceptualizing both environmental-based and persuasive communication-based intervention strategies.

Intervention strategies are frequently categorized in terms of the extent to which they involve coercion (i.e., making people do something they do not want to do, or depriving them from doing something they want to do). At one extreme, the intervention is viewed as being purely facilitative in that it helps individuals perform behaviors and attain goals that they are actively seeking. At the other extreme, a behavior is imposed on people against their will, with little effort at conveying the costs and benefits of the behavior. Even persuasive messages can be viewed as being coercive, when they distort facts and lead people to focus on only narrowly defined aspects of the issue.

The Broader Context

Persuasive strategies and environmental manipulations that guide social action programs occur in the broader context of a cultural system. The nature of this system must be considered to design effective change strategies. Cultural systems include, among other things, knowledge and value systems and a social/political structure. What might seem logical and straightforward to the change agent might be quite illogical from the perspective of the target individual, given the individual's knowledge/value system. For example, in a village in Bolivia, attempts were made by medical doctors to introduce preventive health practices. However, the villagers viewed the function of a "healer" or "doctor" as that of someone who cures the sick. They did not understand why those who appeared to be healthy should be subject to "medical treatment" and behaviors (e.g., obtaining vaccinations), which they believed bordered on the level of molestation (Schweng, 1962).

By the same token, individual behavior evolves in the context of friendship, community, societal, and political structures. To attempt interventions without considering such a context is questionable. For example, it is evident in our development of drunk driving programs that American society is "car-oriented." The private use of automobiles is deeply intertwined with American life and serves vital societal functions for vast numbers of people. This includes such functions as transportation to and from jobs, recreational use, maintaining contact with friends and relatives, not to mention the economic impact of producing and marketing automobiles. The car is a fixture of American society, and the tendency for people is to drive their cars, even when they may be intoxicated. This societal structure places limits on the types of solutions that can be considered when addressing the problem of drunk driving. For example, it may be unreasonable to expect that encouraging individuals through persuasive messages to use public transportation as an alternative to drunk driving will be very effective (except, perhaps, in cities that have extensive and affordable public transportation systems).

The importance of context is well illustrated in an analogy by Niehoff (1966): "The social engineer . . . can be compared to an engineer concerned with building bridges, who certainly must know the problems of stress and the nature of steel. But an engineer must also be aware of the environment in which he constructs his bridges. . . . Intense cold will contract his steel and intense heat will expand it. In a comparable sense, though the [social scientist] . . . must know the techniques of his trade, he also must know something about the environment in which he is working. And primarily this is the cultural system of the people among whom he is working. This cannot safely be assumed to be the same cultural system of the adviser, any more than the physical conditions for building a bridge in a temperate climate can be assumed to be the same as in the arctic or in the tropics'' (p. 5).

Intervention Timing

In addition to the cultural context, attempts to manipulate behavioral determinants should include consideration of the timing of the intervention. Intervention timing refers to the introduction of the program at an opportune time in relation to special circumstances or events. The timing of an intervention can either facilitate or detract from its effectiveness.

Evaluation of the Program

The final step in the design of social action programs is evaluation. Two questions are crucial to answer in this regard: (1) Was the program successful, and (2) if not, why not? A large body of literature on evaluation research has provided guidelines for program evaluation design as well as assessing program utility in terms of its impact and efficiency (e.g., Rossi & Freeman, 1982; Rutman, 1977; Weiss, 1972; see also Ball, 1981; Bickman, 1987). A major difficulty with evaluating program impact is that failure to observe significant impact may be due either to program failure or to faulty evaluation design. In terms of the former, the framework proposed in this chapter may shed insights into why programs are unsuccessful. Specifically, a program may be "unsuccessful" because of failure at any one of the five preceding steps outlined for designing social action programs: (1) specification of program goals, (2) identification of the target population, (3) behavioral analysis, (4) isolation of behavioral determinants, and (5) changing behavioral determinants. In terms of specification of program goals, a social action program may be "unsuccessful" if the initiators of the program have failed to consider issues raised in the context of social ethics and value systems. For example, although a program may effectively produce the intended consequences of the program initiators, it may also produce unintended consequences that subvert certain values basic to the adjustment of the target population. Or the social problem may be conceptualized by the change agent in a fashion that is counter to the cultural context of the target population. Program evaluation must, therefore, consider the nature of the program's objectives.

A social action program might also be ineffective if procedures for identifying the target population are inadequate. As noted earlier, many health education programs require identification of high-risk individuals early, before the onset of illness that results from behavioral deficiencies. If such identification procedures are not available, or are inadequate, a social action program cannot be expected to be effective.

A third source of error in the design of social action programs is the identification of specific behaviors to change and the mapping of these behaviors onto the program objectives. Obviously, if a program has focused its change efforts on behaviors that are irrelevant to the program objectives, it can hardly be said to be successful.

A fourth source of error in designing social action programs concerns the isolation of behavioral determinants or the specification of those variables one should attempt to change. It is here that formal theories of social behavior can be of particular use. Suppose a program was designed to increase blood donations at an upcoming blood drive. Suppose further that a campaign was initiated to convince people that donating blood would help others and, hence, they should donate blood at the upcoming drive. Finally, suppose that this campaign was "ineffective" in that increases in blood donating behavior were not observed. A useful feature of the theories discussed in this chapter is that they provide a framework for understanding why this campaign was ineffective. For example, from the decision-analytic framework, it is clear that the program initiators are making a number of assumptions: (1) The belief that "donating blood would help others" is related to the persons' attitudes toward donating blood at the upcoming drive; (2) increases in this belief will therefore increase persons' intention to donate blood at the upcoming drive (by influencing the attitude and making it the most positive of the two alternatives); and (3) this decision will manifest itself in behavior—namely, people actually going to the blood bank and donating blood. From this perspective, a program may be completely "effective" in that it may indeed change the belief it was intended to change (i.e., donating blood will help others). It may be unsuccessful, however, in that the resulting assumptions made by the programmers may not be correct. Thus, this belief may not have any impact on the attitude and, hence, may be irrelevant to the behavior under consideration. Or, alternatively, the belief may, in fact, change the attitude but not influence the behavioral decision because the attitude associated with donating blood did not exceed the attitude toward not donating blood. Or, the belief may lead to a change in the attitude and, in turn, the behavioral decision, but not influence behavior because of some factor that is affecting the decision–behavior relation. A useful feature of applying a theoretical framework to program evaluation is that it allows the change agent to pinpoint where the program is making a faulty assumption. Once this has been done, procedures can be instituted to rectify the situation.

Finally, a program may be unsuccessful because it has failed to actually change the target beliefs in question (independent of assumptions that changes in this belief will lead to changes in behavior). At this point, an analysis of the persuasive strategies used in the program must be reexamined (McGuire, 1969).

Conclusions

We have outlined a framework for designing social action programs that we have found to be useful within the limited domains of the prevention of drunk driving and the prevention of unintended pregnancies. Because of space constraints, we have described this approach in somewhat general terms. The framework underscores the importance of utilizing strong theory when considering social action programs. Theories can help us better formulate program objectives, understand why people behave as they do, and design and evaluate specific intervention strategies. In this regard, we believe that social psychology has much to offer for purposes of alleviating significant social problems.

References

Abelson, R., & Levi, A. (1985). Decision making and decision theory. In G. Lindzey & E. Aronson (Eds.), *Handbook of social psychology.* New York: Random House.

Ajzen, I., & Fishbein, M. (1980). *Understanding attitudes and predicting social behavior.* Englewood Cliffs, N.J.: Prentice-Hall.

Anderson, N. H. (1981). *Foundations of information integration theory.* New York: Academic Press.

Anderson, N. H. (1982). *Methods of information integration theory.* New York: Academic Press.

Aronson, E., Willerman, B., & Floyd, J. (1966). The effect of a pratfall on increasing interpersonal attraction. *Psychonomic Science, 4,* 227–228.

Axelrod, S., & Aspeche, J. (1982). *The effects of punishment on human behavior.* New York: Academic Press.

Baldwin, W. (1987). Report of the DSBS Branch of the Center for Population Research. National Institute of Health, Bethesda, Maryland.

Ball, S. (1981). *New directions for program evaluation: Assessing and interpreting outcomes.* San Francisco: Jossey-Bass.

Bearden, W. O., Teel, J. E., & Durand, R. M. (1978). Media usage, psychographic, and demographic dimensions of retail shoppers. *Journal of Retailing, 54,* 65–74.

Beck, K. H. (1979). The effects of positive and negative arousal upon attitudes, belief acceptance, behavioral intention, and behavior. *Journal of Social Psychology, 107,* 239–251.

Becker, L. B., & Doolittle, J. C. (1975). How repetition effects evaluation and information seeking about candidates. *Journalism Quarterly, 52,* 611–617.

Bickman, L. (1987). *New directions for program evaluation: Using program theory in evaluations.* San Francisco: Jossey-Bass.

Bogart, L. (1980). *Children, mothers, and newspapers: Newspaper readership project.* New York: Newspaper Advertising Bureau.

Boyd, H. W., Westfall, R., & Stand, S. F. (1986). *Marketing research: Text and cases.* Homewood, IL: Irwin.

Broverman, I. K., Vogel, S. R., Broverman, D. M., Clarkson, F. E., & Rosenkrantz, P. S., (1972). Sex role stereotypes: A current appraisal. *Journal of Sociological Issues, 28*(2), 59–78.

Buck, R. (1985). Prime theory: An integrated view of motivation and emotion. *Psychological Review, 92,* 389–413.

Byrne, D. (1971). *The attraction paradigm.* New York: Academic Press.

Calder, B. J. (1977). Focus groups and the nature of qualitative marketing research. *Journal of Marketing Research, 14,* 353–364.

Campbell, J. P. (1967). *Cross-validation revisited.* Paper presented at the Midwestern Psychological Association, Chicago.

Capaldi, N. (1979). *The art of deception* (2nd ed.). Buffalo, NY: Prometheus.

Cialdini, R. B. (1984). *Influence: How and why people agree to things.* New York: Morrow.

Cleary, H. P. (1972). Health education and health behavior. *Health Education Monographs, 31,* 29–37.

Cook, T. D., & Wadsworth, A. (1981). Attitude change and paired-associates learning of minimal cognitive elements. *Journal of Personality, 40,* 50–61.

Cook, R. D., & Weisberg, S. (1983) *Residuals and influence in regression.* New York: Chapman and Hall.

Cotter, K., & Raju, N. (1982). An evaluation of formula based population squared cross validity estimates and factor estimates in prediction. *Educational and Psychological Measurement, 42,* 493–503.

Cutrow, R. J., Parks, A., Lucas, N., & Thomas, K. (1972). The objective use of multiple physiological indices in the detection of deception. *Psychophysiology, 9,* 578–588.

Daly, E. M., Lancee, W. J., & Polivy, J. (1983). A concial model for the taxonomy of emotional experience. *Journal of Personality and Social Psychology, 45,* 443–457.

Darlington, R. B. (1968). Multiple regression in psychological research and practice. *Psychological Bulletin, 69,* 161–182.

Davidson, A. R., & Jaccard, J. (1979). Variables that moderate the attitude–behavior relation: Results of a longitudinal study. *Journal of Personality and Social Psychology, 37,* 1364–1376.

Dawes, R. A. (1962). A note on base rates and psychometric efficiency. *Journal of Consulting Psychology, 26,* 422–424.

Deaux, K. (1972). Anticipatory attitude change: A direct test of the self-esteem hypothesis. *Journal of Experimental Social Psychology, 8,* 143–155.

Dickson, P. R., & Ginter, J. L. (1987). Market segmentation, product differentiation, and marketing strategy. *Journal of Marketing, 51,* 1–10.

Dillon, W. R., & Goldstein, M. (1981). *Multivariate analysis: Methods and applications.* New York: Wiley.

Dion, K. K., & Stein, S. (1978). Physical attractiveness and interpersonal attraction. *Journal of Experimental Social Psychology, 14,* 97–108.

Donovan, D. M., & Marlett, G. A. (1982). Personality subtypes among driving-while-intoxicated offenders: Relationships to drinking behavior and driving risk. *Journal of Consulting and Clinical Psychology, 50,* 241–249.

Eagly, A. H. (1974). Comprehensibility of persuasive arguments as a determinant of opinion change. *Journal of Personality and Social Psychology, 29,* 758–773.

Eagly, A. H., & Carli, L. L. (1981). Sex of researchers and sex typed communications as determinants of sex differences in influencibility: A meta analysis of social influence studies. *Psychological Bulletin, 90,* 1–20.

Eagly, A. H., Wood, W., & Chaiken, S. (1978). Causal inferences about communicators and their effect on opinion change. *Journal of Personality and Social Psychology, 40,* 384–394.

Ekman, P., & Friesen, W. F. (1974). Detecting deception from the body or face. *Journal of Personality and Social Psychology, 29,* 288–298.

Epstein, S. (1979). The stability of behavior: I. On predicting most of the people much of the time. *Journal of Personality and Social Psychology, 37,* 1097–1126.

Etzioni, A., & Diprete, T. A. (1979). The decline in confidence in America: The prime factor, a research note. *Journal of Applied Behavioral Science, 15,* 520–526.

Exline, R. V. (1972). Visual interaction: The glances of power and preference. In J. K. Cole (Ed.), *Nebraska symposium on motivation, 1971* (pp. 163–206). Lincoln: University of Nebraska Press.

Faden, V., & Bobko, P. (1982). Validity shrinkage in ridge regression: A simulation study. *Educational and Psychological Measurement, 42,* 73–83.

Fern, E. F. (1982). The use of focus groups for idea generation: The effects of group size, acquaintanceship, and moderator on response quantity and quality. *Journal of Marketing Research, 19,* 1–13.

Fink, E. L., Rey, L. D., Johnson, K. W., Spenner, K. I., Morton, D. R., & Flores, E. T. (1975). The effects of family occupation type, sex, and appeal on helping behavior. *Journal of Experimental Social Psychology, 11,* 43–52.

Fishbein, M. (1972). Toward an understanding of family planning behavior. *Journal of Applied Social Psychology, 22,* 214–227.

Fishbein, M., & Ajzen, I. (1974). Attitudes towards objects as predictors of single and multiple behavioral criteria. *Psychological Review, 81,* 59–74.

Fishbein, M., & Ajzen, I. (1975). *Attitude, intention, and behavior: An introduction to theory and research.* Reading, MA: Addison-Wesley.

Frank, R., Massy, W., & Wind, Y. (1972). *Market segmentation.* Englewood Cliffs, NJ: Prentice-Hall.

Gaes, G. G., & Tedeschi, J. T. (1978). An evaluation of self-esteem and impression management theories of anticipatory belief change. *Journal of Experimental Social Psychology, 14,* 579–587.

Green, P. (1977). A new approach to market segmentation. *Business Horizons, 20,* 61–73.

Gropp, M. M. (1980). *Magazine newsletter of research.* New York: Magazine Publishers Association.

Harmon, R. R., & Cooney, K. A. (1982). The persuasive effects of source credibility in buy and lease situations. *Journal of Marketing Research, 19,* 255–260.

Harris, M. B., James, J., Chavez, J., Fuller, M. L., Kent, S., Massanari, C., & Walsh, F. (1983). Clothing: Communication, compliance and choice. *Journal of Applied Social Psychology, 13,* 88–97.

Harrison, A. A., Hwalek, M., Raney, D. F., & Fritz, J. G. (1978). Cues to deception in an interview situation. *Social Psychology, 41,* 156–161.

Hass, R. G. (1981). Effects of source characteristics on cognitive responses and persuasion. In R. E. Petty, T. M. Ostrom, & T. C. Brock (Eds.), *Cognitive responses in persuasion.* Hillsdale, NJ: Erlbaum.

Heilman, M. E. (1976). Oppositional behavior as a function of influence attempt, intensity and retaliation threat. *Journal of Personality and Social Psychology, 33,* 574–578.

Herzberg, P. (1969). The parameters of cross-validation. *Psychometrika Monograph, 34.*

Hiebert, R. A., Ungurait, D. F., & Bohn, T. W. (1982). *Mass media III: An introduction to modern communication.* New York: Longman.

Holbrook, M. B., & Holloway, D. V. (1984). Marketing strategy and the structure of aggregate segment-specific, and differential preferences. *Journal of Marketing, 49,* 62–67.

Hovland, C. I. (1951). Human learning and retention. In S. S. Stevens (Ed.), *Handbook of experimental psychology* (pp. 613–689). New York: Wiley.

Huberty, C. J., & Mourad, S. A. (1980). Estimation in multiple correlation prediction. *Educational and Psychological Measurement, 40,* 101–119.

Insko, C. A., Murashima, F., & Saiyadain, M. (1966). Communicator discrepancy, stimulus ambiguity, and influence. *Journal of Personality, 34,* 262–274.

Jaccard, J. (1974). Predicting social behavior from personality traits. *Journal of Research in Personality, 7,* 358–367.

Jaccard, J. (1975). A theoretical analysis of selected factors important to health education strategies. *Health Education Monographs, 3,* 152–146.

Jaccard, J. (1981). Attitudes and behavior: Implications for attitudes toward behavioral alternatives. *Journal of Experimental Social Psychology, 17,* 286–307.

Jaccard, J., & Becker, M. (1985). Attitudes and behavior: An information integration perspective. *Journal of Experimental Social Psychology, 35,* 1–33.

Jaccard, J., & Dittus, P. (1987). *Personality and decision making.* Unpublished manuscript, Department of Psychology, SUNY, Albany.

Jaccard J., Helbig, D., Wan, C. K., Gutman, M., & Kritz, D. (1987). *Individual differences in attitude-behavior consistency: The prediction of contraceptive behavior.* Unpublished manuscript, Department of Psychology, SUNY, Albany.

Jaccard J., & Turrisi, R. (1987). *Sources of birth control information for teenagers.* Unpublished manuscript, Department of Psychology, SUNY, Albany.

Jaccard, J., & Wan, C. K. (1986). Cross-cultural methods for the study of behavioral decision making. *Journal of Cross-Cultural Psychology, 17,* 123–149.

Jaccard, J., & Wan, C. K. (1987). The case for the description utility of optimum strategies in decision making: The role of attitude. Unpublished manuscript, Department of Psychology, SUNY, Albany.

Jaccard, J., & Wood, G. (1986). An idiothetic analysis of behavioral decision making. In D. Brinberg

& R. J. Lutz (Eds.), *Perspectives on methodology in consumer research*. New York: Springer-Verlag.

Janis, I. L., & Mann, L. (1977). *Decision making: A psychological analysis of conflict, choice and commitment*. New York: Free Press.

Kalter, J. (1987). TV guide: More people rely on newspapers than on TV for news. *The Bulletin, 3*, 42–43.

Kaplan, R. M., & Pascoe, G. C. (1977). Humorous lectures and humorous examples: Some effects on comprehension and retention. *Journal of Educational Psychology, 69*, 61–65.

Kelley, H. H., & Thibaut, J. (1978). *Interpersonal relations: A theory of interdependence*. New York: Wiley.

Kerlinger, F., & Pedhazur, E. (1973). *Multiple regression in behavioral research*. New York: Holt, Rinehart & Winston.

Keyes, L. L. (1972). Health education in perspective—An overview. *Health Education Monographs, 31*, 13–17.

Krasner, L., & Ullman, L. (1973). *Behavior influence and personality*. New York: Holt, Rinehart & Winston.

Landesman S., & Jaccard J. (1987). Family structure and decision. In M. Lewis & S. Feinstein (Eds.), *Social influence*. New York: Academic Press.

Mayo, C., & Henley, N. H. (1981). *Gender and nonverbal behavior*. New York: Springer-Verlag.

McCabe, G. P. (1975). Computations for variable selection in the discriminant-regression analysis. *Technometrics, 17*, 103–109.

McGinley, H., LeFevre, R., & McGinley, P. (1975). The influence of a communicator's body position on opinion change in others. *Journal of Personality and Social Psychology, 31*, 686–690.

McGuire, W. J. (1968). Personality and susceptibility to social influence. In E. F. Borgatta & W. W. Lambert (Eds.), *Handbook of personality theory and research*, pp. 140–162). Chicago: Rand McNally.

McGuire, W. J. (1969). The nature of attitudes and attitude change. In G. Lindzey & E. Aronson (Eds.), *Handbook of social psychology* (1st ed.). Reading, MA: Addison-Wesley.

McGuire, W. J. (1983). A contextualist theory of knowledge: Its implications for innovations and reform in psychology research. In L. Berkowitz (Ed.), *Advances in experimental social psychology* (Vol. 16). New York: Academic Press.

McGuire, W. J. (1985). The nature of attitudes and attitude change. In G. Lindzey & E. Aronson (Eds.), *Handbook of social psychology* (3rd ed.). Reading, MA: Addison-Wesley.

Michener, H. A., & Burt, M. R. (1975). Components of "authority" as determinants of compliance. *Journal of Personality and Social Psychology, 31*, 606–614.

Miller, D. W., & Starr, M. K. (1967). *The structure of human decision*. Englewood Cliffs, NJ: Prentice-Hall.

Miller, N. Maruyama, G., Beaber, R., & Valone, K. (1976). Speed of speech and persuasion. *Journal of Personality and Social Psychology, 34*, 615–624.

Mitchell, T. R., Redicker, K. J., & Beach, L. (1986). Image theory and its implications for organizational decision making. In H. Dims & D. Givia (Eds.), *Social cognition in organization*. San Francisco: Jossey-Bass.

Morris, J. D. (1982). Ridge regression and some alternative weighting techniques: A comment on Darlington. *Psychological Bulletin, 91*, 203–210.

Niehoff, A. (1966). *A casebook of social change*. Chicago: Aldine.

Ogilvy, D., & Raphaelson, J. (1982). Research on advertising techniques that work and don't work. *Harvard Business Review, July–August*, 245–262.

Pagel, M., & Lunneberg, C. (1985). Empirical evaluation of ridge regression. *Psychological Bulletin, 97*, 342–355.

Perelman, C. (1982). *The realm of rhetoric*. (W. Kluback, trans.). Notre Dame: University of Notre Dame Press.

Poltrack, D. (1983). *Television marketing*. New York: McGraw-Hill.

Pruzek, R. M., & Frederick, B. C. (1978). Weighting predictors in linear models: Alternatives to least squares and limitations of equal weights. *Psychological Bulletin, 85,* 254–266.

Radio facts. (1981). New York: Radio Advertising Bureau.

Reynolds, R. A., & Burgoon, M. (1983). Belief processing, reasoning, and evidence. In R. N. Bostrom, *Communication yearbook 7* (pp. 83–104). Beverly Hills, CA: Sage.

Rokeach, M. (1968). *Beliefs, attitudes, and values.* San Francisco: Jossey-Bass.

Rosenstock, I. (1974). Historical origins of the health belief model. In M. H. Becker (Ed.), *The health belief model and personal health behaviors.* Englewood Cliffs, NJ: Slack Thorofare.

Rossi, P. H., & Freeman, H. E. (1962). *Evaluation: A systematic approach.* Beverly Hills, CA: Sage.

Rutman, L. (1977). *Evaluation research methods: A basic guide.* Beverly Hills, CA: Sage.

Sampson, E. E., & Insko, C. A. (1984). Cognitive consistency and conformity in the autokinetic situation. *Journal of Personality and Social Psychology, 68,* 184–192.

Sandage, C. H., Fryburger, V., & Rotzoll, K. (1979). *Advertising theory and practice.* Homewood, IL: Richard D. Irwin.

Santee, R. T., & Jackson, S. E. (1982). Identity implications of conformity: Sex differences in normative and attributional judgments. *Journal of Personality and Social Psychology, 42,* 690–700.

Schweng, L. (1962). An Indian community development project in Bolivia. *America Indigena, 22,* 13–19.

Scotton, D. W., & Zallocco, R. L. (1980). *Readings in market segmentation.* Chicago: American Marketing Association.

Simon, H. (1976). *Administrative behavior: A study of decision making process in administrative organization.* New York: Free Press.

Sines, J. O. (1964). Actuarial methods as appropriate strategy for the validation of diagnostic tests. *Psychological Review, 71,* 517–523.

Sines, J. O. (1966). Acturial methods in personality assessment. In B. A. Maher (Ed.), *Progress in experimental personality research.* New York: Academic Press.

Skinner, H. A. (1978). The art of exploring predictor–criterion relationships. *Psychological Bulletin, 85,* 327–337.

Smith, W. (1956). Product differentiation and market segmentation as alternative marketing strategies. *Journal of Marketing, 21,* 3–8.

Standard Rates and Data Service (1987). Newspaper circulation analysis, *68.*

Stoneman, Z., & Brody, G. H. (1981). Peers as mediators of television food advertisement aimed at children. *Developmental Psychology, 17,* 853–858.

TV and cable factbook. (1986). Washington, DC: TV Digest.

Umesh, U.N. (1987). Transferability of preference models across segments and geographic areas. *Journal of Marketing, 51,* 59–70.

Wainer, H. (1978). On the sensitivity of regression and regressors. *Psychological Bulletin, 85,* 267–273.

Ward, C. D., & McGinnies, E. (1974). Persuasive effects of early and late mention of credible and non-credible sources. *Journal of Psychology, 86,* 17–23.

Weinberg, S. L., & Darlington, R. P. (1976). Canonical analysis when the number of variables is large relative to sample size. *Journal of Educational Statistics, 4,* 313–332.

Weis, C. (1972). *Evaluation research: Methods of assessing program effectiveness.* Englewood Cliffs, NJ: Prentice-Hall.

Wicklund, R. A., & Brehm, J. W. (1976). *Perspectives on cognitive dissonance.* Hillsdale, NJ: Erlbaum.

Wiggins, J. S. (1972). *Personality and prediction: Principles of personality assessment.* Englewood Cliffs, NJ: Prentice-Hall.

Wind, Y. (1978). Issues and advances in segmentation research. *Journal of Marketing Research, 25,* 317–337.

Wind, Y., & Silver, S. E. (1972). Segmenting media buyers. *Journal of Advertising Research, 12,* 14–24.

6

Applying a Social Psychological Model across Health Promotion Interventions
Cigarettes to Smokeless Tobacco

Richard I. Evans and Bettye E. Raines

In writing for a previous volume on applied social psychology (Evans, 1980), we used a social influence-focused model related to the prevention of smoking among adolescents as an illustration of a new challenge to social psychologists. In this chapter, we will discuss how social psychologists who are attacking problems in health promotion and disease prevention, employing a social influence orientation, may consider the cross-application of models from well-studied health problems (i.e., cigarette smoking) to emerging health problems (e.g., smokeless tobacco). An exploration of the utility of such crossover conceptualization and strategies is reflected in ongoing programs of research of our Social Psychology/Behavioral Medicine Research Group, which address the use of both of these substances. Although this volume addresses the application of social influence strategies to preventing social problems, we will also be examining the related behavioral and cognitive processes involved in the initiation and prevention, among adolescents, of the use of tobacco.

Smokeless Tobacco as a Health Problem

Before addressing such crossover conceptualization, it might be in order to briefly discuss why smokeless tobacco use is emerging as a major health problem.

Richard I. Evans and Bettye E. Raines • Department of Psychology, University of Houston, Houston, Texas 77204.

This is reflected in a number of recent reports, including that of the Advisory Committee to the Surgeon General (1986), a recent review article by Connolly *et al.* (1986), and a statement from the U.S. surgeon general (Koop, 1986). As health problems, cigarette smoking and smokeless tobacco use share, physiologically, the potentially addictive nicotine component and, socially, availability and acceptability in the youth culture as legitimized and legally sanctioned practices. Because the potential risks of smokeless tobacco are just beginning to be emphasized in health promotion campaigns, its use may be perceived by adolescents as a "safe" alternative to cigarette smoking (Chassin, Presson, Sherman, McLaughlin, & Gioia, 1985). While some recent smokeless tobacco studies (Ary, Lichtenstein, & Severson, 1987; Schinke, Gilchrist, Schilling, & Senechal, 1986) have begun to demonstrate conceptual rigor, the present field reflects primarily incidence data. It seemed important to us to explore the possibility of applying at least some aspects of our smoking prevention social influence model to prevention of the use of smokeless tobacco from the standpoint of both the health risks involved and the reported incidence of use among adolescents (Evans, 1988b).

This chapter will first briefly review current knowledge regarding the health risks associated with smokeless tobacco use. It will then summarize reports of contemporary incidence of use of smokeless tobacco and age of onset, with a particular focus on the relationship between the use of cigarettes and smokeless tobacco. After a brief discussion of some important behavioral and cognitive differences between the use of the two substances, the chapter will explicate our hypotheses concerning the extension of our already developed and applied social psychological model of the initiation of cigarette smoking among adolescents (Figure 1) to the use of smokeless tobacco (Figure 2). Some of these hypotheses are operant in our current process analysis/long-term longitudinal intervention study, which employs a study population of 270 Little League Baseball teams. One component of the study involves major league baseball players serving as "role models" as the investigation proceeds through its various stages.

While epidemiological evidence based on long-term longitudinal investigations is not yet available, as is the case with cigarette smoking, the U.S. Surgeon General's report (Advisory Committee, 1986) on the health consequences of using smokeless tobacco concludes that there is strong scientific evidence linking the use of smokeless tobacco to oral cancer, oral leukoplakias, and nicotine dependence or addiction. Studies related to its impact on the cardiovascular system (e.g., Gritz, Baer-Weiss, Benowitz, Van Vunakis, & Jarvik, 1981; Squires *et al.*, 1984) are not as definitive but suggest that the absorption of nicotine through the buccal tissues results in plasma nicotine concentrations typical of those found in cigarette smokers who inhale. Other serious disorders that have been associated with the use of smokeless tobacco include a higher rate of stillbirths and low birthweight infants among women who are users (Krishna, 1978), neuromuscular disease (Patten, 1984), an peptic ulcer (Benowitz, 1986).

The health risks associated with the use of smokeless tobacco, as with any potentially harmful substance, are related to incidence of use. Over the past de-

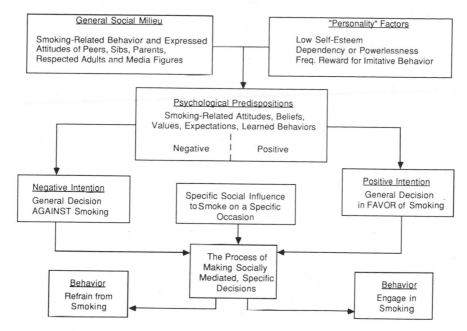

Figure 1. A model of smoking-related social psychological processes affecting behavior.

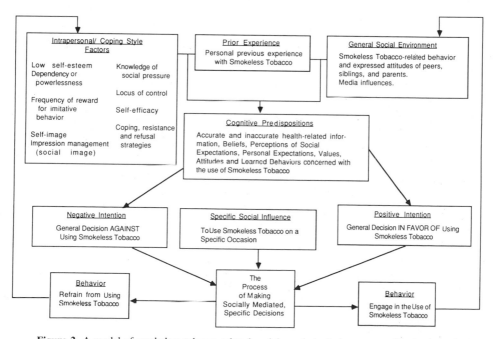

Figure 2. A model of smokeless tobacco-related social psychological processes affecting behavior.

cade, production of fine-cut tobacco used in snuff and chewing tobacco has tripled (Boyd & Associates, 1987), and sales of these products have increased at an average of 11% per year (Dent, Sussman, Johnson, Hansen, & Flay, 1987). A business section report (Harper, 1980) estimated that the number of smokeless tobacco users in the United States may have reached 22 million, or almost 10% of the population.

Incidence data from the 1986 U.S. Surgeon General's report indicate that the highest prevalence of use is among male adolescents and young adults. Several recent surveys (Ary *et al.*, 1987; Dent *et al.*, 1987; Dignan, Block, Steckler, Howard, & Cosby, 1986; Glover, 1986; Lichtenstein, Severson, Friedman, & Ary, 1984; Marty, McDermott, & Williams, 1986; Poulson, Lindenmuth, & Greer, 1984; Schinke, Gilchrist, Schilling, Walker, *et al.*, 1986) report that the percentage of use among male adolescents ranges between 7 and 43%, with wide variations associated with age, geographic location, and race. The rates of use for female adolescents are lower, ranging from 0 to 3%, suggesting that this group may not yet have begun to exhibit the "following" pattern that women have previously demonstrated in cigarette smoking. Among Native American adolescents, however, Schinke, Gilchrist, Schilling, Walker, *et al.* (1986) report equally high usage among boys and girls. Careful study of female adolescent smokeless tobacco users might be useful in understanding the factors that could lead to increased usage among young women.

Regarding age of onset, in a study of 7th- through 12th-graders from 17 schools scattered throughout Texas (Schaefer, Henderson, Glover & Christen, 1985), 55% of male regular users were found to have started at or before age 12. An investigation involving 1500 7th- through 10th-grade males in Oregon (Ary *et al.*, 1987) indicates the mean age of initial experience to be 11.2 years. A study conducted in Wyoming (Gritz, Ksir, & McCarthy, 1985) determined the median age of initiation to be 11 years. Results from a study carried out in rural Ohio (Bonaguro, Pugh, & Bonaguro, 1986) indicate a mean age of 9.5 years for beginning the use of chewing tobacco. The early onset of use reflected in these figures will require investigators concerned with social influence factors to give close attention also to age-related developmental factors. The Houston Group Little League Baseball Study mentioned earlier was designed to take advantage of a naturally occurring cohort of 9-year olds, the entry-level age for Little League baseball teams.

Most significantly, in terms of the focus of the present chapter, evidence has begun to emerge suggesting that the tendency to use smokeless tobacco may be related to the tendency to smoke cigarettes (Severson, 1986), although the results of contemporary investigations appear to differ regarding the precise nature of this relationship (Ary *et al.*, 1987; Hunter *et al.*, 1986; Lichtenstein *et al.*, 1984).

In order to assist in conceptualizing the similarities in the social influence processes underlying the use of cigarettes and smokeless tobacco, it may be useful to consider several behavioral and cognitive differences related to their use.

Behavioral differences include convenience and detectability, duration, and frequency of use. Smokeless tobacco, which requires no sustained use of the hands, may be more convenient to use than cigarettes, particularly during periods of physical activity. This factor has been promoted in the context of ease of use during athletic activity. Its use requires no special paraphernalia such as matches or ashtrays. The fact that smokeless tobacco produces no smoke may be highly significant within the present climate of social sanctions regarding public cigarette smoking. This lack of smoke or strong, identifiable odor may also be significant to adolescents considering whether or not they will be detected in performing the behavior. Duration and frequency of use appear to vary considerably between smokeless tobacco and cigarettes. An individual cigarette burns away in a very brief period of time, whereas empirical data indicates that adult users retain smokeless tobacco in their mouth for approximately 24 minutes per dip/chew (Gritz et al., 1981), with adolescent male users reporting duration ranges of from 10 to 20 minutes (Ary et al., 1987). An investigation among adolescent users (Marty et al., 1986) indicates that 52% of the subjects report using more than three dips/chews per day. Ary and his associates (1987) report an average of 5.3 dips per day among adolescent users.

Cognitive differences between smokeless tobacco use and cigarette smoking include misconceptions regarding smokeless tobacco use and the sources of social influences related to its use. Among adolescents, misconceptions include the belief that the use of smokeless tobacco is a relatively safe alternative to cigarette smoking (Chassin et al., 1985; Schaefer et al., 1985). Lichtenstein and his colleagues (1984) report that only 24% of teenagers in their sample agreed that chewing and smoking are both bad for a person's health. In another study (Schinke, Gilchrist, Schilling, & Senechal, 1986), only 60% of tobacco nonusers, 41% of smokers, and 33% of smokeless tobacco users agreed that smokeless tobacco is harmful to health. Most significantly, Chassin and her associates (1985) present evidence suggesting not only that adolescents perceive smokeless tobacco as less of a health threat than smoking, but that beliefs about the health consequences of smokeless tobacco are related, among nonusers, to the intention to use such products in the future. The revision of our original smoking-related processes model (see Figure 1) includes health-related misconceptions in the process of initiating and maintaining smokeless tobacco use (see Figure 2, Cognitive Predispositions). It should also be considered that unlike the overt influence to smoke cigarettes, which appears to strongly reflect peer pressure (Evans, 1984), overt influences to use smokeless tobacco may also come from adult authority figures, either in media or real-life contexts. For example, in one study (Ary et al., 1987), 19.8% of boys surveyed who had tried smokeless tobacco had received the product from an adult. Regarding more covert influences such as modeling, in the world of athletics some coaches actually use smokeless tobacco. One study (Marty et al., 1986) reports that 6% of high school smokeless tobacco users identified coaches as the primary source of influence to initiate use. Resisting such influences within the context of competitive athletics may require different strategies from those appropriate to resisting pressure from peers.

Social Psychological Influences on Using Smokeless Tobacco

At this point, it might be in order to review the concepts included in our model of smokeless tobacco-related social psychological processes affecting behavior (Figure 2).

General social environment, as related to the decision to engage in a behavior, includes both the relevant behavior and expressed attitudes of peers, siblings, and parents and the images of users that are promoted in the media. Data from a variety of sources (e.g., Evans, Dratt, Raines, & Rosenberg, 1988; Hirschman, Leventhal, & Glynn, 1984; Levitt & Edwards, 1970) support the notion that the behavior and expressed attitudes of significant others (e.g., parents, peers) bear a strong relationship to an individual's initiation of smoking. There is also some evidence suggesting a similar relationship regarding smokeless tobacco use (Ary et al., 1987; Bonaguro et al., 1986; Hunter et al., 1986; Lichtenstein et al., 1984; Marty et al., 1986). For a number of years, Christen and his associates (Christen, 1980; Christen & Swanson, 1983; Glover, Christen, & Henderson, 1982) have been pointing out an intensive media campaign by the tobacco industry aimed at persuading individuals to adopt the practices of dipping snuff and chewing tobacco. Blum's (1983) report of a campaign including endorsements by well-known professional athletes (e.g., major league baseball players) illustrates the advertising tactics that have been used. Ernster (1986) suggests that teenage males are a major target of campaigns that include such endorsements and sponsorship of baseball games on television. At the press conference announcing our Little League Baseball Smokeless Tobacco Prevention Project (Cantwell, 1987), Houston Astros baseball pitcher Nolan Ryan, who serves as chair of our Players' Advisory Committee, recounted how he quit using smokeless tobacco partly because of his awareness of the influence of his example to young people. Although current regulations prevent broadcast media advertising, print advertisement and other forms of promotion, including free product samples, continue to be employed.

The relationships between an adolescent's smokeless tobacco use and influences stemming from the general social environment may be explained conceptually in various ways, of course. One explanation might involve the use of two very widely applicable theories—social learning (Bandura, 1977) and the theory of reasoned action (Ajzen & Fishbein, 1980; Fishbein & Ajzen, 1975). Social learning theory explicates the process through which observation, or vicarious experience, leads to the acquisition of expectations and learned behaviors. In the case of smokeless tobacco, the observation of others' apparently enjoyable use followed by no discernible negative consequences may, through the process of vicarious learning, result in positive expectations toward, and disinhibition of, the behavior. The theory of reasoned action suggests the mechanism through which these expectations, or beliefs, and the expressed attitudes of significant others have an impact on behavior. The theory suggests that these beliefs and the perceptions of attitudes held by significant others regarding an individual's engaging in a specific behavior combine in the form of a personally held attitude and sub-jective norm to produce an intention to behave. The intention is then translated into actual behavior. Support for the application of this theory in developing an understanding of the initiation of smoking behavior comes from a variety of sources (e.g., Chassin *et al.*, 1981). A recent preliminary investigation (Brubaker & Lof-tin, 1987) has provided an indication of the utility of applying the theory of rea-soned action to the study of smokeless tobacco use among early adolescents. Im-plicit in the hypotheses we are testing is the possibility that both social learning theory and the theory of reasoned action can be utilized in the examination of the process leading to the use of smokeless tobacco and to cigarette smoking.

The component of the process model concerning *intrapersonal/coping style factors* that may relate to the decision to engage in a behavior also seems impor-tant to the investigation of the process of becoming a user of smokeless tobacco. Bandura (1977) lists three characteristics that appear to facilitate imitative learn-ing, as discussed above: low self-esteem, dependency or powerlessness, and a history of receiving frequent rewards contingent upon engaging in imitative be-havior. An additional possible link between intrapersonal factors and participation in behaviors such as cigarette smoking and the use of smokeless tobacco is the need for a positive self-image and for effective impression management. Several investigators have pointed to the roles of self-image and impression management in adolescent cigarette smoking (e.g., Barton, Chassin, Presson, & Sherman, 1982; Botvin & Eng, 1980; Leventhal & Cleary, 1980). The possibility of a similar relationship existing in the use of smokeless tobacco will also be explored. Schlenker (1980) states that "given an existing set of beliefs about what images are related to particular appearance cues, people can coordinate and control their . . . props . . . in order to construct specific identities before . . . audiences" (p. 284). He provides the example of projecting a "macho identity" by decorating one's den with guns, gun racks, and mounted animal heads. An adolescent seeking to dis-play a similar "macho image" might choose to do so by using smokeless tobacco or by displaying a distinctive faded snuff-can mark on the rear pocket of his blue jeans whether or not he is an actual user. Other factors subsumed under this com-ponent of the model which are related to the need for a positive self-image and effective impression management, and which may well have an impact on the use of smokeless tobacco, are knowledge of social pressure, coping, resistance and refusal strategies, locus of control, and self-efficacy. These factors will be further explicated in the discussion on specific influences to initiate behaviors.

A third component of the process model, *prior experience,* includes factors such as actual previous experience with the substance in question. Prior experi-ence is likely to contribute to the disinhibition of future behavior. It also provides the opportunity for the individual to experience the physiological effects of the substance. These include, in the case of both cigarettes and smokeless tobacco, a nicotine "rush." As several investigators (e.g., Hirschman *et al.,* 1984) have suggested, future behavior is likely to be influenced in a direction contingent on the way in which such physical reactions are interpreted. These interpretations lead to specific beliefs about the behavior, these beliefs being part of the next component of the model, *cognitive predispositions.*

Cognitive predispositions that may influence the decision of whether or not to engage in a behavior include information (both accurate and inaccurate), beliefs, related attitudes, values, perceptions of social expectations, personal expectations, and learned behaviors, all products of those categories of factors that have previously been discussed. It is at this point in the process that we postulate that the individual forms general intentions regarding whether or not to engage in a specific behavior—in this case, use of smokeless tobacco. In a survey of 230 junior high school students (Evans & Smith, 1980), nonsmokers were found to hold strong negative beliefs, attitudes, and values concerning smoking. These young adolescents appeared to have very strong reasons *not* to smoke. Their classmates who did intend to smoke in the future, however, seemed to have relatively neutral opinions about smoking. These data suggest that only teenagers who are cognitively predisposed to a strong antismoking bias may be successful in maintaining their resistance to influences to smoke. This possibility may be applicable to the relationship between attitudes and behaviors regarding smokeless tobacco. As discussed above, evidence exists suggesting that the intention to use smokeless tobacco is, in part, contingent on beliefs concerning the health consequences of such use (Chassin *et al.*, 1985).

The component of the model that addresses *specific social influence* affecting the decision of whether or not to engage in a behavior is primarily concerned with peer pressure. Christen, McDaniel, and Doran (1979) report retrospective, anecdotal evidence from high school and college student users of smokeless tobacco suggesting that peer pressure is one of the reasons they began to chew tobacco and/or dip snuff. It has been suggested that unless individuals exposed to peer pressure possess knowledge of social-pressure coping and resistance strategies (Evans, 1984), an internal locus of control (Chassin *et al.*, 1981), and a sense of high self-efficacy (Leventhal, Safer, & Panagis, 1983), they are not likely to deal effectively with peer pressure and will engage in the behavior about which they are being pressured. It should be noted that the importance of these factors may vary depending on the developmental stage of the adolescents (Chassin, Presson, Sherman, Corty, & Olshavsky, 1984).

The component of the model that concerns the process of making socially mediated, specific decisions refers to a distinction between general descriptive and mediating process variables (Evans *et al.*, 1988). For example, peer pressure can be a specific, direct social influence to use tobacco or it can be an influence that contributes to a decision to use tobacco that is directly the result of a specific friend offering an individual a cigarette or a chew of smokeless tobacco on a particular occasion.

So far, this chapter has dealt with a rationale for applying a social psychological model we employed in our smoking-prevention research to an emerging health problem, use of smokeless tobacco. Literature on health risks and recent incidence of use data were reviewed in order to convey the extent of the problem. Particular emphasis was placed on evidence suggesting a relationship between smokeless tobacco use and cigarette smoking, a relationship interpreted as indicating that these two behaviors may be seen as functionally equivalent by some adolescents. Prefaced by a discussion of some of the more salient behavioral and cognitive differences between smokeless tobacco use and cigarette smoking, our conceptual model designed to understand the decision to smoke cigarettes was employed as a basis for exploring the decision to use smokeless tobacco. In essence, this chapter is designed to provide a psychosocial-behavioral perspective on the emergence of still another apparently health-threatening behavior among adolescents.

Preventive Strategies

The presentation of such a cognitive-psychosocial-behavioral model of the determinants of the use of smokeless tobacco by adolescents may illustrate how the social psychologist entering the field of behavioral medicine or health psychology may be able to capitalize on the considerable body of existing conceptualizations and findings related to disease prevention research programs. In this instance, it appears that several concepts or techniques that have emerged from the smoking prevention literature might be considered for inclusion in investigations of methods for effectively preventing smokeless tobacco use.

In the area of intrapersonal factors, techniques employed within smoking prevention efforts that directly or indirectly target factors such as self-esteem (Fishbein, Ajzen, & McArdle, 1980) may have an impact on prevention of smokeless tobacco use. In addition, one method that might prove successful in deterring the use of smokeless tobacco is to reinforce the use of other devices for impression management. Addressing this as it concerns cigarette smoking, Leventhal and Cleary (1980) wrote, "It suggests that efforts be made to show that the exciting aspects of the image are illusory and that good health, attractive appearance, neat dress, and not smoking are linked to greater success in sex, greater strength and daring, and so forth" (p. 385). The fact that adolescents may choose between smokeless tobacco use and cigarette smoking as being functionally equivalent may be taken as encouragement that behavioral substitutions may be fairly readily accepted by them, providing that equivalence of the substitute behaviors can be established.

Considering efforts to influence the effects of prior behavior, it has been suggested (Leventhal et al., 1983) that effective interpretations might include targeting those interpretations of physiological reactions which are incorrect and which lead to positive cognitive predispositions toward unhealthy behaviors. For example, if the experience of a nicotine "rush," a state of a feeling mildly euphoric, is construed as a potentially dangerous cardiovascular assault, rather than as a harmlessly pleasant experience, the next component of the model related to cognitive predispositions might be influenced in the desired direction.

Regarding efforts to influence cognitive predispositions, it seems quite clear that persuasive communications may be constructed in order to increase knowledge and to alter positive beliefs, expectations, and attitudes toward use of smokeless tobacco. It is essential to note two things in constructing these communications. First, in order to have a maximal effect on behavior, persuasive communications must be highly specific, focusing on those cognitions that underlie the behavior (Fishbein et al., 1980). Second, unless sensitive to the possibility, these specific communications targeting smokeless tobacco use may deter such use while producing a concomitant increase in smoking. This potential side effect must be vigilantly monitored. In fact, smokeless tobacco use prevention programs should also contain components that are designed to decrease the likelihood of smoking cigarettes. Although, as Lando (1985) points out, prevention programs may have an impact that generalizes across substances, such generalizations cannot be expected from highly specific persuasive communications. Despite these cautions, it should be noted that since the use of smokeless tobacco may be consciously perceived as an alternative to smoking, cognitive persuasion techniques that point out why using smokeless tobacco is not an acceptable alternative to cigarette smoking may be unusually effective in preventing such use.

In addition to the potentially useful techniques discussed above, techniques developed for teaching peer-pressure resistance and refusal skills may also play a role in deterring smokeless tobacco use. Such techniques originated in the context of a ''social inoculation'' concept (Evans, 1976; Evans et al., 1978, 1981). One spin-off of this concept has been the now widely disseminated ''Just Say No'' to peer pressure, part of the refusal training component of ''social inoculation'' (Evans, 1988a). As described in more detail elsewhere (Evans, 1984), inoculation against social influences to smoke is the primary focus of our social inoculation interventions.

To guide the development of our interventions, we found McGuire's (1968) communication-persuasion model to be relevant. This model analyzes the impact of communications according to five components: attention, comprehension, acceptance, retention, and action. It is obvious that, to be effective, a communication must hold the person's attention and be understandable to that person. In addition, the communication must elicit acceptance on the part of the person exposed to the message. Induced acceptance must be maintained over time (retention) for it to be translated into action in appropriate situations.

Various elements of the social inoculation filmed messages we produced address problems of attention, comprehension, and acceptance (Evans, Smith, & Raines, 1984). First, instead of adults, adolescent narrators present scientific information. In keeping with their role as information brokers, however, these student narrators make no claim to having scientific expertise of their own. Thus, such phrases as ''the researchers asked me to tell you . . .'' and ''the researchers found that . . .'' are included at appropriate points.

Second, much of the content of the films and discussions dealing with social influences to smoke and with strategies for coping with these influences is based on data from students who are similar to those in the audience (Evans, Raines, & Hanselka, 1984). Most of the footage in the films shows students acting out situations that their peers have described to us in preintervention surveys and focused group interviews. Our process evaluation suggests that these scenes and situations are perceived by the student audience as realistic.

Third, the messages in the films and the discussions that follow them are presented in a manner directed toward reinforcing self-attributions or the ability of the members of the audience to self-determine their decision whether or not to smoke. The student narrators repeatedly tell the audience, "You can decide for yourself," "Knowing these facts might help you to decide," and "Here's something you might want to think about." Process evaluations have indicated that the student audiences are favorably impressed by this self-attributional aspect of the films and discussions.

In addition to tailoring our intervention to the model, as suggested above, our "social inoculation" strategy may be described as a behavioral variation of McGuire's (1961) congnitive inoculation approach to attitude change. McGuire suggests that existing attitudes may be strengthened by inoculating individuals against counterarguments to which they might be exposed. By explicating the nature of various social influences to smoke, our intervention program attempts to inoculate the audience against these influences. Further, we suggest to the students specific strategies that they might use to cope with the social influences when they encounter them.

To increase the probability of impact of the social inoculation interventions, information is presented that is intended to motivate the student to develop a *negative* smoking intention—an intention *not* to smoke. Information presented includes the immediate health effects of smoking, the negative social consequences of smoking, and the cost of smoking. A film depicting immediate health effects includes statements of commonly held beliefs about smoking followed by demonstrations that either confirm or refute the accuracy of these beliefs. Another message attempts to increase students' awareness of the dangers of experimental smoking.

Prior to the presentation of the social inoculation messages, other messages familiarized the students with various social influences to smoke. Three social influences were defined in our pilot study (Evans *et al.,* 1978)—modeling, peer pressure, and cigarette advertising—and scenes representing examples of each of these influences were presented. During further investigations, we have incorporated adult nagging, since responses in a preintervention survey indicated that this was a more frequently cited factor in adolescent smoking than had previously been apparent. In the case of cigarette advertising, content analyses of ads are used to reveal to students the technique employed by advertisers. When students subsequently encounter a situation in which a social influence to smoke is present, they will be better able to recognize that social influence consciously and to understand how it operates. This recognition and understanding might well enable the student to make a specific decision that is based more on personal intention than on the demands of the particular situation. Throughout the films and the classroom discussions that follow their screening, the students are encouraged to make a *conscious* decision about smoking, rather than be swayed by external influences without being sufficiently vigilant concerning the effects of such external influences.

Briefly summarized, the social inoculation consists of the presentation of strategies and skills for coping with social influences to smoke that the students might encounter in the future. Various films depict specific strategies that nonsmoking students indicate they use for coping with peer pressure to smoke. Students are then given the opportunity to role-play peer-pressure situations that they might encounter and to rehearse ways of coping with them.

Variations of this social influence-centered approach have subsequently been developed and evaluated by several other investigators (Flay, 1985) and do appear to be effective components of programs designed to prevent cigarette smoking in adolescents. The similarities between social pressures to smoke cigarettes and pressures to use smokeless tobacco could lead to an adaptation of this social inoculation or "refusal training strategy" to programs designed to prevent the use of smokeless tobacco. Some support for the efficacy of this approach in affecting smokeless tobacco use has been provided in the investigations of Schinke, Gilchrist, Schilling, and Senechal (1986). Furthermore, with the development of even more specific peer-pressure resistance skills (Hops *et al.*, 1986), measures that allow for systematic feedback on performance, these techniques may become even more effective.

In conclusion, although smokeless tobacco use among adolescents appears to be increasing, efforts toward prevention of its use may profit from exploring the applicability, in this new context, of the knowledge and techniques acquired through cigarette smoking prevention programs that have already been developed and evaluated. Of course, these techniques may not be applied without some modification based on the identification of attributes specific to smokeless tobacco. In this chapter, by discussing applications of addressing prevention of cigarette smoking to the use of smokeless tobacco, we have attempted to illustrate how social psychologists might use an extant social-psychological model designed to deal with one health risk as a basis for formulating hypotheses to address other health risks.

ACKNOWLEDGMENTS. We acknowledge the invaluable contribution to this chapter of the late Lewis M. Dratt, through his role in assisting us in integrating the conceptualization in our current research program as we concurrently are investigating prevention of the use of both cigarettes and smokeless tobacco. This work was supported by research grants from the NCI (5 RO1 CA41471-03 and 1 RO1 CA 41722-02) to Richard I. Evans.

References

Advisory Committee to the Surgeon General. (1986). *The health consequences of using smokeless tobacco* (NIH Publications No. 86-2874). Washington, DC: U.S. Government Printing Office.

Ajzen, I., & Fishbein, M. (1980). *Understanding attitudes and predicting social behavior.* Englewood Cliffs, NJ: Prentice-Hall.

Ary, D. V., Lichtenstein, E., & Severson, H. N. (1987). Smokeless tobacco use among male adolescents: Patterns, correlates, predictors and the use of the drug. *Preventive Medicine, 16,* 385–401.

Bandura, A. (1977). *Social learning theory.* Englewood Cliffs, NJ: Prentice-Hall.

Barton, J., Chassin, L., Presson, C. C., & Sherman, S. S. (1982). Social image factors as motivators of smoking initiation in early and middle adolescence. *Child Development, 53,* 1499–1511.

Benowitz, N. L. (1986, January). Smokeless tobacco, nicotine, and human disease. In W. J. Blot & G. Boyd (cochairs), *Health implications of smokeless tobacco use.* NIH Health Implications of Smokeless Tobacco Consensus Development Conference, Bethesda, MD.

Blum, A. (1983). Using athletes to push tobacco to children: Snuff-dippin' cancer-lipped man. *New York State Journal of Medicine, 83,* 1365–1367.

Bonaguro, J. A., Pugh, M., & Bonaguro, E. W. (1986). Multivariate analysis of smokeless tobacco use by adolescents in grades four through twelve. *Health Education, 17,* 4–7.

Botvin, G. J., & Eng, A. (1980). A comprehensive school-based smoking prevention program. *Journal of School Health, 50,* 209–213.

Boyd, G., & Associates. (1987). Use of smokeless tobacco among children and adolescents in the United States. *Preventive Medicine, 16,* 402–421.

Brubaker, R. G., & Loftin, T. L. (1987). Smokeless tobacco use by middle school males: A preliminary test of the reasoned action theory. *Journal of School Health, 57,* 64–67.

Cantwell, G. (1987). Smokeless tobacco use in Little League studied: Astros team up for oral cancer battle. *Houston Post,* September 29, p. 12A.

Chassin, L., Presson, C. C., Bensenberg, M., Corty, E., Olshavsky, R. W., & Sherman, S. J. (1981). Predicting adolescents' intentions to smoke cigarettes. *Journal of Health and Social Behavior, 22,* 445–455.

Chassin, L., Presson, C. C., Sherman, S. J., Corty, E., & Olshavsky, R. W. (1984). Predicting the onset of cigarette smoking in adolescents: A longitudinal study. *Journal of Applied Social Psychology, 14,* 224–243.

Chassin, L., Presson, C. C., Sherman, S. J., McLaughlin, L., & Gioia, D. (1985). Psychosocial correlates of adolescent smokeless tobacco use. *Addictive Behavior, 10,* 431–435.

Christen, A. G. (1980). The case against smokeless tobacco: Five facts for the health profession to consider. *Journal of the American Dental Association, 101,* 464–465.

Christen, A. G., McDaniel, R. K., & Doran, J. E. (1979). Snuff dipping and tobacco chewing in a group of Texas college athletes. *Texas Dental Journal, 97,* 6–10.

Christen A. G., & Swanson, B. A. (1983). Orally used smokeless tobacco as advertised in the metamorphic trade cards of 1870–1900. *Bulletin History of Dentistry, 31,* 82–86.

Connolly, G. N., Winn, D. M., Hecht, S. S., Henningfield, J. E., Walker, B., Jr., & Hoffman, D. (1986). The reemergence of smokeless tobacco. *New England Journal of Medicine, 314,* 1020–1027.

Dent, C. W., Sussman, S., Johnson, C. A., Hansen, W. B., & Flay, B. R. (1987). Adolescent smokeless tobacco incidence: Relations with other drugs and psychosocial variables. *Preventive Medicine, 16,* 422–431.

Dignan, M., Block G., Steckler, A., Howard, G., & Cosby, M. (1986). Locus of control and smokeless tobacco use among adolescents. *Adolescence, 21,* 377–381.

Ernster, V. L. (1986, January). Advertising of smokeless tobacco products. In W. J. Blot & G. Boyd (cochairs), *Health implications of smokeless tobacco use.* NIH Health Implications of Smokeless Tobacco Consensus Development Conference, Bethesda, MD.

Evans, R. I. (1976). Smoking in children: Developing a social psychological strategy of deterrence. *Preventive Medicine, 5,* 122–127.

Evans, R. I. (1980). Behavioral medicine: A new applied challenge to social psychologists. In L. Bickman (Ed.), *Applied social psychology annual* (Vol. 1, pp. 279–305). Beverly Hills: Sage.

Evans, R. I. (1984). A social inoculation strategy to deter smoking in adolescents. In J. Matarazzo, S. Weiss, N. Miller, J. Herd, & S. Weiss (Eds.), *Behavioral health: A handbook of health enhancement and disease prevention* (pp. 765–774). New York: Wiley.

Evans, R. I. (1988a). Health promotion: Science or ideology? *Health Psychology, 7*, 203–219.

Evans, R. I. (1988b). Smokeless tobacco vs cigarette use among adolescents. *The Cancer Bulletin, 40*, 355–359.

Evans, R. I., Dratt, L. M., Raines, B. E., & Rosenberg, S. S. (1988). Social influences on smoking initiation: Importance of distinguishing descriptive vs. mediating process variables. *Journal of Applied Social Psychology, 18*, 925–943.

Evans, R. I., Raines, B. E., & Hanselka, L. L. (1984). Developing data-based communications in social psychological research: Adolescent smoking prevention. *Journal of Applied Social Psychology, 14*, 289–295.

Evans, R. I., Rozelle, R. M., Maxwell, S. E., Raines, B. E., Dill, C. A., Guthrie, T. J., Henderson, A. H., & Hill, P. C. (1981). Social modeling films to deter smoking in adolescents: Results of a three-year field investigation. *Journal of Applied Psychology, 66*, 339–414.

Evans, R. I., Rozelle, R. M., Mittelmark, M. B., Hansen, W. B., Bane, A. L., & Havis, J. (1978). Deterring the onset of smoking in children: Knowledge of immediate physiological effects and coping with peer pressure, media pressure, and parent modeling. *Journal of Applied Social Psychology, 8*, 126–135.

Evans, R. I., & Smith, C. K. (1980). *Cigarette smoking in teenage females: A social-psychological-behavioral analysis and further evaluation of a model prevention strategy.* Preliminary report to the National Cancer Institute of a survey with 500 seventh grade students.

Evans, R. I., Smith, C. K., & Raines, B. E. (1984). Deterring cigarette smoking in adolescents: A psychosocial-behavioral analysis of an intervention strategy. In A. Baum, J. Singer, & S. Taylor (Eds.), *Social psychological aspects of health* (pp. 301–318). Hillsdale, NJ: Erlbaum.

Fishbein, M., & Ajzen, I. (1975). *Belief, attitude, intention and behavior: An introduction to theory and research.* Reading, MA: Addison-Wesley.

Fishbein, M., Ajzen, I., & McArdle, J. (1980). Changing the behavior of alcoholics: Effects of persuasive communication. In I. Ajzen & M. Fishbein (Eds.), *Understanding attitudes and predicting social behavior.* Englewood Cliffs, NJ: Prentice-Hall.

Flay, B. R. (1985). What do we know about the social influences approach to smoking prevention? Review and recommendations. In C. Bell & R. Battjes (Eds.), *Prevention research: Deterring drug abuse among children and adolescents.* Washington, DC: NIDA Research Monograph #63.

Glover, E. D. (1986, January). Regional prevalence of smokeless tobacco use. In W. J. Blot & G. Boyd (cochairs). *Health implications of smokeless tobacco use.* NIH Health Implications of Smokeless Tobacco Consensus Development Conference, Bethesda, MD.

Glover, E. D., Christen, A. G., & Henderson, A. H. (1982). Smokeless tobacco and the adolescent male. *Journal of Early Adolescence, 2*, 1–13.

Gritz, E. R., Baer-Weiss, V., Benowitz, N. L., Van Vunakis, H., & Jarvik, M. E. (1981). Plasma nicotine and cotinine concentrations in habitual smokeless tobacco users. *Clinical Pharmacological Therapy, 30*, 201–209.

Gritz, E. R., Ksir, C., & McCarthy, W. J. (1985). Smokeless tobacco use in the United States: Past and future trends. *Annals of Behavioral Medicine, 7*, 24–27.

Harper, S. (1980). In tobacco, where there's smokeless fire. *Advertising Age*, June 23.

Hirschman, R. S., Leventhal, H., & Glynn, K. (1984). The development of smoking behavior: Conceptualization and supportive cross-sectional survey data. *Journal of Applied Social Psychology, 14*, 184–206.

Hops, H., Weissman, W., Biglan, A., Thompson, R., Fuller, C., & Severson, H. H. (1986). A taped situation test of cigarette refusal skill among adolescents. *Behavioral Assessment, 8*, 145–154.

Hunter, S. MacD., Croft. J. B., Burke, G. L., Parker, F. C., Webber, L. S., & Berenson, G. S. (1986). Longitudinal patterns of cigarette smoking and smokeless tobacco use in youth: The Bogalusa Heart Study. *American Journal of Public Health, 76*, 193–195.

Koop, C. E. (1986). The campaign against smokeless tobacco. *New England Journal of Medicine, 314*, 1042–1044.

Krishna, K. (1978). Tobacco chewing in pregnancy. *British Journal of Obstetrics and Gynecology, 85*, 726–728.

Lando, H. A. (1985). The social influences approach to smoking prevention and progress toward an integrated smoking elimination strategy: A critical commentary. In C. Bell & R. Batjes (Eds.), *Prevention research: Deterring drug abuse among children and adolescents.* Washington, DC: NIDA Research Monograph #63.

Leventhal, H., & Cleary, P. D. (1980). The smoking problem: A review of the research and theory in behavioral risk modification. *Psychological Bulletin, 88,* 370–405.

Leventhal, H., Safer, M. A., & Panagis, D. M. (1983). The impact of communications on the self-regulation of health beliefs, decisions, and behavior. *Health Education Quarterly, 10,* 3–29.

Levitt, E. E., & Edwards, J. A. (1970). A multivariate study of correlative factors in youthful cigarette smoking. *Developmental Psychology, 2,* 5–11.

Lichtenstein, E., Severson, H., Friedman, L., & Ary, D. (1984). Chewing tobacco use by adolescents: Prevention in relation to cigarette smoking. *Addictive Behavior, 9,* 351–355.

Marty, P. J., McDermott, R. J., & Williams, T. (1986). Patterns of smokeless tobacco use in a population of high school students. *American Journal of Public Health, 76,* 190–192.

McGuire, W. J. (1961). The effectiveness of supportive refutational defenses in immunizing and re-storing beliefs against persuasion. *Sociometry, 24,* 184–197.

McGuire, W. J. (1968). The nature of attitudes and attitude change. In G. Lindzey & E. Aronson (Eds.), *Handbook of social psychology, Vol. 3: The individual in a social context* (pp. 136–314). Reading, MA: Addison-Wesley.

Patten, B. M. (1984). Neuromuscular disease due to tobacco use. *Texas Medicine, 88,* 47–51.

Poulson, T. C., Lindenmuth, J. E., & Greer, R. O., Jr. (1984). A comparison of the use of smokeless tobacco in rural and urban teenagers. *Cancer Journal for Clinicians, 34,* 248–261.

Schaefer, S. D., Henderson, A. H., Glover, E. D., & Christen, A. G. (1985). Patterns of use and incidence of smokeless tobacco consumption in school-age children. *Archives of Otolaryngology, 111,* 639–642.

Schinke, S. P., Gilchrist, L. D., Schilling, R. F. II, & Senechal, V. A. (1986). Smoking and smoke-less tobacco use among adolescents: Trends and intervention results. *Public Health Report, 101,* 373–378.

Schinke, S. P., Gilchrist, L. D., Schilling, R. F. II, Walker, R. D., Locklear, V. S., & Kitajima, E. (1986). Smokeless tobacco use among Native American adolescents. *New England Journal of Medicine, 314,* 1051–1052.

Schlenker, B. R. (1980). *Impression management.* Monterey, CA: Brooks/Cole.

Severson, H. H. (1986, January). Psychosocial factors in the use of smokeless tobacco by adolescent males. In W. J. Blot & G. Boyd (cochairs), *Health implications of smokeless tobacco use.* NIH Health Implications of Smokeless Tobacco Consensus Development Conference, Bethesda, MD.

Squires, W. G., Jr., Brandon, T. A., Zinkgraf, S., Bonds, D., Hartung, G. H., Murray, T., Jackson, A. S., & Miller, R. R. (1984). Hemodynamic effects of oral smokeless tobacco in dogs and young adults. *Preventive Medicine, 13,* 195–206.

7

Heart Health Program

Applying Social Influence Processes in a Large-Scale Community Health Promotion Program

Barbara Loken, Janet Swim, and Maurice B. Mittelmark

Social influence processes have played an important role in the conceptual under-pinnings, development, and implementation of the Minnesota Heart Health Pro-gram (MHHP). MHHP is a communitywide program developed to prevent illness and disability by helping people reduce their own risk factors associated with heart disease. This chapter describes the program as a way of illustrating how social influence processes have been used in a primary prevention program. (The pro-gram has been described at length elsewhere; see Blackburn *et al.*, 1984; Mittel-mark *et al.*, 1986).

Background of MHHP

The MHHP is a 10-year research and demonstration project that is designed to promote healthy life-styles in three communities in Minnesota. An underlying theme of the program is that a population's psychological, social, and cultural characteristics influence that population's risk of cardiovascular diseases (CVD), and that changes in these characteristics should produce significantly lower rates

Barbara Loken • Department of Marketing, Carlson School of Management, University of Minne-sota, Minneapolis, Minnesota, 55455   **Janet Swim** • Department of Psychology, The Pennsylva-nia State University, University Park, Pennsylvania 16802   **Maurice B. Mittelmark** • Bowman-Gray School of Medicine, Wake Forest University, Winston-Salem, North Carolina 27103.

of known risk factors for CVD and subsequent reductions in premature disease and death incidence (Mittelmark *et al.*, 1986). The MHHP project, funded by the National Heart, Lung, and Blood Institute (NHLBI), is consistent with NHLBI guidelines for demonstration projects in that the interventions are primarily those that "have already been found to be efficacious in other studies and include, but are not limited to, education strategies and modifications in health care and health-related practices" (NHLBI, 1983, p. 2).

Multiple intervention strategies—including mass media, community organization, youth education, and population-based screening—are used to persuade people within the targeted communities to adopt more "heart-healthy" life-styles. The underlying philosophy of the MHHP is to advocate change through positive educational messages. For example, the smoking cessation programs advocate quitting smoking through positive cessation messages (e.g., quitting smoking will lower one's risk of cardiovascular diseases) and social support from the community (Murray, 1986). Information about diet and nutrition focuses on the positive food choices people can make. The target audience for the MHHP programs varies depending upon the program, but across all programs, the ultimate goal is to reach individuals between the ages of 25 and 74.

Program Evaluation

As a demonstration study (Phase VIII of Flay's 1986 model of research phases), the MHHP uses a quasi-experimental design in which three pairs of matched communities are surveyed and observed over a 9-year period. The MHHP is evaluated in two major ways. Annual surveys are conducted of both cross-sectional samples and panels. Samples for these surveys are drawn from the adult population ages 25 to 74 randomly selected from the three educated and three comparison communities. Questionnaires assess program awareness, demographics, cognitive variables (e.g., knowledge about heart disease risk factors), and self-reported behaviors relating to primary risk factors (blood pressure control, smoking, physical activity, and diet). Measures also include physiological assessments (e.g., blood pressure, weight, serum thiocyanate, blood total, and HDL cholesterol levels) and morbidity and mortality (see Mittelmark *et al.*, 1986, for more detail).

A second "education evaluation" survey activity conducts up to 30 evaluation studies each year, primarily telephone surveys, to provide such information as the usefulness of particular messages and educational strategies, overall program awareness and awareness of specific program elements within the educated communities, and cognitive, attitudinal, and behavioral changes within the educated communities. Typical response rates for these surveys are 90 to 95%. A more complete description of the evaluation programs can be found elsewhere (Blackburn *et al.*, 1984; Mittelmark *et al.*, 1986).

The present report focuses on a discussion of the social influence theories that have provided an overarching conceptual theme for development of educational programs. Also, selected projects within MHHP are described that have incorporated social influence theories such as social learning theory and models of attitude structure and attitude change.

Theory Guiding the Overall Program

MHHP's 10-year plan has been guided by perspectives from at least two sets of theories: (1) action research, originally conceived by Kurt Lewin (1948), and (2) models of innovation-diffusion (e.g., Rogers, 1983; Rogers & Shoemaker, 1971). Other sociological theories, including community or social exchange theories, have also guided program implementation and maintenance, but they are not included in this chapter (see, e.g., Finnegan, Bracht, & Viswanath, 1989, for a review of additional theories and programs).

Lewin's Action Approach

Lewin (1948) advocated research programs that would alleviate social problems rather than research "that produces nothing but books" (p. 203). According to Lewin, there are three basic stages in planning such social programs. In the first, fact-finding, stage an "overall plan" of how to reach program objectives and the first steps of the plan are formed. In the second stage, the first steps are executed and additional fact-finding occurs to evaluate the action, learn the strengths and weaknesses of the steps taken, plan the next step, and modify the overall plan. The third, "circle of planning," stage consists of repeating the cycle of planning, acting, and fact-finding.

The MHHP's goal of reducing the nation's number one cause of death, heart disease, is consistent with Lewin's goals of action research, and the MHHP strategy follows the cyclical process outlined by Lewin. Programs successfully conducted by former community health projects were incorporated, where possible, into the MHHP. For example, past community research (see Blackburn *et al.*, 1984) suggested that direct intervention had been effective at changing health-threatening behaviors of those at high risk for heart disease. MHHP's Heart Health Educational Centers, which provide personalized behavioral health education information such as blood pressure and cholesterol levels, have reached their target goal of screening at least 60% of members ages 25 to 74 in the community. Furthermore, MHHP researchers (Murray *et al.*, 1986) found that although body weight and smoking did not change significantly for a group randomly assigned to attend the screening center, this group did have lower cholesterol levels, improved eating patterns and physical activity scores, lower heart rates, or lower diastolic blood pressure, and they were taking more blood pressure medication. Thus, the screening centers have been successful in both reaching people and providing the educational tools necessary for behavior change.

The MHHP also is guided by Lewin's action approach in that programs that have *not* yielded the expected outcomes have been replaced by other, more appropriate programs. For example, adult education classes incorporated at the beginning of the project were attended by a very small minority (about 6%) of screening center participants. In response to this low rate of attendance, the classes were discontinued, and other innovative programs were developed to educate and motivate adults. For example, a ''Quit and Win'' program with an incentive of a free family vacation was begun. Those who signed up for a Quit and Win contest and remained abstinent for an entire month were eligible for a series of prizes (such as a family vacation in Florida) from a lottery at the end of the month. Subsequent variations of this program included the use of an ''Adopt a Smoker'' program, whereby the smoker signed up for the contest along with a support person. The support person was chosen by the smoker as one who would support him or her during the first month of abstinence.

Programs on nutrition were also developed in response to the need for innovative programs and were designed to make it easier to choose healthful foods, and thus act upon one's knowledge. The programs encouraged people to eat greater quantities of fruits and vegetables, grains, legumes, poultry and fish, lean cuts of meat, and low-fat dairy products. Specific programs included a grocery labeling program, in which low-sodium and low-fat foods were identified on the food shelves with color-coded labels, and a restaurant-labeling program, in which items that met specified guidelines in their sodium and fat content were marked with small red hearts. The demonstrated success of both the Quit and Win and the food-labeling programs has led to their continuation. Thus, the MHHP's overall plan has not been wedded to theory testing but has been a self-correcting empirical approach.

Innovation Diffusion

No particular theory has guided the MHHP, but because the program is a community-based program, many of its conceptual themes have been adopted from innovation-diffusion models. According to Rogers and Shoemaker (1971), the diffusion process is the spread of innovations over time to the members of a social system. The time element has two dimensions: the time required for individuals to move from knowledge of an innovation to decision to adopt the innovation, and the time required for an entire social system to adopt the change.

Rogers and Shoemaker conceptualized four stages in the decision to adopt an innovation that provide a useful framework for understanding the impetus of several MHHP programs (see Finnegan *et al.*, 1989, for an alternative framework for community-based programs). First is *knowledge and understanding* of the innovation. Second, individuals are *persuaded* to hold favorable or unfavorable attitudes toward the innovation. Third, individuals decide to *engage in behavior* that leads to adopting or rejecting the innovation. Last, individuals seek *confirmation* of the decision made. A failure to receive confirmation leads to reversal of the decision.

Knowledge

The MHHP has sought to accelerate the adoption of heart-healthy behaviors in the intervention communities through mass media attempts to increase program awareness and knowledge. For instance, the MHHP has used traditional mass media channels such as a TV broadcast of a five-part program called "A Video Guide to the Best of Health" and provided free pamphlets on how to quit smoking. The Heart Health Screening centers and the grocery store and restaurant labeling programs, in which items low in salt and cholesterol are marked for the consumer, have also increased awareness of the program.

Data on general awareness of the heart health program in the community and awareness of specific programs within the MHHP are gathered biannually by the evaluation staff. It has taken about 2½ years for the communities to reach their maximal awareness level of 50 to 60% correct unaided recall and 80 to 90% correct recognition (of "a recent program in your community to prevent heart disease"). These percentages, based upon general population samples ages 25 to 74, are exceptionally high and demonstrate that high levels of awareness can be achieved for an innovation at the community level. Furthermore, awareness of specific programs within MHHP has been high. For instance, the general population's awareness of the grocery store program reached 60 to 70% and awareness of the restaurant labeling program reached 80 to 90% within 2 years of the programs' inceptions.

Persuasion

Although research on innovation diffusions (Rogers & Shoemaker, 1971) has found that mass media may be best at increasing knowledge of an innovation, the first stage in the diffusion process, interpersonal channels may be most important for persuasion, the second stage. In order to promote interpersonal channels, the MHHP has involved community members in its implementation of the program (see Finnegan et al., 1989; Carlaw, Mittelmark, Bracht, & Luepker, 1984). For example, a community advisory board (CAB) composed of prominent community leaders identified from previous analyses of the community was formed. Initially, leading citizens with stated interests or a commitment to MHHP were invited to be members. They were asked to suggest names of others that would be helpful. The leaders that were identified were similar to those identified in personal interviews in which, after the MHHP was described to the interviewee, he or she provided names of critical leaders and "doers" in the community.[1] Next, task

[1]The community board can also be seen as legitimizing the project and investing local resources for a long-term partnership with the communities, and, as such, it relates more broadly to community social change theory (see Finnegan et al., 1989).

forces chaired by members of the CAB for each of the four targeted risk areas (eating patterns, physical activity, smoking, and blood pressure) and *ad hoc* advisory boards, such as a board composed of representatives from major medical centers, were formed. The members of the CAB represented opinion leaders who would presumably encourage favorable attitudes toward the program and heart-healthy behaviors. The interactions in the task force facilitated program commitment and helped develop an environment and norms supportive of heart health.

Decision

In order to encourage the decision to adopt and maintain heart-healthy behaviors, social systems of support such as skill-building sessions and workshops in churches, schools, trade unions, and service and health clubs were established. Organizations that engaged the largest participation of community members, such as churches (membership ranged from 43% to 48% in the communities), were chosen. For instance, an organization study (MacBride, Pirie, Sorenson, & Kurth, 1986) consisted of distributing a promotion kit to 6 churches and 6 worksites, conducting training sessions for coordinators at the 12 locations, and making speakers and on-site classes available. Additionally, 3 of the churches and 3 of the worksites received greater contact and support by MHHP field staff. Pre- and postsurveys of members of the organizations revealed changes over time on measures of awareness of the community program, adopting social norms supporting heart health behaviors (such as greater discussion by participants at church or work about health issues), and decrease in consumption of high-sodium foods. Although these differences may be attributable to changes in the community at large (history effects) or changes due to the survey itself (testing effects), other surveys conducted at this time showed support for neither of these competing explanations.

Confirmation

Finally, certain MHHP programs have sought to strengthen the community's commitment to heart-healthy behaviors. For instance, at worksites employers have been encouraged to support regular exercise by their employees through competitive point systems for teams from different worksites. Additionally, insurance companies, banks, and other related organizations have been encouraged to provide favorable rates to clients who engage in more heart-healthy behaviors.

A basic principle of the innovation-diffusion model (as well as other models of community organization and change; see Finnegan *et al.*, 1989) is that ideas travel through networks of people. The effectiveness of using community networks to increase adoption of the heart health program message was examined within certain neighborhoods in an intervention community. The program consisted of neighborhood parties revolving around heart health themes, neighborhood exercise classes, and having volunteers canvas their neighborhoods to encourage other neighbors to attend the Heart Health Center programs.

As compared with a demograhically similar neighborhood that did not receive the program (Swim, Loken, Lesley, & Bracht, 1988), participation by residents in the intervention program and engaging in heart-healthy behaviors did not significantly increase. While these results were disappointing, it became clear that reasons besides the lack of effect of the treatment could also explain them. For instance, members of both the intervention and comparison neighborhoods were from an intervention community, and changes in both groups (e.g., attending classes, the heart health centers, and increasing exercise behaviors) occurred over time. Both groups had received persuasion attempts both prior to and during the intervention, and a ceiling on participation may have occurred. Thus, the influence of neighborhood recruitment may not have been able to increase involvement above the involvement obtained already from existing methods of recruitment.

Summary

In sum, Lewin's action approach and the diffusion of innovations model have served as valuable frameworks for the MHHP in developing and implementing programs over time. Programs that have been successfully evaluated from past community research (e.g., direct intervention through screening centers) or that have shown to be effective through program awareness and evaluation (e.g., the smoking cessation or grocery labeling programs) have been continued. Programs that have been unsuccessful have been replaced or revised.

Furthermore, evaluation data indicate that awareness of the Minnesota Heart Health program and its specific programs has diffused over time in all three intervention communities. A variety of programs have been systematically developed to accelerate the adoption process (e.g., development of the community advisory board) and to increase each community's commitment to heart-healthy behaviors (e.g., incorporation of programs into community neighborhoods, churches, and worksites). In the next section we discuss selected theories that have guided research studies and specific programs within MHHP.

Theory Guiding Specific Programs

Social Learning Theory

Elements of social learning theory that other researchers have found to be useful have been incorporated into MHHP programs. For example, Jessor and Jessor's (1977) problem behavior theory has served as a guide to MHHP researchers, particularly those working with youth education. This section will describe, first, major elements of social learning theory and, second, MHHP's adoption of problem behavior theory. Examples of how MHHP has incorporated elements of these theories will also be described.

Major Elements of Social Learning Theory

Three elements of social learning theory that have influenced MHHP programs are observational learning, self-efficacy, and reciprocal determinism. Although there are a number of social learning theorists with similar perspectives, Bandura's work (e.g., 1977a, 1977b, 1978) has been the most influential among MHHP researchers.

Observational Learning. According to social learning theories, behavior is the direct result of anticipated rewards that accompany behavior. People anticipate these rewards because they have previously received the rewards themselves, or they have observed someone else receiving them—hence, observational learning. Generally the most effective models in observational learning (other than the self) are those individuals who have similar goals and values as the observer, have high status, or are demographically similar to the observer.

The community advisory board may be seen as models of high status in the MHHP communities. Communications by these board members about rewards associated with heart-healthy behaviors have regularly appeared in the local newspapers and other media. Furthermore, prizes in the Quit and Win Contest programs provide incentives for people to attempt to quit smoking. Data support this contention. We found that 2 months after the contest ended, the contest prize (a free trip to Disney World for a family of four) was the most frequently mentioned reason for signing up for the contest (mentioned by 36% of a sample of contest participants), followed by the contest's providing an incentive to quit (mentioned by 29%). Furthermore, nearly 50% of contestants indicated 6 months after the contest that they would not sign up for a contest without a prize. A majority (78%) also indicated that the prize would be somewhat or very important in their decision to sign up for a contest. The smoking contests also have promoted successful quitters as models for other smokers by publishing their names in local newspapers.

Self-Efficacy. The second key element in social learning theory is self-efficacy (Bandura, 1977a), which also is enhanced through modeling behaviors. Self-efficacy results from observers' convictions that they can perform certain behaviors to produce certain outcomes. Observers' confidence in their own ability is strengthened.

The use of self-efficacy, as well as observational learning, has been most clearly used in MHHP's school-based youth education programs. Youth education to induce heart-healthy life-styles is based on the assumption that healthy behaviors and attitudes are learned at an early age, and that changes can be directed at the youth as well as the adults in the community (Klepp, Halper, & Perry, 1986; Perry, 1986; Perry & Jessor, 1985; Perry & Murray, 1982). School-based programs are designed to change health behavior norms, teach health-related skills, and reinforce the adoption of health behaviors. For instance, a smoking and drug abuse prevention program called "Keep it Clean" uses a 6-hour program taught by same-age peer leaders and facilitated by classroom teachers. This program is part of a large set of studies that have tested the use of social influence to prevent smoking behaviors in adolescents (see Flay, 1985, for a review). In the MHHP programs five students, elected as the most popular, are trained to be peer leaders (Klepp *et al.*, 1986). Theoretically, popular peers should be effective models because they provide vicarious reinforcement for healthy behaviors, are of high status, and are similar to the rest of the students. In addition to using peer leaders, the "Keep It Clean" program has taught students skills such as saying "no" to peer pressures and uses role playing to reinforce alternative healthy behaviors (Perry & Jessor, 1985). Thus, self-efficacy is enhanced by vicariously experiencing success from the models, from direct persuasion, and from skill-building exercises and role playing.

Reciprocal Determination. A third key element of social learning theory is Bandura's conception of reciprocal determinism (Bandura, 1978). Rather than assuming that people passively react toward stimuli in the environment or act independently of environmental influences, Bandura describes behavior, person, and environment factors as all interacting with one another. This conception, called reciprocal determinism, argues that people regulate their own behavior through self-managed incentives. That is, people choose standards of comparison by which to positively or negatively evaluate their own behaviors. These standards are internal cognitive structures that may be based upon other people's behavior or one's own past behavior. The evaluation occurs because the person has set goals that form the standards and has monitored his or her own behaviors to see if they meet the standards. Through goal setting and self-monitoring, people control their behaviors and their incentives.

Goal setting and self-monitoring have been used in MHHP's weight-loss program "A Pound of Prevention" (Forster, Jeffreys, Schmid, & Kramer, 1988). Most people who are overweight in their later years were not overweight when they were younger. Thus, this program was designed to prevent typical future weight gain by participants who were within 15% of their ideal weight by making them aware of their current eating habits. On a monthly basis half the participants received information on healthy eating and were encouraged to either self-report their weight or come to the health screening center to be weighed. Participants also invested $120, which was refunded on a monthly basis if they met their weight-maintenance goals (i.e., if they did not weigh more than they had at their initial weighin). Over a year later, 82% of the program participants maintained or lost weight, compared with 56% of the control group.

Goal setting and self-monitoring also have been used in worksite physical activity programs. In these programs, participants are encouraged to set specific behavioral goals, such as "I will exercise three times a week." They monitor their own behavior by recording their success on company charts visible to all members of the organization. At the end of the program the company with the greatest activity participation points wins a prize. Thus, in addition to personal goal setting and self-monitoring, group norms are known and social pressures are present to encourage physical activity.

Problem Behavior Theory

Jessor and Jessor (1977) developed a model to describe adolescent problem behavior, including drug use, alcohol use, and premarital sex. Cheryl Perry, in her work with MHHP's youth education program, has developed a theoretical framework, shown in Figure 1, based on Jessor's problem-behavior theory and Bandura's social learning theory (Perry & Jessor, 1985). As with Jessor and Jessor's model and Bandura's reciprocal determinism, Perry has focused on three major dimensions of analysis: behavior, person, and environment. Additionally, she uses two main strategies to promote healthful behavior: (1) weakening, reducing, and eliminating *health-compromising* behavior and (2) introducing, strengthening, and reinforcing *health-enhancing* behaviors. Past research has tended to be limited to the reduction of health-compromising behavior rather than the adoption of health-enhancing behavior. Like Jessor and Jessor's model, Perry's model includes perceived norms and expectations as environmental attributes, and the functional meanings attributed to health-enhancing and health-compromising behavior as person attributes. Like social learning, attributes such as modeling, re-

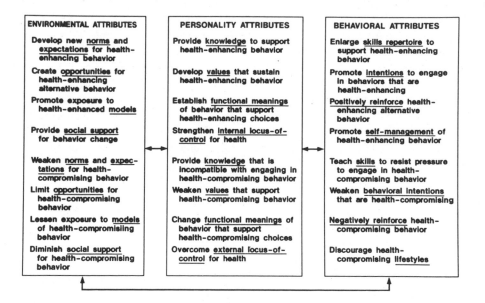

Figure 1. Theoretical attributes at each focus of intervention. (From Perry & Jessor, 1985.)

inforcement, and skill training are also included in the model. Additionally, Bandura's influence is seen in the conception of behavior as both a cause and an effect of person and environmental variables.

The Keep It Clean program mentioned earlier was designed to incorporate elements of environment, personality, and behavior. On the environmental level, the program focuses on perceived social norms by having students estimate the number of students in their schools who smoke. The students' perceptions are adjusted by pointing out how they overestimated this number. On the personal level the program attempts to change attitudes about the acceptability of smoking behavior and provides knowledge about the social and physiological consequences of smoking and drug abuse. Last, on the behavioral level, students learn to scrutinize tobacco advertising, make statements about their intentions to remain nonsmokers, and role-play alternative behaviors to smoking.

Attitude and Attitude-Change Theories

Overview

Most primary prevention programs include persuasive communications that include specific information targeted to a population that is expected to influence members of that population to behave in a desired manner. In general, communitywide health promotion programs are based on the assumption that changes in health-related behaviors will occur if members of the community (a) are made aware of the health problem and (b) are informed about preventive measures. Models of attitude change make further assumptions that argue that the nature of the information disseminated to people is important, and will vary depending upon the population.

In this section we discuss the use of attitude and attitude-change theories within the context of the MHHP. In particular, we discuss influences at the individual level in the context of a theory of "reasoned" behavior (Ajzen & Fishbein, 1980; Fishbein & Ajzen, 1975) and report the results of a study on the comparative effects of positive, negative, and neutral messages on people's knowledge and perceptions about heart disease, investigated in a direct-mail study.

The Theory of Reasoned Action

Overview and Relevance to MHHP. The theory of reasoned action has been tested and used extensively (see Ajzen & Fishbein, 1980, for a review), and readers unfamiliar with the theory are referred to these sources for a more detailed description of the model. The complete model is shown in Figure 2. According to this model, most behaviors of interest to social psychologists can be explained in terms of relatively few concepts, and, as shown in the figure, a person's behavior can be traced back ultimately to his or her cognitions about performing the behav-

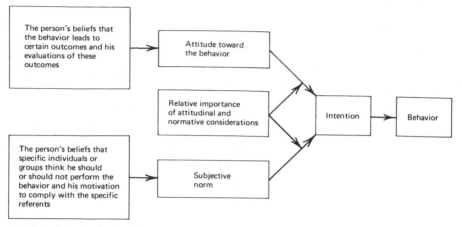

Note: Arrows indicate the direction of influence.

Figure 2. The theory of reasoned action. (From Ajzen & Fishbein, 1980.)

ior. Several assumptions underlying the theory of reasoned action have relevance to and may be used as guidelines for understanding certain of the MHHP objectives:

1. People make systematic use of the information that is available to them about health-related behaviors. Therefore, information is at the core of the persuasion process.
2. Most disease-prevention behaviors are under the volitional control of the individual.
3. The cognitions that influence a person's attitudes toward a health behavior are those that are salient to the individual. In order for changes to occur at a behavioral level, change generally needs to occur for multiple beliefs.
4. Past health behaviors and social structural variables (e.g., occupation, gender) have indirect rather than direct influences on future intentions and behavior.

Each of these assumptions is discussed below in greater detail.

Systematic Use of Information. According to the theory of reasoned action, people are rational information-processors. Information that is available in memory is used systematically in making choices. This notion is not unique to the theory of reasoned action; it is an assumption that underlies most theories of information processing (e.g., Anderson, 1971, 1974; Wyer 1974) and theories of health promotion (e.g., Becker, 1974; Rosenstock, 1966). The information available in memory relevant to health behaviors may derive from various sources, including past experiences as well as information from the media, schools, books, and other people. Educational goals or informational campaigns may be reasonable methods, then, to try to provide individuals with the appropriate information for making healthy choices. The broadly based objectives of the MHHP are to provide the education necessary to change people's beliefs about healthy choices and about a person's own ability to control his or her risk of heart disease. Similarly, from such things as taste tests of heart-healthy recipes in grocery stores or school-based activities, new experiences in the MHHP communities provide information about heart-healthy choices. Several programs, including media education, adult education classes, and restaurant and grocery store labels, have focused specifically on community education.

Volitional Control. Related to the above is the assumption that most disease-prevention behaviors are under the volitional control of the individual. According to the theory of reasoned action, a person's behavior is best predicted by his or her intentions to perform the behavior. The theory predicts, for example, that a person's intention to quit smoking is the best predictor of actual smoking-cessation behavior. Similarly, getting regular exercise is best predicted by intentions to exercise regularly, and eating food low in fat is best predicted by intentions to eat foods low in fat. An educational campaign is successful, therefore, to the extent that it influences a person's intentions to perform heart-healthy behaviors.

The relationships between behavioral intentions and behavior for several health issues were tested in a longitudinal survey of 267 residents in an MHHP educational and a matched comparison community. Respondents were asked their intentions in the next 6 months to eat vegetables, salt their food at the table, do strenuous exercise, and get their blood pressure checked. Six months later respondents reported whether they had engaged in these behaviors. Correlations with intentions across both communities for the first three behaviors were significant ($r(265) = .59$, $r(265) = .71$, $r(265) = .41$, respectively; all p's $< .01$) and were not significant for the last behavior ($r(265) = .13$, $p > .05$). This latter intention–behavior relationship for blood pressure was based on a continuous variable, the number of times blood pressure was measured in the past 6 months. The behavioral measure was highly skewed (most responses ranged from 0 to 5, but a few individuals reported estimates of 50 or more), perhaps accounting for the lack of relationship for this health behavior.

Hoverstad and Howard-Pitney (1986) found that the intention–behavior relationship varied as a function of involvement. For salt-use behavior, the correlation between behavioral intention and behavior was significantly greater ($z = 2.33$, $p < .05$) when people were highly involved with the issue ($r(42) = .43$, $p < .01$) than when they were not ($r(51) = .11$, $p > .05$). These authors argue that for the high involvement group, intentions may have been based on "central processing" (Petty & Cacioppo, 1981), leading to more persistent intentions and a greater likelihood of acting on these intentions.

Salient Beliefs. According to the theory of reasoned action, the cognitions or beliefs that determine a person's attitudes, norms, intentions, and, finally, behavior are those beliefs that are salient to the individual. This assumption has three important implications for prevention programs. First, the amount of information that is available to the individual is limited. A person retrieves from memory only a subset of what is known about an issue in forming a behavioral choice. Therefore, regardless of how much is learned by the individual about a particular issue, only a part of this information will be available for use by the individual.

A second implication of the salience hypothesis is that different people or groups of people will have different salient beliefs. For example, the cognitive factors underlying exercise behavior for one group of people (e.g., low-educated males) are likely to be different from the cognitive factors underlying exercise behavior for another group of people (e.g., highly educated females). As a result, an educational campaign developed for highly educated females could be largely unsuccessful when directed toward low-educated males.

A third implication of the salience hypothesis is that health-related behaviors may be at least partly determined by non-health-related beliefs. A particular target group may engage in an aerobic activity primarily because it makes them feel and look better, not because it could reduce their risk of heart disease. Thus, "looking good" and "feeling good" may be salient beliefs about performing the behavior, and may be desirable target beliefs to change in a social influence attempt. Or, a particular group may continue to smoke cigarettes not because they don't believe the health consequences but because the pleasurable outcomes of smoking are more salient than the health hazards. In this case, a campaign to inform people about the health hazards of smoking would be largely unsuccessful, since these individuals are already knowledgeable, whereas a campaign to increase the salience of health hazards might be more worthwhile. A different target group may decide to quit smoking because the health hazards have become salient (e.g., a close relative has died of lung cancer), and still another group may quit smoking because of social pressure to quit from spouses, friends, or co-workers. Thus, depending upon the beliefs salient within a population, the nature and focus of the social influence attempt should vary.

Data from a study by Loken and Shimanski (1988) show that the salient beliefs in the general population underlying certain heart health behaviors may include both health- and non-health-related consequences of performing the behavior. Questions were standard items (from Ajzen & Fishbein, 1980) used to identify modal salient beliefs. The most frequently mentioned advantages and disadvantages of smoking cigarettes and using salt at the table were tabulated.

The health-related consequences of smoking and salt use were, while clearly important to respondents, only some of the concerns mentioned. For example, for smoking behaviors, disadvantages included the expense, odor on clothing and furniture, bad breath, the social unacceptability of smoking, and stained teeth. With respect to health concerns, cancer and breathing problems were still far more prevalent concerns than heart problems. Thus, despite the growing attention in the United States to heart disease risk factors, the link between heart disease and smoking may not yet be top of mind to most individuals. The positive outcomes of smoking that were most frequently mentioned included relaxation and preventing weight gain.

For both behaviors tested, health issues were clearly among the most salient consequences reported. However, it was also clear that a variety of non-health-related beliefs were salient to respondents, and that an understanding of these latter issues is useful for developing programs designed to change behavior. In order to change a person's attitudes, norms, intentions, and behavior, it is therefore important to focus upon changing the cognitive structure that currently underlies behavior.

Taste tests in grocery stores within the MHHP communities demonstrate the principle of focusing on both health-related and non-health-related beliefs in the general population. In these demonstrations, the savory qualities of the food are considered along with its nutritive properties. Similarly, such tests imply that multiple factors may underlie behavior. The theory of reasoned action, as well as others (e.g., Becker, 1974; Rosenstock, 1966; Triandis, 1977), implies that behavior is ultimately a function of a set of beliefs that are salient to the individual. Changes in attitudes are accomplished by changing the beliefs or cognitions underlying that attitude, or by making additional beliefs salient. Consequently, social influence attempts that focus on multiple salient belief changes (e.g., focusing on both health and nonhealth concerns) and that, like the MHHP, include multiple targets and interventions, should increase the probability of change.

Indirect Influences on Intentions and Behavior. The theory of reasoned action argues that variables not included in the model components, such as demographics, past behaviors, or personality characteristics, influence health intentions only indirectly through their effects on cognitions, attitudes, and norms underlying those intentions. That is, variables "external" to the model affect behavioral intentions and behavior only to the extent that they are mediated by the normative and attitudinal components of the model (see Figure 2). Furthermore, the effects of attitudes and subjective norms on behavior are indirect in that they are mediated by effects on behavioral intentions.

Bentler and Speckart (1979) proposed and found support for two modifications to this model when predicting drug-use behavior (see Figure 3). In the Bentler-Speckart model attitudes directly influence not only behavioral intentions but also behavior. Furthermore, prior behavior was included in the model as a direct predictor of behavioral intentions and behavior (rather than mediated by attitudes and norms). A number of studies have attempted to replicate Bentler and Speckart's findings and test a direct path from subjective norms to behavior. Replications generally support a path from past behavior to future behavior, but the results are inconsistent with respect to differences in time lags (Bagozzi, 1981; Fredricks & Dossett, 1984; Godin, Valois, Shephard, & Desharnais, 1987; Shimp & Kavas, 1984). However, evidence for a direct causal path from attitudes and

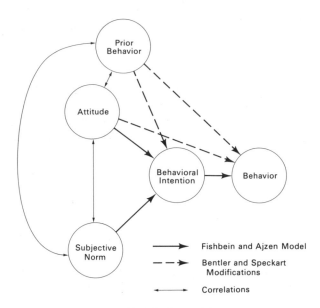

Figure 3. Attitude behavior models.

subjective norms to behavior is weak. Tests of direct paths from subjective norms to behavior have not been as strong as tests of direct paths from attitudes to behavior.

In the heart health program, we tested further the causal paths of several competing models for two heart-related issues: exercise and salt use (Swim, Loken, & Howard-Pitney, 1987). This study tested for evidence of direct causal paths from both attitudes and subjective norms to behavior, as well as from past behavior to behavioral intentions and behavior.

Adult respondents in two Minnesota communities were surveyed by telephone three times in 1 year. Because of constraints in telephone surveying and in order to keep the goodwill of the respondents, multiple measures of each construct were not obtained. The first survey assessed respondents' attitudes, norms, and intentions; the second, attitudes, norms, intentions, and behavior; and the third, behavior. Two behaviors, salt use and getting regular physical exercise, were tested with a time frame of 6 months.

Full and reduced models were analyzed with LISREL VI (Joreskog & Sorbom, 1984) using single indicator variables. The reduced model, representing Fishbein and Ajzen's model, is nested within the full model. The full model includes Bentler and Speckart's proposed addition of past behavior in the model and the addition of a direct causal path from attitudes to behavior. The full model also includes a direct causal path from subjective norms to future behavior.

Because the data were longitudinal, covariances were used to test the model and stability paths were included in both the reduced and full models. The stability paths directly linked the measures of attitudes, subjective norms, and behavioral intentions from time 1 to time 2.

Figures 4 and 5 present the standardized path coefficients fitted for the full models for exercise and salt use. The significance of the paths support Fishbein and Ajzen's original paths and Speckart's modification of adding a direct link from past behavior to future behavioral intention and past behavior to future behavior. However, consistent with Fishbein and Ajzen, the significance of the paths does not support adding a direct path from attitudes or subjective norms to future behaviors. The chi-square goodness-of-fit tests indicate that neither the full model nor the reduced model fit the data well (full model, $\chi^2(9) = 35.48$ for exercise and 40.96 for salt use; reduced model, $\chi^2(15) = 99.46$ for exercise and 113.82 for salt use).

As in previous studies, the present models generally did not attain adequate goodness of fits as assessed by the chi-squares. However, as Bentler and Speckart (1979) point out, this is true for both the full and the reduced models. Furthermore, the significance of the path coefficients from prior behavior to future behavioral intentions and to future behavior support prior research findings (Bagozzi, 1981; Fredricks & Dossett, 1984; Godin *et al.*, 1987). This support, as well as support for Fishbein and Ajzen's (1975) original path from prior behavioral intentions to future behavior, were found even from data with 6-month intervals be-

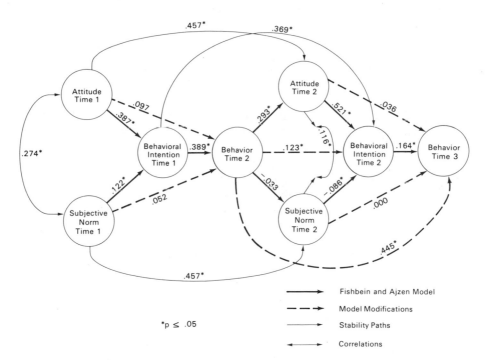

Figure 4. Standardized paths for model testing "regular exercise."

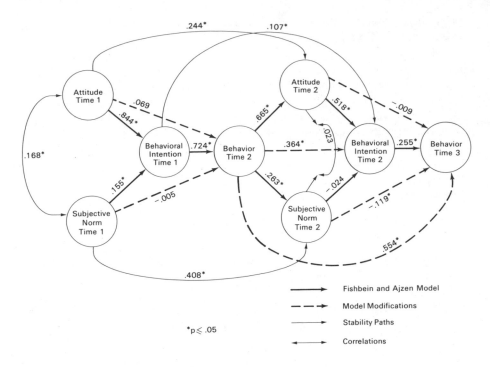

Figure 5. Standardized paths for model testing "salt use at the table."

tween measurements. Also consistent with prior research (Fredricks & Dossett, 1984; Godin *et al.*, 1987; Shimp & Kavas, 1984), the path coefficients do not support including direct paths from attitudes and subjective norms to behavior. However, like other studies (Fredricks & Dossett, 1984; Godin *et al.*, 1987), the paths from subjective norm to behavioral intention at time 1 and time 2 were small.

Attitude Change: A Direct-Mail Study

Traditional models of attitude and behavior change (e.g., Hovland, Janis, & Kelley, 1953) have focused on the effects of source, message, and receiver variables on awareness, comprehension, and acceptance of the persuasive communication. Source variables studied most often include the credibility, atttractiveness, and expertise of the source. Message variables studied have included such factors as the use of fear appeals, "rational" versus "emotional" messages, the number and order of arguments presented, positive versus negative appeals, one-sided versus two-sided arguments, and the frequency of appeals. Finally, receiver variables include individual differences, such as the self-esteem, intelligence, gender, social class, or level of recipient involvement in the message (see McGuire, 1969, 1985). Certain of these source, message, and receiver variables have been more effective than others, and frequently work in combination with one another. With regard to message factors, high fear appeals have been found to be effective when the receiver is also given specific recommendations for carrying out the appeal. Two-sided arguments are more effective than one-sided arguments when the audience is highly educated. As noted by Fishbein and Ajzen (1975), however, the specific message arguments manipulated under different levels of these variables are rarely similar in content.

As part of the MHHP, a study using a specific mass medium, direct mail, was conducted to determine the effectiveness of different appeals on people's awareness and knowledge levels regarding three controllable cardiovascular risk factors: cigarette smoking, high blood pressure, and high-fat, high-salt diets (Salmon, Loken, & Finnegan, 1985). The three message strategies included a neutral "straight facts" appeal, a positive appeal focusing on the benefits of heart health changes, and a negative appeal focusing on the hazards of an unhealthy life-style.

In the health-promotion area, probably the most frequently researched strategy for informational campaigns has been the use of fear appeals (e.g., Janis & Feshbach, 1953; Ray & Ward, 1970; Sternthal & Craig, 1974; Webb, 1974). Less frequently researched has been the relative effectiveness of negative, positive, and neutral appeals. Negative appeals, as defined in the present context, are those that relate the adverse consequences of behaving or failing to behave in a certain way, whereas positive appeals focus on the benefits derived from performing a behavior. Both types of appeals are generally designed to motivate message recipients through positive or negative emotions or thought. A neutral appeal, in the present context, was designed to motivate learning more about the facts associated with the issue.

To test the effectiveness of the three appeals (see Salmon 1985), a small brochure was designed by the media division of MHHP. All three message appeals provided the same basic information concerning the controllable risk factors: smoking, high blood pressure, and high-fat, high-salt diets; also, the appearance of all three brochures—the color, size, and graphics—was identical. Brochures were mailed to randomly selected households in each of the three message appeal conditions. A control condition was added to the design, in which members were not sent any brochure. A subsample of households in each condition received a posttest phone survey 1 week after the brochures were received.

Results of the study (see also Salmon *et al.*, 1985) showed that awareness of receiving the brochure was significantly higher in the neutral appeal condition (28%) than in either the positive (15%) or negative (14%) conditions. No significant differences occurred in the groups' perceptions of risk factor importance, so all three were equally effective in influencing these beliefs. However, while sample sizes were small, the neutral group tended to recall more items pertaining to specific risk factors than the other groups, and the positive appeal group was better than the other groups in recalling the name of the sponsoring organization, i.e., MHHP.

An analysis of specific thoughts generated about the brochure suggested that, again, the neutral group generated more thoughts about specific, controllable risk factors than the other two groups; conversely, the positive appeal generated more general, positive thoughts (about the heart program, the brochure, desire for more information) than the negative group. Finally, the negative appeal generated more negative affect (e.g., "I tore it up," "It doesn't apply to me") or reminders of specific friends or relative who have heart disease.

One theoretical rationale that may account for these data is the recent theorizing on the effects of mood and information processing (Isen, 1984). People in a positive mood (which may have been induced by the positive appeal condition) may process information differently than people in a neutral (or negative) mood. In particular, the depth of processing may be greater among those in a neutral mood; consistent with a levels-of-processing notion (Petty & Cacioppo, 1981), such individuals may focus more on the specific message arguments, such as specific risk factor information. Conversely, if people in a positive mood process information less deeply, they may focus more on peripheral cues, such as source cues (hence, greater recall of the source of the message).

Summary

In summary, a number of theories have been used to guide specific programs within MHHP. Social learning and problem behavior theories have guided the use of observational learning and modeling (e.g., the use of peer leaders in youth education) and the development of incentives (e.g., in weight maintenance or as contest prizes). Attitude and attitude-change theories have been used to understand the cognitive processes underlying attitude, intention, and behavior change, and the nature of persuasive messages required to encourage and maintain heart-healthy behaviors.

Conclusions

This chapter has described how theories about social influence may be used to guide and develop a large-scale communitywide health program. For several reasons, such programs often reflect a highly eclectic approach to theory application. First, as noted earlier, the National Heart, Lung, and Blood Institute guidelines for demonstration projects suggest that interventions should be based upon previously tested programs or theories. Prior intervention programs reflect a diverse array of theoretical and applied approaches to health behavior change. Second, the large-scale communitywide programs involve the input of many researchers and program specialists, who, by nature of their diverse backgrounds, necessitate diverse theoretical approaches. Third, the primary outcome variables associated with such projects focus on health behavior change rather than theory testing.

As our data show, several social psychological theoretical frameworks are capable of, and useful for, explaining heart health awareness, cognitions, attitudes, and behavior. The uses for each have been dependent upon the program investigated and the research investigation. Lewin's action approach and the innovation-diffusion paradigm have provided useful frameworks for developing the MHHP objectives and guiding the development of programs, particularly during the initial stages of the project. Social learning theory has been useful for understanding, explaining, and developing programs for youth education, smoking incentives programs and weight incentives programs. Finally, attitude theory and measurement has been useful for understanding and explaining the nature of the information that underlies heart health behaviors and therefore potential foci for attitude and behavior change in informational campaigns.

In addition to the use of theory as a guide to the project, the large-scale scope of this project has allowed for testing of basic research issues where innovative strategies for implementing that research can be devised. The direct-mail study and tests of the Fishbein-Ajzen model are examples of this research. Thus, an interchange exists between theory testing and application. Theory can be used to guide specific programs, and the applied nature of the program has allowed for the testing of specific theoretical propositions.

ACKNOWLEDGMENTS. Barbara Loken was associate director of education evaluation, Janet Swim was a research assistant, and Maurice Mittelmark was the education director of the Minnesota Heart Health Program, School of Public Health, University of Minnesota, Minneapolis, Minnesota 55455. The authors are grateful to Phyllis Pirie, Cheryl Perry, John Finnegan, and Neil Bracht for their thoughtful comments on an earlier version of this chapter, and to Jan Shimanski, Colleen MacBride, Beth Howard-Pitney, Dave Boush, Chuck Salmon, and Ron Hoverstad for assistance with data analysis.

References

Ajzen, I., & Fishbein, M. (1980). *Understanding attitudes and predicting social behavior*, Englewood Cliffs, NJ: Prentice-Hall.

Anderson, N. H. (1971). Integration theory and attitude change. *Psychological Review, 78*, 171–206.

Anderson, N. H. (1974). Cognitive algebra: Integration theory applied to social attribution. In L. Berkowitz (Ed.), *Advances in experimental social psychology* (Vol. 7). New York: Academic Press.

Bagozzi, R. P. (1981). Attitudes, intentions, and behavior: A test of some key hypotheses. *Journal of Personality and Social Psychology, 41*, 607–627.

Bandura, A. (1977a). Self-efficacy: Toward a unifying theory of behavioral change. *Psychological Review, 84*(2), 191–215.

Bandura, A. (1977b). *Social learning theory*. Englewood Cliffs, NJ: Prentice-Hall.

Bandura, A. (1978). The self system in reciprocal determinism. *American Psychologist, 32*, 344–358.

Becker, M. H. (1974). The health belief model and sick role behavior. *Health Education Monographs, 2*, 409–419.

Bentler, P. M., & Speckart, G. (1979). Models of attitude-behavior relations. *Psychological Review, 86*, 452–464.

Blackburn, H., Luepker, R., Kline, F. G., Bracht, N., Carlaw, R., Jacobs, D., Mittelmark, M., Stauffer, L., & Taylor, H. L. (1984). The Minnesota Heart Health Program: A research and demonstration project in cardiovascular disease prevention. In J. D. Matarazzo, S. M. Weiss, J. A. Herd, N. E. Miller, & S. W. Weiss, *Behavioral health: A handbook of health enhancement and disease prevention.* New York: Wiley.

Carlaw, R. W., Mittelmark, M. B., Bracht, N., & Luepker, R. (1984). Organization for a community cardiovascular health program: Experiences from the Minnesota Heart Health Program. *Health Education Quarterly, 11*(3), 243–252.

Finnegan, J. R., Bracht, N. F., & Viswanath, K. (1989). Community power and leadership analyses: Formative research strategies for lifestyle campaigns. In C. Salmon (Ed.), *Information campaigns: Managing the process of social change* (Annual Review of Communication Research, Vol. 18). Newbury Park, CA: Sage.

Fishbein, M., & Ajzen, I. (1975). *Beliefs, attitude, intentions, and behavior.* Reading, MA: Addison-Wesley.

Flay, B. R. (1985). What we know about social inference approach to smoking prevention: Review and recommendations. In C. Bell, *Prevention research: Deterring drug abuse among children and adolescents* U. S. Department of Health and Human Services Publication No. (APN) 85, 67–112. Washington DC: U. S. Government Printing Office.

Flay, B. R. (1986). Efficacy and effectiveness trials (and other phases of research) in the development of health promotion programs. *Preventive Medicine, 15,* 451–474.

Forster, J. L., Jeffreys, R. W., Schmid, T. L., & Kramer, M. (1988). Preventing weight gain in adults: A pound of prevention. *Health Psychology, 7*(6), 515–525.

Fredricks, A. J., & Dossett, D. L. (1983). Attitude-behavior relations: A comparison of the Fishbein-Ajzen and Bentler-Speckart models. *Journal of Personality and Social Psychology, 45,* 501–512.

Godin, G., Valois, T., Shephard, R. J., & Desharnais, R. (1987). Prediction of Leisure-time exercise behavior: A path analysis (LISREL V) model. *Journal of Behaviour Medicine, 10*(2), 145–158.

Hoverstad, R., & Howard-Pitney, B. (1986). Involvement in heart health issues: A field experiment. In *Advances in health care research* (pp. 18–21). Snowbird, Utah: American Association for Advances in Health Care Research.

Hovland, C. I., Janis, I. L., & Kelley, H. H. (1953). *Communication and persuasion.* New Haven: Yale University Press.

Isen, A. M. (1984). Toward understanding the role of affect in cognition. In R. S. Wyer & T. Srull (Eds.), *Handbook of social cognition* (pp. 179–235). Hillsdale, NJ: Erlbaum.

Janis, I. L., & Feshbach, S. (1953). Effects of fear-arousing communications. *Journal of Abnormal and Social Psychology, 48,* 78–92.

Jessor, R., & Jessor, S. L. (1977). *Problem behavior and psychosocial development: A longitudinal study of youth.* New York: Academic Press.

Joreskog, K. G., & Sorbom, D. (1984). *LISREL VI: Analysis of linear structural relationships by the method of maximum likelihood.* Mooresvile, IN: Scientific Software.

Klepp, K. I., Halper, A., & Perry, C. L. (1986). The efficacy of peer leaders in drug abuse prevention. *Journal of School Health, 56*(9), 407–411.

Lewin, K., (1948). Action research and minority problems. In G. W. Lewin (Ed.), *Resolving social conflicts.* New York: Harper.

Loken, B., & Shimanski, J. (1988). *Salient beliefs underlying salt use and smoking behaviors.* Working paper.

MacBride, C., Pirie, P., Sorenson, G., & Kurth, C. (1986). *Organizational study involving Bloomington churches and worksites.* Internal report to MHHP investigators.

McGuire, W. J. (1969). The nature of attitudes and attitude change. In G. Lindzey & E. Aronson (Eds.), *The handbook of social psychology* (2nd ed., vol. 3, pp. 136–314). Reading, MA: Addison-Wesley.

McGuire, W. J. (1985). Attitudes and attitude change. In G. Lindzey & E. Aronson (Eds.), *The handbook of social psychology,* (3rd. ed., vol. 2, pp. 233–346). New York: Random House.

Mittelmark, M. B., Luepker, R. V., Jacobs, D. R., Bracht, N. F., Carlaw, R. W., Crow, R. S., Finnegan, J., Grimm, R. H., Jeffrey, R. W., Kline, F. G., Mullis, R. M., Murray, D. M., Pechacek, T. F., Perry, C. L., Pirie, P. L., & Blackburn, H. (1986). Community-wide prevention of cardiovascular disease education strategies of the Minnesota Heart Health Program. *Preventive Medicine, 15,* 1–17.

Murray, D. M. (1986). Dissemination of community health promotion programs: The Fargo-Moorhead Heart Health Program. *Journal of School Health, 56*(9), 375–381.

Murray, D. M., Luepker, R. V., Pirie, P. L., Grimm, R. H., Jr., Bloom, E., Davis, M. A., & Blackburn, H. (1986). Systematic risk factor screening and education: A community-wide approach to prevention of coronary heart disease. *Preventive Medicine, 15,* 661–672.

National Heart, Lung, and Blood Institute. (1983). *Guidelines for demonstration and education research grants.* Washington, DC: Author.

Perry, C. L. (1986). Community-wide health promotion and drug abuse prevention. *Journal of School Health, 56*(9), 359–363.

Perry, C. L., & Jessor, R. (1985). The concept of health promotion and the prevention of adolescent drug abuse. *Health Education Quarterly, 12*(2), 169–184.

Perry, C. L., & Murray, D. M. (1982). Enhancing the transition years: The challenge of adolescent health promotion. *Journal of School Health, May,* 307–310.

Petty, R. E., & Cacioppo, J. T. (1981). *Attitudes and persuasion: Classic and contemporary approaches.* Dubuque, IA: Wm. C. Brown.

Ray, M. L., & Ward, S. (1970). Fear: The potential of an appeal neglected in advertising. *Journal of Marketing, 34,* 54–62.

Rogers, E. M. (1983). *Diffusion of innovations.* New York: Free Press.

Rogers, E., & Shoemaker, F. (1971). *Communication of innovations: A cross-cultural approach.* New York: Free Press.

Rosenstock, I. M. (1966). Why people use health services. *Milbank Memorial Fund Quarterly, 44,* 97–127.

Salmon, C. T., Loken, B., & Finnegan, J., Jr. (1985). Direct mail in a cardiovascular health campaign: Use and effectiveness. *Evaluation and the Health Professions, 8*(4), 438–52.

Shimp, T. A., & Kavas, A. (1984). The theory of reasoned action applied to coupon usage. *Journal of Consumer Research, 11,* 795–809.

Sternthal, B., & Craig, C. S. (1974). Fear appeals: Revisited and revised. *Journal of Consumer Research, 1,* 22–34.

Swim, J., Loken, B., & Howard-Pitney, B. (1987). *A longitudinal test of attitude behavior models.* Paper presented at the Midwestern Psychological Association, Chicago.

Swim, J., Loken, B., Leslie, M., & Bracht, N. (1988). *Bloomington neighborhood "pilot" study.* Internal report to MHHP investigators.

Triandis, H. C. (1977). *Interpersonal behavior.* Monterey, CA: Brooks/Cole.

Webb, R. A. J. (1974). Fear and communication. *Journal of Drug Education, 4,* 97–103.

Wyer, R. S., Jr. (1974). *Cognitive organization and change: An information-processing approach.* Hillsdale, NJ: Erlbaum.

8

Social Influence and Antiprejudice Training Programs

Althea Smith

Social influence refers to actions used to change the attitude or behavior of another person. There are two types of social influences that can be used to reduce prejudice and prevent discrimination. The first type occurs between the influencer and the audience: between a teacher and a student in a course, trainer and participants in a training workshop, or facilitator and staff at a community mental health center. The second type of influence process is within a person. In self-influence, the influencer and the target audience are the same. In this chapter, I will focus primarily on work that emphasizes self-influence strategies rather than influencer-to-target strategies. The purpose here is to explain how and why self-influence concepts are used to reduce prejudice and discrimination and to make classroom, community-based training programs and workshops effective.

The term *antiprejudice training* refers to preventive strategies used to increase participants' awareness and sensitivity in order to keep them from making prejudgments based on racial stereotypes and discriminating behaviors. It is assumed that racial stereotypes are pervasive in our culture, and people need to be trained to evaluate the stereotypic images conveyed about racial ethnic groups. Major goals of antiracism training are to prevent the acquisition of new stereotypes, to change old stereotypes, or to prevent the inclusion of additional groups in an existing stereotype.

Throughout this chapter, situations that involve instances of institutional and personal racism will be presented. Many of the same principles also apply to other "isms," such as sexism, classism, homophobia/heterosexism, anti-Semitism, ageism, and prejudice toward the handicapped. Because examples of racism rather than other forms of oppression are presented, this does not mean that one form of

Althea Smith • Visions Incorporated, 68 Park Avenue, Cambridge, Massachusetts 02138.

oppression is more important than another. Nor is it intended to obscure the significant differences among anti-Semitism, sexism, racism, and other "isms." Rather, racism is used here as an exemplar, with parallels being drawn from it for learning how to reduce bias and discrimination in all areas (Katz & Taylor, 1988). The title of this chapter refers to "antiprejudice" training because the principles apply to all training dealing with "isms." However, for present purposes the focus will be on racial prejudice or racism.

Definitions of Racism

The term *racism* has been defined in different ways in the psychological literature (Katz & Taylor, 1988). Dictionaries define *racism* as the belief that race is the primary determinant of human traits and capacities and that racial differences produce an inherent superiority of a particular race. Racism can incorporate behavioral bias (discrimination) or attitudinal prejudgment (prejudice), but both are not necessary to produce unequal treatment (Katz, 1976; Taylor, 1984). In his book *Prejudice and Racism,* Jones (1972) describes two forms of racism: institutional and personal. According to Jones, personal racism relates to interpersonal attitudes and behaviors that are racially biased. Chesler (1976) defines institutional racism as standard practices and procedures that help create or perpetuate advantages or privileges for some group and exclusions or deprivations for other groups. Jones makes it clear that one form of racism supports and reinforces the other. The institutional form of racism involves power and control over resources, policies, and cultural values. In general, whites control the major economic, political, and social institutions in the United States, whether directly or indirectly. Therefore, they are the ones primarily exclusively responsible for institutional racism.

Elsewhere in the psychology literature, three types of individual racism have been described: dominative, aversive, and symbolic (Dovidio & Gaertner, 1985; Kovel, 1970; McConahay, 1986; McConahay & Hough, 1976). These three types vary in the degree of overt hostility and will be defined in detail later on. *Oppression* is a broader, more encompassing term referring to forms of institutionalized prejudice and discrimination toward certain groups. Here, racism is just one example of oppression. Throughout this discussion I will make references mostly to examples of individual racial prejudice and discrimination.

The Changing Nature of Prejudice

Changes in the quantity of contact, quality of stereotypes, and interracial contact have occurred in the past 25 years. Prior to the 1960s in most of the United States, the nature of interracial relations were a few brief contacts between blacks and whites, with whites always in higher status and power positions than blacks (Woodward, 1966). Since the civil rights movement in the 1960s, several noteworthy changes have occurred in the nature of racial prejudice.

Social Experience of Racism

First, there has been a change in social norms, which make it unacceptable now to express prejudice and stereotypes about black and other racial ethnic groups in many settings. Busing conflicts, racial riots, and bombings, all vividly portrayed in the media, evoked national shame and embarrassment (McConahay, Hardee, & Batts, 1981) but occurred less frequently in the 1980s than in the past. The new norms have been publicized in intercultural training programs in schools, in the workplace, and through local community groups like the YMCA and YWCA. Changes in these social norms have implications for antiracism work because they make it unacceptable to admit to prejudice. It is widely accepted not to talk about race unless one is liberal, totally accepting, and unbiased in one's racial attitudes and behaviors. People interested in reducing prejudices need to develop more creative ways to tap and change subtle prejudice than ever before.

Second, the form and frequency of interracial contact and interracial relations has also changed. Contact between the races prior to 1954 was highly circumscribed, with separate schools, public facilities, restaurants, transportation, and hotel accommodations. However, the Civil Rights Act, busing, affirmative action, higher numbers of college-educated blacks, and integrated neighborhoods have increased regular interracial contact. Such contacts have increased in variety and extent with greater exposure by whites to different types of black people. Exposure through the movies and TV programs has also expanded whites' familiarity with certain types of black images. For instance, during the 1960s alone equality and friendship in black and white relationships was portrayed in films such as *Paris Blues, Lilies of the Field, A Patch of Blue, In the Heat of the Night,* and *Guess Who's Coming to Dinner?*

Increased contact and exposure give more opportunity for disconfirming old, negative stereotypes and increasing the opportunity to develop new images based on personal experiences and new information. Prejudice is both the devaluation and glorification of groups, although usually we do not consider both positive and negative valuations in racial stereotyping. The prevalent image of Asian-Americans, for example, is a case in point. As the model minority, Asian-Americans are viewed as quiet, passive, obedient, industrious, and mathematically inclined. Some of these are generally seen as positive traits in the white middle-class value orientation (Endo, Sue, & Wagner, 1980). Others, such as "passive" and "quiet," are not generally seen as positive attributes in whites but are seen as positive when attributed to oppressed groups. A different standard is applied to racial minorities, wherein some negative traits are considered "positive" when applied to racial minorities. The opposite is also true. Positive traits take on a negative connotation. In the Eddie Murphy *Beverly Hills Cop* movies, the black hero is always a brilliant, unflappable, macho detective. In contrast, all whites are portrayed as incompetent idiots. Unlike Clint Eastwood, who played a similar character and was seen as a hero, Eddie Murphy was judged by critics to be too smart, too fearless. He was too perfect, unbelievable as a black character, almost superhuman.

Regardless of the specific content, positive or negative, modern stereotypes are still simplistic overgeneralizations that minimize or ignore individual differences. They fail to recognize diversity within the group being stereotyped. There is developing evidence that stereotyping is likely to be mixed, with positive as well as negative evaluations, with favorable and unfavorable content (Karlins, Coffman, & Walter, 1969). This makes prejudice appear to be less prevalent.

Planners of antiracism programs often include activities for identifying and sorting stereotypes that form the cornerstone of prejudice. For those who do such analyses, efforts should be taken to distinguish between social and personal stereotypes. Agreed-upon cultural values portrayed in books, television, magazines, and newspapers represent normative social stereotypes (Jones, 1972; Secord & Backman, 1964). In contrast, an individual's views about the traits and behaviors of blacks or Hispanics could be based on personal experience, hearsay, or conformity to a reference group. Social stereotypes are likely to be hidden, embedded in daily routines, and therefore less obvious and more unconscious. Still, by silence, comments, or humor, our reference groups, friends, and families identified who was acceptable and what the limits of behavior should be with minority groups.

Subtle Expressions of Racism

Changes in racism and race prejudice are also reflected in the subtleties of individual racial behavior. Behavior has shifted from the Kovel (1970) concept of the hate-motivated acting-out of the dominative racist to the well-intentioned behavior of the color-blind "humanist" described by Janice Ruffin (1973). Joel Kovel has described two types of racism, dominative and aversive. His book (Kovel, 1970) defines the two types of racists as follows:

> [The dominative racist is] . . . the type who acts out bigoted beliefs . . . he represents the open flame of race hatred. The true white bigot expresses a definitive ambition through all his activity: he openly seeks to keep the black man down, and he is willing to use force to further his ends. . . . The aversive racist is the type who believes in white race superiority and is more or less aware of it but does nothing overt about it. He tries to ignore the existence of black people, tries to avoid contact with them and at most, tries to be polite, correct and cold in whatever dealings are necessary between the races. (p. 54)

In comparison, Ruffin (1973) outlines four more subtle types of racist roles often played by "liberals," including "the democrat," who persists in the belief that American institutions are fair and equitable and does not view racism and poverty as societal problems but as problems of the individual. Second, according to Ruffin, "the white expert" is an insensitive person who professes to be an expert on black behavior. She says that this person acknowledges socioeconomic differences between blacks and whites. This person blames blacks for the problem and puts the sole responsibility for the solution on black people. For this type, she says, the answer lies in blacks competing with whites and pulling themselves up by their bootstraps. Ruffin's third type, "the humanist," has a naive, color-blind approach to racial issues. The humanist believes we are all the same, brothers and sisters under the skin. By seeing only people, the humanist strips blacks of their cultural and ethnic identity. Another recent category is the "Marxist," who acknowledges the economic oppression and exploitation of blacks but does not see differences between blacks and any other lower-class group. Race, then, is just another name for class, and no attention is given to the role of racial discrimination.

The Kovel "types" imply a consistent, unitary, stable personality, whereas Ruffin suggests a more variable, situational basis for whites' attitudes and behaviors toward blacks. Other conceptualizations have reflected more of the complexity of whites' attitudes and behaviors towards blacks, such as cultural racism (Jones, 1985), symbolic racism (Sears & Kinder, 1970), and modern racism (McConahay, 1982). In society at large, racism has changed in the past 25 years in social acceptability, subtlety, and complexity.

Antiprejudice Training Principles

Changes in the nature of prejudice are also reflected in the group norms observed in prejudice reduction training and teaching situations. In this next section, aspects of courses, group training, or workshops are used to point out some changes in the social psychology of racism in groups. These groups are varied in size as well as in racial composition and the motivations of the members. In undergraduate university courses, most students are young (e.g., 18–24), white, and middle class and have selected the course as an elective in a psychology department. In required graduate or professional school courses, students are more diverse in age (e.g., 24–50). In both courses students are required to keep journals of their personal reactions to racism materials both in the course and out.

Workshops conducted in human service programs in the community are quite different from courses. Such workshops have been offered in settings such as a community mental health center, a state-run public health program for women and children, and a residential facility for teenagers as part of a staff training workshop. Because these workshops are conducted at the request of the program director or the board of directors, they begin with an endorsement from the top administrator and proceed to build staff interest and support. The effectiveness of the courses and workshops is reflected in increased awareness of race-related attitudes and behaviors, increased sensitivity to racial stereotyping, and increased advocacy against oppression. The evidence for these changes is found in the written journal entries or evaluation statements made at the end of training.

Since most participants in these classes and community workshops are willing participants who are open to becoming more aware of racism, teachers and trainers might be seen as preaching to the converted. Although the participants may be more aware of racism than is the general population, there are still many parallels in their personal behaviors to racial attitudes and behaviors of the population at large. These parallels are reflected in the following four themes that help guide our training programs.

First, people have said they come to these sessions to prove they are not prejudiced. This is not surprising because prejudice is so socially undesirable by most contemporary norms. Many people come to the sessions defensive or resistant to the idea that they might be biased and stereotypic in their reactions to blacks, Puerto Ricans, or Cambodians, for example. For some, their willingness to volunteer reflects self-ascribed blamelessness. Some say very early in the training or courses that they want to learn more about other groups, to increase their self-awareness, and, sometimes, to prove to themselves and to others that they really are not prejudiced. Those participants who think of themselves as unprejudiced see no need to engage themselves fully in these sessions. Such attitudes can, of course, create a sense of detachment and complacency. Detachment and complacency coupled with knowledge of the pervasiveness of oppression in our culture can create hopelessness and apathy among the participants.

The approach I take in my courses and training programs is to acknowledge that racism cannot be fully eliminated throughout our society but that we can stop using old biased ways and not perpetuate bias toward new groups. Therefore, I begin with establishing new norms in the group that assume that everyone is prejudiced and has bias against certain groups simply because they grew up in a prejudiced culture. This norm acknowledges that some level of prejudice is not something to be defensive or guilty about. It recognizes the pervasiveness of prejudice through exposure to the media, family and peer attitudes, and school textbooks. Then the goals of the training are to increase tolerance, learn to identify negative stereotyping, and learn to accept diversity. This norm helps to remove the element of emotional blame that can paralyze ways of thinking about how to change personal behavior.

Second, individual racism has, for the most part, become very subtle and hidden. Differences in levels of prejudice and the apparent reduction in systemic oppression toward different groups have made denial about the extent of the problem and personal wrongdoing easy for some. For example, most of us have not "bashed" a Cambodian or Vietnamese person. We probably have not consciously denied housing or employment because of a person's race or ethnicity. The racial jokes, inappropriate sexual comments to women, put-downs, and avoidance behavior, especially when they are not "intended to hurt anyone," pale by comparison to the overtly hostile behavior of the dominative racist or the self-proclaimed racist. This makes the more subtle forms of prejudice appear more acceptable and "harmless." I start the training by pointing out that not everyone needs to get arrested or demonstrate to reduce injustice or send his or her child to an inner-city, segregated school to fight racism. However, all people can combat racism in small ways by encouraging their children to play, socialize, and get along with culturally diverse people; they can refuse to laugh at racist jokes; or they can voice disapproval at racial slurs. The point is, the level of protest or intervention is variable, just as is the level of oppression.

Third, racial attitudes are complex, ambiguous, and confusing. Those who participate in an elective course or seek our information about a racial/ethnic group all hold some stereotypes, believe some inaccurate ideas, lack information about a group, and want to change their attitudes. When asked why they have signed up or volunteered for the training, many participants say they had recently witnessed some form of racism, wanted to learn if they had the "disease," and wanted to learn to recognize their own prejudices. Usually they were in the "mixed" position of wanting to change if they held racist attitudes but really not wanting to know if their attitudes were racist.

Fourth, in antiprejudice training, especially among whites who have experiences working with people of color, the question is often raised: "How can I be helpful without being patronizing since I can never really know what it is like to be black, or Native American, Haitian, or Cuban?" A fear of rejection keeps many people inactive, emotionally distant, and cautious about antiracism training. My approach here is that we all have some experience with being oppressed because of class, religion, gender, or education. This gives us intimate experience with oppression. I point out that it is true that unless you have lived as a person of color you will not fully know what it is really like to be racially oppressed; however, that does not mean you do not have any relevant experiences with the thoughts and feelings of oppression that could be drawn on for understanding and empathy.

These factors of social desirability, subtlety, complexity, and fear of rejection drive prejudice and discrimination underground and call for special attention to make prejudice visible again. Course and workshop "ground rules" act to acknowledge the victim's experience of prejudice and give participants permission to explore their attitudes and experience with prejudice. Saying we all are prejudiced removes the blame for being prejudiced from the individual and offers an avenue for individuals to find specific ways to choose to change their own behavior.

Social Psychology and Antiracism Activities

A number of simulations designed to improve intergroup relations have been reported in the social psychological literature. These simulations were based on the notions of the contact hypothesis (Allport, 1954). This hypothesis suggests that prejudicial attitudes will be decreased by (a) increases in equal status contact through a manipulation of the power differential of the two groups, (b) the creation of norms supporting contact, and (c) giving participants the experience of "walking in the others' shoes."

Eye of the Storm

An example simulation that is often cited in introductory social psychology textbooks was developed by an Iowa schoolteacher to give children some experience of what it would be like to be discriminated against on the basis of eye color. One day soon after the death of Rev. Martin Luther King, she assigned brown-eyed students to be the favored group. For one day the blue-eyed students had to eat and play alone, were ridiculed, or were ignored. The next day the roles were reversed and the brown-eyed students were discriminated against. The experience was filmed and titled "Eye of the Storm." In follow-up television interviews 20 years later, participants still reported the tremendous impact that day had on helping them become aware of what discrimination felt like. After similar programs adults consistently report heightened awareness and empathy for oppressed groups.

Robber's Cave

Another simulation, called "robber's cave," was conducted at a boys' camp by Sherif, Harvey, White, Hood, and Sherif (1961). In it two teams of previously unfamiliar campers were encouraged to compete, thus increasing intergroup conflict. In a short time, competition in sports and other camp activities led to hostility and anger; competitiveness occurred even while the groups were watching a movie. Positive intergroup relations were restored only after the boys were required to work cooperatively to achieve a common task. This simulation pointed out how the norms of cooperation or competition can create friendly or hostile intergroup contact.

Jigsaw Puzzle

In a series of field experiments, Aronson, Blaney, Sikes, Stephan, and Snapp (1978) used a classroom setting to structure an environment of interdependence and equality. Students in six-person groups were given the day's lesson plan divided into six segments, one for each student. The individual student had to learn her or his unique and vital part of the information and then to teach it to the other members of the team. All six segments had to be put together, like a jigsaw puzzle, for the entire lesson to be complete. The jigsaw method encourages interdependence and, most importantly, shows that each member of the group makes a unique contribution. In racially mixed groups this is the key dimension to give equal status to all racial/ethnic members. These experiments contribute to understanding the importance of power in interracial contact. Although each of these activities and experiments contributes to our understanding of norms or conditions of contact, it is not clear how or why the participants change their attitudes and behavior. That is, how were they convinced? What persuaded them to change?

Attribution and Self-Persuasion

Research on self-awareness, empathy with the oppressed, and proattitudinal advocacy provide some ideas about the causes of our own and others' behaviors. Antiracism activities usually increase personal involvement and awareness about the causes of behaviors. This probably accounts for the large number of people who report learning a great deal about themselves through the training programs. Self-persuasion tactics, whether attribution- or advocacy-based, form the basis of a number of role-playing exercises and simulations used in antiracism training.

Attribution facilitates self-persuasion if we attribute our behaviors to some underlying attitude or belief. Self-attributional processes can reinforce and intensify attitudes and make them harder to change. Proattitudinal advocacy and the foot-in-the-door technique are important self-attribution strategies to use with those who are sympathetic and experienced in working with oppressed populations. With an experienced group, the goal is not to identify attitudes and opinions but to reaffirm and strengthen the commitment to work in eliminating racism. In proattitudinal advocacy, the goal is to discuss, debate, and argue for an attitudinal position within the limits of acceptance to strengthen desirable attitudes (Fazio, Zanna, & Cooper, 1977).

The foot-in-the-door phenomenon builds on a small commitment in order to motivate people to make a more substantial investment (Freedman & Fraser, 1966). Learning to interrupt a co-worker or dormitory mate who makes racist remarks can be transferred to objecting to racial slurs uttered by parents and close relatives. It usually takes time to practice the behaviors and build the commitment to take on a relative or close friend.

Attitudes and attributions that are socially unacceptable (such as racial prejudice) are more likely to be unconscious. Researchers disagree about extent of awareness of our attitudes and belief. There are those who assume that individuals are fully conscious of their attitudes and attributions (Langer, 1978). In fact, Tedeschi, Schlenker, and Bonoma (1971) believe that "the individual [is an] internally active processor of information who sorts through and modifies a multitude of cognitive elements in an attempt to achieve some type of cognitive coherence" (p. 685). In contrast to the idea that people are fully aware of their attitudes, others believe that people are controlled either by unconscious drives or the social situation. Research on self-awareness as defined as self-consciousness and self-monitoring style (Snyder, 1974) reflects this line of thinking.

Self-consciousness is particularly important when the attitudes are socially taboo, forbidden, or undesirable. In the workshop training, I assume that self-awareness is important to avoid defensiveness and resistance. It is also crucial to facilitate development of new attitudes and behaviors. One exercise that heightens self-awareness is called "BAFA BAFA." BAFA BAFA is a cultural simulation that involves two mock cultures with different languages, social norms, values, beliefs, and systems of personal relationships. In this simulation, the group divides into two groups who then visit one another and try to figure out each other's culture. One group, interested in trading, is task-focused and competitive. The other group values personal relationships and is not at all interested in money or competition. Very quickly the trading culture begins to exploit the relationship-oriented culture during the visits, and the relationship culture begins to ignore and isolate the trading-oriented visitors, who do not seem to follow the rules. The following group discussion raises questions about the primary components for defining a culture, acceptable behavior toward those not in our culture, and the nature of the feelings of outsiders and members of a visiting group. Then parallels can be drawn to different racial and other oppressed groups. In one form or another an individual's own prejudice comes out during the game, even if it is only about playing such a "silly game," which is, of course, itself culturally defined. Even these discussions can be used to point out the subtleties of prejudice.

One attributional difference in awareness involves perspectives of the actor and the observer. When we observe people from a different culture, we want to make sense of the actor's behavior (Hieder, 1958; Kelley, 1972; Jones & Nisbett, 1971). Although we often interpret and explain our own behavior by saying it is situational (i.e., caused by circumstances outside ourselves), we often interpret and explain others' behaviors as dispositional (i.e., caused by intrinsic qualities of the other). From this observer stance, we can believe that we have perfectly good reasons for our stereotypic images of ethnic groups such as Japanese, blacks, and Native Americans. Our attitudes include stereotypes with a "kernal of truth" in them. In other words, our situational attributions are based in an objective reality (e.g., I live in run-down housing conditions that are dirty because I am poor; I am poor because I am discriminated against). In contrast, dispositional attributions of others (Buss, 1979) are personality-based (e.g., blacks are dirty, lazy people; that is why they live in run-down housing projects). The combination of believing in situational justifications for our own prejudice and dispositional explanations for the conditions of oppressed groups makes identifying and changing prejudice very difficult. In this case, a training program could try to reduce the actor/observer bias with the use of role-playing techniques.

Role Playing and Self-Persuasion

During role playing, people are asked to "act as if" they are experiencing a certain event. They are to imagine what it would be like to put themselves in a particular situation. First used by psychotherapists, role playing required patients to imagine what it would be like if they were a specified other. Adolescents role-playing their adult parents or depressed patients role-playing happy people have gained some insight into the motivations and consequences of the others' behavior (Kelly, 1955; Moreno, 1953). Later, Janis and Mann (1965) used role-playing techniques successfully with smokers acting out the role of cancer patients. The forms of role playing used in research have varied from debates to psychodrama. The primary ingredient is the attempt to present the attitudes, beliefs, opinions, or behaviors of another person in a convincing manner. The experimental research on role playing shows it is an excellent way to allow subjects to get actively involved in identifying their attitudes toward different groups with whom they may or may not have had experiences in the past (Janis & King, 1954; Janis & Mann, 1965). In general, there are two sources of information about the consequences of being in the other person's position. One source is external information such as direct experiences and role playing. The other source includes the internal self-monitoring systems of self-evaluation and critique. The techniques addressed below focus changes in external information. They are then followed by a discussion of internal knowledge sources.

Attribution processes will facilitate the change process only if a person attributes racial prejudice to his or her own disposition. The factors that should be incorporated into the persuasion process that promote dispositional self-attributions include (1) our tendency to claim responsibility for acts that lead to desirable outcomes, (2) the strong effect of behaviors we repeat across situations (or how we can do them in different settings), (3) lack of strong situational pressures to perform in a certain way, (4) our attitudes that are reinforced by positive feedback from others, and (5) increasing time passage between our behavior and the reason for it, reducing the salience of situational pressures on our behavior (Smith, 1982).

Let me describe two of the role-playing exercises that I have used that involve attribution process. I want to add the caution that these should not be used without some training or experience with group dynamics or some professional experience with groups because the techniques have been surprisingly painful for some participants. The leader/trainer strategies for handling painful situations should be planned before they happen.

One proadvocacy exercise I have used in a newly formed group is one based on controversial statements. These are mostly policy statements, such as "Anyone who wants to work can find a job unless he is just lazy," "The welfare system undermines worker motivation because of coddling and fraud," or "Interracial marriages are OK but it is the children who really suffer." In this exercise the activist, liberal students speak freely with sensitivity and understanding about the conditions of the oppressed. They are aware of, and sensitive to, the anger, fear, frustration, and hopelessness that many blacks, Hispanics, women, gays, and disabled people feel about being discriminated against in the welfare, employment, and educational systems. However, their intolerance is directed toward those (especially other whites) who are not as aware of, or sympathetic to, these issues. They display bigotry toward the bigot. A major task in these training programs is to engage participants to persuade others, changing their own attitudes and behaviors, or reaffirming their attitudes and commitment to equality and social justice. Role-playing the position of the bigot can sensitize the more liberal-minded to issues that support resistance and hatred in others.

Another antiprejudice training exercise, known as the "rebirth fantasy," allows participants to imagine themselves as born again as another race and to get emotionally involved with the images, feelings, thoughts, and expectations of being born black (for white subjects). As one subject put it: "I never thought about what it would be like to be black before. I wasn't sure if I should just have black skin, and everything else stayed the same. Or whether I should have different parents, live in a different neighborhood, go to different schools. Like, would my whole life course have been different as a black. I just never thought about it before." Another student said: "Being born again as a black really depressed me. When I thought about my childhood, I was warm, happy, healthy, well cared for by my big family. But from a teenager on my life was hopeless, pretty bleak!"

Antiracism exercises using role playing are likely to be effective in decreasing prejudice by evoking empathy with blacks (as well as Asians, Hispanics, or Native Americans), developing sympathy for the plight of racial groups, providing opportunity for rehearsing plausible antiracism arguments, and acting as a reminder of guilt, embarrassment, or shame about previous behavior.

A contribution of role-playing simulations over the previous activities used in social psychology is that these make use of all aspects of a person's attitudes-thoughts, behaviors, and emotions. Some of the activities require members to think about Afro-Americans, Puerto Ricans, or Mexicans as equal in status and instrumental in achieving the group's goal. Other simulations could engage group members' emotions or thoughts but usually not both. Affecting and involving all three aspects of the attitude could increase the probability of attitude change.

In an exercise called "role reversal," groups are broken into two groups, one group playing the role of the majority group and the other playing the role of a minority group the group members know. Each group spends 15 minutes or so generating a list of behaviors that the other group does that makes them feel angry, frightened, or uneasy. In the second phase of the exercise, the individual instances are fed back by one member at a time from the minority group speaking to one member of the majority group. From personal involvement in actual incidents, individuals practice sending and listening to emotionally charged information. Although in most instances all of the the participants are white, the simulation has a lasting effect on everyone. One person taking on the role of people of color at a workshop on prejudice at a community health center said: "As soon as it was my turn, I immediately became angry about the fact that white administrators always talk down to the mental health assistants who are mostly black and Haitian. I really felt the indignity and wanted other people to know how angry I was. I knew it was a game but suddenly it felt so real."

One woman, who was an administrator for the Department of Social Services and a student in an MSW training program, became angry, hostile, and defensive when addressed by a white classmate who was role-playing a black teenager. In discussions after the simulation the administrator said she felt as if she had to defend herself and all white people when "attacked" by the black teen. She said she felt guilty and ashamed about racism in this country, in her family, and in her agency and always felt personally responsible for it when interacting with black clients. During the discussion afterwards she realized how much responsibility she had placed on herself.

Summary

Several persuasion tools are used in the antiracism training program that can be used in programs to counteract other "isms." When lack of information or familiarity is a basis for prejudice, contact (under certain condition) seems appropriate (Allport, 1954). When "blaming the victim" seems to be the problem, empathy or shared experiences with prejudice can increase self-awareness through reversing the roles of the actor and the observer.

There are several advantages to using the self-persuasion paradigm in antiprejudice training over the intergroup relations models. One of the more practical advantages is that it is not necessary for out-group members to participate in the training. In many of the classes I teach and in a number of the training situations I lead, there are few people of color. A second advantage is that persuasion-based training empowers individuals by allowing them to change any aspects of their own behavior that they choose. It gives individual participants a sense of control in reducing prejudice. It also gives a sense of optimism in that one can combat personal prejudice that in the past has often seemed hopeless.

References

Allport, G. (1954). *The nature of prejudice*. Reading, MA.: Addison-Wesley.

Aronson, E., Blaney, N., Sikes, J., Stephan, C., & Snapp, M., (1978). *The jigsaw classroom*. Beverly Hills, CA.: Sage.

Buss, A. R. (1979). On the relationship between causes and reasons. *Journal of Personality and Social Psychology, 37*, 1458–1461.

Chesler, M. A. (1976). Contemporary sociological theories of racism. In P. A. Katz (Ed.), *Towards the elimination of racism*. New York: Pergamon Press.

Dovidio, J. F., & Gaertner, S. L. (Eds.). (1985). *Prejudic, discrimination and racism*. New York: Academic Press.

Endo, R. S., Sue, S., & Wagner, N. (Eds.). (1980). *Asian Americans: Social and psychological perspectives* (Vol. 2). Palo Alto, CA: Science and Behavior.

Fazio. R. H., Zanna, M., & Cooper, J. (1977). Dissonance and self perception: An integrative view of each theory's proper domain of applications. *Journal of Experimental Social Psychology, 13*, 464–479.

Freedman, J., & Fraser, S. C. (1966). Compliance without pressure: The foot-in-the-door technique. *Journal of Personality and Social Psychology, 4*, 195–202.

Heider, F. (1958). *The psychology of interpersonal relations*. New York: Wiley.

Janis, I. L., & King, B. T. (1954). The influence of role playing on opinion change. *Journal of Abnormal and Social Psychology, 49,* 211–218.

Janis, I. L., & Mann, L. (1965). Effectiveness of emotional role-playing in modifying smoking habits and attitudes. *Journal of Experimental Research in Personality, 1,* 84–90.

Jones, E. E., & Nisbett, R. E. (1971). The actor and the observer: Divergent perceptions of the cause of behavior. Morristown, NJ: General Learning Press.

Jones, J. M. (1972). *Prejudice and racism.* Reading, MA.: Addison-Wesley.

Jones, J. M. (1985). Racism: A cultural analysis of the problem. In J. F. Dovidio & S. L. Gaertner (Eds.), *Prejudice, discrimination and racism.* New York: Academic Press.

Karlins, M., Coffman, T. L., & Walter, G. (1969). On the fading of social sterotypes: Studies in 3 generations of college students. *Journal of Personality and Social Psychology, 13,* 1–16.

Katz, P. (1976). *Towards the elimination of racism.* New York: Pergamon Press.

Katz, P., & Taylor, D. (Eds.). (1988). *Eliminating racism: Profiles in controversy.* New York: Plenum Press.

Kelley, H. H. (1972). Attributions in social interactions. In E. E. Jones *et al., Attribution: Perceiving the causes of behavior,* Morristown, NJ: General Learning Press.

Kelly, G. A. (1955). *The psychology of personal constructs.* New York: W. W. Norton.

Kovel, J. (1970). *White racism: A psychological history.* New York: Pantheon.

Langer, E. (1978). Re-thinking the role of thought in social interaction. In J. H. Harvey, W. Ickes, & R. F. Kidd (Eds.), *New directions in attribution research.* Hillsdale, NJ: Erlbaum.

McConahay, J. B. (1982). Self interest versus racial attitudes as correlates of anti-busing attitudes in Louisville: Is it the buses or the blacks? *Journal of Politics, 44,* 692–720.

McConahay, J. B. (1986). Modern symbolic racism. In J. F. Dividio & S. L. Gaertner (Eds.), *Prejudice, discrimination and racism.* New York: Academic Press.

McConahay, J. B., Hardee, B. B., & Batts, V. (1981). Has racism declined in America? *Journal of Conflict Resolution, 25,* 563–580.

McConahay, J. B., & Hough, J. C. (1976). Symbolic racism. *Journal of Social Issues, 32,* 23–45.

Moreno, J. L. (1953). *Who shall survive?* (2nd ed.). New York: Beacon House.

Ruffin, J. (1973). Racism as countertransference in psychotherapy groups. *Perspectives in Psychiatric Care, 11* (4), 172–178.

Sears, D. O., & Kinder, D. R. (1970). *The good life, "white racism" and the Los Angeles voter.* Paper presented at the Annual meeting of the Western Psychological Association, Los Angeles.

Secord, P. F., & Backman, C. W. (1964). *Social psychology,* New York: McGraw-Hill.

Sherif, M., Harvey, O. J., White, J., Hood, W., & Sherif, C. (1961). *Intergroup conflict and cooperation: The robbers cave experiment.* Norman: University of Oklahoma Institute of Intergroup Relations.

Smith, M. J. (1982). *Persuasion and human action: A review and critique of social influence theories.* Belmont, CA: Wadsworth.

Snyder, M. (1974). The self-monitoring of expressive behavior. *Journal of Personality and Social Psychology, 30,* 526–537.

Taylor, D. (1984). Race, prejudice, discrimination and racism. In A. Kahn, E. Donnerstein, & M. Donnerstein (Eds.), *Social psychology.* Dubuque, IA: Wm. C. Brown.

Tedeschi, J. T., Schlenker, B. R., & Bonoma, T. V. (1971). Cognitive dissonance: Private raciocination or public spectacle. *American Psychologist, 26,* 655–695.

Woodward, C. V. (1966). *The strange career of Jim Crow.* New York: Oxford University Press.

9

Reducing Aggression in Children through Social Interventions

Eric F. Dubow and Constance L. Cappas

Recent research has demonstrated that aggressive behavior develops early in life and is a relatively stable characteristic over time and across situations (Huesmann, Eron, Lefkowitz, & Walder, 1984; Olweus, 1979; Roff & Wirt, 1984). Huesmann *et al.* (1984) reported an impressive relation for males between peer-rated aggression in the third grade and aggression measured 22 years later by self-ratings of aggression, spouse abuse, and punishment of children, and by objective assessments (traffic violations and criminal offenses). An aggressive style of solving problems in childhood is related concurrently to other potentially handicapping problems, such as academic disability (Huesmann, Eron, & Yarmel, 1987) and peer rejection (Dubow & Cappas, 1988). Such evidence underscores the need to develop interventions to mitigate aggression in childhood before it becomes a deeply ingrained method of solving problems.

Aggression is an overdetermined behavior likely caused by a combination of genetic, biological, and learning/environmental factors (Eron, 1987). Learning/environmental factors are of primary importance for designing intervention programs to reduce aggression. Interventions have focused on sources of social influence in the child's environment that may act as the major instigators to aggression (e.g., family, media, peers). The processes through which these sources of influence might operate have been described by Huesmann (1982). Theoretical models have evolved from reinforcement theory to social learning theory to a current cognitive information-processing view that focuses on how children learn attitudes

Eric F. Dubow and Constance L. Cappas • Department of Psychology, Bowling Green State University, Bowling Green, Ohio 43403.

and develop schemata (i.e., internalized representations about people and events) conducive to aggressive behavior.

Two powerful sources of social influence that are widely recognized as contributors to the development of aggression are the family and the media. This chapter will review relevant research on the learning of aggression in these contexts and will describe specific interventions designed to prevent this process. Next, a variety of group interventions will be reviewed, the goal of which is to train children to utilize behavioral and cognitive skills that are incompatible with aggression. These programs rely on the peer-group training context for its presumed social influence processes (e.g., modeling effects, normative influence pressures). Finally, a newly developing model of the development of aggression— the "social-cognitive information-processing approach"—will be described along with its implications for intervention.

The Influence of the Family on Aggressive Behavior

Jones and Gerard (1967) stated that owing to the child's dependence on parents, the parents have a "virtually monopoly" over the development of the child's behavioral and cognitive outcomes. Parents control what Raven and Rubin (1983) refer to as the "six bases of social power," which enable parents to exert tremendous influence over the child's behavior, including the development of aggression: rewards, coercion (threats, physical punishments), expertise (e.g., special skills), information, referent power (i.e., the child desires to emulate the parents), and legitimate authority (i.e., the powerful social role of "parent").

A great deal of research has examined the family environment as a training ground for aggressive behavior. Child aggression and delinquency can be predicted from parent aggression. Huesmann *et al.* (1984) reported that parents who used harsh child-rearing strategies (e.g., physical punishment) raised children who were rated as aggressive by their peers; in turn these children, when they grew up, tended to have aggressive children. West and Farrington (1977) reported that delinquent children tended to be raised by parents who themselves had a history of crime. A similar conclusion can be drawn from child abuse studies and investigations of family violence. Individuals reared in abusive homes are more likely than those reared in nonabusive homes to be abusive toward their own children (Straus, Gelles, & Steinmetz, 1980), and abused children are more aggressive toward their peers and caretakers than are nonabused children (George & Main, 1979). These results suggest that children learn aggressive behaviors from exposure to the physically aggressive behaviors of their parents.

The learning of aggression in children was extensively studied by Eron, Walder, and Lefkowitz (1971), who theorized that there were specific antecedent-consequent relations between parental behaviors and child aggression. Following the frustration-aggression hypothesis that frustrating circumstances might generate a propensity to aggression, the authors posited that parental rejection and lack of nurturance would serve to instigate child aggression. Eron *et al.* also hypothesized that parental punishment would frustrate the child as well as serve as a model for aggressive behavior. Finally, the authors predicted that children who failed to internalize parental standards—those who did not identify with the parent or show guilt for transgressions—would be more aggressive than children who did internalize parental standards and exhibit a sense of guilt. In a field study of 871 third-graders and their parents, the researchers found that each of these variables related independently to a child's peer-nominated aggression score.

Other investigators have likewise focused on aspects of child-rearing that might be associated with the development of aggression in children. Baumrind (1971) described three patterns of child-rearing. The "authoritative" parent exhibits firm control, inductive discipline, and positive encouragement of the child's autonomy and independence; authoritative parents tend to have mature, self-controlled children. The "authoritarian" parent relies on power-assertive discipline and is typically less nurturing, affectionate, and empathic toward the child than is the authoritative parent. The "permissive" parent generally displays ineffective, lax discipline and is noncontrolling and nondemanding. The two latter child-rearing styles were associated with aggression and lack of self-control in children. Sears, Maccoby, and Levin (1957) suggest that children of authoritarian parents imitate power-assertive, coercive approaches to solving problems; children of permissive parents have no limits or aversive consequences applied to their aggressive behavior, and thus their aggression is reinforced.

Patterson and his colleagues at the Oregon Social Learning Center have developed a "family coercion model" to explain how specific aspects of family management of child behavior influence the development of aggression. Patterson (1976) argues that aggressive families engage in significantly more coercive behaviors than nonaggressive families. Coercive behaviors are attempts by one family member to influence another member in a manner experienced as aversive to the other. Such behaviors include disapproval, whining, noncompliance, ignoring, humiliating, teasing, crying, and physical and verbal aggression. The failure of parents to manage coercive behaviors, which may first appear trivial (e.g., whining), can lead to a sequence of interactions resulting in habitually aggressive behavior. A coercive sequence is characterized by reciprocity; that is, if one member initiates a coercive action, the victim is likely to respond in kind (e.g., the mother will respond to the child's tantrum by yelling). The interaction is further characterized by escalation; a high rate of coercion in one member is likely to be matched in intensity and rate by the other member. Positive and negative reinforcement play crucial roles in maintaining coercive behaviors. Patterson (1986) reported that 70% of a child's counterattacks are functional; they are followed by the attacker's withdrawal. Thus, the child's coercive act is reinforced, while the attacker is negatively reinforced by escaping or terminating the counterattack.

Interventions Based on Family Management Techniques

Several parent-training interventions have been developed on the basis of research on parent child-rearing practices and aggression (Barkley, 1987; Forehand & McMahon, 1981; Patterson, 1976). These interventions are typically based on learning principles, and thus they emphasize antecedents and consequences of aggressive behavior. The goal is to modify parent–child interaction. Patterson's (1976) parent-training intervention will be presented as an example of such programs owing to its extensive development and the availability of supportive evaluation research.

Patterson (1976) contends that the coercive process leads to several disruptions in the family: (1) Escape-avoidance becomes a learned behavior, (2) families become sidetracked from working on effective negotiation and communication skills, (3) prosocial reinforcers lose their reinforcing quality, (4) parents evaluate themselves negatively, and (5) marital satisfaction decreases. The interventions developed by Patterson and his colleagues (e.g., Patterson, 1976; Patterson, Chamberlain, & Reid, 1982) target these disruptive processes. First, parents are taught the fundamental concepts of child management, including awareness of positive and negative reinforcement and the coercive process. Second, an effort is made to enhance parental awareness of developmentally appropriate child behavior and explore parents' expectations for their child. Next, parents are instructed in negotiation and communication skills. Finally, parents are taught disciplinary skills to apply to coercive child behaviors (e.g., time-out, extinction) and are instructed in the administration of social/tangible reinforcement contingent on prosocial behavior.

In a study of 27 families receiving a 6-week intervention (Patterson, 1976), 66 to 75% of the problem children exhibited significant reductions in coercive behaviors, and 66% of the parents learned skills that effectively reduced coercive interactions and promoted prosocial behaviors. However, a 2-year follow-up indicated that many families did not continue to use these skills. Patterson *et al.* (1982) extended the length of treatment to 17 weeks and utilized well-trained therapists to offer additional treatment for marital conflicts and other major crises. Parent training was compared with a waiting-list comparison group on the frequency of observed deviant child behaviors at home and in the clinic. The parent-training group showed a 63% reduction in coercive child behavior compared with a 17% reduction for the comparison group.

Kazdin (1987) noted that Patterson's parent-training intervention is probably the most effective technique for reducing aggression in severely antisocial children in terms of its demonstrated effectiveness in well-controlled studies, potential radiation of treatment effects to siblings, and availability of treatment manuals. Kazdin (1987) also noted that the limitations of the intervention include the lack of focus on family processes outside of the parent–child relationship, and the significant demands made on parents who participate in the program.

The Influence of the Media on Aggressive Behavior

Early laboratory studies by Bandura, Ross, and Ross (1961, 1963a, 1963b) illustrated that the mere observation of aggressive models led children to imitate aggression even though the subjects did not have the opportunity to perform the responses or to receive any direct reinforcement during the observation period. Bandura et al. (1963b) also found that children viewing a filmed model who was rewarded for his aggressive behavior subsequently imitated the behavior, while children viewing the same model who was punished for his aggressive behavior subsequently inhibited their aggression. Thus, the imitation of aggression was shown to be a function of both having observed the behaviors and having vicariously experienced the response consequences.

Several laboratory and field studies have since corroborated Bandura's findings; they indicate that viewing of TV violence influences the development of aggression regardless of the subject's initial level of aggression (e.g., Huesmann, Lagerspetz, & Eron, 1984; Lefkowitz, Eron, Walder, & Huesmann, 1977; Singer & Singer, 1981). Parke, Berkowitz, Leyens, West, and Sebastian (1977) exposed institutionalized juvenile delinquents in the United States and Belgium to 5 days of either violent or nonviolent movies. Behavior observations recorded during the 5 days indicated that children exposed to the violent films were more aggressive than those who viewed the control films. In a widely cited field study, Lefkowitz et al. (1977) reported that one of the best predictors of a 19-year-old's peer-nominated aggression score was his preference for violent television at age 8. This relation was higher than that obtained between the child's aggression at age 8 and his preference for TV violence at age 19.

On the basis of studies like these, Bandura (1977) has developed a social learning theory to account for the acquisition of a wide variety of behaviors, including aggression. A fundamental aspect of the theory is that new behaviors are acquired through observing behaviors modeled or performed by others. Of special interest are the processes involved in observing the consequences of responses emitted by others. The consequences of others' behaviors inform us about the appropriateness of certain behaviors in certain situations. In addition, the consequences resulting to others' behaviors lead us to develop expectations regarding the potential benefit to us for performing those behaviors. For these modeling influences to occur, four component processes must take place: (1) We must attend to the model's behavior. We are more likely to attend to models whom we perceive as powerful, of high status, attractive, and competent, and those with whom we identify. (2) We must commit the model's behavior to our memory in symbolic form (e.g., a visual or verbal code) in order to access this code to guide our future performance. (3) We must have the opportunity to enact our symbolic representation of the behavior by cognitively organizing it, imitating it, monitoring our performance, and making any necessary corrections to match the modeled behavior. (4) We are more likely to be influenced by observed behavior if it has resulted in outcomes that we value rather than if it has resulted in outcomes that are likely to be punished.

Media-Oriented Interventions Based on Social Learning Theory

If aggressive behavior can be learned by observing models in the media, then it is equally plausible that prosocial behaviors (e.g., helping, sharing) can be learned in this way. Since prosocial behavior and aggression are viewed as mutually incompatible response classes (Bandura et al., 1963b), aggressive behaviors should begin to drop out of the child's repertoire as the child increasingly acquires prosocial behaviors. While Rushton's review (1982) of media-oriented prosocial skills training studies indicates positive training effects on prosocial behavior, effects on reducing aggression are less clear.

In a study that utilized modeling of prosocial skills as a primary training component, Friedrich-Cofer, Huston-Stein, Kipnis, Sussman, and Clewett (1979) exposed 141 Head Start children to one of four film conditions spanning 20 sessions. One group viewed neutral films devoid of prosocial content (e.g., circuses). A second group viewed prosocial Mr. Rogers films teaching helping and sharing. A third group viewed the same Mr. Rogers films but were also exposed to relevant materials such as books to build on the prosocial themes taught by Mr. Rogers. The fourth group viewed the Mr. Rogers films, had access to the relevant materials, and also received the benefit of a 12-hour teacher training course designed to encourage children's performance of prosocial behaviors through verbal labeling and rehearsal of such behaviors in songs. Children exposed to this last condition showed higher levels of positive social interaction with peers and lower levels of aggression compared with the other groups. Thus, rehearsal of the modeled behaviors added to the effectiveness of the prosocial films.

Goldstein and Glick (1987) developed a prosocial skills training program, "Structured Learning," which has been conducted with samples of aggressive children and adolescents with some degree of success. The program makes extensive use of models presented on videotape. The models portray such behaviors as assertiveness, following instuctions, and alternatives to aggression. As in the Friedrich-Cofer et al. (1979) study, mere observation of the models' behaviors was not the only influence strategy used. Participants also engaged in overt behavioral rehearsal of the skills, participated in group discussion of the videotape, and received feedback from the trainer. These training elements are theoretically tied to Bandura's component processes, which determine modeling influences. For example, behavioral rehearsal facilitates retention of the behavior in memory and enhances motor reproduction. Modeling and repeated behavioral rehearsal increase the actor's perceived self-efficacy, or expectations about future success using the behavior, and thus motivate the actor to use the behavior outside of the training session. Feedback from the trainer ensures that the trainee will attend to relevant aspects of the behavior, facilitates retention by encouraging a more precise internal representation of the behavior, and enhances motor reproduction by coaching the subject to match his or her response more closely to the modeled behavior. Group discussion may further enhance retention of the behavior in memory.

Unfortunately, these additional training elements do not always exert their intended effect. For example, Sprafkin and Rubinstein (1983) manipulated the television diets of institutionalized behavior-disordered youngsters over a 1-month period. Youngsters exposed to prosocial programs increased their prosocial behavior and decreased their aggression compared with those who viewed popular, often violent, programs. However, adding a group discussion component to the prosocial TV diet had an unexpected effect; the youngsters exhibited high levels of aggression. Perhaps these highly aggressive children perceived a threat to their freedom of choice and actively resisted the intervention. It is also possible that a group contagion effect occurred, in which the discussion stimulated rebellious behavior that spread throughout the group (Sears, Peplau, Freedman, & Taylor, 1988). The effect of group discussion will be discussed in more detail later, but it is important to note that researchers must carefully consider the potential effects of this training element on different types of children (e.g., highly aggressive children).

It appears that media-oriented prosocial skills interventions generally lead to the acquisition of the modeled behaviors, particularly when modeling tapes are combined with other training techniques (e.g., feedback, behavioral rehearsal). However, interventions based primarily on prosocial modeling have not convincingly demonstrated a simultaneous or durable decrease in aggressive behavior (e.g., Friedrich & Stein, 1973). The next section examines media-oriented interventions that target cognitive skills to discourage the development of aggression.

Media-Oriented Interventions Based on Cognitive Processes

Huesmann (1982, 1988) proposed a cognitive information-processing interpretation of observational learning that focuses on the child's attitudes and cognitions likely to facilitate the imitation of aggression. In a 3-year longitudinal study of children in the United States and Finland, Huesmann, Lagerspetz, and Eron (1984) found that in both countries the aggressive child was one who believed that TV presented an accurate portrayal of real life, identified with aggressive TV characters, and engaged in high levels of aggressive fantasy. The authors hypothesized that the child who is repeatedly exposed to aggressive portrayals may encode (or represent in memory) these scenarios. The child is more likely to encode and store scenarios that have subjective utility as likely solutions to real-life social problems. Thus, aggressive acts that are perceived as realistic and performed by characters with whom the child highly identifies are more likely to be encoded and stored than acts that do not satisfy these criteria. In addition, the more the child views TV violence and engages in aggressive fantasy, the more opportunity the child has to learn and rehearse aggressive cognitions, attitudes, and solutions.

In light of this cognitive model, Huesmann, Eron, Klein, Brice, and Fischer (1983) conducted an intervention with high TV violence-viewing children designed to change their cognitions and attitudes about TV violence. Part of the intervention included a formal attitude-change approach apparently based on cognitive consistency theories (Sears *et al.*, 1988). According to this perspective, people strive for consistency in their cognitive structures. One specific theory, Festinger's theory of cognitive dissonance, states that when people engage in counterattitudinal behaviors, the inconsistency between their attitudes and behaviors leads to cognitive conflict (dissonance). One method of reducing such conflict is to change one's attitude to be consistent with the behavior. Sears *et al.* (1988) discuss the conditions that facilitate attitude change subsequent to engaging in counterattitudinal behavior. It is critical that the individual believe that he or she has freely chosen to perform the behavior without threat. The individual must also feel committed to the behavior. In addition, the individual must feel responsible for the consequences of engaging in the behavior. The attitudes of an individual's reference group (those people whom the individual identifies with and values) can be used as extremely powerful sources of influence to persuade the individual to adopt those attitudes valued by the group.

In their intervention, Huesmann *et al.* (1983) creatively applied these influence strategies. Children in the experimental group were asked to help produce a film to alter the attitudes of schoolchildren in Chicago who have been fooled by TV, and have gotten in trouble for imitating violent TV portrayals. The subjects were told they "knew better" than to believe that TV was a realistic portrayal of real life. These manipulations were intended to create in the children a feeling of personal choice to participate, encourage a commitment to such an important cause, produce a sense of responsibility for the consequences of their behaviors, and generate attitudes that the experimenters wished the children to adopt. The intervention consisted of two training sessions in which the children developed arguments about the negative aspects of TV violence, how it is not like real life, why it is undesirable to imitate TV violence, and similar ideas. The subjects wrote their arguments and then read them during a "talk-show" format, which was videotaped and replayed to them. This format was intended to create a perception that an anti-TV-violence group norm existed. Children in a placebo group performed the same procedures but were ostensibly producing a film about their "favorite hobbies."

Four months after the intervention, the experimental group showed a decrease in peer-nominated aggression compared with the placebo group. The experimental subjects who had decreased most in aggression were those who were less identified with the TV characters prior to the intervention and who came to believe that TV violence viewing could be harmful. The authors attributed the success of the program to the attitude changes that perhaps reduced the likelihood that the subjects would encode and later access the aggressive scenarios observed on TV.

Other investigators have made efforts to teach young children "critical TV viewing skills," cognitive abilities more typical of older children, in the hopes that these skills might decrease their vulnerability to the negative effects of TV viewing (Corder-Bolz, 1980; Singer, Zuckerman, & Singer, 1980). Singer *et al.* (1980) devised an eight-lesson curriculum to enhance children's awareness of the different types of TV programs, the degree of reality of TV portrayals, how TV influences the viewer's feelings and behaviors (especially violence viewing and aggression), and the purposes and types of commercials, among others. While such an approach increased children's knowledge about TV compared with a control group at 3-month follow-up, there was no assessment of the children's subsequent aggressive behavior or attitudes. Corder-Bolz (1980) reported on a series of studies that utilized an adult ''mediator'' who offered explanatory comments and attitudes toward the TV portrayals. In one study, children viewed a Batman episode that was edited to include inserts in which a man and a woman commented that while Batman is fun to watch, it is not realistic, and that in real life one would solve problems differently than did Batman. Children exposed to the mediation were less likely to endorse aggression as the societal norm compared with children who viewed the film without such mediation. Such interventions suggest that parents might take a more active, mediating role in viewing TV with their children by fostering critical viewing skills.

Unfortunately, it may be difficult to encourage parents to play such a role. Corder-Bolz (1980) found that only 55% of the parents in a sample of 3,321 Texas families reported talking to their children about TV program content. In addition, some evidence shows that parents may resist the intended effects of TV-oriented interventions. Singer and Singer (1981) conducted an intervention for the parents of 141 nursery school children. One group of parents attended three TV training sessions designed to educate parents on the positive and negative aspects of TV viewing, the evidence of a TV violence viewing–aggression link, the factors to consider in choosing which programs to watch, and the need to become active rather than passive viewers. This intervention produced no significant effect on children's observed aggressive behavior or TV viewing habits. Parental report further indicated that direct efforts at training parents to monitor and limit children's TV viewing were met with resistance.

Taken together, the interventions reviewed in this section indicate that modifying children's beliefs and attitudes about media presentations offers a promising approach to reducing children's imitation of aggression. However, these programs have yet to demonstrate long-term effectiveness. In addition, since only a small proportion of the variance in aggression is accounted for by exposure to violent media portrayals, interventions focused on reducing the TV violence viewing–aggression relation might not be as powerful as developing in children behaviors and cognitive skills incompatible with aggression that they can use across contexts.

Group Interventions to Mitigate Aggressive Behavior

Over the past few decades, many types of peer-group interventions have been developed to reduce aggression in children; no assumption is made regarding the contexts in which aggression is learned (e.g., family, media). The goal of these interventions is to modify children's aggressive behaviors and cognitions across settings. One set of programs follows from the principles of behavior theory, while another set follows a cognitive-behavioral viewpoint. We will focus primarily on interventions for children in regular elementary schools identified as aggressive relative to their peers. The reader is referred to Kazdin (1987) for a review of treatment approaches for more seriously antisocial children who have been clinically referred for conduct-disorder problems. Before describing these interventions, we present a discussion of the theoretical rationale behind group training.

Much of the theory supporting peer-group training is not made explicit by those investigators who develop programs to decrease children's aggression. However, developmental and social psychologists have proposed various theories to account for the powerful influence of groups, particularly peer groups, on the acquisition of behaviors and cognitions. In the developmental psychology literature, peer relationships are viewed as serving different functions than adult–child relationships. Since peer relationships are egalitarian (e.g., Hartup, 1978), peer interactions are more conducive to socializing normative sexual behaviors and to helping the child learn to master aggressive impulses. Through the processes of modeling and reinforcement, peer groups are also seen as critical in the development of, for example, social competence, empathy, expression of emotions, and motor skills necessary in sports. Hartup (1978) also notes that peers provide information regarding group norms and the appropriateness of behaviors in different settings.

Social psychologists have also advanced theories on the social influence of groups that are relevant to this discussion. Jones and Gerard (1967) described group pressures toward uniformity. We seek validation for our attitudes and beliefs, and thus we may use others in our environment as standards of reference. We are likely to turn to "cooriented peers," those whom we believe to have perspectives and social experiences similar to our own. We are more likely to use others as a reference group if we admire and identify with them. Reference groups exert informational influence to the extent that they provide useful information to help us develop our cognitions. They also exert normative influence because in our desire to be accepted by the group, we may change our attitudes and beliefs to conform to those of the group. To ensure acceptance by the group, we may be inclined to adopt the group's norms as standards for our behavior.

These potential group influences might prove to be important in interventions to decrease aggression in children. As noted earlier, several interventions rely on group discussion as a major training element. Through the processes of informational and normative influence, exposure to the group's discussion of attitudes might lead the trainees to adopt similar ones. In addition, developmental psychologists argue that cognitive growth may be stimulated by exposure to new and discrepant information. According to Flavell (1977), psychologists such as Piaget and Kohlberg believe that when children become aware of information slightly more advanced than their current stage of cognitive development, a state of cognitive conflict, or disequilibrium, ensues. These children actively attempt to organize and integrate this new information into their cognitive structure and may thus conceptualize the problem in a new way. Exposure to peers whose views are only slightly more advanced than the given child's is thought to be a powerful method of influencing cognitive growth.

Group Interventions Based on Behavioral Techniques

Early attempts to reduce children's aggression were based on reinforcement and extinction. The assumption was that children became aggressive as a result of being rewarded for their aggressive acts. One way to extinguish such behavior was by ignoring it on a consistent basis, while simultaneously attending to (and thus reinforcing) appropriate behavior. Several successful examples of this approach can be found (e.g., Madsen, Becker, & Thomas, 1968; Slaby & Crowley, 1977). Reinforcement was the primary technique used in a series of studies reported by Durlak (1986) based on the Primary Mental Health Project developed by Cowen (see Cowen, Gesten, & Weissberg, 1980). Children in regular primary-grade classrooms were identified by teachers as having behavioral and learning problems. Small groups received approximately 10 sessions emphasizing social and token reinforcement for appropriate cooperative behavior during activity sessions that included arts and crafts and puppet and board games. These children exhibited significant reductions in school maladjustment (learning, acting-out, withdrawn problems) after treatment and up to 7 months following the intervention, compared with children who received nondirective relationship treatment or no treatment. While the behavioral techniques may have been the active ingredients producing behavior change, the possible effects of peer-group influences described above must also be considered.

In order to potentiate the effect of behavioral interventions, some investigators have directly manipulated the influence of the peer group (e.g., Grieger, Kaufman, & Grieger, 1976; Walker, Hops, & Greenwood, 1981). Walker et al. (1981) developed a program to decrease aggression and promote cooperation in primary-school children. The program utilizes reinforcement techniques (in the classroom, playground, and home). A behavioral consultant first designs a specific behavioral program for the target child depending on that child's initial frequency of negative social interactions; the child receives points for increases in cooperative behavior and decreases in aggression toward peers. The component designed to maximize the influence of the peer group is that if the child meets his or her criteria for success (i.e., a previously determined number of points indicating positive social behavior) during the recess period, a group activity is rewarded for the entire class. Thus, the child is subject to the normative influence exerted by the group. Initial research indicated significant decreases in aggression both on the playground and in the classroom. In addition, the target children's aggressive behavior was deemed to be within the normal range.

Walker et al. (1981) stress that in order to achieve a durable and generalizable change in aggressive behavior, behavioral techniques should include simultaneous instruction in cooperative behaviors. Consistent with this suggestion, researchers have hypothesized that unpopular and aggressive children may be deficient in their knowledge of what constitutes appropriate social skills (Gottman, Gonso, & Schuler, 1976; Renshaw & Asher, 1982). Through the use of modeling and explanation of the new skill, behavioral rehearsal, feedback, and group discussion, social skills training programs have instructed children in friendship-making, group participation, cooperation, and question-asking skills, but have yielded inconsistent findings with regard to reducing aggression (e.g., Gottman, Gonso, & Schuler, 1976; Ladd, 1981). Such mixed findings may be attributed to the possibility that some aggressive children are not in fact deficient in their knowledge of prosocial skills (Dubow, 1988), and that these programs have not simultaneously applied negative consequences for aggression or made attempts to change perceptions about aggression. Such problems have led researchers to focus on modifying children's cognitions with the hopes that this approach might lead to more long-lasting behavior change.

Group Interventions Based on Cognitive-Behavioral Techniques

"Cognitive-behavioral" interventions focus on modifying cognitive strategies assumed to mediate social behavior. It is hypothesized that we typically employ covert mediating responses to facilitate control over our behavior. Such strategies include internal cognitive phenomena such as covert self-verbalizations (self-instructions), cognitive problem-solving skills, and empathy or role-taking abilities. These skills have been encoded and stored in memory and are used as guides for how we interpret and react to events. Since these cognitive skills would likely interfere with the commission of aggressive behavior, it is assumed that aggressive children are deficient in these processes. This section will review interventions for aggressive children aimed at modifying empathy, self-verbalizations, and problem-solving skills.

Piaget introduced the term *egocentrism* to describe the preschool child's inability to infer another's cognitive and affective perspectives (see Flavell, 1977). With development, children become better able to infer the thoughts and feelings of others; that is, their role-taking skills increase. Feshbach (1982) presented a three-component model of empathy that includes two types of role-taking skills (the ability to discriminate the affective states of others, and the ability to assume the cognitive perspective of others) and an affective component (the ability to actually experience the emotion witnessed in the other). The development of these skills may be mediated by the child's exposure to new and discrepant information, which the child accommodates to change his or her current cognitive structures. It has been hypothesized that empathy or role-taking skills reduce the likelihood of aggressive behavior because observing the negative consequences of aggression to others (pain, injury) should elicit distress responses in the empathic observer even if the observer is the instigator of the aggressive act (Feshbach, 1979). Researchers have found a negative relation between empathy and aggression in children and adults (Miller & Eisenberg, 1987). Thus, investigators have developed empathy-training interventions to reduce aggression in children (e.g., Feshbach, 1979; Iannotti, 1978).

Feshbach (1979) designed a 30-session empathy training program for 60 elementary school children rated as aggressive by teachers. In an "affective-cognitive" condition, children were trained to infer both the emotions and the cognitions of others. In a "cognitive" condition, children were trained to identify nonemotional states of others, such as their intentions and thoughts. Training stimuli were presented in the form of games, including identifying emotions from pictures, reconstructing stories from others' viewpoints, role-playing, listening to and making audiotapes, and viewing videotapes. Another group received problem-solving skills training, and a control group read stories. Results indicated that the greatest reductions in aggression were associated with "affective-cognitive" empathy training. However, investigators have suggested that empathy training may have stronger effects on enhancing prosocial behavior than on mitigating aggression (Feshbach, 1982; Iannotti, 1978).

Another popular cognitive-behavioral intervention for aggressive, impulsive children is self-instructional training, the goal of which is to encourage children to "talk to themselves," using mediational, covert, self-guiding speech to inhibit impulsive behavior (Meichenbaum & Goodman, 1971). This approach is based on Luria's (1961) theory of the development of verbal self-regulation. Luria argues that until age 3, a child's behavior is generally controlled by the overt speech of others. Between ages 3 and 4, the child is able to produce and be governed by his or her own overt speech if the child is instructed. However, the ability of overt speech to control behavior during these first two stages is unreliable because the child may respond to speech as meaningless noise without semantic content. As development proceeds, semantic content of speech increasingly comes to control behavior. By age 4½, the child can begin to regulate his or her own behavior by inaudible, internal speech. It has been hypothesized that aggressive, impulsive children are deficient in verbal self-regulation to control their behavior. In fact, Camp (1977) has found that aggressive boys respond with more rapid response styles to impersonal tasks than do nonaggressive boys, and also fail to use mediational activity unless requested to do so.

In a typical self-instructional training study (e.g., Camp, Blom, Herbert, & van Doorninck, 1977) children are instructed to analyze a variety of impersonal (e.g., math exercises) and interpersonal (e.g., hypothetical social conflicts) tasks by self-verbalizing the following questions: What is my problem? What is my plan? Am I using my plan? How did I do? First, these self-instructions are modeled overtly by the trainer. Next, the child is instructed to perform the task while the trainer gives the instructions aloud. Then, the child performs the task verbalizing the instructions aloud. Next, the child performs the task while whispering the instructions, and gradually utilizes the self-instructions covertly. While the self-instructional approach appears to improve impulsive, aggressive children's performance on cognitive and motor tasks, improvement in disruptive-aggressive behavior that generalizes across settings and over time has been inconsistent (e.g., Bugental, Whalen, & Henker, 1977; Camp et al., 1977; Kendall & Wilcox, 1980). However, studies in which self-instructions are applied intensively to interpersonal problems, and which have included other treatment elements (e.g., problem-solving training, behavioral rehearsal) have had a somewhat greater impact on reducing aggression (e.g., Goodwin & Mahoney, 1975; Snyder & White, 1979).

Another widely used intervention to decrease aggression in children is the training of problem-solving skills. This approach, derived from D'Zurilla and Goldfried's (1971) model of problem-solving behavior, views problem solving as a covert cognitive process that makes available a variety of potentially effective response alternatives for dealing with a problem. Through the training of specific cognitive problem-solving strategies, the individual becomes able to create or discover symbolically the solutions to unfamiliar problems. Spivack, Platt, and Shure (1976) hypothesized the existence of a group of specific cognitive skills that mediate the quality of our social adjustment. These interpersonal cognitive problem-solving (ICPS) skills are (1) the capacity to generate alternative solutions to interpersonal problems, (2) the ability to consider the consequences of one's social acts in terms of the impact on oneself and others, and (3) the ability to formulate step by step the means necessary to carry out a solution. Spivack et al. (1976) found that these abilities emerge at different ages. For example, alternative solution thinking appears to mediate preschoolers' adjustment, while consequential thinking becomes important during early elementary school.

The program developed by Spivack and Shure (Shure & Spivack, 1979; Shure, Spivack, & Gordon, 1972; Spivack et al., 1976) served as a model program for other researchers. Shure et al. (1972) developed a 50-session ICPS training program for groups of preschoolers and kindergarten children identified as impatient and withdrawn. Daily lessons ranging from 5 to 20 minutes were presented in game form. Early lessons focused on prerequisite skills thought to be necessary for ICPS abilities: listening, paying attention, understanding multiple attributes of people, labeling feelings. In later lessons, children were presented with pictured interpersonal problem situations involving peers and parents, and children were encouraged to generate alternative solutions to the problems as well as to recognize the consequences to their solutions. Such training led not only to enhanced ICPS skills but also to improvements in teacher-rated withdrawn and acting-out behavior. ICPS training for 2 consecutive years led to greater improvement than training for only 1 year (Shure & Spivack, 1979).

Attempts by other researchers to replicate these results using similar but modified ICPS programs have not always been successful, with some studies finding that such training is more likely to enhance ICPS skills than to reduce aggressive or acting-out behavior (e.g. Allen, Chinsky, Larcen, Lochman, & Selinger, 1976; Weissberg et al., 1981). In addition, in interventions that have led to improvement in children's behavior, behavioral gains have not always generalized across settings/measures (e.g., Lochman, Burch, Curry, & Lampron, 1984; Lochman & Curry, 1986). The variability of program design across studies (e.g., number of sessions, specific ICPS skills trained) might in part account for the mixed findings. It also appears that involving a wider range of influential social agents (e.g., parents) in the program enhances the generalization of behavior change (e.g., Yu, Harris, Solovitz, & Franklin, 1986). Finally, it has been suggested that children may require simultaneous training in cognitive strategies to control their thinking as well as instruction in alternative prosocial behaviors to substitute for their well-practiced aggressive responses. Interventions combining cognitive and behavioral approaches have shown mixed results with severely antisocial children (Dubow, Huesmann, & Eron, 1987; Goldstein & Glick, 1987) but much more positive results with aggressive children in regular classrooms (Pitkanen, 1974; Robin, Schneider, & Dolnick, 1976).

In summary, while interventions to reduce aggression in children have shown some success, the overall picture includes failures to replicate and lack of maintenance and generalization of training effects. One problem with the programs is their short-term design. In addition, the more severely antisocial youths may resist the intended effects of interventions (Dubow *et al.*, 1987; Sprafkin & Rubinstein, 1983), suggesting that we need to focus efforts on changing their attitudes about aggression. Interventionists must also begin to explore the normative and informational influences of the peer group in training sessions; it is necessary to study the conditions under which these influences exert beneficial or deleterious effects on reducing aggression. Finally, and perhaps most important, many of the interventions are not derived from a comprehensive theory of the development of aggression based on longitudinal studies supporting a cause–effect relation between skill deficits and aggression. The next section will describe a newly developing model of the development of aggression and will note its implications for intervention programs.

Social-Cognitive Information Processing and Aggressive Behavior

Dodge's Social Information-Processing (SIP) Model

Dodge, Pettit, McClaskey, and Brown (1986) developed a model to study the relation between cognitive processes and social behavior in children. The key determinant of a child's behavior in response to a social stimulus is his or her social information-processing (SIP) skills, a sequence of cognitive processes that occur rapidly and often at a nonconscious level. First, the child must encode the available cues in the situation (e.g., the peer's tone of voice, facial expression). Next, the child must interpret, or attach meaning to, these cues. For example, the child might attribute "anger" to the peer's tone of voice. Third, the child must generate alternative solutions to the social problem. Fourth, the child must evaluate the potential consequences of the generated alternatives. Finally, the child must choose a response and enact it. Dodge *et al.* devised methods to assess these SIP skills by examining children's responses to videotaped stimuli.

Dodge *et al.* (1986) studied the social information-processing skills of 43 teacher- and peer-rated aggressive and 36 nonaggressive children in response to two social-stimulus situations: peer group entry and peer provocation. In response to the peer provocation situation, significant SIP differences were found between aggressive and nonaggressive children for each of the five social information-processing skills. (1) Nonaggressive children utilized more of the presented cues, consistent with earlier findings by Dodge and Newman (1981) that aggressive boys searched for fewer relevant cues in making intent attributions. (2) Nonaggressive children were more accurate at identifying prosocial intentions of the actors, while aggressive children were more accurate at identifying aggressive intentions. Aggressive children have been shown to be biased toward hostile attributions when interpreting ambiguous behaviors of others (Dodge & Frame, 1982). (3) Aggressive children generated a higher proportion of aggressive alternative solutions, replicating earlier findings (Richard & Dodge, 1982). (4) Nonaggressive children were more likely to evaluate competent responses positively. (5) Nonaggressive children were judged to be better skilled at verbally enacting responses.

Dodge *et al.* failed to find significant group differences in SIP skills in response to the "peer-group entry" problem, suggesting that aggressive children may exhibit social information-processing deficiencies in only some situations. However, competent behavior in each situation (peer provocation, peer-group entry) was predicted by SIP skills in response to that situation. These findings indicate that children who attended to relevant situational cues, generated competent and nonaggressive solutions to social problems, evaluated incompetent solutions negatively, and were judged as competent in their verbal enactment of solutions were in fact more likely to behave competently in actual social situations. Thus, interventions based on Dodge's model to enhance socially competent behaviors would attempt to modify the sequence of social information-processing steps used by the child to solve social problems.

Huesmann's Cognitive Information-Processing Model

Huesmann and his colleagues have developed a cognitive information-processing interpretation of observational learning to explain the acquisition and maintenance of aggressive behavior (Huesmann, 1982, 1988; Huesmann & Eron, 1984). Fundamental to this approach is the notion of the schema, "a cognitive structure that represents organized knowledge about a given concept or type of stimulus" (Fiske & Taylor, 1984, p. 140). According to Huesmann (1988), behavior is controlled by event schemata or "scripts" learned early in the individual's life. Fiske and Taylor (1984) describe a script as a schema that reflects our knowledge of the typical sequence of events in a particular social situation (e.g., being provoked on the playground). A script contains props or objects commonly encountered during the event, social roles of event participants (e.g., provoker), and rules describing the steps to be expected during the social sequence. Scripts guide our information processing and greatly facilitate our social behavior. We attempt to fit incoming information into the appropriate script; in fact, our interpretation and memory of a given social event is often distorted so that it is consistent with the script. Scripts are believed to develop through repeated exposure to similar situations, leading the script to become more and more abstract and complex.

Huesmann proposed several factors associated with the learning of a relatively high proportion of aggressive scripts. It is possible that the child has been reinforced for aggression, which would lead aggressive strategies to be highly valued. Further, through observational learning, the child might encode salient aggressive scenes and perhaps integrate them into previously encoded scripts. To maintain the aggressive script in memory, the child might fantasize about and rehearse these scenes. Elaborative rehearsal of aggressive scripts might lead the child to develop more general strategies for behavior than the specific ones initially encoded. In addition, the more likely the observed scene is perceived as realistic and the more the child identifies with the actor, the more likely is the scene to be encoded into a script for behavior. Consistent with these notions, Huesmann and Eron (1984) found that aggressive fantasy, perceptions of observed violence as realistic, and identification with aggressive characters are associated with higher rates of aggressive behavior.

The retrieval of scripts is influenced by several cognitive processes that are similar to Dodge's social information-processing skills. One element influencing script retrieval is the child's attention to, and interpretation of, cues in the situation. Fitzgerald and Asher (1987) found that the aggressive child's interpretation of a situation was influenced by the cue of peer preference; aggressive children exhibited less hostile bias toward liked than toward disliked peers. The importance of the child's attribution about the protagonist's behavior cannot be overstated. As Sears *et al.* (1988) note, if the child perceives an attack or frustration as under the personal, internal control of the protagonist, the child is more likely to arrive at a hostile interpretation, resulting in anger, and thus a greater likelihood of retrieving an aggressive script.

Huesmann considers the search for alternative scripts to be the next important cognitive process. The search process is affected by several factors: (1) the proportion of encoded aggressive and competing prosocial scripts, (2) the frequency and elaborateness of rehearsal of each script, (3) the degree to which cues presented during an actual event match those present at encoding time, and (4) the depth and persistence of the child's search for alternatives. Aggressive children appear to be deficient in some of these processes. Richard and Dodge (1982) found that compared with popular children, aggressive children generated higher proportions of aggressive solutions and fewer effective subsequent solutions (those deeper in their repertoires).

Finally, Huesmann views the child's evaluation of alternative-generated scripts as critical to script retrieval. Factors influencing script evaluation include prediction of the consequences of enacting the script, judgment of one's self-efficacy to execute the script successfully, and perception of the behavior as congruent with one's internalized standards and perceived societal norms. Aggressive and non-aggressive children appear to differ on some of these variables. Deluty (1983) found that aggressive children evaluated aggressive solutions more positively (e.g., good, strong, wise, brave, successful, and kind) than either submissive or assertive children. Perry, Perry, and Rasmussen (1986) found that compared with non-aggressive children, aggressive children reported that it was "easier" to perform aggressive acts and more difficult to control aggression; aggressive children were also more likely to expect the consequence of an aggressive act to bring tangible rewards and to curtail the future aversive behavior of others.

In summary, Huesmann's model views aggressive children as deficient in several cognitive information-processing skills that influence the retrieval of aggressive scripts. The aggressive child attends to irrelevant social stimuli and, in some situations, may be more likely to attribute hostility to others' behavior, thus feeling provoked and therefore justified in his or her aggression. Of primary importance, the aggressive child accesses a high proportion of aggressive scripts and evaluates positively the consequences of enacting these scripts since aggression is perceived as normative, effective, realistic, and an easy response to emit. Thus, Huesmann's model and the Perry *et al.* (1986) research suggest that cognitive social-learning variables (e.g., the child's self-efficacy for performing certain behaviors, outcome expectancies, perceived societal norms regarding aggression) be incorporated into a comprehensive social information-processing model such as Dodge's to explain the development of aggression. Interventions based on Huesmann's model would attempt to modify the child's approach to script retrieval, focusing on the cognitive processes influencing script search and evaluation.

Summary and Conclusions

The family and the media have been described as potentially powerful sources of social influence affecting the development of aggression in children, and interventions designed to reduce their deleterious effects have been presented. Parents can discourage the acquisition of aggressive responses by utilizing various forms of social influence: (1) learning new disciplinary, negotiation, and communication skills, (2) applying environmental contingencies (rewards and response consequences) more consistently, (3) modeling both positive social behaviors and attitudes consistent with such behaviors, and (4) helping their children analyze critically all environmental and media portrayals of violence.

Peer-group interventions have also been developed to train children in behavioral and cognitive skills incompatible with aggression. Social skills training programs might help to teach children specific alternative behaviors to aggression.

Cognitive skills believed to mediate aggression (e.g., empathy, covert self-verbalizations, problem-solving skills) might encourage children to plan strategies more deliberately. The advantages of using the peer group in such training studies include its potential to exert normative and informational influences on its members. Group modeling and discussion might provide children with opportunities to learn new behaviors and attitudes incompatible with aggression. However, if the norms of the peer group are consistent with aggressive behavior, such groups may actually encourage disruptive behavior in their members.

The effectiveness of the interventions reviewed in this chapter has not been uniformly positive. Behavioral improvements have not often been maintained over time and across settings. We have suggested several reasons for this. (1) Aggressive behavior is so well learned, and perhaps self-reinforcing, that short-term interventions are not likely to eradicate the problem. (2) Aggressive children may resist the obvious intended effects of the intervention. (3) Interventions have not been based on comprehensive models of how children learn and subsequently enact aggressive behavior.

Recent applications of cognitive information-processing models to the development of aggression have led to a more promising picture for future intervention programs. Aggressive children appear to possess deficits in a sequence of social information-processing skills necessary to encode and interpret presented information, and to plan, evaluate, and enact responses to social problem situations. These skills may be influenced by children's perceptions of aggression as a normative, effective, realistic, and easily enacted response. Future research clarifying information-processing deficits of aggressive children would inform the design of interventions to reduce aggression. Future research might also more systematically study and apply attitude change techniques to modify children's perceptions of the normativeness of aggression. Such interventions might include the modeling of antiaggressive attitudes and behaviors by popular TV and sports personalities with whom children highly identify. Similarly, creative methods to utilize the influence of the peer group in interventions should be more extensively explored. Overall, it appears that for improvement in aggression to generalize across settings, key socialization agents (e.g., parents, the media, teachers, peers) must work together to discourage the learning of aggressive behavior and to promote the acquisition and maintenance of positive social behavior.

References

Allen, G. J., Chinsky, J. M., Larcen, S. W., Lochman, J. E., & Sellinger, H. V. (1976). *Community psychology and the schools: A behaviorally oriented multilevel preventive approach.* Hillsdale, NJ: Erlbaum.

Bandura, A. (1977). *Social learning theory.* Englewood Cliffs, NJ: Prentice-Hall.

Bandura, A., Ross, D., & Ross, S. A. (1961). Transmission of aggression through imitation of aggressive models. *Journal of Abnormal and Social Psychology, 63,* 575–582.

Bandura, A., Ross, D., & Ross, S. A. (1963a). Imitation of film-mediated aggressive models. *Journal of Abnormal and Social Psychology, 66,* 3–11.

Bandura, A., Ross, D., & Ross, S. A. (1963b). Vicarious reinforcement and imitative learning. *Journal of Abnormal and Social Psychology, 67,* 601–607.

Barkley, R. A. (1987). *Defiant children: A clinician's manual for parent training.* New York: Guilford Press.

Baumrind, D. (1971). Current patterns of parental authority. *Developmental Psychology Monographs, 4.* (Monograph I), 1–103.

Bugental, D. B., Whalen, C. K., & Henker, B. (1977). Causal attributions of hyperactive children and motivational assumptions of two behavior change approaches: Evidence for an interactional position. *Child Development, 48,* 874–884.

Camp, B. W. (1977). Verbal mediation in young aggressive boys. *Journal of Abnormal Psychology, 86,* 145–153.

Camp, B. W., Blom, G. E., Herbert, F., & van Doorninck, W. J. (1977). "Think Aloud": A program for developing self-control in young aggressive boys. *Journal of Abnormal Child Psychology, 5,* 157–169.

Corder-Bolz, C. R. (1980). Mediation: The role of significant others. *Journal of Communication, 30,* 106–118.

Cowen, E. L., Gesten, E. L., & Weissberg, R. P. (1980). An integrated network of preventively oriented school-based mental health approaches. In R. H. Price & P. E. Polister (Eds.), *Evaluation and action in the social environment* (pp. 173–210). New York: Academic Press.

Deluty, R. H. (1983). Children's evaluations of aggressive, assertive, and submissive responses. *Journal of Clinical Child Psychology, 12,* 124–129.

Dodge, K. A., & Frame, C. L. (1982). Social cognitive biases and deficits in aggressive boys. *Child Development, 53,* 620–635.

Dodge, K. A., & Newman, J. P. (1981). Biased decision-making processes in aggressive boys. *Journal of Abnormal Psychology, 90,* 375–379.

Dodge, K. A., Pettit, G. S., McClaskey, C. L., & Brown, M. M. (1986). Social competence in children. *Monographs of the Society for Research in Child Development, 51* (2, Serial No. 213).

Dubow, E. F. (1988). Aggressive behavior and peer social status of elementary school children. *Aggressive Behavior, 14,* 315–324.

Dubow, E. F., & Cappas, C. L. (1988). Peer social status and reports of children's adjustment by their teachers, by their peers, and by their self-ratings. *Journal of School Psychology, 26,* 69–75.

Dubow, E. F., Huesmann, L. R., & Eron, L. D. (1987). Mitigating aggression and promoting prosocial behavior in aggressive elementary schoolboys. *Behaviour Research and Therapy, 25,* 527–531.

Durlak, J. A. (1986, May). *Secondary prevention of school maladjustment: Programs, outcomes, and issues.* Paper presented at the meeting of the Midwestern Psychological Association, Chicago.

D'Zurilla, T. J., & Goldfried, M. R. (1971). Problem-solving and behavior modification. *Journal of Abnormal Psychology, 78,* 107–126.

Eron, L. D. (1987). The development of aggressive behavior from the perspective of a developing behaviorism. *American Psychologist, 42,* 435–442.

Eron, L. D., Walder, L. O., & Lefkowitz, M. M. (1971). *Learning of aggression.* Boston: Little, Brown.

Feshbach, N. D. (1979). Empathy training: A field study in affective education. In S. Feshbach & A. Fraczek (Eds.), *Aggression and behavior change: Biological and social processes* (pp. 234–249). New York: Praeger.

Feshbach, N. D. (1982). Sex differences in empathy and social behavior in children. In N. Eisenberg (Ed.), *The development of prosocial behavior* (pp. 315–338). New York: Academic Press.

Fiske, S. T., & Taylor, S. E. (1984). *Social cognition.* Reading, MA: Addison-Wesley.

Fitzgerald, P. D., & Asher, S. R. (1987, August). *Aggressive-rejected children's attributional biases about liked and disliked peers.* Paper presented at the meeting of the American Psychological Association, New York.

Flavell, J. H. (1977). *Cognitive development.* Englewood Cliffs, NJ: Prentice-Hall.

Forehand, R., & McMahon, R. J. (1981). *Helping the non-compliant child: A clinician's guide to parent training*. New York: Guilford Press.

Friedrich, L. K., & Stein, A. H. (1973). Aggressive and prosocial television programs and the natural behavior of preschool children. *Monographs of the Society for Research in Child Development, 38* (4, Serial No. 151).

Friedrich-Cofer, L. K., Huston-Stein, A., Kipnis, D. M., Sussman, E. J., & Clewett, A. S. (1979). Environmental enhancement of prosocial television content: Effects on interpersonal behavior, imaginative play, and self-regulation in a natural setting. *Developmental Psychology, 15*, 637–646.

George, C., & Main, M. (1979). Social interactions of young abused children: Approach, avoidance, and aggression. *Child Development, 50*, 306–318.

Goldstein, A. P., & Glick, B. (1987). *Aggression replacement training: A comprehensive intervention for aggressive youth*. Champaign, IL: Research Press.

Goodwin, S. E., & Mahoney, M. J. (1975). Modification of aggression through modeling: An experimental probe. *Journal of Behavior Therapy and Experimental Psychiatry, 6*, 200–202.

Gottman, J., Gonso, J., & Schuler, P. (1976). Teaching social skills to isolated children. *Journal of Abnormal Child Psychology, 4*, 179–197.

Grieger, T., Kaufman, J. M., & Grieger, R. M. (1976). Effects of peer reporting on cooperative play and aggression of kindergarten children. *Journal of School Psychology, 14*, 307–313.

Hartup, W. W. (1978). Children and their friends. In H. McGurk (Ed.), *Issues in childhood social development* (pp. 130–170). London: Methuen.

Huesmann, L. R. (1982). Television violence and aggressive behavior. In D. Pearl, L. Bouthilet, & J. Lazar (Eds.), *Television and behavior: Ten years of scientific progress and implications for the eighties. Volume 2: Technical reviews* (pp. 126–137). Washington, DC: U.S. Government Printing Office.

Huesmann, L. R. (1988). An information-processing model for the development of aggression. *Aggressive Behavior, 14*, 13–24.

Huesmann, L. R., & Eron, L. D. (1984). Cognitive processes and the persistence of aggressive behavior. *Aggressive Behavior, 10*, 243–251.

Huesmann, L. R., Eron, L. D., Klein, R., Brice, P., & Fischer, P. (1983). Mitigating the imitation of aggressive behavior by changing children's attitudes about media violence. *Journal of Personality and Social Psychology: Attitudes and Social Cognition, 44*, 899–910.

Huesmann, L. R., Eron, L. D., Lefkowitz, M. M., & Walder, L. O. (1984). The stability of aggression over time and generations. *Developmental Psychology, 20*, 1120–1134.

Huesmann, L. R., Eron, L. D., & Yarmel, P. W. (1987). Intellectual functioning and aggression. *Journal of Personality and Social Psychology: Personality Processes and Individual Differences, 52*, 232–240.

Huesmann, L. R., Lagerspetz, K., & Eron, L. D. (1984). Intervening variables in the television violence-aggression relation: Evidence from two countries. *Developmental Psychology, 20*, 746–775.

Iannotti, R. J. (1978). Effects of role-taking experiences on role-taking, empathy, altruism, and aggression. *Developmental Psychology, 14*, 119–124.

Jones, E. E., & Gerard, H. B. (1967). *Foundations of social psychology*. New York: Wiley.

Kazdin, A. E. (1987). Treatment of antisocial behavior in children: Current status and future directions. *Psychological Bulletin, 102*, 187–203.

Kendall, P. C., & Wilcox, L. E. (1980). Cognitive-behavioral treatment for impulsivity: Concrete versus conceptual training in non-self-controlled problem children. *Journal of Consulting and Clinical Psychology, 48*, 80–91.

Ladd, G. (1981). Effectiveness of a social learning method for enhancing children's social interaction and peer acceptance. *Child Development, 52*, 171–178.

Lefkowitz, M. M., Eron, L. D., Walder, L. O., & Huesmann, L. R. (1977). *Growing up to be violent*. New York: Pergamon Press.

Lochman, J. E., Burch, P. R., Curry, J. F., & Lampron, L. B. (1984). Treatment and generalization effects of cognitive-behavioral and goal-setting interventions with aggressive boys. *Journal of Consulting and Clinical Psychology, 52*, 915–916.

Lochman, J. E., & Curry, J. F. (1986). Effects of social problem-solving training and self-instruction training with aggressive boys. *Journal of Clinical Child Psychology, 15*, 159–164.

Luria, A. R. (1961). *The role of speech in the regulation of normal and abnormal behavior.* New York: Boni and Liveright.

Madsen, C. H., Becker, W. C., & Thomas, D. R. (1968). Rules, praise, and ignoring: Elements of elementary classroom control. *Journal of Applied Behavior Analysis, 1*, 139–150.

Meichenbaum, D., & Goodman, J. (1971). Training impulsive children to talk to themselves: A means of developing self-control. *Journal of Abnormal Psychology, 77*, 115–126.

Miller, P. A., & Eisenberg, N. (1987, August). *The relation of empathy to aggression and psychopathology: A meta-analysis.* Paper presented at the meeting of the American Psychological Association, New York.

Olweus, D. (1979). The stability of aggression reactions in human males: A review. *Psychological Bulletin, 85*, 852–875.

Parke, R. D., Berkowitz, L., Leyens, J. P., West, S., & Sebastian, R. J. (1977). Some effects of violent and non-violent movies on the behavior of juvenile delinquents. In L. Berkowitz (Ed.), *Advances in experimental social psychology* (Vol. 10, pp. 135–172). New York: Academic Press.

Patterson, G. R. (1976). The aggressive child: Victim and architect of a coercive system. In E. J. Mash, L. A. Hamerlynck, & L. C. Handy (Eds.), *Behavior modification and families: Volume 1. Theory and research.* New York: Brunner/Mazel.

Patterson, G. R. (1986). Performance models for antisocial boys. *American Psychologist, 41*, 432–444.

Patterson, G. R., Chamberlain, P., & Reid, J. B. (1982). A comparative evaluation of a parent-training program. *Behavior Therapy, 10*, 168–185.

Perry, D. G., Perry, L. C., & Rasmussen, P. (1986). Cognitive social learning mediation of aggression. *Child Development, 57*, 700–711.

Pitkanen, L. (1974). The effects of simulation exercises on the control of aggressive behavior in children. *Scandinavian Journal of Psychology, 15*, 169–177.

Raven, B. H., & Rubin, J. Z. (1983). *Social psychology.* New York: Wiley.

Renshaw, P. D., & Asher, S. R. (1982). Social competence and peer status: The distinction between goals and strategies. In K. H. Rubin & H. S. Ross (Eds.), *Peer relationships and social skills in childhood* (pp. 375–395). New York: Springer-Verlag.

Richard, B. A., & Dodge, K. A. (1982). Social maladjustment and problem-solving in school-aged children. *Journal of Consulting and Clinical Psychology, 50*, 226–233.

Robin, A., Schneider, M., & Dolnick, M. (1976). The turtle technique: An extended case study of self control in the classroom. *Psychology in the Schools, 13*, 449–453.

Roff, J. D., & Wirt, R. D. (1984). Childhood aggression and social adjustment as antecedents of delinquency. *Journal of Abnormal Child Psychology, 12*, 111–126.

Rushton, J. P. (1982). Television and prosocial behavior. In D. Pearl, L. Bouthilet, & J. Lazar (Eds.), *Television and behavior: Ten years of scientific progress and implications for the eighties. Volume 2: Technical reviews* (pp. 248–257). Washington, DC: U.S. Government Printing Office.

Sears, R. R., Maccoby, E. E., & Levin, H. (1957). *Patterns of child-rearing.* Evanston, IL: Row, Peterson.

Sears, D. O., Peplau, L. A., Freedman, J. L., & Taylor, S. E. (1988). *Social psychology.* Englewood Cliffs, NJ: Prentice-Hall.

Shure, M. B., & Spivack, G. (1979). Interpersonal cognitive problem-solving and primary prevention: Programming for preschool and kindergarten children. *Journal of Clinical Child Psychology, 8*, 89–94.

Shure, M. B., Spivack, G., & Gordon, R. (1972). Problem-solving thinking: A preventive mental health program for preschool children. *Reading World, 11*, 259–273.

Singer, J. L., & Singer, D. G. (1981). *Television, imagination, and aggression: A study of preschoolers.* Hillsdale, NJ: Erlbaum.

Singer, D. G., Zuckerman, D. M., & Singer, J. L. (1980). Helping elementary school children learn about TV. *Journal of Communication, 30,* 84–93.

Slaby, R. G., & Crowley, C. G. (1977). Modification of cooperation and aggression through teacher attention to children's speech. *Journal of Experimental Child Psychology, 23,* 442–458.

Snyder, J. J., & White, M. J. (1979). The use of cognitive self-instructions in the treatment of behaviorally disturbed adolescents. *Behavior Therapy, 10,* 227–235.

Spivack, G., Platt, J. J., & Shure, M. B. (1976). *The problem-solving approach to adjustment.* San Francisco: Jossey-Bass.

Sprafkin, J., & Rubinstein, E. A. (1983). Using television to improve the social behavior of children. In J. Sprafkin, C. Swift, & R. Hess, (Eds.), *Prevention in human services. Rx television: Enhancing the preventive impact of TV* (pp. 107–114). New York: Haworth Press.

Straus, M. A., Gelles, R. J., & Steinmetz, S. K. (1980). *Behind closed doors: Violence in the American family.* Garden City, NY: Anchor Press/Doubleday.

Walker, H. M., Hops, H., & Greenwood, C. R. (1981). RECESS: Research and development of a behavior management package for remediating social aggression in the school setting. In P. S. Strain (Ed.), *The utilization of classroom peers as behavior change agents* (pp. 261–303). New York: Plenum Press.

Weissberg, R. P., Gesten, E. L., Carnike, C. L., Toro, P. A., Rapkin, B. D., Davidson, E., & Cowen, E. L. (1981). Social problem-solving skills training: A competence building intervention with second- to fourth-grade children. *American Journal of Community Psychology, 9,* 411–423.

West, D. J., & Farrington, D. P. (1977). *The delinquent way of life.* London: Heineman.

Yu, P., Harris, G. E., Solovitz, B. L., & Franklin, J. L. (1986). A social problem-solving intervention for children at high risk for later psychopathology. *Journal of Clinical Child Psychology, 15,* 30–40.

10

The "Psycho-Logic" of Fear-Reduction and Crime-Prevention Programs

Dennis P. Rosenbaum and Linda Heath

Since the early 1960s, the United States has been a country besieged by crime at levels never before observed in the Western world. Between 1960 and 1976 the rate of property crime in urban areas more than doubled and the rate of violent crime more than tripled (Jacob & Lineberry, 1982). Although crime rates have stabilized and even dropped slightly over the past few years, Americans suffered an estimated 34.9 million victimizations in 1985, touching 25% of all households (Bureau of Justice Statistics, 1987).

Crime had infiltrated virtually all aspects of our lives and our culture, from the daily behaviors of individuals to the continuous presentations of the mass media. Our pervasive concern about (and even fascination with) crime has taken a major psychological toll on most members of our society. Some of the biggest costs include a substantial fear of victimization and a loss of behavioral freedom for many Americans. National survey data indicate that fear of crime increased substantially between the mid-1960s and the mid-1970s (Baumer & DuBow, 1977) and has remained at this higher level. For example, a 1983 Gallup poll found that 45% of the nation admitted that there was an area within 1 mile of their homes where they were afraid to walk alone at night—up from 31% in 1967 (Gallup, 1983). Fear of walking alone at night often exceeds 60% in urban areas and can exceed 75% for the urban elderly (Skogan & Maxfield, 1981).

In recent years fear of crime has been the primary focal point of research on reactions to crime (e.g. DuBow, McCabe, & Kaplan, 1979; Lavrakas *et al.*, 1980;

Dennis P. Rosenbaum • Center for Research in Law and Justice and Department of Criminal Justice, University of Illinois at Chicago, Chicago, Illinois 60680.   **Linda Heath** • Department of Psychology, Loyola University of Chicago, Chicago, Illinois 60626.

Skogan *et al.*, 1982), the primary focal point of evaluation research on community crime prevention programs (e.g. Rosenbaum, 1986), and a powerful tool for politicians and the mass media. Interest in fear of crime was formalized in 1978 when the National Institute of Law Enforcement and Criminal Justice[1] decided that "fear" should be listed next to "crime" on the agency's research agenda as a major social problem worthy of federal attention. Thus, while the decade from 1968 to 1977 can be characterized as the "war on crime," the next decade can be defined as the "war on fear of crime." In other words, we have witnessed the unusual elevation of a psychological construct to the level of a major social problem, with numerous fear-reduction programs emerging in the context of larger "crime-prevention" activities.

Elevating fear of crime to a place of prominence on the national agenda did not, however, lead to its speedy alleviation. A decade ago we were beginning to see that most experimental changes in police response, such as increasing random patrols, providing quicker responses to citizen calls, or conducting more follow-up investigations, were not successful at reducing either crime or fear of crime in the community (Eck & Spellman, 1987; Sherman, 1986). This recognition of the limits of "professional responses to crime" has led to a rapid growth in "community crime prevention" programs, which are based on the premise that citizens play a key role (indeed the primary role) in the prevention of crime and the creation of public safety (Lavrakas, 1985; Rosenbaum, 1988). Over the past decade, the policy agenda at the national and local level has been geared toward encouraging citizens to engage in various crime-prevention behaviors to protect themselves, their family members, their belongings, and/or their immediate neighborhoods.

In this chapter we will take a critical look at the "psycho-logic" that underlies several popular strategies for reducing crime and fear in the community. In particular, a "rational fear" model will be articulated and the evidence supporting its causal links will be reviewed. Our analysis suggests that certain efforts to *strengthen* the individual's crime prevention responses may be incompatible with efforts to *weaken* the individual's fear response.

Although the available research is limited, the results are not very supportive of the fear-reduction hypothesis. The situation may be worse than simply discovering that community interventions to reduce fear have been ineffective. In fact, there is some evidence to suggest that fear levels have *increased* as a result of these social influence attempts (see Rosenbaum, 1987). How is this possible? Perhaps by identifying the social processes that are believed to be operating in these settings we can shed some light on these unexpected (and presumably unwelcome) outcomes. Our analysis will suggest that certain crime prevention strategies are based on implicit assumptions about social behavior that are difficult to defend. Social psychological research and theorizing, with a bit of "20/20 hindsight," will guide our analysis of this prevention area.

---

[1] Currently known as the National Institute of Justice, U.S. Department of Justice.

The Rational Fear Model

What is the best way to reduce fear of crime in the community? A look at the literature on community crimes prevention programs leads to the conclusion that reducing objective risk of victimization is considered the best method of reducing fear. Stated differently, program designers have generally assumed that fear of crime is a rational response to the objective risk of criminal victimization. A high level of fear is assumed to be caused by a high level of criminal activity in the individual's environment, which is cognitively interpreted as a threat to one's own safety. Therefore, citizen-based strategies to reduce fear should focus on encouraging residents to engage in behaviors that will prevent criminal activity in the neighborhood or reduce one's own risk of victimization. Thus, rather than directly attacking fear, this rational approach attacks the crime problem, and assumes that fear will decline accordingly as residents become aware that the objective risk of victimization has been reduced.

The next basic question is how do we encourage or stimulate the necessary crime-prevention behaviors? Most programs begin with the premise that residents need (in addition to knowledge or skill) the motivation to participate in crime-prevention activities. Thus, some type of arousal must be provided to get citizens to the point where preventive action is likely. The majority of citizen crime-prevention programs try to stimulate this arousal or concern about crime by providing citizens with crime-related information. Local messages designed to motivate citizens (whether formal or informal) often contain information about the nature and extent of criminal activity in the neighborhood or the likelihood of criminal victimization.

The rational fear model is illustrated in Figure 1. Whether the program is

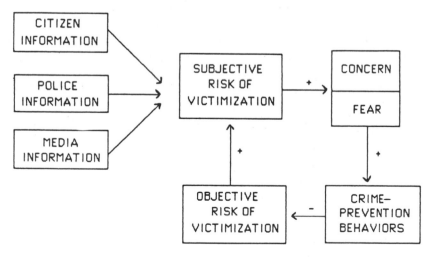

Figure 1. Rational fear-reduction model guiding citizen crime-prevention programs.

initiated by citizens, police, or the media, information is disseminated or communicated about the risk of crime. The main message is: "We have, or may soon have, a crime problem in this neighborhood, and you could be a victim." This information should increase public concern and/or individual fear, which in turn should stimulate crime-prevention behaviors. These added precautions should reduce the level of crime in the local environment and/or reduce the individual's own risk of criminal victimization, which, in turn, should cause residents to feel safer.

This model of crime prevention and fear reduction contains an inherent disequilibrium. If the relationships among fear, prevention actions, objective crime risk, and subjective crime risk are as indicated in the model, after one complete cycle through the model the process should reverse direction. That is, fear should decrease, leading to a decrease in crime-prevention behaviors, followed by an increase in objective crime risk and a subsequent increase in subjective crime risk and fear of crime. This aspect of the model illustrates the importance of naturally self-sustaining or permanent crime-prevention actions. For example, better window and door security and light timers will continue to operate without continuous effort on the part of the individual and should continue to protect even after fear has decreased. Activities such as attending meetings, patrolling neighborhoods, and general territorial surveillance demand considerable effort over time and, therefore, would be less likely to be maintained after fear reduction has occurred, if the model is correct. Indeed, the maintainence of collective crime-prevention activities is a serious problem in this field (Rosenbaum, 1987), but whether changes in fear and/or concern levels is the major determinant of this decline in participation rates remains uncertain.

One troubling question in this model is whether these programs are designed to increase "concern" and/or "fear." Few practitioners or community organizers would admit that their efforts are designed to increase fear of crime as a motivational tactic, but all would contend that they are intended to raise residents' level of concern about crime. This distinction between fear and concern has a long history in crime research (Baumer & Rosenbaum, 1981; Fowler & Mangione, 1974; Furstenburg, 1971; Lavrakas *et al.*, 1980; Tyler, 1980). Essentially, *concern* is a term that refers to beliefs about the magnitude or severity of the crime problem in society or in a prescribed geographic area, while *fear* is used to indicate an individual's affective worry about being victimized or cognitive estimates of his or her risk of criminal victimization.[2] Many practitioners would argue that their crime

---

[2] We should note that "fear" in the crime literature is not defined or measured the same way as would be found in the psychological literature on fear. As Rosenbaum and Baumer (1981) note, the psychological literature treats fear as having a major physiological component, including rapid heartbeat, focused perceptions, and increased reaction time, preparing us for "fight or flight." In contrast to these visceral reactions to immediate stimuli, the crime literature refers to self-reported anxieties about future misfortune. Although these crime-related fear measures have been questioned by some, we have been able to document the reliability and validity of several multiitem scales (see Baumer & Rosenbaum, 1981).

prevention programs are intended to make citizens aware of the crime problem (i.e., increase concern) without making them more fearful of victimization.

Although researchers have successfully demonstrated that concern and fear are empirically distinct constructs, the ability of social interventions to raise concern without simultaneously raising fear remains in question. In a quasi experiment specifically addressing the question, Lavrakas, Rosenbaum, and Kaminski (1983) found that a community newsletter containing crime statistics and crime-prevention tips was successful at elevating concern without affecting fear levels. However, efforts to replicate this effect in Houston, Texas, and Newark, New Jersey, were unsuccessful, indicating that neither concern nor fear was affected by the newsletter (Lavrakas, 1986). Evaluations of other strategies involving interpersonal communication indicate that these two perceptions are not easy to separate and are positively correlated at the neighborhood level. For example, in a quasi-experimental assessment of community crime-prevention activities in Chicago, we found that concern about crime increased significantly over a 1-year period in two of four experimental neighborhoods, but so did fear—in fact, fear of crime increased in three of four neighborhoods (Rosenbaum, Lewis, & Grant, 1986). Thus, practitioners may find it difficult to influence levels of concern without also affecting levels of fear.

Regardless of the impact of concern, there is evidence, both compelling and suggestive, that crime-prevention efforts can and do exacerbate fear of crime. In terms of police influence strategies, Rosenbaum and Bickman (1989) found, using a randomized experimental design, that crime-prevention officers can increase fear of crime and inhibit psychological recovery by recommending home security improvements shortly after victimization—a very common practice in the United States. Police have also played a major role in crime-prevention awareness campaigns, including film presentations, public addresses, workshops, and the distribution of crime-prevention materials. As DuBow *et al.* (1979) note, "a frequent premise underlying such presentations is the need to teach people that crime is more extensive and serious than they think" (p. 23).

Even among people who are not recent crime victims, programs aimed at increasing crime prevention behaviors sometimes increase fear. In the "Take a Bite Out of Crime" national public information campaign, which featured Mc-Gruff, the crime dog, evaluations showed that media presentations aroused fear among parts of the population. This fear is not necessarily seen as a negative outcome. Rather, in keeping with the rational fear-reduction model, O'Keefe (1986) noted, "Fear arousal to a limited degree may well enhance the persuasive impact of a message" (p. 264).

Is fear arousal an *intentional* strategy by crime-prevention practitioners, or is it an unexpected consequence of providing citizens with information about local crime? There is no clear answer to this question at present, but our field experience over the years leads us to suspect that both intentional and untoward effects are operating. We do know that community organizers use techniques that would seem to generate fear as easily as they would generate concern. For example, in attempting to explain why fear of crime might increase as a result of participating in a Block Watch meeting, Rosenbaum (1987) notes that organizers in Seattle and Chicago are trained to encourage attendees to share victimization experiences:

> The *Citizens Guide to Organize a Block Watch* (Seattle Police Department, n.d.) suggests that the organizer begin the meeting with a discussion of local crime statistics and then "ask if anyone present has been a victim of crime recently" (p. 6). In Chicago, "people are encouraged to talk about recent victimization experiences" (Citizen Information Service of Illinois, 1982, p. 12). As the Seattle guide explicitly states "the purpose of this information is to let people know there is crime in their neighborhood and anyone can be a victim" (p. 6). (Rosenbaum, 1987, p. 120)

These interventions are apparently intended to arouse both fear and concern among local participants. If fear is heightened, then the proposed rational fear model would suggest that initial *fear arousal* will eventually lead to *fear reduction*. The role of fear in the crime-prevention process is an important issue and thus will be the central focus of our remaining discussion. Although practitioners and policy makers are often disturbed by the thought of programs seeking to arouse fear as a motivational device, perhaps moderate levels of arousal are highly effective at influencing crime-prevention behaviors. Hence, the remainder of this chapter will look at the theoretical assumptions underlying the rational fear model in relationship to the available empirical evidence. The key questions to be addressed are the following: (1) Is fear a rational response to crime or is it influenced by nonrisk factors? (2) What are the effects of fear on crime-prevention behaviors? (3) What are the effects of engaging in crime-prevention behaviors on fear of crime? (4) Does social psychology help us to understand the processes at work and possibly suggest alternative intervention strategies?

The Rationality of Fear

Is fear a rational response to crime or is it influenced by nonrisk factors? To some extent, people's perceptions and fears are accurate, or at least covary with objective conditions in the environment. A number of studies have shown that residents who live in high crime areas perceive more crime, feel a higher risk of victimization, and report greater fear than persons living in lower crime areas (e.g. Block & Long, 1973; Boggs, 1971; Fowler & Mangione, 1974; Furstenburg, 1972; McPherson, 1978; Reiss, 1967). On the other hand, researchers have identified communities and cities with crime rates that are quite different, but with fear levels that are surprisingly similar (Reiss, 1967; Waller & Okihiro, 1976). Moreover, the research on *changes* in crime rate suggests that fear is not a direct function of objective crime rates. Analysis of national data over a number of years has shown that fear of crime has not increased as quickly as the official crime rate (Hindelang, 1974) and that fear has not always even changed in the same direction as the crime rate (Erskine, 1974). Perhaps the most interesting aspect of this fear–

crime relationship is highlighted by DuBow *et al.* (1979)—namely, that rises in crime seem to be more effective in boosting fear than decreases in crime are at lowering fear. Thus, fear may be easier to increase than it is to decrease with crime risk information.

Perceived changes in crime rates (as opposed to actual changes) may play a critical role in altering fear levels. The case studies of "crime waves" (i.e., sudden apparent increases in crime after a period of low crime rates) often conclude that *perceived* change is the driving force behind the heightened fear; this perception is often due to changes in the behavior of the police or the media rather than changes in the objective risk of victimization (e.g. Baker, Nienstedt, Everett, & McCleary, 1983; Fishman, 1977). These observations do not suggest that citizens are irrational in their fear response. Given the information available to them, citizens may be responding quite appropriately. However, these observations, along with documentation of citizen reactions to singular crimes that are unusual or well-publicized (see Conklin, 1975), suggest that citizens' fears are subject to manipulation by factors other than the objective risk of victimization.

While the above neighborhood-level analyses suggest a correspondence between fear and objective risk, a look at individual-level analyses offers an entirely different picture. Indeed, the most compelling evidence to support the argument that fear is not a direct by-product of an unsafe environment comes from a sizable body of research on the individual correlates of fear (e.g., for reviews, see Baumer, 1978; Skogan & Maxfield, 1981). The primary findings can be described as the fear paradox: Persons who perceive the highest crime rates, the greatest personal risk, and the greatest fear of crime are the least likely to be victimized (Health, Riger, Gordon, & Le Bailly, 1979; Hindelang, Gottfredson, & Garofalo, 1978; Skogan *et al.*, 1982). In particular, research has repeatedly shown that women are much more fearful than men, and older residents are much more fearful than younger residents, yet women and the elderly are less frequently victimized by crime than their counterparts.

There has been a longstanding debate in the field about whether fear levels are inappropriately high for certain groups (e.g., President's Crime Commission, 1967) or are appropriate to a situation in which women are more physically vulnerable and may have a lower sense of self-protection efficacy (Riger, LeBailly, Gordon, & Heath, 1979; Stinchcombe *et al.*, 1977).[3] Without entering this debate, we can conclude that the observed inverse relationship between fear and risk is evidence to suggest that fear is determined at least partially by factors other than the objective crime conditions.

What are these "other" factors that help to account for fear of crime? Social psychologists and criminologists have suggested that perceptions of crime are influenced by three basic sources of information: (1) direct experience with crime,

---

[3] Another position is that fear levels are appropriate for the elderly, who may have a higher risk of victimization *per unit of exposure* than other age groups (Antunes, Cook, Cook, & Skogan, 1977; DuBow *et al.*, 1979), but have lower exposure levels owing to reduced mobility.

(2) social interactions with relatives, friends, and neighbors, and (3) exposure to the mass media (DuBow *et al.,* 1979; Skogan & Maxfield, 1981; Tyler, 1980; Tyler & Lavrakas, 1986). What do we know about the effects of personal experience with crime and socially transmitted information on fear of crime?

Victimization Experience

The early research on the effects of personal experience found that fear was unrelated to victimization experience (Biderman, Johnson, McIntyre, & Weir, 1967; Conklin, 1971; Ennis, 1967; Fowler & Mangione, 1974; Hindelang, 1974), while several later studies did find victims to be more fearful than nonvictims (Lavrakas, 1982; Skogan & Maxfield, 1981; Tyler, 1980). Other researchers have uncovered fear differences by separating personal from property crimes, older from younger victims, and/or multiple from single incidents, (e.g. Garofalo, 1977; Rifai, 1976). Unfortunately, all of the above-mentioned research is cross-sectional in nature (comparing victims and nonvictims), thus greatly weakening the inference that victimization experience explains the difference in fear levels. However, more powerful panel studies (where individuals were victimized between the pretest and the posttest) reveal that victimization by either personal or property crime is a fear-arousing experience (Rosenbaum & Lurigio, 1989; Skogan, 1987).

In sum, we now know that victimization experience is an important contributor to fear of crime. However, we must keep in mind that 3 out of 4 households are *not* touched by crime during the year, and of those that are, 8 out of 10 are *not* touched by violent crimes known to be the most fear-arousing. Data from the National Crime Survey yield a victimization rate for violence (rape, robbery, and assault) of only 35 per 1,000 persons age 12 and over (Bureau of Justice Statistics, 1983). Thus, while victimization is certainly one source of fear, it remains a relatively rare set of events and thus is unable to account for the magnitude of the current fear response.

Social Interaction

The role of informal social networks in coping with environmental stress has received considerable attention by psychologists in recent years (Gottlieb, 1981; Unger & Wandersman, 1985). Researchers now recognize the importance of relatives, neighbors, and friends as a major source of information and support. In the area of crime, the Reactions to Crime Project (Skogan *et al.,* 1982) was instrumental in focusing attention on the role of informal contacts and interpersonal communication in the formation of perceptions and fears regarding crime. Although serious crime directly touches the lives of only a small segment of the population during any given year, the majority have exchanged crime stories, perceptions, and assessments of the crime problem. Knowing about the victimization experiences of friends, family, and neighbors is now referred to as "vicarious victimization" (Skogan *et al.*, 1982) or "indirect victimization" (Tyler, 1980). Several studies have found that such indirect contact with crime is associated with higher levels of fear (Lavrakas, 1982; Skogan & Maxfield, 1981; Tyler, 1980). Thus, fear of crime may be influenced as much by interpersonal communication as it is by other sources of information. Indeed, for residents of Chicago, Lavrakas (1982) found that vicarious victimization was a stronger predictor of fear than actual victimization experience.

Although our knowledge of the content of interpersonal communication about crime is quite limited, field research indicates that community residents talk to one another about specific crimes that have occurred (locally and elsewhere), specific local incivilities (or signs of disorder), and general perceptions and concerns regarding these problems (Lewis, Grant, & Rosenbaum, 1988; Podolefsky & DuBow, 1981; Skogan & Maxfield, 1981). Although some researchers have interpreted their findings to suggest that social interaction *reduces* fear of crime (Gubrium, 1974; Merry, 1981; Sundeen & Mathieu, 1976), the bulk of available research supports the alternative hypothesis that social interaction and communication about crime *increase* fear among those exchanging the information (Greenberg, Rohe, & Williams, 1982; Newman & Franck, 1980; Rosenbaum *et al.*, 1986; Skogan & Maxfield, 1981; Tyler, 1980). Thus, talking about crime seems to arouse rather than alleviate the fear response. The nature and content of the communication may help to clarify this effect, although mediating variables have yet to be empirically identified. For example, in local meetings, the amount and severity of local violence can be distorted and crime victims may be overrepresented (Skogan & Maxfield, 1981). There is some evidence that crime victims become "communication nodes" for crime information, attracting and disseminating other victimization stories (LeJeune & Alex, 1973).

Mass Media

Another source of information about crime, particularly crime beyond the immediate neighborhood, is the mass media. Fishman (1977) documented how a "crime wave against the elderly" in New York City was created by newspaper and television coverage, with no actual increase in the rate of crimes against the elderly. Here, perceptions of the crime rate followed the mass media rather than any information about objective risk of victimization in the local environment. Similarly, Heath and Petraitis (1986) found that the perception of crime danger in distant places (i.e., another city or downtown in the local city) is positively correlated with the amount of television viewing. The perception of crime danger in one's own neighborhood, on the other hand, is positively related to television viewing only among those who live in high crime, urban areas (Doob & MacDonald, 1979; Heath & Petraitis, 1986). This pattern is consistent with the "double dose'' notion (Gerbner & Gross, 1976), which posits that media images gain added power when they are a close match to reality.

The effects of mass media presentations of crime on fear are further qualified by details about crime location and motivation. Crime news that contains no information about crime motive arouses greater fear than news with motive content, particularly if the crimes are local (Heath, 1984). Similarly, accounts of gruesome local crimes increase fear, while accounts of gruesome crimes that occur elsewhere seem to reassure people regarding the safety of the local environment (Heath, 1984). Finally, mass media effects have been found to operate more on the level of general concern about crime or danger to the average person than on the level of personal danger or fear of victimization (Tyler & Cook, 1984).

In sum, there is growing evidence that indirect experience with crime via socially transmitted information can have a significant impact on fear of crime. Social interaction and discussion about crime can lead to fear arousal. The mass media can also increase fear of crime, but the effects appear to be less powerful and more qualified than the effects of social interaction. Unfortunately, the information being communicated by other persons or the mass media (information that serves as the basis for changes in fear levels) is likely to be quite distorted and highly selective (Heath, Gordon, & LeBailly, 1981). Thus, fear is not always based on an objective assessment of risk. Furthermore, for community organizers who quietly claim that they have achieved their objective of motivating local residents, the research community would respond that most of the observed effects cannot be attributed to planned social interventions, but rather to informal processes. Nevertheless, we will proceed to ask whether the arousal actually leads to preventive behaviors.

The Effects of Fear on Crime-Prevention Behaviors

One of the most important assumptions in the rational fear model is that fear arousal will lead to crime-prevention behaviors. The efficacy of fear-arousing communications in changing behavior or behavioral intentions in areas such as dental hygiene, safe driving practices, and smoking was the focus of considerable social psychological research in the 1960s (see Tedeschi & Lindskold, 1976). Consistent with the literature, DuBow and his colleagues (DuBow et al., 1979) concluded, after reviewing the crime-related literature, that persons who are afraid of criminal victimization are more likely to engage in various crime-prevention behaviors than persons who are not afraid. Before updating and clarifying this conclusion, we should define what we mean by "crime-prevention behaviors."

Crime-prevention behaviors have been conceptualized in many different ways (for reviews, see Baumer & Rosenbaum, 1981; DuBow et al., 1979; Lavrakas & Lewis, 1980). The most straightforward and empirically tested typology offers three categories of behaviors—personal protection behaviors, household protection behaviors, and neighborhood/community protection behaviors (cf. Lavrakas *et al.*, 1980; Skogan, 1981). Personal protection behaviors include all efforts to protect oneself from victimization, ranging from not going out alone at night to carrying a weapon to taking a self-defense class. Household protection behaviors include all efforts to reduce the probability that potential offenders will gain illegal entry into one's home. These behaviors can be directed at creating physical barriers (e.g., installing better locks) or psychological barriers (e.g., using timers on indoor lights). Neighborhood protection behaviors include all efforts directed at preventing crime in a specific geographic area. Often these are collective actions that require citizen participation in public meetings (e.g., Block Watch meetings).

One of the most consistent findings in the literature is that fear of crime is positively correlated with certain personal protection behaviors. In particular, fear of crime is associated with restricted mobility or risk-avoidance activities. Persons who are fearful of crime, as compared with persons less fearful, are more likely to avoid going out in the evening, and when they do go out, they are more likely to avoid areas perceived as dangerous and take someone with them (Gordon & Riger, 1979; Lavrakas, 1982; Maxfield, 1977; 1987; Riger *et al.*, 1979; Savitz, Lalli & Rosen, 1977; Skogan & Maxfield, 1981; Tyler, 1980). However, as others have noted (Hindelang *et al.*, 1978; Maxfield, 1987), the strong relationship between fear and behavioral restrictions in the evening is confounded by differences in life-styles. Women and older persons (the most fearful subgroups) go out less frequently in the evening for recreational activities than do men and younger persons, regardless of their fear levels. Nevertheless, closer analysis suggests that fear does exert an independent influence on avoidance behavior, although it is less important than these demographic predictors of leisure activities (Maxfield, 1987).

Although fear seems to provide sufficient motivation to activate avoidance behaviors, there is little evidence that it consistently stimulates other types of personal protection or home protection measures (Furstenberg, 1972; Heath & Davidson, 1988; Kim, 1976; Maxfield, 1977; Sundeen & Mathieu, 1976; Wilson, 1976). Even among the elderly, who express high fear levels, few preventive actions are taken other than locking doors (Lawton, Nahemow, Yaffe, & Feldman, 1976; Market Opinion Research, 1977). Fear does not seem to drive most citizens to carry a weapon, take self-defense classes, buy a dog, dress differently, carry one's purse in a certain way, purchase and install hardware, or take other precautions. While household protection behaviors (usually for burglary prevention) are more common than personal protection behaviors (Skogan, 1981), they are less consistently association with fear of crime. In a major study of citizen participation, Lavrakas (1981) found that fear was unrelated to home protection behaviors, and that many demographic and social factors were stronger predictors of these behavioral responses.

The research literature is quite ambiguous regarding the motivating effects of fear on participation in *collective* neighborhood crime-prevention activities. There is some evidence that fear is positively related to interpersonal and collective actions against crime. For example, studies have found that higher fear is associated with asking neighbors to watch one's home (Kim, 1976) and with participating in collective crime-prevention meetings (Conklin, 1971; Kim, 1976; Yaden, Folkstand, & Glazer, 1973). However, several researchers have argued that residents' motivation to join community anticrime groups does *not* stem primarily from fear or risk avoidance but rather from a concern about crime as a neighborhood problem (Lavrakas et al., 1980; Podolefsky & DuBow, Tyler & Lavrakas, 1986). The lack of consistent findings in this area may be due to researchers' focusing on different forms of collective anticrime behaviors. Research indicating no fear motivation has focused primarily on the individual's motivation for joining stable *multiissue community organizations,* while research indicating fear-based motivations has been largely directed at *ad hoc single-issue groups* that are created to address pressing crime problems. For example, the national evaluation of Neighborhood Watch programs (Garofalo & McLeod, 1986) documents how these crime-focused programs often emerge quickly in middle-class neighborhoods in response to a rash of burglaries or other crimes. This popular program is a good illustration of how collective participation can be the product of fear arousal (cf. Rosenbaum, 1987; Skogan, 1987). But generally speaking, community research can be interpreted as indicating that fear levels are negatively correlated with collective action. That is, high crime, high fear neighborhoods are characterized by an absence of collective crime-prevention behaviors, high levels of distrust, and high levels of self-protective behaviors (Conklin, 1975; Rosenbaum, 1987; Skogan, 1986).

The relationship between fear and crime-prevention behaviors can be cast in terms of the reactance/learned helplessness integration proposed by Wortman and Brehm (1975). According to this formulation, initial threats to control (such as a rash of burglaries in a normally safe neighborhood) instigate attempts to reestablish control. Long-lasting threats to control (such as consistently high crime rates in a neighborhood) lead to the giving-up response, termed *learned helplessness,* according to this reformulation. This framework accounts for the data that show collective action as a response to crime threats in middle-class, normally safe neighborhoods but not in more needy, high crime neighborhoods (Garofalo & McLeod, 1986). A new threat to safety is met with resistance; a long-standing threat is met with self-restrictions (Gordon & Riger, 1979; Lavrakas, 1982). Heath and Davidson (1988) found this reactance/learned helplessness pattern regarding threat of sexual assault and self-protective behaviors. Initial threats to safety were met with increased attempts at self-protection, but long-standing threats to safety were accompanied by decreased self-protective behaviors.

To summarize, research on the relationship between fear and crime-prevention behaviors allows the following conclusions: Fear of crime seems to activate a limited set of personal protection behaviors (primarily avoidance and restriction), but is *not* strongly related to either home protection behaviors or collective neighborhood protection behaviors (with the exception of encouraging initial attendance at crime-focused meetings in middle-class areas following recent crime upturns). Unfortunately, the types of self-protection that are stimulated by fear arousal have been accused of contributing to a cycle of increased fear, increased criminal activity,and ultimately neighborhood decline. The National Advisory Commission on Criminal Justice Standards and Goals (1973), in reference to a widespread citizen "retreat behind locks, bars, alarms, and guards," argued that "although these prophylactic measures may be steps in self-protection, they can lead to a lessening of the bonds of mutual assistance and neighborliness" (p. 46). Whether self-protection measures or other forms of crime-prevention behavior are effective in preventing crime, and thus reducing fear, is an empirical question that will be addressed in the next section. But in fairness to the fear-arousal advocates, there is some limited evidence that fear does more than motivate residents to stay home and lock their doors—in certain neighborhoods, rapid changes in the perceived risk of victimization seems to push local residents to attend one or more anticrime meetings to discuss the perceived problem that has developed.

The Effects of Crime-Prevention Behaviors on Fear

If the rational fear model is correct, then newly acquired crime-prevention behaviors (produced by fear arousal) should result in a reduced risk of victimization, which, in turn, should result in a reduced level of fear. As noted earlier, one can also hypothesize a direct route for fear reduction—namely, social interaction and discussion. Given some evidence that fear can stimulate certain types of individual and collective action, the key question becomes: What do we currently know about the effects of these preventive actions on subsequent fear and crime levels?

The effectiveness of crime-prevention behaviors is a long-standing issue that has yet to receive adequate research attention. Many national meta-type evaluations in the 1970s conclude that we simply do not have adequate high-quality data to estimate the effects of community crime-prevention programs (see Lurigio & Rosenbaum, 1986). Nevertheless, let us summarize some of the observed relationships and issues that surround the question of behavioral impact on fear and victimization.

Individual and Household Behaviors

When an individual engages in preventive behaviors for self-protection or property protection purposes, do these behaviors reduce the individual's fear of crime, either directly (by producing a sense of control, efficacy, or perceived reduction in risk) or indirectly (by reducing the level of crime or risk of victimization)? Unfortunately, the literature pertinent to the direct behavior–fear link is the same literature cited earlier regarding the fear–behavior link. That is, most of the research in this field is based on cross-sectional correlations and therefore does not allow for an easy determination of causality or even the direction of causality.

If we reverse the direction of causality, as DuBow and his colleagues (1979) have proposed, we would conclude that risk-avoidance behaviors cause people to be more fearful of victimization and to perceive a higher risk of falling prey to crime, but that home protection behaviors have little effect upon fear levels. The argument that behavior causes fear (as opposed to fear causing behavior) is certainly consistent with Bem's (1967) self-perception theory. Residents who find themselves locking their doors and restricting their behavior on a daily basis may be creating a behavioral foundation for drawing the inference that they are afraid. Repetitious behavior could strengthen the fear response.

Thinking that panel data would help clarify the direction of causality between fear and behavior, we reanalyzed some community survey data collected earlier by one of the authors (Rosenbaum et al., 1986). Figure 2 shows the zero-order correlations between a fear-of-personal-crime index and an avoidance index using data collected from 1636 Chicago residents in a 1-year panel design. Although these data further document the strong positive relationship between fear and avoidance behavior, the identical cross-lag coefficients provide little guidance in determining the direction of causality. Additional partial correlations did not clarify the relationships.

Whether one interprets these data as indicating that fear serves as a motivator for protective behavior or protective behavior enhances fear, the results are inconsistent with the hypothesis that fear is reduced as a result of engaging in individual crime-prevention behaviors. The observation that high levels of fear and high levels of behavioral restriction go hand in hand suggests that, even if these precautionary measures are highly effective in lowering risk, fear is not responsive to changes in safety. This brings us to the most basic question that remains unanswered: Is the risk of victimization lowered as a result of engaging in crime-

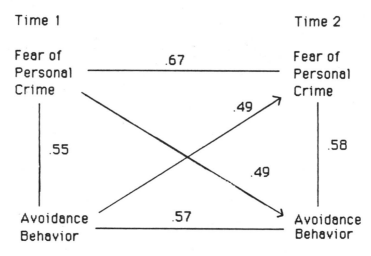

Figure 2. Cross-lagged panel view of fear and avoidance behavior (zero-order correlations).

prevention behaviors? In other words, is there some benefit that is reaped given the high price of fear and protective action?

Here again, the verdict is still out regarding the effectiveness of most crime-prevention measures. However, we should begin with the consistent finding cited earlier that behavioral restrictions are the highest among groups that have some of the lowest rates of victimization. Lavrakas (1982) found that being female and being older—two low victimization groups—are among the best predictors of behavioral restrictions (defined in this study as not carrying lots of cash, not walking near certain types of strangers, and not going out alone at night), a relationship some researchers have attributed to increased vulnerability and fear of sexual assault (Gordon, Riger, LeBailly, & Heath, 1980).

Preventive behaviors are also possible once a confrontational crime has been initiated. There is some evidence gathered from crime victims to suggest that certain self-protection strategies are more effective than others at thwarting an attack that is under way. For example, Furby and Fuschoff (1986), in a review of the literature on avoiding sexual assault, concluded that forceful strategies such as screaming and physical resistance were more effective at avoiding rape than nonforceful strategies such as moral reasoning or pleading with the offender. However, we still lack good evidence about the effectiveness of strategies commonly employed to avoid the attack in the first place.

The effectiveness of home protection behaviors is another issue that must be addressed in the proposed crime-prevention model. There is some evidence to suggest that home protection behaviors are effective in preventing property victimization. For example, a number of studies have found that participation in a property-marking (engraving) program is associated with lower rates of victimization (see Heller, Stenzel, Gill, Kold, & Schimerman, 1975, for a review). However, selection biases loom as a threat to the inferrence that property marking was responsible for lower victimization rates (Lurigio & Rosenbaum, 1986). Persons who participated in property marking may have elected to engage in a number of additional home protection behaviors or may have enjoyed a lower rate of victimization prior to participation. However, one panel study (Wilson & Schneider, 1978) tested, and did not find support for, these rival hypotheses.

Other types of "target hardening" behaviors *appear to be* effective at lowering rates of property victimization for participants. A national evaluation of crime-prevention security surveys found that persons who receive and implement recommendations for improving home security are less likely to be victimized by burglary than persons who do no participate in this program (International Training, Research and Evaluation Council, 1977). Again, the potential problems associated with self-selection could be sizable. Furthermore, we know very little about which home protection behaviors, if any, were adopted. Researchers have identified a wide range of protective behaviors that are initiated with varying levels of frequency, but little is known about the relative effectiveness of these choices.

Although the available research has been used to suggest that certain home protection behaviors may reduce the risk of victimization, many of these behaviors are not responsive to fear arousal, as indicated earlier. Rather, home protection behavior is largely determined by other social and economic factors. Furthermore, to reduce one's own risk of victimization is not the same as reducing crime rates in the neighborhood. The displacement of crime is a real possibility (although limited data are available on this issue). To the extent that the offender's disposition to commit crime is not altered and the practice of individual crime prevention is not widespread, crime levels in the neighborhood should remain unchanged, and the threat of victimization would be ever-present. This has important implications for all self-protection and home protection behaviors that are not one-time investments but require continuous repetition. Acting in a manner that lowers your risk of victimization on one day does not eliminate the threat of crime for subsequent days, especially in high crime areas.

Neighborhood Crime-Prevention Behaviors

Participating in neighborhood crime-prevention behaviors is often viewed as having greater promise for lowering neighborhood crime and fear levels, since they reach beyond the individual and his or her own property. In theory, collective citizen actions can influence fear of crime directly or indirectly. The empirical support for both paths is discussed below.

Direct Fear Reduction

Considering the possibility of direct fear reduction, DuBow *et al.* (1979) note that "there is considerable belief among organizers of collective crime responses that certain programs make people less afraid" (p. 64). Rosenbaum (1987) has articulated the rationale behind this belief—namely, that social interaction and discussion at anticrime meetings is expected to alleviate anxiety about a mutual problem via social comparison processes (cf. Festinger, 1954), and/or enhanced personal efficacy (cf. Bandura, 1982). Similarly, criminologists have argued that talking about crime may serve a cathartic purpose to "reduce inner tensions" (Conklin 1975; DuBow *et al.,* 1979).

Clearly, one of the primary reactions to crime is to talk about it with others, even if nothing else is accomplished. Unfortunately, we know very little about the direct effects of group discussion on fear of crime. Earlier, we cited research suggesting that persons who talk frequently about crime are more fearful than persons who do not have regular discussions about the crime problem. However, the direct effects of group meetings and other collective behaviors on fear have been studied only rarely. When we look at only the more rigorous evaluations, the results provide very little support for the fear-reduction hypothesis and some support for the alternative fear-exacerbation hypothesis (see Rosenbaum, 1988). Thus, summarizing to this point, there is a real possibility that (1) residents come to specific anticrime meetings, such as Neighborhood Watch (as opposed to regular voluntary organization meetings) as a result of fear arousal and (2) once at the meeting, these people may be further aroused by the information being communicated either explicitly or implicitly. Considerably more research is needed to substantiate these hypotheses since most of the available work is either correlational or quasi-experimental and adopts as "black box" approach to understanding group meetings.

Surprisingly, social psychological research on small-group processes sheds little light into this black box. The primary focus of this diverse body of research has been the specification of conditions under which social influence will or will not occur (with considerable attention paid to the relative size of the minority and majority groups), rather than the effects of these influence attempts (see Tanford & Penrod, 1984, for a review). The vast majority of small-groups research has examined the effects of social influence on either *perceptual judgments* (e.g., Asch's classic line-length judgments; Moscovici's color judgments) or *decisions* (e.g., jury decisions, following Schachter's classic "Johnny Rocco" case). Opinions and preferences have been the object of social influence in a few studies, but researchers have not ventured beyond these areas of impact. Specifically, our main area of interest—human emotion and perception of risk—has received almost no attention in the social influence literature. For example, we do not know whether "collective polarization" (i.e., a shift toward extremization of response as a result of group discussion) is a phenomenon that will occur with emotions and risk perceptions in the same manner that it occurs with attitudes (e.g. Moscovici & Doise, 1974; Myers & Bishop, 1970).

Schachter (1959), in his classic research on affirmation, was among the first to theorize about the effects of group behavior on emotions. Applying Festinger's (1954) social comparison theory to human emotions, Schachter argued that people affiliate with one another to compare emotional states and to achieve socially mediated fear reduction. To date, there is a paucity of research testing the fear-reduction hypothesis, but the available work does not support Schachter's proposition that the *mere presence* of other anxious persons similar to oneself will reduce anxiety (Cottrell & Eply, 1977). There is some evidence that a companion model will affect fear levels by modeling either a calming or a fearful response (Amoroso & Walters, 1969; Shaver & Liebling, 1976). However, laboratory settings that induce fear by threatening painful shocks or injections and use a single companion (rather than a group) have questionable applicability to urban fear of crime at neighborhood or block meetings. In sum, whether group discussion about crime will increase, decrease, homogenize, or have no effect on the fear levels of group participants is not easily discernible from current social psychological theory or research.

Indirect Fear Reduction

The next basic question is whether collective action holds promise for reducing fear indirectly by means of reducing crime in the neighborhood. This is the most fundamental and often-asked question in this field—do neighborhood crime prevention activities prevent crime? Although there are literally hundreds of "success stories" about neighborhood crime-prevention programs, there is a paucity of rigorous evaluation research in this field (for critical reviews, see Lurigio & Rosenbaum, 1986; Rosenbaum, 1987, 1988; Skogan, 1979; Yin, 1979). Among the stronger evaluations, the evidence is mixed. While reductions in community-wide victimization rates have been reported, most of these efforts also involved strategies that supplemented citizen crime-prevention behaviors, such as environmental redesign and/or changes in policing practices. The stronger evaluations of programs directed primarily at community organizing efforts have tended, with few exceptions, to show either no effect or an apparent negative effect upon victimization rates (Rosenbaum, 1988). Part of the problem has been the absence of high levels of citizen participation and little evidence that citizens engage in the hypothesized behaviors (other than attending meetings) that are believed necessary for preventing crime (e.g., social interaction on the streets, territorial surveillance, crime reporting, bystander intervention, and numerous personal and home protection behaviors). Generally speaking, it is fair to say that participation in neighborhood crime-prevention behaviors—including meetings—is low and very difficult to increase in neighborhoods where the need is greatest—i.e., where the objective risk of victimization is greatest and fear of crime is high (Greenberg, Rohe, & Williams, 1985; Pate, McPherson, & Silloway, 1987). In neighborhoods where fear levels are high, distrust of neighbors is also high and residents often feel a sense of helplessness in responding to social problems. Thus, individual protective actions (associated with high fear) are preferred in high-fear areas to collective crime-prevention measures designed to improve the neighborhood (Skogan, 1987).

The rational fear model assumes that fear is reduced when crime is reduced. The failure of crime-prevention programs to effectively reduce crime rates may help to explain their parallel failure to reduce fear levels. However, even if the evaluation research literature contained strong evidence of reductions in crime (which it does not), we have suggested that community residents may be insensitive to these actual changes in levels of crime and instead may turn to other sources of information to determine the "appropriate" level of fear. The lack of fear reduction, therefore, is probably not simply attributable to the ineffectiveness of community programs in reducing actual crime levels.

Summary and Conclusions

To summarize, we have suggested that fear of crime is not an entirely rational response to crime. Discrepancies between victimization rates and fear levels have caused researchers to look for other processes that are responsible for multiplying the psychological impact of crime on the individual. Fear of crime is largely influenced by the *perceived* risk of victimization, and risk information is obtained from two sources other than personal victimization experience—informal interaction with others (neighbors, family, friends, and relatives), and exposure to the mass media. Crime- and fear-reduction programs have sought to exploit these sources of risk information to stimulate crime-prevention behaviors. The motivational strategy often employed is to disseminate risk information that will raise concern about crime and/or raise fear of crime. Successful efforts to raise concern without raising fear have been few, since fear and concern are often correlated. Intentional efforts to manipulate fear are justified by organizers on the assumption that fear arousal will influence compliance with crime-prevention recommendations—a strategy similar to prevention campaigns in other areas, such as the health field.

Our knowledge of the relationship between fear and crime-prevention behavior can be summarized as follows: Although fear of crime does not appear to influence a wide variety of personal protection behaviors, it does seem to have a strong effect on avoidance/restriction behaviors such as not going out as often after dark or avoiding areas or persons perceived as dangerous. While this reduction in mobility is associated with a lower risk of victimization, it does not appear to result in a substantial reduction in fear. In fact, extreme restrictions on behavior could produce an increase in fear and, if practiced enough by residents, could lower the constraints on crime by allowing criminally minded persons to act without surveillance (although this is largely speculation at this point). Thus, fear of crime may be responsive to risk information in only one direction—it may be easier to increase fear than it is to decrease fear, but further research is needed.

The strong covariation between behavioral restriction and fear of crime could be interpreted, in psychological terms, as a phobic response. By avoiding exposure, the person also avoids victimization and attributes the lack of victimization to the precautions. The continued lack of victimization is seen as evidence of the efficacy of the restrictive precautions and the dangerousness of the world without such precautions. In much the same way that the elevator phobic avoids plunging to her death by avoiding elevators, the "crime phobic" avoids crime victimization by locking herself inside at night and distrusting her neighbors.

This is not to say that all fear of crime is bad and counterproductive. An unrealistically low level could lead to an "illusion of invulnerability" (Perloff, 1984), thus causing the individual to take needless risks and possibly incur more crime victimization. At the other end of the continuum, however, we also find that extremely high levels of fear of crime are accompanied by lower self-protective behaviors (Heath & Davidson, 1988). So, although *some* fear of crime serves a self-protective function, very high and very low levels of fear are probably dysfunctional in terms of precautionary behaviors.

Generally speaking, fear of crime does *not* motivate citizens to enact home protection behaviors, which are largely determined by social and economic factors, nor does fear exert significant influence on most collective/neighborhood and related social needs. As predicted by reactance theory, the one important exception is to this pattern is participation in crime-specific meetings (e.g., Watch meetings), where fear levels in middle-class neighborhoods may be subject to manipulation by local organizers, the media, or police. However, in this situation, the assumption that fearful citizens can have their fears alleviated by attending a local meeting of concerned residents is not supported by the available data, and in fact, the opposite effect may occur. The social processes that take place at neighborhood or block meetings are poorly understood, but field research suggests that these groups are not simply a forum for the dissemination of objective information about crime, and they may serve to exacerbate emotional reactions to crime. In sum, when the total body of available research is considered, it does not bode well for the rational fear model. Fear is an important psychological response for coping with the threat of crime, but efforts to manipulate fear do not produce the kinds of preventive behaviors that are conducive to permanent fear reduction in the community.

Future Research and Policy Implications

The social processes that produce changes in fear of crime are poorly understood. In particular, the effects of neighborhood or block meetings on residents' perceptions and emotions is one important area where research is needed for theory testing and policy development. Despite the large body of research on small-group processes, there is a paucity of social psychological studies that examine group effects on emotions and risk perceptions. The existing work is helpful at least in identifying factors that may be operating in small-group settings to raise, lower, or homogenize fear levels. Social processes worthy of consideration include modeling, labeling, information persuasion, and minority/majority influence. In addition, initial fear levels of participants (prior to group discussion) and the degree of group structure are important variables that should be examined when polarization hypotheses are being tested.

To the extent that fear exacerbation is occurring, our best guess is that a combination of influence processes are operating at *ad hoc* anticrime meetings to produce this effect—namely, social comparison and direct information persuasion. We suspect that persons who are somewhat fearful/concerned about the local crime environment, but yet are uncertain about the validity of recent rumors and pamphlets proclaiming a "crime problem," will attend a block/neighborhood meeting for social validation of perceptions and emotional support. Upon arrival at the meeting, they listen to victimization stories from other (similar) residents, offer a few of their own personal experiences with crime, and listen to "organizers" make the persuasive argument that the crime problem has increased in severity and will only get worse if citizens do not act. These conditions, if accurate, could lead to fear arousal via "anxious" modeling, information persuasion, and social validation of risk perceptions.

From a policy standpoint, greater attention should be paid to what actually happens at community crime prevention meetings; i.e., who says what to whom in what manner? The fundamental assumption that "nothing but good" can result from well-intended meetings must be challenged and community organizers must take more responsibility for the social by-products of their organizing strategies. First, organizers must be clear about their intent as "social engineers." If, on the one hand, fear arousal at anticrime meetings is their objective, then organizers have a greater responsibility for offering a sound plan for fear reduction after the meeting has concluded. As suggested in this chapter, however, encouraging citizens to engage in personal crime-prevention behaviors is not sufficient, since these behaviors alone are not effective at reducing fear levels and may even sustain or enhance fear of victimization. If, on the other hand, organizers believe that meetings should serve to solidify the community and directly reduce fear (perhaps after distributing fear-arousing invitations), then they should take a greater interest in the content of these meetings and the *"social support needs"* of the participants.

Social support has been defined in many ways in the community mental health literature, but three dimensions seem to be particularly relevant to "neighboring" and fear of crime in urban communities: *Personal/emotional support* (ranging from sociability to socioemotional needs), *functional/instrumental support* (informal helping), and *informational support*. (Weiss, 1982). Unger and Wandersman (1985) have hypothesized that personal/emotional and instrumental support lead to fear reduction, while informational support leads to fear arousal. This is consistent with our assessment of the literature that talking about crime only serves to exacerbate fear, but more controlled research is needed on the specific effects of these types of support. In practice, efforts to provide emotional support at community crime-prevention meetings are uncommon, but instrumental support has been offered in crime-prevention programs such as Block Watch.

For those who intend to arouse fear at local meetings with crime statistics and stories, the bigger problem is that risk-information strategies by themselves have not been terribly effective at stimulating a wide variety of crime-prevention behaviors that could eventually reduce crime and fear in the community. Prevention experts in other fields have learned that perceived risk or fear is only one of the key ingredients necessary for stimulating preventive behaviors. Rosenstock's (1966; 1974) health-belief model posits three factors that determine the likelihood of engaging in preventive action: (1) perceived risk, (2) perceived seriousness of the threat, and (3) perceived efficacy of preventive action. Rarely has perceived efficacy been studied in the crime-prevention area, but the available research has shown it to be an important predictor of individual protection behaviors (Lavrakas *et al.*, 1980). Other factors that may influence crime-prevention behavior are relative costs and opportunities (Skogan, 1981). Thus, after communicating information about crime risk and severity, organizers cannot be content to offer a random list of crime-prevention tips. We know that local residents are discriminating in their crime-prevention behaviors, and therefore, efforts must be made to "market" prevention activities that are seen as efficacious, affordable, and available.

Social psychological theory and evaluation research can also be used to offer some general policy suggestions regarding program development in this topic area.

First, in light of past evaluations of crime-prevention programs, we know that communities react differently to programs depending on the social characteristics and crime problems in the area. Not only is the rational fear model probably incorrect in many regards, but the notion of a "one size fits all" crime-prevention/ fear-reduction program is also probably ill-advised. Community analysis should precede efforts at organizing to determine local community needs, thus allowing organizers to tailor the program to fit these needs.

For heuristic purposes, neighborhoods can be grouped into three types, each with different crime-prevention/fear-reduction needs. The first type is the proto-typic "healthy" neighborhood, where people know each other, share common values, and feel responsible for each other's safety and of the quality of life in the neighborhood. In these communities a suspicious noise brings out several neigh-bors to investigate, an abandoned auto is quickly identified, and neighbors work with authorities to remedy problems as they arise. This is the prototype that com-munity organizers attempt to transplant into other neighborhoods. Indeed, this "healthy neighborhood" needs little outside intervention and has created the in-formal social control processes needed to keep crime and fear at low levels.

A second type of neighborhood is one characterized by psychological "re-actance" stimulated by recent threats to safety. Fear levels have recently increased in this neighborhood (whether by design or not), as has residents' motivation to remove this new threat. In this situation, residents are ready to be mobilized, feel some sense of control over their environment, and should be receptive to com-munity organizing efforts. Collective activities such as Neighborhood Watch would be appropriate so long as they included emotional and/or instrumental support to those who participate as well as specific behavioral recommendations for prevent-ing crime. Block parties and other social events would also be appropriate for increasing social networking and social support without focusing on the crime issue *per se*. To the extent possible, security recommendations should encourage the one-time purchase of good hardware that provides a continuing source of se-curity (e.g., dead-bolt locks) without the constant reminder of the crime threat (e.g., peepholes and door chains).

The third type of neighborhood is one where "learned helplessness" has taken root. Fear is constantly high but motivation to lessen crime danger is low, perhaps precipitated by feelings of low self-efficacy. (This is not an unfamiliar description to urban scholars who have studied low-income, high-crime neighbor-hoods). In this situation, the manipulation of fear and perceived risk will not be effective in stimulating preventive behaviors other than enhancing avoidance or withdrawal. Therefore, organizers must move from the crime issue to other social problems that residents astutely recognize as the source of the crime problem, such as drug abuse, unemployment, and a lack of constructive activities for neigh-borhood youth. Given the limited prospects for improving security *directly* through collective citizen action (for reasons of both motivation and cost), government has a greater responsibility to provide adequate security hardware in these "learned helpless" neighborhoods (cf. Rosenbaum, 1988). In the absence of adequate cit-izen participation in preventive behaviors, the one-time purchase and installation of security devices should go a long way toward improving public safety in the most troubled neighborhoods. However, social policy and funding must continue to support innovative self-help programs designed to enhance efficacy in these neighborhoods and to provide better social services.

The above suggestions are based on research findings and theoretical formulations from many different areas and should be treated as preliminary policy ideas. To proceed in a more orderly fashion, research and policy ideas must be integrated both at the point of program design and during the evaluation stage. Only then can we achieve a clear understanding of how fear, risk, behavior, and intervention are pieced together to form a coherent social environment.

References

Amoroso, D. M., & Walters, R. H. (1969). Effects of anxiety and socially mediated anxiety reduction on paired-associates learning. *Journal of Personality and Social Psychology, 11*, 388–396.

Antunes, G. E., Cook, F., Cook, T., & Skogan, W. (1977). Patterns of personal crime against the elderly: Findings from a national survey. *Gerontologist, 17*, 321–327.

Baker, M. H., Nienstedt B., Everett, R. S., & McCleary, R. (1983). The impact of a crime wave: Perceptions, fear, and confidence in the police. *Law and Society Review, 17*, 319–336.

Bandura, A. (1982). Self-efficacy mechanism in human agency. *American Psychologist, 37*, 122–147.

Baumer, T. L. (1978). Research of fear of crime in the United States. *Victimology, 3*, 254–264.

Baumer, T. L., & DuBow, F. (1977, May). *Fear of crime in the polls: What they do and do not tell us.* Paper presented at the American Association of Public Opinion Research, Bush Hills Falls, PA.

Baumer, T. L., & Rosenbaum, D. P. (1981). *Measuring fear of crime.* Final Report to the National Institute of Justice. Evanston, IL: Westinghouse Evaluation Institute.

Bem, D. J. (1967). Self-perception: An alternative interpretation of cognitive dissonance phenomena. *Psychological Review, 74*, 183–200.

Biderman, A. D., Johnson, L. A., McIntyre, J., & Weir, A. W. (1967). *Report on a pilot study in the District of Columbia on victimization and attitudes toward law enforcement.* Washington, DC: U.S. Government Printing Office.

Block, M. S., & Long, G. J. (1973). Subjective probability of victimization and crime levels: An econometric approach. *Criminology, May*, 87–93.

Boggs, S. L. (1971). Formal and informal crime control: An exploratory study of urban, suburban and rural orientations. *Sociological Quarterly, 12*, 319–327.

Bureau of Justice Statistics. (1983). *Report to the nation on crime and justice: The data.* Washington, DC: U.S. Department of Justice.

Bureau of Justice Statistics. (1987). *Criminal victimization in the United States, 1985.* NCJ-104273. Washington, DC: U.S. Department of Justice.

Citizen Information Service of Illinois. (1982). *Community-Directed Crime Prevention: An Alternative That Works.* Final Report to the National Institute of Justice. Chicago: Author.

Conklin, J. E. (1971). Dimensions of community response to the crime problem. *Social Problems, 18*, 373–384.

Conklin, J. E. (1975). *The impact of crime.* New York: Macmillan.

Cottrell, N. B., & Epley, S. W. (1977). Affiliation, social comparison, and mediated stress reduction. In J. M. Suls & R. L. Miller (eds.), *Social comparison processes: Theoretical and empirical perspectives.* Washington, DC: Hemisphere.

Doob, A. N., & MacDonald, G. E. (1979). Television viewing and fear of victimization: Is the relationship causal? *Journal of Personality and Social Psychology, 37*, 170–179.

DuBow, F., McCabe, E., & Kaplan, G. (1979). *Reactions to crime: A critical review of the literature.*

U.S. Department of Justice, National Institute of Justice. Washington, DC: U.S. Government Printing Office.

Eck, J. E. & Spelman, W., with Hill, D., Stephens, D. W., Stedman, J. R., & Murphy, G. R. (1987). *Problem solving: Problem-oriented policing in Newport News*. Washington, DC: Police Executive Research Forum.

Ennis, P. H. (1967). *Criminal victimization in the United States: A report of a nationwide survey*. Washington, DC: U.S. Government Printing Office.

Erskine, H. (1974). The polls: Fear of violence and crime. *Public Opinion Quarterly, 38*, 131–145.

Festinger, L. (1954). A theory of social comparison processes. *Human Relations, 7*, 117–140.

Fishman, M. (1977). *Crime waves as ideology*. Paper presented at the 1977 annual meetings of the Society for the Study of Social Problems, Chicago.

Fowler, F. J., & Mangione, T. W. (1974). *The nature of fear*. Survey Research Program, University of Massachusetts, and the Joint Center for Urban Studies of M.I.T. and Harvard University.

Furby, L., & Fischoff, B. (1986). *Rape self-defense strategies: A review of their effectiveness*. Technical Report 86-3. Eugene, OR: Eugene Research Institute.

Furstenberg, F. F., Jr. (1971). Public reaction to crime in the streets. *American Scholar, 40*, 601–610.

Furstenberg, F. F., Jr. (1972). Fear of crime and its effects on citizen behavior. In A. Biderman (ed.), *Crime and justice: A symposium*. New York: Nailburg.

Gallup, G. H. (1983). *The Gallup report*. Report No. 210. Princeton, NJ: Gallup Poll.

Garofalo, J. (1977). *Public opinion about crime: The attitudes of victims and non-victims in selected cities*. Washington, DC: U.S. Government Printing Office.

Garofalo, J., & McLeod, M. (1986). *Improving the effectiveness and utilization of neighborhood watch programs*. Draft Final Report to the National Institute of Justice. Albany, NY: State University of New York at Albany, Hindelang Criminal Justice Research Center.

Gerbner, G., & Gross, L. (1976). Living with television: The violence profile. *Journal of Communication, 26*, 172–199.

Gordon, M.T., & Riger, S. (1979). Fear and avoidance: A link between attitudes and behavior. *Victimology, 4*, 395–402.

Gordon, M.T., Riger, S., LeBailly, R., & Heath, L. (1980). Crime, women, and the quality of urban life. *Signs: A Journal of Women in Culture and Society, 54*, 5144–5160.

Gottlieb, B. H. (Ed.). (1981). *Social networks and social support*. Beverly Hills, CA: Sage.

Greenberg, S., Rohe, W. M., & Williams, J. R. (1982). Safety in urban neighborhoods. *Population and Environment, 5*, 141–165.

Greenberg, S., Rohe, W. M., & Williams, J. R. (1985). *Informal citizen action and crime prevention at the neighborhood level: Synthesis and assessment of the research.* U.S. Department of Justice, National Institute of Justice. Washington, DC: U.S. Government Printing Office.

Gubrium, J. F. (1974). Victimization in the old age. *Crime and delinquency, 20*, 245–250.

Heath, L. (1984). Impact of newspaper crime reports on fear of crime: Multimethodological investigation. *Journal of Personality and Social Psychology, 47*, 263–276.

Health, L., & Davidson, L. (1988). Dealing with the threat of rape: Reactance or learned helplessness. *Journal of Applied Social Psychology, 18*, 1334–1351.

Heath, L., Gordon, M. T., & LeBailly, R. (1981). What newspapers tell us (and don't tell us) about rape. *Newspaper Research Journal, 2*, 48–55.

Health, L., & Petraitis, J. (1986). Television viewing and fear of crime: Where is the scary world? *Basic and Applied Social Psychology, 8*, 97–123.

Heath, L., Riger, S., Gordon, M., & LeBailly, R. (1979, September). *Rape stereotypes and fear: A control paradox*. Paper presented at the Meetings of the American Psychological Association, New York.

Heller, N. B., Stenzel, W. W., Gill, A. D., Kold, R. A., & Schimerman, S. R. (1975). *Operation identification projects: Assessment of effectiveness*. National Evaluation Program—Phase I. Washington, DC: U.S. Department of Justice, National Institute of Law Enforcement and Criminal Justice.

Hindelang, M. J. (1974). Public opinion regarding crime, criminal justice, and related topics. *Journal of Research in Crime and Delinquency, July,* 101–106.

Hindelang, M. J., Gottfredson, M. R., & Garofalo, J. (1978). *Victims of personal crime.* Cambridge: Ballinger.

International Training, Research and Evaluation Council. (1977). *National Evaluation program phase I summary report: Crime prevention security surveys.* Washington, D.C.: National Institute of Law Enforcement and Criminal Justice.

Jacob, H. & Lineberry, R. L. (1982). *Governmental responses to crime.* Executive Summary Report to the National Institute of Justice. Evanston, IL: Northwestern University, Center for Urban Affairs and Policy Research.

Kim, Y. J. (1976). *The social correlates of perceptions of neighborhood crime problems and fear of victimization.* A Reaction to Crime Project Working Paper, Center for Urban Affairs, Northwestern University.

Lavrakas, P. J. (1981). On households. In D. A. Lewis (Ed.), *Reactions to crime.* Beverly Hills, CA: Sage.

Lavrakas, P. J. (1982). Fear of crime and behavioral restrictions in urban and suburban neighborhoods. *Population and Environment, 5,* 242–264.

Lavrakas, P. J. (1985). Citizen self-help and neighborhood crime prevention policy. In L. A. Curtis (Ed.), *American violence and public policy.* New Haven, CT: Yale University Press.

Lavrakas, P. J. (1986). Evaluating police-community anti-crime newsletters: The Evanston, Houston, and Newark field studies. In D. P. Rosenbaum (Ed.), *Community crime prevention: Does it work?* Beverly Hills, CA: Sage.

Lavrakas, P. J., & Lewis, D. A. (1980). The conceptualization and measurement of citizens' crime prevention behaviors. *Journal of Research in Crime and Deliquency, July,* 254–272.

Lavrakas, P. J., Normoyle, J., Skogan, W. G., Hertz, E. J., Salem, C., & Lewis, D. A. (1980). *Factors related to citizen involvement in personal, household, and neighborhood anti-crime measures.* Final Report to the National Institute of Justice. Evanston, IL: Northwestern University, Center for Urban Affairs and Policy Research.

Lavrakas, P. J., Rosenbaum, D. P., & Kaminski, F. (1983). Transmitting information about crime and crime prevention: The Evanston newsletter quasi-experiment. *Journal of Police Science and Administration, 2,* 463–473.

Lawton, M. P., Nahemow, L., Yaffe, S., & Feldman, S. (1976). Psychological aspects of crime and fear of crime. In J. & S. S. Goldsmith (Eds.), *Crime and the elderly* (pp. 21–29). Lexington, MA: Lexington Books.

LeJeune, R., & Alex, N. (1973). On being mugged: The event and its aftermath. *Urban Life Culture, October,* 259–287.

Lewis, D. L., Grant, J. A., & Rosenbaum, D. P. (1988). *The social construction of reform: Crime prevention and community organizations.* New Brunswick, NJ: Transaction Publishers.

Lurigio, A. J., & Rosenbaum, D. P. (1986). Evaluation research in community crime prevention: A critical look at the field. In D. P. Rosenbaum (ed.), *Community crime prevention: Does it work?* Beverly Hills, CA: Sage.

Market Opinion Research. (1977). *The Michigan public speaks out on crime.* Detroit, MI: Author.

Maxfield, M. G. (1977). *Reactions to fear.* A working paper based on an examination of survey data from Portland, Kansas City and Cincinnati. Evanston, IL: Northwestern University, Center for Urban Affairs.

Maxfield, M. G. (1987). *Explaining fear of crime: Evidence from the 1984 British crime survey.* Research and Planning Unit Paper 43. London, England: Her Majesty's Stationery Office.

McPherson, M. (1978). *Realities and perceptions of crime at the neighborhood level.* Minneapolis: Minnesota Crime Prevention Center.

Merry, S. E. (1981). *Urban danger: Life in a neighborhood of strangers.* Philadelphia: Temple University Press.

Moscovici, S., & Doise, W. (1974). Decision making in groups. In C. Nemeth (Ed.), *Social psychology: Classic and contemporary integrations.* Chicago: Rand McNally.

Myers, D. G., & Bishop, G. D. (1970). Discussion effects on racial attitudes. *Science, 169,* 778–779.

National Advisory Commission on Criminal Justice Standards and Goals. (1973). *Community crime prevention.* Distributed by National Technical Information Service, U.S. Department of Commerce.

Newman, O., & Franck, K. A. (1980). *Factors influencing crime and instability in urban housing developments.* Washington, DC: U.S. Government Printing Office.

O'Keefe, G. J. (1986). The McGruff national media campaign: Its public impact and future implications. In D. P. Rosenbaum (Ed.), *Community crime prevention: Does it work?* Beverly Hills, CA: Sage.

Pate, A., McPherson, M., & Silloway, G. (1987). *The Minneapolis community crime prevention experiment.* Draft Evaluation Report. Washington, DC: Police Foundation.

Podolefsky, A., & DuBow, F. (1981). *Strategies for community crime prevention: Collective responses to crime in urban America* Springfield, IL: Charles C Thomas.

The President's Commission on Law Enforcement and Administration of Justice. (1967). *Task force report: Crime and its impact—An assessment.* Washington, DC: U.S. Government Printing Office.

Reiss, A. J., Jr. (1967). *Studies in crime and law enforcement in major metropolitan areas.* Field Survey III, Vol. 1 of of the Presidential Commission of Law Enforcement and the Administration of Justice. Washington DC: U.S. Government Printing Office.

Rifai, M. A. (1976). *Older Americans' crime prevention research project.* Multnomah County Division of Public Safety, Portland, OR.

Riger, S., LeBailly, R., Gordon, M., & Heath, L. (1979, September). *Fear of crime and women's use of self-protective measures.* Paper presented at the Meetings of the American Psychological Association, New York.

Rosenbaum, D. P. Ed. (1986). *Community crime prevention: Does it work?* Beverly Hills, CA: Sage.

Rosenbaum, D. P. (1987). The theory and research behind neighborhood watch: Is it a sound fear and crime reduction strategy? *Crime and Delinquency, 33,* 103–134.

Rosenbaum, D. P. (1988). Community crime prevention: A review and synthesis of the literature. *Justice Quarterly, 5,* 323–395.

Rosenbaum, D. P., & Baumer, T. L. (1981). *Measuring fear of crime: A set of recommended scales.* Evanston, IL: Westinghouse Evaluation Institute..

Rosenbaum, D. P., & Bickman, L. (1989). *Scaring people into crime prevention: The results of a randomized field experiment.* Manuscript in preparation.

Rosenbaum, D. P., Lewis, D. A., & Grant, J. A. (1986). Neighborhood-based crime prevention: Assessing the efficacy of community organizing in Chicago. In D. P. Rosenbaum (Ed.), *Community crime prevention: Does it work?* Beverly Hills, CA: Sage.

Rosenbaum, D. P., & Lurigio, A. J. (1989). Isolating the effects of victimization on perceptions and behaviors. Chicago, IL: University of Illinois at Chicago, manuscript in preparation.

Rosenstock, I. M. (1966). Why people use health services. *Milbank Memorial Fund Quarterly, 44,* 94–127.

Rosenstock, I. M. (1974). The health-belief model and preventive health behavior. *Health Education Monographs, 2,* 354–386.

Savitz, L. D., Lalli, M., & Rosen, L. (1977). *City Life and Delinquency—Victimization, fear of crime and gang membership.* Washington, DC: National Institute for Juvenile Justice and Delinquency Prevention, Office of Juvenile Justice and Delinquency Prevention.

Schachter, S. (1959). *The psychology of affiliation.* Palo Alto, CA: Stanford University Press.

Shaver, P., & Liebling, B. (1976). Explorations in the drive theory of social formation. *Journal of Social Psychology, 99,* 259–271.

Sherman, L. W. (1986). Policing communities: What works? In A. J. Reiss, Jr., & M. Tonry (Eds.), *Communities and crime,* Vol. 8 of M. Tonry & N. Morris (Eds.), *Crime and Justice: A Review of Research.* Chicago: University of Chicago Press.

Skogan, W. G. (1979). Community crime prevention programs—Measurement issues in evaluation. In *How well does it work.* Washington, DC: U.S. Government Printing Office.

Skogan, W. G. (1981). On attitudes and behaviors. In D. A. Lewis (Ed.), *Reactions to crime.* Beverly Hills, CA: Sage.

Skogan, W. G. (1986). Fear of crime and neighborhood change. In A. J. Reiss, Jr., & M. Tonry (Eds.), *Communities and crime,* Vol. 8 of M. Tonry & N. Morris (Eds.), *Crime and justice: A review of research.* Chicago: University of Chicago Press.

Skogan, W. G. (1987). Community organizations and crime. In M. Tonry & N. Morris (Eds.), *Crime and justice: A Review of Research.* Vol. 10. Chicago: University of Chicago Press.

Skogan, W. G., Lewis, D. A., Podolefsky, A., DuBow, F., Gordon, M. T., Hunter, A., Maxfield, M. G., & Salem, G. (1982). *Reactions to crime project: Executive summary.* Washington, DC: Department of Justice, National Institute of Justice.

Skogan, W. G., & Maxfield, M. G. (1981). *Coping with crime: Individual and neighborhood reactions.* Beverly Hills, CA: Sage.

Stinchcombe, A. L., Heimer, C., Iliff, R. A., Scheppele, K., Smith, T. W., & Taylor, D. G. (1977). *Crime and punishment in public opinion: 1948–1974.* Chicago, IL: National Opinion Research Center.

Sundeen, R. A., & Mathieu, J. T. (1976). The fear of crime and its consequences among elderly in three urban areas. *Gerontologist, 16,* 211–219.

Tanford, S., & Penrod, S. (1984). Social influence model: A formal integration of research on majority and minority influence processes. *Psychological Bulletin, 95,* 189–225.

Tedeschi, J. Y., & Lindskold, S. (1976). *Social psychology: Interdependence, interaction, and influence.* New York: Wiley.

Tyler, T. R. (1980). The impact of directly and indirectly experienced events: The origin of crime-related judgements and behaviors. *Journal of Personality and Social Psychology, 39,* 13–28.

Tyler, T. R., & Cook, F. L. (1984). The mass media and judgments of risk: Distinguishing impact on personal and societal level judgments. *Journal of Personality and Social Psychology, 47,* 693–708.

Tyler, T. R., & Lavrakas, P. J. (1986). Mass media effects: Distinguishing the importance of personal and societal level effects. In R. Perloff & S. Krauss (Eds.), *Mass media effects and political information processing.* Beverly Hills, CA: Sage.

Unger, D. G., & Wandersman, A. (1985). The importance of neighbors: The social, cognitive, and affective components of neighboring. *American Journal of Community Psychology, 13,* 139–169.

Waller, I., & Okihiro, N. (1976). *Burglary and the public.* Unpublished manuscript.

Waller, I., & Okihiro, N. (1978). *Burglary: The victim and the public.* Toronto, Canada: University of Toronto Press.

Weiss, R. S. (1982). Relationship of social support and psychological well-being. In H. G. Schulberg & M. Killilea (Eds.), *The modern practice of community mental health.* San Francisco: Jossey-Bass.

Wilson, L. A. (1976). *Private and collective choice behavior in the provision of personal security from criminal victimization.* Doctoral dissertation, Department of Political Science, University of Oregon.

Wilson, L. A., & Schneider, A. L. (1978). *Investigating the efficacy and equity of public initiatives in the provision of private safety.* Paper presented at the Annual Conference of the Western Political Science Association, Los Angeles.

Wortman, C. B., & Brehm, J. W. (1975). Responses to uncontrollable outcomes: An integration of reactance theory and the learned helplessness model. In L. Berkowitz (Ed.), *Advances in experimental social psychology* (Vol. 8, pp. 277–336). New York: Academic Press.

Yaden, D., Folkstand, S., & Glazer, P. (1973). *The impact of crime in selected neighborhoods: A study of public attitudes in four Portland census tracts.* Portland, OR: Campaign Information Counselors.

Yin, R. K. (1979). What is citizen crime prevention? In *How well does it work?* Washington, DC: U.S. Government Office.

11

Preventing Injuries and Deaths from Vehicle Crashes
Encouraging Belts and Discouraging Booze

E. Scott Geller

Injury is the primary cause of lost person-years of productive life in the United States (Waller, 1987). The number of years lost annually to injuries of Americans exceed those lost from cancer by 2.4 million years and heart disease by 2.0 million years of life (*Injury in America,* 1985). Injury from motor vehicle crashes account for approximately 45% of the total (Sleet, 1987). In 1985 alone, approximately 43,800 people in the United States died in traffic accidents, and 3.5 million were injured (National Highway Traffic Safety Administration, 1986). Vehicle crashes are the single leading cause of death and injury to Americans between the ages of 4 and 35 (McGinnis, 1984) and were estimated to cost the nation approximately $69.5 billion in 1984 (National Highway Traffic Safety Administration, 1985), ranking second only to cancer (Hartunian, Smart, & Thompson, 1981).

The 1979 report from the surgeon general (Califano, 1979) identified people and their behavior as the major contributor to poor health, injuries, and death. This theme of improved health and reduced injuries through behavior change has been emphasized in other government reports (e.g., Harris, 1980, 1981), in journal articles (e.g., Roberts, 1987; Roberts, Fanurik, & Layfield, 1987; Sleet, 1987), at recent conference proceedings (e.g., Geller, 1988; Kalsher & Geller, 1988; Tolsma, 1987), and throughout entire journal issues (e.g., Lawson, Sleet, & Amoni, 1984; Roberts & Brooks, 1987). The basic idea is that unhealthy or injury-prone

E. Scott Geller • Department of Psychology, Virginia Polytechnic Institute and State University, Blacksburg, Virginia 24061.

life-styles result from excessive unhealthy and unsafe behaviors and deficient healthy and safe behaviors (Gelfand & Hartmann, 1984). "What people *do* influences the quality of life, and people *doing* is the realm of psychology; the science of behavior" (Roberts *et al.,* 1987, p. 105).

One behavioral excess and one behavioral deficit have been identified as contributing most to injuries and fatalities from vehicle crashes. As promulgated by the U.S. Department of Transportation (DOT) for a decade, the behavioral excess is alcohol consumption and the behavioral deficit is safety belt use. In the United States, alcohol is estimated to have contributed to 50–55% of fatal vehicle accidents and 18–25% of injury-producing crashes (Fell, 1982). The use of shoulder and lap belts is the single most protective measure that can be conveniently taken to reduce the risk of death or injury in a vehicle crash. In fact, it is estimated that 55% of all fatalities and 65% of all injuries from vehicle crashes would be prevented if safety belts were used (*Federal Register,* 1984), yet recent observational surveys indicate that about 75% of adults and 50% of children (0 to 4 years) fail to use a vehicle safety belt or a child safety seat (Ziegler, 1986). It is estimated a mere 10% increase in safety belt use would prevent as many as 30,000 injuries and save 1,500 lives and $800 million in direct costs (Sleet, 1987).

From a policy or legal perspective, significant steps have been made in recent years to reduce alcohol-impaired driving and increase use of safety belts and child safety seats. Stricter penalties for driving under the influence of alcohol (DUI), liability legislation for servers of alcoholic beverages, and increased enforcement of anti-drunken-driving legislation (including police roadblocks for DUI checks) are commonplace throughout the United States. Moreover, 41 states have increased the minimum legal drinking age to 21 (Steed, 1988). In the domain of occupant protection, all 50 states have now passed legislation requiring young children (from 0 to 4 years in most states) to be protected in child safety seats (Steed, 1987), and at the time of this writing, 31 states had enacted mandatory safety belt use laws (MUL) for adults (Steed, 1988).

The legislative attempts to reduce behavioral excess and increase behavioral deficit that contribute to injuries and fatalities from vehicle crashes have made a difference, but much more behavior change is necessary. The deterrence effect of stricter DUI laws and increased enforcement has been mild and transitory, largely because of the low probability of punishment—about one DUI arrest per 5,000 miles of alcohol-impaired driving (Ross, 1987). Raising the legal drinking age has significantly reduced injuries and deaths in the affected age group (Wagenaar, 1983), but this impact is actually miniscule considering the overall drunk-driving problem (Ross, 1982, 1985; Russ & Geller, 1985).

Safety belt use has increased dramatically in virtually every state that has passed a mandatory use law (MUL). For example, during the last 6 months of 1985, observations of safety belt use by front-seat occupants in 17 states without an MUL revealed 21.6% buckled up (Ziegler, 1986), whereas mean post-MUL belt use across 27 states with MULs was 48% (Campbell, Stewart, & Campbell, 1987). Unfortunately, safety belt use following an MUL declines markedly when the initial media attention wanes, and it has rarely stabilized above 50%. Therefore, legislation is insufficient to change the behavioral deficit of low nationwide safety belt use. In fact, it is generally believed that the safest drivers are the first to comply with an MUL, and most prominent decreases in injuries from vehicle crashes won't occur until the remaining 50% buckle up—the individuals currently resisting the belt-use mandates (Campbell *et al.*, 1987). Although the rate of buckling infants and toddlers in child safety seats has increased dramatically as a result of child restraint laws (Steed, 1987), a recent study of pre- versus postlaw fatality rates among young children in 11 states showed minimal differences (Wagenaar, Webster, & Maybee, 1987). This is partially because of the ineffective use of available safety seats by as many as 70% of the users (Cynecki & Goryl, 1984; Shelness & Jewett, 1983), and perhaps also because drivers at higher risk for a crash are least likely to protect their children in an appropriate safety seat.

It is obvious that no single approach will be sufficient to prevent injuries and fatalities resulting from alcohol-impaired driving and nonuse of safety belts. Indeed, a theme of the 1987 Conference on Injury was the urgent need for a comprehensive nationwide attack on these behavioral excesses and deficits by politicians, corporate leaders, employee groups, health and medical professionals, educators, media writers and producers, grass roots agencies, civic and service clubs, and family members. The remainder of this chapter reviews the role of applied behavior analysis in a large-scale effort to prevent injuries and deaths from vehicle crashes.

Applied Behavior Analysis

Applied behavior analysis was founded on the approach to behavioral science developed by B. F. Skinner (e.g., 1938, 1958). Skinner emphasized the importance of overt behavior and its observable environmental, social, and physiological determinants. The independent variables in Skinner's "science of behavior" are environmental stimuli and behavioral contingencies, analyzed as determinants of response occurrence. Applications of behavior analysis are generally more effective at correcting behavioral deficits (i.e., increasing response rate) than at removing behavioral excess (i.e., decreasing response rate), and usually the impact of a behavior-change intervention varies directly with the convenience of the desired behavior. For these reasons, the behavior analysis approach has been applied more frequently and successfully to increase safety belt use than to decrease alcohol-impaired driving. The applied behavior analysis research targeting safety belt promotion is reviewed first.

Antecedent Approaches to Increased Safety Belt Use

Antecedent strategies for encouraging safety belt use take many forms, including (a) verbalizations, signs, or stimulus cues that remind or urge safety belt use (referred to as "persuasive messages" in the communication literature), (b) another individual modeling or demonstrating appropriate belt use, (c) the signing of a pledge card that commits one to buckle up, (d) incentives that announce the availability of rewards following safety belt use, and (e) disincentives that publicize a monetary fine following nonuse of a safety belt.

Vehicle Reminder Systems

Over the years, a variety of buzzer-light reminder systems have been included in motor vehicles. Most intrusive was the buzzer that continued to sound until front-seat belts were buckled. Another intrusive device was the ignition interlock system that required front-seat belts to be buckled in order to start one's vehicle. These systems were undermined, however, by a majority of vehicle owners who disconnected the buzzer or sat on a buckled belt (Geller, Casali, & Johnson, 1980; Robertson, 1975). Thus, these intrusive systems were short-lived.

Buzzer-light reminders in contemporary vehicles consist only of a panel light and a buzzer or chime that initiates when the ignition key is turned on if the driver is unbuckled and terminates in 4 to 8 seconds. It is not possible to avoid the reminder tone when people start their vehicles before buckling up, which was the case for about 50% of 1,492 field observations (von Buseck & Geller, 1984). This prompted General Motors Research Laboratories to lend the author a research vehicle (a 1984 Cadillac) that provided any one of the following reminder systems: the standard 4- to 8-second buzzer or chime that initiates upon engine ignition, a 4- to 8-seccond buzzer or chime that initiates 5 seconds after engine ignition, a voice reminder ("Please fasten your safety belt") that initiates 5 seconds after engine ignition and offers a "thank you" after the driver's belt is buckled, and a second reminder option whereby the 4- to 8-second buzzer, chime, or verbal prompt initiates if the driver is unbuckled when the vehicle makes its first stop after exceeding 10 miles per hour. This special vehicle had a computer in its trunk for recording each instance of driver belt use.

We studied the relative effects of these different reminder systems by having college students drive the experimental vehicle on a planned community route under the auspices of an energy conservation study. During the 2-mile driving course, the subject was required to stop and park the vehicle at six specific locations and get out of the car to flip a toggle switch in the trunk, presumably to reset the apparatus that was measuring efficiency of gasoline use. This gave the driver six opportunities to buckle up during a 1-hour session. Each subject returned periodically to participate in this so-called energy conservation study, and safety belt use was examined on an individual basis in an attempt to show functional control of a particular reminder system.

So far, we have run 30 subjects with this research paradigm and found substantial variability between sessions and across subjects. Two consistent findings were that the vocal reminder, in lieu of the buzzer or chime, increased belt use prominently for 3 out of 5 cases, and the second reminder (buzzer or voice) increased safety belt use for 2 out of 7 subjects. Delaying the buzzer reminder 5 seconds after engine ignition had no impact. Obviously, many more subjects need to be run before reliable conclusions can be made. And before presuming external validity for specific relationships between reminder systems and safety belt use, it will be necessary to study belt use when subjects borrow the experimental vehicle for ad libitum use. At any rate, the potential of different vehicle reminder systems has been shown with a field paradigm that closely parallels experimental behavior analysis (Skinner, 1938, 1958). Indeed, our experimental vehicle could be considered a "Skinner box on wheels."

Buckle-Up Reminder Stickers

Simple buckle-up reminder stickers are available in various formats for display on vehicle dashboards. Thyer and Geller (1987) studied the behavioral impact of a 1.5×2.5-inch sticker with the message "Safety Belt Use Required in This Vehicle" by asking 24 graduate students to keep systematic records of the safety belt use of passengers traveling in the front seat of their vehicles before, during, and after sticking the reminder to the passenger-side dashboard of their vehicle. The vehicle drivers (i.e., the data recorders) always used their safety belt. During an initial 2-week baseline period, the mean belt use of 476 total passengers was 34%. Subsequently, during a 2-week period with the stickers in place, passenger belt use increased to 70% ($n = 448$). The stickers were removed for 2 weeks, and passenger belt use dropped to 41% ($n = 406$). When the reminder stickers were restored for two additional weeks, 78% of 392 front-seat passengers buckled up. Rogers (1984) found similar dashboard reminders to increase safety belt use by approximately 400% (i.e., from 10 to 38%) among drivers of state-owned vehicles.

The "Flash for Life" Reminder

A few years ago, the author developed a flash-for-life approach to safety belt promotion, whereby a person displayed to vehicles occupants the front side of an 11×14-inch flash card that read: "Please Buckle Up—I Care." If the vehicle occupant buckled up after viewing this message, the "flasher" flipped the card over to display the bold words "Thank You For Buckling Up." For the first evaluation of this behavior-change tactic (Geller, Bruff, & Nimmer, 1985), the "flasher" was in the front seat of a stopped vehicle and the "flashee" was the driver of an adjacent, stopped vehicle. The flash card was shown to 1,087 unbuckled drivers, and of the 82% who looked at the flash card, 22% complied with the buckle-up request on the spot.

Thyer, Geller, Williams, and Purcell (1987) demonstrated the efficacy of another application of the flash for life reminder by posting college students at the entrance/exit areas of campus parking lots and had them "flash" vehicle occupants as their vehicles entered or exited the lot. Mean safety belt use by vehicle drivers increased from 19.5% ($n = 629$) during an initial 1-week baseline period to 45.5% ($n = 635$) during a subsequent week of daily flashing. The intervention was withdrawn during the third week and average belt use decreased to 28.5% ($n = 634$). When the intervention was reinstated during the fourth week, the percentage of drivers observed buckled up increased to 51.5% ($n = 625$).

Roberts, Alexander, and Knapp (1987) extended the flash for life procedure by disseminating vinyl folders with the same "buckle-up" and "thank you" messages to 10,000 schoolchildren. They found higher rates of safety belt use among flash-card recipients and observed children "flashing" throughout the community. I have distributed more than 3,000 flash for life cards nationwide (usually upon request by an individual who heard about the intervention procedure), and some safety belt groups (e.g., in Ohio and Virginia) have personalized the flash card for distribution and use throughout their state.

The "Airline Lifesaver" Reminder

The author initiated this buckle-up reminder by handing a 3×5-inch card to the airline pilot and/or flight attendants when boarding an airplane. The card indicates that airlines have been the most effective promoters of seat belt use, and requests that someone in the flight crew make an announcement similar to the following near the end of the flight: "Now that you have worn a seat belt for the safest part of your trip, the flight crew would like to remind you to buckle up during your ground transportation." To date, the author has distributed the airline lifesaver on 328 flights (from November 1984 through August 1988), and on 31.5% of these occasions a buckle-up reminder was given at the end of the flight. TWA and Eastern Airlines have been especially cooperative, even adding this buckle-up prompt to their regular end-of-the-flight announcements. On the other hand, an airline that the author uses most often (Piedmont Airlines) actually distributed a memo to its staff stating specifically "to ignore the request of the Virginia Tech professor with the blue card."

The direct buckle-up influence of the airline lifesaver would be difficult (or impossible) to assess, but it is safe to assume that the beneficial large-scale effect of this antecedent strategy is a direct function of the number of individuals who deliver the reminder card to airline personnel. In this regard, it is encouraging that several corporations (e.g., Ford Motor Company, Tennessee Valley Authority, and Air Products of Allentown, Pennsylvania) have distributed airline lifesaver cards to their employees for their own use during air travel. If the delivery of an airline lifesaver does not influence a single airline passenger to use a safety belt during ground transportation, at least the act of handing an airline lifesaver card to another person should increase the card deliverer's commitment to personal safety belt use.

Education

Over the years, educational strategies for promoting safety belt use have been numerous, varying from simple television prompts to comprehensive public education campaigns involving communitywide dissemination of signs, billboards, radio and TV advertisements, school programs, films, slide shows, and pamphlets. Typically, the impact of these educational efforts on safety belt use has been negligible, whether applied in employee safety programs (Geller, 1982b; Phillips, 1980), through home television (Robertson et al., 1974), or throughout an entire community in varied formats (Cunliffe et al., 1975).

Geller and Hahn (1984) implemented a 20-minute educational program in a corporate setting that tripled safety belt use among blue-collar workers for a 1-month period. Following a 3-minute film, the author led an informal group discussion about the value of safety belts and factors that inhibit people from buckling up. Presumably, the key to the success of this program was the active involvement of the workers in the group discussion. This educational approach toward safety belt promotion was replicated successfully with different discussion leaders at two large industries—at Buroughs Wellcome in Greenville, North Carolina (Cope, Grossnickle, & Geller, 1986), and at the Reeves Brothers Curon Plant in Cornelius, North Carolina (Kello, Geller, Rice, & Bryant, 1988). Similarly, Kurt Lewin's (1958) classic research demonstrated maximum behavior change following an educational intervention that got participants actively involved in the presentation (i.e., through group discussions) and stimulated "group-carried" decisions.

Modeling

This antecedent refers to actual demonstration of specific behaviors that can have prominent effects on the behaviors of observers (Bandura, 1977). For example, when TV stars buckle up, some viewers learn how to put on a safety belt; others are reminded they should buckle up on every vehicle trip; still others realize that safety belt use is normative behavior. On the other hand, frequent nonuse of safety belts on TV can create or support the attitude that certain types of individuals (e.g., macho males or sexy females) do not use safety belts.

Our systematic observation and analysis of driving behavior on prime-time TV over recent viewing seasons (i.e., 1984, 1985, 1986) was based on the premise that use or nonuse of vehicle safety belts has large-scale modeling effects. Although there has been steady improvement across the three seasons, safety belt use by our network stars has been alarmingly low. Table 1 summarizes the results of our observations of 5,544 total driving scenes across 538 episodes of 21 different prime-time TV shows. The overall rate of safety belt use on TV has doubled over the past 3 years (from 8% in 1984 to 17% in 1986), consistent with changes in national belt-use statistics. It is unfortunate that the TV medium is only reflecting the unsafe driving practices of the general public, rather than attempting to model safe behavior and setting appropriate standards.

Table 1 shows that one macho TV character (i.e., T. J. Hooker) did model appropriate belt use in 1984 and was responsible for giving ABC the relatively high belt-use average that year. The prominent increase in safety belt use from 1985 to 1986 by "MacGyver" (3 to 34% belt use) and "Spenser for Hire" (0 to

Table 1. Safety Belt Use for Prime Time Network Shows during the 1984, 1985, and 1986 Seasons

Network	1984 season			1985 season			1986 season		
	Episodes	Driving scenes	Belt use	Episodes	Driving scenes	Belt use	Episodes	Driving scenes	Belt use
ABC shows									
Fall Guy	12	163	13%	7	222	0%	—	—	—
Hardcastle & McCormick	15	155	3%	11	110	39%	—	—	—
T.J. Hooker	11	149	47%	—	—	—	—	—	—
Matt Houston	12	99	2%	—	—	—	—	—	—
MacGyver	—	—	—	11	64	3%	4	41	34%
Moonlighting	—	—	—	12	54	37%	4	27	81%
Spenser	—	—	—	3	13	0%	3	61	28%
ABC totals	50	566	17%	44	463	14%	11	129	42%
CBS shows									
Cagney & Lacey	—	—	—	10	36	39%	6	38	42%
Dukes of Hazard	15	413	0%	—	—	—	—	—	—
Equalizer	—	—	—	14	102	14%	6	30	20%
Magnum PI	15	74	0%	6	34	0%	11	145	11%
Scarecrow & Mrs. King	14	118	16%	12	74	26%	5	60	15%
Simon & Simon	18	143	0%	22	148	2%	6	51	29%
CBS totals	62	748	3%	64	394	13%	34	324	19%
NBC shows									
A-Team	18	236	1%	15	139	20%	6	62	39%
Helltown	—	—	—	6	47	2%	—	—	—
Highway to Heaven	—	—	—	12	55	0%	6	26	0%
Hill Street Blues	13	71	0%	12	46	13%	10	58	3%
Hunter	13	133	7%	9	103	38%	12	136	38%
Miami Vice	17	112	0%	13	71	0%	16	192	3%
Remington Steele	18	104	2%	13	87	0%	—	—	—
Riptide	14	123	20%	11	73	37%	—	—	—
NBC totals	93	779	5%	91	621	16%	50	474	18%
OVERALL	205	2,093	8%	199	1,478	15%	95	927	22%

28% belt use) was also encouraging. The prominently low use of safety belts by Colt ("Fall Guy") in 1984 and 1985 is quite disappointing and unrealistic, since Colt played the role of a stunt driver. The driver who performed the vehicle stunts on this show obviously wore a safety harness on every trip.

Mr. T's unusually high rate of safety belt use in 1985 (up from no belt use in 1984) was very noticeable on the show, since he was the only member of his "A-Team" to buckle up that season. However, during 1986, his colleagues were often seen using their safety belts. The dramatic change in Mr. T's belt-use behavior may have been partially due to a nationwide campaign that my students and I initiated in 1984 to bring public attention to the inappropriate nonuse of safety belts by TV stars. First, we circulated a petition throughout the United States that described the presumed detrimental modeling effects of low safety belt use on TV, and we received approximately 50,000 signatures from 36 different states. Subsequently, we distributed a list of 30 names and addresses of TV stars, along with instructions to write letters requesting safety belt use by those who didn't buckle up and to write "thank you" notes to those who already buckled up on TV. In 1984 Mr. T was mailed more than 800 "buckle-up" letters. During the summer of 1987, the author was invited to Hollywood and gave an invited safety belt workshop to writers, producers, and TV stars from all three networks.

Commitment and Goal Setting

Commitment and goal-setting tactics request verbal or written statements from individuals or groups that they will perform certain behaviors. Substantial increases in safety belt use were observed after "buckle-up" pledge cards were distributed and signed at an industrial site (Geller & Bigelow, 1984; Horne & Terry, 1983), a community hospital (Nimmer & Geller, 1988), during a church service (Talton, 1984), and throughout a university campus (Geller, Kalsher, Rudd, & Lehman, 1989). For an application of a similar commitment procedure in the domain of energy conservation, see Pallak, Cook, and Sullivan (1980).

The Geller et al. study was a long-term and large-scale investigation conducted on the Virginia Tech campus with 22,000 students. During the spring and fall academic quarters, 1986 buckle-up pledge cards were available throughout the campus (10,000 in the spring 18,000 in the fall). Signing this pledge card implied a commitment to use vehicle safety belts for an entire academic quarter, and depositing a detachable portion of the pledge card in one of several raffle boxes located throughout the campus enabled entry into weekly random drawings of prizes donated by local merchants. The remainder of the pledge card was designed to be hung from a vehicle's inside rearview mirror as a reminder of one's commitment to buckle up.

By requesting pledge card signers to write their vehicle's license plate number on the pledge card and by recording vehicle license plate numbers during systematic observation of campus safety belt use, we were able to dichotomize the belt observations according to whether or not the driver had signed a pledge card. Since parking decals were also recorded during belt audits, it was possible to categorize the belt-use data according to whether the vehicle driver was faculty/ staff or a student.

During each phase of the study, faculty/staff drivers used safety belts significantly more often than students ($p < .01$), and those who signed a buckle-up pledge were buckled up more often than those who did not ($p < .01$). During both the spring and fall pledge-card lotteries, faculty/staff pledgers ($n = 208$) went from a high prepledge belt use level of 56.4% to a postpledge level of 75.9%, and students who signed pledge cards ($n = 252$) increased their belt use from a prepledge level of 49.3% to a postpledge level of 69.8%.

Incentives and Disincentives

Research has shown quite dramatically that the impact of a legal mandate (e.g., safety belt use law) varies directly with the amount of media promotion (i.e., the disincentive). The success of our campus pledge-card program described above was dependent upon making faculty, staff, and students aware of the possible rewards for turning in signed pledge cards. This promotional aspect of the program was an incentive, whereas delivering prizes to raffle winners was a rewarding consequence, contingent upon a person's pledge card being selected during weekly raffles.

Rewards to Increase Safety Belt Use

Promoting safety belt use by rewarding individuals for signing a buckle-up pledge card has been termed an *indirect* reward strategy, in contrast to the *direct* approach of rewarding an individual directly for using a safety belt (cf. Geller, 1984b, 1985b). Rewards are *direct* and *immediate* response consequences when vehicles are stopped and occupants are rewarded on the spot for being buckled up. On the other hand, vehicles with occupants using safety belts can be identified (e.g., by recording license plate numbers) and the occupants can be contacted later to receive rewarding consequences for being buckled up. This is a *direct* and *delayed* reward strategy (cf. Geller, 1984a).

The direct and immediate approach should be most effective at increasing safety belt use, and the indirect rewards should be least effective when considering basic learning theory. However, reviews of the literature (Geller, 1984b; Geller & Bigelow, 1984) and comparative research (Geller, Rudd, Kalsher, Streff, & Lehman, 1987) have generally shown these reward strategies to be equivalently effective at motivating the use of safety belts.

Direct and Immediate Rewards

As reviewed by Geller (1984b), the on-the-spot consequences for direct and immediate reward programs have usually been inexpensive and have varied widely in type (e.g., flowers, candy, balloons, trinkets, lottery tickets, or coupons exchangeable for money or food). It has been particularly worthwhile to solicit donations for prizes from community businesses. This reduces the program expense while involving the local community in a worthwhile safety effort. Most community merchants appreciate the special goodwill advertising available for their support of a local safety belt program (Geller, 1985a, 1985b; Streff & Geller, 1986). Direct rewards for safety belt use have at least doubled the baseline percentage of those buckled up in target vehicles, whether implemented at industrial sites (Geller, 1983; Geller, Davis, & Spicer, 1983; Spoonhour, 1981; Stutts, Hunter, & Campbell, 1984), shopping malls (Elman & Killebrew, 1978), bank exchange windows (Geller, Johnson, & Pelton, 1982; Johnson & Geller, 1984), high schools (Campbell, Hunter, & Stutts, 1984), or universities (Geller, Paterson, & Talbott, 1982). Although belt use has dropped substantially after the removal of an incentive/ reward program, in most cases the posttreatment follow-up levels of belt use have remained significantly higher than the pretreatment baseline levels.

None of the direct and immediate reward programs referred to so far targeted young children, perhaps the most critical age group for developing a buckle-up habit. Michael Roberts and his colleagues have successfully applied direct and immediate rewards to protect children in vehicles by (a) rewarding parents with lottery tickets redeemable for prizes if their children (ages 0.5 to 6 years) were buckled up appropriately when arriving at day care centers (Roberts & Turner, 1986), (b) rewarding preschool-aged children with colorful stickers when they arrived at day care centers (Roberts & Layfield, 1987), and (c) teaching PTA volunteers to reward elementary school children with lapel stickers, lottery tickets for pizzas, bumper stickers and coloring books if all vehicle occupants were buckled up when arriving at school (Roberts & Fanurik, 1986; Roberts, Fanurik, & Wilson, 1988). In all of these child-directed studies, the use of safety belts or child safety seats increased dramatically, from baseline buckle-up averages as low as 5% (Roberts & Fanurik, 1986) and 11% (Roberts & Turner, 1986) to usage levels of 70% and 64%, respectively. When these reward programs were withdrawn, safety belt use did decline, but it remained prominently higher than the initial baseline levels, as with the reward programs that targeted adults (e.g., see reviews by Geller, 1982a, 1984b). Actually, the residual effects of the child-directed programs have been notably higher than typically found with the safety belt programs that targeted adults (i.e., high school students, college students, and company employees).

Direct and Delayed Rewards

Because vehicles cannot always be stopped conveniently and safely, rewards for safety belt use must sometimes be delayed. For these types of programs, shoulder belt use is observed as vehicles enter or exit the program site, and without stopping the vehicles, the license plate number of vehicles with buckled occupants are recorded for a subsequent prize drawing. The winning license plate numbers are publicly posted, and the owners of the identified vehicles claim their prizes at an announced location.

Rudd and Geller (1985) applied this procedure throughout a large university campus with 21,000 registered vehicles by having the university police record license plate numbers for weekly raffles. Kalsher, Geller, Clarke, and Lehman (in press) adapted this delayed-reward strategy for the largest naval base in the world (with approximately 75,000 vehicles entering the base daily) by using the navy base police to collect license plate numbers for weekly prize lotteries. The use of indigenous personnel (i.e., police officers) to administer the large-scale campus and navy base programs was particularly advantageous. Even though 22 officers recorded a total of 6,859 entries for 9 intervention weeks of the campus program and 20 officers recorded a total of 16,000 raffle entries during the 4-week navy base program, none of the officers reported disruption in their daily duties. This suggests that a police-administered, delayed-reward program for safety belt promotion is feasible for communitywide or even statewide application. It is likely that such a program would make the enforcement of a state mandatory belt use law more palatable to both the police and the public, and would increase the number of safety belt users.

Geller *et al.* (1987) compared the impact of six corporate-based direct and *immediate* reward programs for safety belt promotion with the results of five direct and *delayed* programs and found no significant differences. The six immediate reward programs increased safety belt use among employees an average of 137% above baseline, and the five delayed programs increased employee belt use an average of 101% above the baseline levels. Those programs that included long-term follow-up assessment (i.e., four immediate- and four delayed-reward programs) found steady declines in belt use but with some residual effects. The follow-up records of the immediate reward programs (taken 1 month to 2 years after the program; $M = 7.0$ months) showed an average belt use that was 62% above the preintervention baseline levels. The residual effects for the delayed-reward programs averaged only 15% above the initial baseline levels, but these follow-up measures were taken later than those for the direct-reward programs (i.e., 3 months to 2½ years; $M = 2.8$ years).

Indirect Rewards

The pledge card strategy mentioned earlier as an antecedent commitment and goal-setting strategy is considered an *indirect* reward technique when rewards are given for signing the buckle-up pledge (Geller *et al.*, 1989; Horne & Terry, 1983). That is, rewards were not given directly for individual safety belt use. Instead, individuals signed buckle-up pledge cards in order to enter raffle drawings. Thus, the behavior of making an explicit commitment to buckle up was rewarded. For example, it was impossible to develop an equitable system for choosing winners among the 6,000 potential safety belt users entering or exiting the six gates across two work shifts at the General Motors Technical Center. Therefore, an indirect-reward strategy was developed and implemented. Specifically, all employees were given a chance to enter the GM "Seatbelt Sweepstakes" if they signed a buckle-up pledge card that committed the signers to use vehicular safety belts for 1 year. This program increased safety belt use at the GM Tech Center from 36% to an average belt use percentage of 60% 2 years after the program was terminated (Horne, 1984).

Group-Based Rewards

In addition to the individual pledge-card contingency, the GM Seatbelt Sweepstakes included a group contingency to motivate safety belt use. Specifically, the entire work force of 6,000 employees had to reach a certain percentage of safety belt use (i.e., the group goal) before each of three successive prize drawings were held in which a new automobile was the first prize. Employees reported incidents of peer pressure to buckle up in order to achieve each goal, and the successively increasing belt use goals per raffle of 55, 65, and 70% were in fact reached.

Another group-based reward contingency was implemented by Geller and Hahn (1984) to increase the impact of their corporate-based safety belt program. For this direct- and delayed-reward program, a single cash prize was raffled off each week from the pool of license plate numbers collected from daily observations of safety belt use. The amount of the cash award for each weekly raffle was determined by the average percentage of safety belt use by the work group during the preceding week (i.e., the cash prize amounted to $1 per percentage point). A feedback chart displayed the mean safety belt use each day and reminded workers of their group-based reward contingency. This public posting of daily group progress probably had motivating properties of its own, as found in a variety of community-based programs for motivating behavior change (cf. Geller, Winett, & Everett, 1982), and as predicted from Lewin's (1958) group dynamics tactic referred to earlier in this chapter.

Are Extrinsic Rewards Necessary?

Geller *et al.* (1987) reviewed five corporate safety belt programs that did not use rewards, but rather applied an interactive small-group discussion format (as discussed earlier). After a 20- to 25-minute group discussion, buckle-up pledge cards were distributed and participants were urged by the group leader and by other participants to make a buckle-up commitment. A portion of each signed pledge card was detached and deposited in a "pledge box" as the participants left the room. From their comparisons of these *no-reward* programs (detailed in Cope *et al.*, 1986; Geller & Bigelow, 1984; Kello *et al.*, 1988) with 13 reward programs, Geller *et al.* (1987) concluded that the immediate impact of reward versus no-reward programs was equivalent. However, after program termination there was consistently greater maintenance of safety belt use for the no-reward programs.

Several theoretical formulations and laboratory investigations suggest that extrinsic rewards may not be the optimal approach for motivating lasting behavior change. Indeed, the conceptualization and investigation of the "minimal justification principle" (Lepper, 1981), "overjustification" (e.g., Lepper, Green, & Nisbett, 1973), "intrinsic motivation" (Deci, 1975; Deci & Ryan, 1980), and "cognitive dissonance and attribution" (e.g., Aronson, 1966; Aronson & Carlsmith, 1963; Wilson & Lassiter, 1982) predict greater long-term behavior change with interventions that minimize extrinsic controls. Powerful extrinsic motivators are assumed to inhibit individuals from gaining an internal justification for performing the target behavior after the external controls are withdrawn. Clearly, more research is needed to define the parameters for obtaining enough extrinsic control to initiate the buckle-up response but not too much so as to obviate perceived internal control and intrinsic justification.

Applied Behavior Analysis and Drunk-Driving Prevention

From the perspective of applied behavior analysis, excessive alcohol consumption and alcohol-impaired driving are target behaviors influenced by certain environmental events or conditions that precede and follow these responses. For example, incentives might be available to encourage excessive drinking (e.g., two-for-one prices during "happy hour") or the assignment of sober individuals to do the driving (e.g., free food and soft drinks for a "designated driver"). Alternatively, a disincentive antecedent could discourage alcohol consumption (e.g., the checking of ID cards by servers of alcohol) or DUI (e.g., the announcement of a nearby police roadblock). Likewise, certain response consequences can encourage continued alcohol consumption (e.g., peer support and social attention for participating in drinking games) or discourage future alcohol-impaired driving (e.g., being stopped at a DUI checkpoint). In addition, the efficacy of particular intervention strategies to prevent DUI (e.g., feedback from meters that display blood alcohol concentration, DUI-prevention training for the servers of alcohol, the availability of safe driving alternatives) depends upon the antecedent conditions and the reinforcing or punishing consequences. The remainder of this chapter highlights research related to this particular perspective of the critical societal problem of alcohol-impaired driving.

The DUI problem is substantially more complex and difficult to influence than the problem of low safety belt use, and thus requires more than an antecedent-behavior-consequence analysis. For example, the impact of a behavior-change intervention for DUI prevention will be determined by various individual factors (e.g., age, gender, genetics, attitudes, and drinking history) that predispose a person to drink excessively or DUI. In addition, the addictive element of alcohol abuse adds physiological dependency to the complexities in reducing the incidence of DUI. In other words, one cannot assume that a given set of antecedent conditions and response consequences will have the same effect across individuals. The outcome of a particular intervention strategy will be influenced by dynamic inter-actions between individual and environmental factors (e.g., Geller & Lehman, 1988; Jessor & Jessor, 1975). This is not to say that individual variables do not influence interventions to increase safety belt use—they certainly do. Rather, the behaviors and environs related to the DUI problem are much more complex than those related to the protection of vehicle occupants with safety belts, and thus they allow for many more unanticipated and nonpredictable interactions among person, behavior, and situational variables. This difference is exemplified by the following selective review of approaches to change DUI-related behaviors. What follows is not an exhaustive review of legal, education, and community-based interventions to prevent DUI—more comprehensive reviews are available elsewhere (e.g., Laurence, Snortum, & Zimring, 1988; Moskowitz, 1988; Russ & Geller, 1985). Instead, the research reviewed here was selected to typify a behavior analysis approach to the DUI problem, to show the need for additional behavior-change research, and to illustrate innovative intervention procedures that could benefit from a behavior analysis perspective. Clearly, behavior analysts have far fewer success stories in the domain of DUI prevention than safety belt promotion.

Feedback Interventions

Some have argued that drinkers are not always aware of their alcohol impair-ment, and that receiving personal feedback about one's blood alcohol concentra-tion (BAC) may reduce the probability of DUI (e.g., Geller, Altomari, Russ, & Harwood 1985; Geller & Russ, 1986). Feedback regarding a drinker's level of alcohol impairment can be readily available at bar and party settings (a) in the form of a BAC chart called a "nomogram," (b) by means of a breath alcohol test that can be self-administered, or (c) through one's performance on certain "field sobriety tests."

BAC Nomograms

Body weight and the number of drinks consumed within 2 hours can be used readily to estimate BAC. For example, a 120-pound individual who consumes four 12-ounce beers in 2 hours could have a maximum BAC of .10% (U.S. DOT, 1979). Nomograms have been printed on key chains and bar napkins and have been distributed widely as part of some anti-drunk-driving campaigns, but they are not foolproof. Although these scales were derived from carefully controlled laboratory studies with calculations based on an "average" individual, O'Neill, Williams, and Dubowski (1983) showed that the actual range of BACs can vary greatly for a given weight and within a certain time period. Thus, nomograms may lead individuals to over- or underestimate their BACs substantially (Waller, 1986). In the case of underestimation, nomograms may be a menace to DUI prevention, since they tell intoxicated individuals that they are not legally drunk. Therefore, it has been suggested that nomograms be removed from circulation and a better index of alcohol impairment be developed (Dubowski, 1984).

Self-Testing BAC Meters

Minimal effort is required to obtain accurate BAC measurements from the relatively inexpensive, portable BAC meters (Picton, 1979). Such devices can be placed in drinking establishments to provide immediate, individualized BAC feedback for guiding individuals in their drinking/driving decisions. However, research assessing the utility of BAC meters has not been completely favorable. For example, in a field study with drinking and driving information provided to bar patrons, Oates (1976) reported that subjects who received BAC feedback were no more likely to use the public transportation services (i.e., taxi or bus) than were nonparticipants.

Calvert-Boyanowsky and Boyanowsky (1980) placed BAC meters in several bars in British Columbia to study whether BAC feedback influenced DUI of bar patrons. They administered questionnaires to assess the driving plans of those patrons who volunteered to take the breath test. The patrons' decisions about subsequent driving were assessed by self-report and unobtrusive observation of a patron's mode of transportation upon leaving the tavern. The authors concluded that, although breath testing was popular, knowledge of BAC did not deter the majority of alcohol-impaired subjects from driving.

A particular concern of this approach to DUI prevention is that BAC feedback might indeed exacerbate alcohol consumption, because drinkers may view the feedback as a game score rather than information to prevent DUI. Support for this notion was observed in a study by Harwood (1984) conducted at a university fraternity party. During the party, a few students actually urged others to obtain higher BAC levels, cheering enthusiastically as "players" successively increased their BAC levels. The BAC measures taken from all students when they left the party showed significantly higher mean BAC among those who used the BAC meter at least once during the party. It is likely, however, that his finding resulted from a self-selection sampling bias, with those who consumed more alcohol being more apt to assess their BAC during the party.

Field Sobriety Tests

Given that alcohol affects performance adversely along several dimensions, including reaction time and standing steadiness (e.g., see Carpenter, 1962 for a review), Geller and Russ (1986) argued that behavioral tests of impairment might be useful in a social context for determining a person's level of intoxication. The validity of this thesis was studied by asking students at college beer parties to participate in simple behavioral tasks that might indicate alcohol impairment (Geller & Russ, 1986; Russ & Geller, 1986). These tests were modified from laboratory studies and were designed to be easily administered and scored. Subjects were asked, for example, to catch a ruler as it dropped between their thumb and fore-finger. The number of inches it fell was used as an indication of reaction time. The subjects were also asked to participate in a five-step, progressive body-bal-ance task. Participants were given points for maintaining their balance at each increasingly difficult level of the task.

Performance on both the ruler drop and body-balance tasks contributed sig-nificantly to the prediction of actual BAC. Many subjects reported that poor per-formance on these tasks would likely dissuade them from driving. However, this favorable reaction to the field sobriety tests decreased as the participant's BAC increased. More research is needed to investigate how simple performance tests can be used to persuade alcohol-impaired individuals not to drive. Indeed, field sobriety tests may be more valid than BAC as an index of performance deficits related to driving (Johnson, 1983). Furthermore, simple sobriety tests could be administered by party hosts, drink servers, or friends to increase a respondent's awareness of the debilitating effects of excessive alcohol consumption.

The Drinking Milieu

Comparatively little research has addressed the environmental determinants of drinking in naturalistic settings. Yet the environmental context within which drinking occurs certainly influences whether alcohol consumption is excessive and whether behaviors occur to prevent DUI. This section reviews the relatively min-imal research that examined the effect of specific environmental factors on drink-ing and DUI risk. This is an area that demands much additional investigation from a behavior-change perspective. Most of this field research has occurred in bars or tavern settings, although about as much alcohol consumption occurs at home and at parties or social gatherings (O'Donnell, 1985), and these latter settings are places where socially responsible drinking could potentially be taught. For ex-ample, the home is the usual place for receiving one's first alcoholic beverage (Hanson, Engs, & Katter, 1985), and parental reaction to such drinking behavior can certainly have a major influence on subsequent alcohol consumption.

The party or social gathering of friends and acquaintances is an ideal setting in many respects for introducing techniques that reflect socially responsible drink-ing. For example, such events could provide opportunities to serve low-alcohol or nonalcoholic beverages, or to administer field sobriety tests, or to make BAC feedback meters available. Interactive discussions can evolve naturally among friends to provide the rationale and support (i.e., reinforcing consequences) for appro-priate server intervention strategies. Indeed, such discussions may result in prac-tical refinements of procedures to control drinking and driving.

High school and college settings often represent the last chance to gather a "captured audience" for increasing group awareness of drinking and driving is-sues and teaching a socially responsible approach to alcohol consumption. In fact, alcohol-awareness groups based at high schools (e.g., SADD) and colleges (e.g., BAUCUS) have been among the most innovative and active in encouraging socially responsible drinking. Thus, organizations and individuals are available at high schools and colleges to implement party-based interventions for reducing excessive alcohol consumption and preventing DUI. We hope the field studies reviewed in this section are only the beginning of a promising research domain to define setting-specific determinants of drinking and driving.

The Bar Environment

Results from an investigation of 185 bars in Vancouver (Graham, 1984) suggested that intoxication and aggression were related to larger seating capacity, rows of tables, no decor theme, and lower standards of furnishings and upkeep. Graham suggested that decor and upkeep in bars may convey a message to patrons about the kinds of behaviors expected. Other activities and general atmosphere characteristics that Graham identified as significant determinants of intoxication included the type of entertainment, availability of food, ventilation, noise, and crowding. Additional naturalistic studies of relationships between alcohol consumption and setting variables are urgently needed.

The "Happy Hour"

The "happy hour" typically refers to a period of time after the workday has ended and before the evening meal. In order to attract a greater volume of business during this off-peak period, some entrepreneurs offer alcohol at bargain prices. As many as 16 states prohibit happy hours or other forms of sales promotion, and 22 additional states have such legislation pending (Waller, 1986).

The effect of reduced drink prices on individual drinking patterns was explored by monitoring the same persons as they drink in experimental and natural settings (Babor, Mendelson, Uhly, & Souza, 1980). In both settings, reduced prices (during happy hour) significantly increased the frequency of drinking episodes and the amount of alcohol consumed among both casual and heavy drinkers. In a controlled setting, Babor, Mendelson, Greenberg, and Kuchnle (1978) found that an eightfold increase in alcohol consumption during happy hours was not a substitute for consumption at other times of the day. In fact, patterns of drinking influenced by the happy hour (i.e., gulping drinks, massing successive drinks, and consuming straight drinks) were likely to be learned and repeated at other times.

Size of Drinking Group

Sommer (1965) observed isolated male drinkers sitting alone in 32 Edmonton beer parlors, and contrasted their drinking behavior with that of drinkers in groups. He found that isolated drinkers ordered an average of 1.69 drinks, whereas individual drinkers in groups ordered 3.51 drinks. However, when the amount of time spent in the barroom was taken into account, the data suggested that the reason persons in groups drank more than isolated drinkers was not because they drank faster but because they remained in the barroom longer.

These seminal findings of Sommer were replicated 20 years later by the naturalistic observation of college students drinking beer (Geller, Russ, & Altomari, 1986). Of the 243 college students (mean age about 19) observed, 19% drank alone, 48% drank in pairs, 16% drank in triads, and 17% drank in groups of four or more. Students drinking in groups drank significantly more beer per individual than those drinking alone, but those drinking alone spend significantly less time in the bar. Thus, the rate of beer consumption was nearly identical for those drinking alone (.49 ounces per minute) and individuals drinking with others (.48 ounces per minute).

Rosenbluth, Nathan, and Lawson (1978) also observed that male and female college students drank more beer in groups than in dyads. An intriguing finding from these field observations that requires follow-up research was that same-gender dyads showed less rapid beer consumption than mixed-gender dyads.

Glasses versus Pitchers

Geller et al. (1986) offered convincing evidence from their bar observations that the sale of beer in pitchers may contribute to excessive alcohol consumption and subsequent risk for DUI. These investigators obtained systematic, reliable, and unobtrusive observations of drinking behavior at six bars that sold large quantities of beer to college students in 40-ounce pitchers, 10-ounce plastic cups and 12-ounce bottles. Of the 243 drinkers observed during their entire stay in a bar, 77% were male and 68% ordered their beer in a pitcher. By far the most beer was consumed per person when it was ordered in a pitcher (i.e., mean per capita beer consumption was 35.2 ounces from pitchers, 15.1 ounces from bottles, and 10.0 ounces from cups). But *rate* of drinking did not vary significantly as a function of drink container, because those who ordered their beer in a pitcher stayed in the bar significantly longer (mean of 66 minutes) than those ordering beer in a bottle (mean of 34 minutes) or in a cup (mean of 23 minutes).

The Barroom Server

An especially critical aspect of the drinker's social environment is the server of alcoholic beverages. "Dram shop" laws permit tavern owners to be held liable if they serve alcohol to an intoxicated patron who later causes an accident while DUI. In response to these laws, servers of alcoholic beverages are receiving special training aimed at preventing their customers from DUI (Mosher, 1979, 1983; Peters, 1986). Most intervention training programs teach servers to identify the specific warning signs that indicate when a customer may overindulge. Servers learn to use a variety of tactics, including delaying alcoholic drink service, offering food, serving nonalcoholic beverages, and suggesting that the patron not drive.

Some programs include the use of video vignettes and role playing to help servers evaluate customers' behavior and to practice intervention skills.

The first systematic evaluation of server intervention was accomplished by Russ and Geller (1987). These investigators obtained direct measures of servers' intervention behaviors and patrons' BAC levels both before and after 50% of the servers at two bars received "Training Intervention Procedures for Servers of Alcohol," a 6-hour training program referred to as TIPS and used nationwide by major corporations such as Anheuser-Busch, Heublein, Miller Brewers, Ogden Foods, and Ramada Inn. Research assistants, who were unaware of which 17 servers had received the training, posed as regular patrons ("pseudopatrons") and set the occasion for server intervention to occur by drinking three alcoholic beverages per hour for 2 consecutive hours. Using a hidden microphone, a partner taped all interactions between the server and the pseudopatron, and at the end of the session measured the pseudopatron's BAC. Servers were unable to distinguish the pseudopatrons from regular patrons during the observation sessions, even though the servers were told during training about the use of pseudopatrons and agreed to the evaluation.

The comparison of data from pseudopatrons served by trained versus untrained bar personnel revealed a substantial impact of the TIPS program, at least over the short term. The trained servers initiated significantly more interventions to reduce the probability of DUI than did untrained personnel, and the pseudopatrons served by trained personnel exhibited fewer signs of intoxication. Most important, when pseudopatrons were served by trained personnel, they had significantly lower BAC levels than the pseudopatrons served by untrained servers.

Although the Russ and Geller evaluation indicates promise for a server-training approach to DUI prevention, much more research and development of this concept is needed. For example, the impact of any training program will be transitory if the behaviors taught during the training are not supported by the environmental context in which they are to occur. Thus, trained competencies to monitor alcohol consumption for potential DUI risk will not be used consistently unless reinforced by natural or contrived contingencies. Some bar management policy, for example, provides a guaranteed 15% gratuity if a drinker must be "cut off" from excessive consumption or forcibly prevented from driving a vehicle. Geller, Russ, and Delphos (1987) reported a natural contingency that might be effective, particularly in maintaining the behaviors taught during server-intervention training; namely, customers' gratuities tended to be higher after the servers received the TIPS program. Further field research along these lines is critically needed, as well as comparative studies of different techniques to teach and maintain server-intervention behaviors. The priority for this type of research is based on the behavior analysis principle that the optimal time to intervene for behavior change is at the place where the target behavior has an opportunity to occur. Server intervention is a DUI prevention strategy that meets this behavior-change criterion, in contrast with the standard DUI education and awareness messages that are typically delivered to persons when they are sober and remote from the setting that sets the occasion for DUI risk.

Drinking at Parties

Geller and his students (Geller et al., 1986; Kalsher & Geller, 1989; Russ & Geller, 1988) have found some intriguing environment–behavior relationships from systematic observations of students' drinking behavior at university parties. The general procedure for these field studies was as follows:

1. When entering a party, subjects were informed that their drinking would be monitored, that they would be asked some drinking-related questions, and that they would be given a breath test (BAC) upon leaving the party.

2. Subjects were given a blind taste-test whereby they successively sampled three 2-ounce samples of different beer types (i.e., Budweiser, Bud Light, and LA or low-alcohol beer), and then were asked which sample they preferred to drink at the party.

3. Each subject was given a numbered cup and ID badge.

4. Two or more research assistants recorded the subject's ID number and the time whenever a subject obtained a drink. Individuals approaching the bar with more than one cup were requested to announce the ID number of the person(s) for whom they were getting beer.

5. When a subject left the party, a brief exit interview was administered and a measure of BAC was taken using an Alco-Sensor breath-testing device.

6. Those with a BAC of 0.10% or greater were informed that they were above the state's legal limit of intoxication and were urged not to drive home. A member of the research team offered a free ride home to any person who wanted to use this service.

In one study (Kalsher & Geller, 1989) the stimulus control (or marketing impact) of beer brand labels was demonstrated. At an initial fraternity party, the three available beer kegs were *not* labeled according to the three different beers available—Budweiser, Bud Light, and low-alcohol (LA). At a second party 1 month later, the three kegs were labeled according to brand name. At the first party (86 males and 72 females), the drinking preferences during the party matched the results of the taste-preference tests obtained at the start of both parties (i.e., Budweiser was most preferred and selected most often, LA was least preferred and selected least often). When the beer kegs were labeled according to brand name, the subjects (151 males and 220 females) showed a significant preference for Bud Light over Bud.

The LA beer was only consumed to any extent at the party with unlabeled kegs, suggesting a social stigma attacked to ordering a low-alcohol drink and for a desire to get drunk. The preference for Bud Light over Budweiser implies a powerful influence of marketing strategies. Indeed, it is possible that most individuals perceive light beers as having only fewer calories and not less alcohol.

Would Bud Light have been more popular than Budweiser if the kegs were labeled according to their alcohol content as well as brand name (i.e., 3.8% alcohol for Budweiser and 2.8% alcohol for Bud Light)?

Even though low-alcohol beer is not typically the "beer of choice" when other beers are available, it may reduce the risk of alcohol impairment and DUI if served at a party without the guests being informed. Geller and Kalsher (1989) researched this empirical question with the general party observation procedures described above. Both mixed drinks and beer were available at no cost to the subjects at two fraternity parties. At the start of the party, each participant was required to select one drink alternative (beer or mixed drinks) and to continue with that choice throughout the evening. At one party (64 males and 43 females), the only beer was Budweiser, whereas at the other party (70 males and 48 females) the beer was LA. Subjects were unaware of the brand of beer being served. The BAC levels at the end of the party were significantly lower among those students who drank LA beer than for those who drank Budweiser ($p < .01$), and no one complained about beer taste. Also, those who drank beer (approximately half of the persons at each party) did *not* drink at significantly higher rates or get more impaired than those who chose mixed drinks. This finding contradicts the conclusion from interview research that beer drinkers get more impaired than those who consume mixed drinks (Berger & Snortum, 1985).

Summary and Conclusions

The challenge for everyone who could receive an unintentional injury at home, at the workplace, or on the road is to focus on prevention. Motivating individuals to act for prevention, however, is most difficult because rewards to support such behavior are usually not available. In fact, the unsafe or unhealthy alternatives are often followed by immediate pleasures. Therefore, not only do prevention behaviors usually lack immediate rewarding consequences, they often compete with alternative unsafe or unhealthy behaviors that are rewarded. This chapter reviewed research that focused on the development and evaluation of interventions to change two of the most critical behaviors responsible for unintentional injury: nonuse of vehicle safety belts and driving a vehicle while under the influence of alcohol.

Compared with most prevention strategies that require repeated responding in order to be preventive (e.g., regular exercise, daily use of protective work clothing, brushing teeth, proper nutrition), using a vehicle safety belt is not only most convenient, it is also most likely to pay off in substantial dividends. Since safety belt use requires minimal response cost and is intuitively protective (once certain myths about belts and crashes are dispelled), basic principles of large-scale behavior change are directly applicable; and because safety belt use or nonuse can be readily observed in field settings, it has been possible to evaluate the relative efficacy of different applications of behavior-change principles. As a result, a number of antecedent and consequence strategies have been developed for increasing safety belt use in a variety of community settings, including schools, universities, industries, banks, churches, and naval bases. It is encouraging that most of these interventions can be delivered successfully by indigenous staff or volunteer groups, and they have been sponsored willingly by both the private and public sectors.

Because a variety of cost-effective techniques for increasing safety belt use have been identified, it cannot be assumed that continued research on safety belt promotion is any less important. In fact, the opposite is true. Most of the research reviewed in this chapter raised important empirical questions. For example, in order to increase the greatest number of safety belt users over the longest period of time, it is necessary to study (a) various schedules for delivering and fading buckle-up rewards; (b) different combinations of extrinsic incentives and intrinsic commitment procedures; (c) the differential effects of various intervention strategies on adults versus children, blue-collar versus white-collar workers, and employees versus retired persons; (d) the comparative cost-effectiveness of implementing safety belt programs at corporations, schools, recreational facilities, churches, and local businesses; (e) the long-term impact of combining behavior-change strategies, such as incentives/rewards for safety belt use and disincentives/punishers for safety belt nonuse; and (f) techniques for mobilizing groups of people and resources to implement communitywide programs for safety belt promotion.

Attacking drunken driving with applied behavior analysis has not been nearly as straightforward as intervening to increase safety belt use. To decrease inappropriate behavior, behavior-change specialists typically focus on increasing the occurrence of behaviors incompatible with the undesired behavior. This is a more appropriate approach to DUI prevention than the current punishment strategies receiving increased attention in the United States. Because it has been impossible to administer the kind of punishment contingency for DUI that works—one with a consequence that is frequent, consistent, immediate, and adequately severe—catching an alcohol-impaired driver is usually not corrective or rehabilitative, and the threat of such punishment for DUI is not a long-term deterrent.

The initial challenge for a positive reinforcement approach to DUI prevention is defining situations and behaviors that decrease the risk of DUI. The possibilities for study seem endless; however, there has been only a minimal amount of research related to this essential aspect of DUI prevention. There have been some promising beginnings, and these were highlighted in this chapter. In particular, certain environmental conditions have been studied as potential facilitators or inhibitors of excessive drinking (e.g., size of drinking groups and drink containers, the availability of BAC feedback meters, "happy hour" incentives, labels on beer kegs), and one mechanism for applying the results of this research to prevent DUI (i.e., through server intervention) has been addressed. Unfortunately, these studies are few in number, and the findings cannot be generalized beyond a particular type of drinker (e.g., a college student) and environmental setting (e.g., college bar or fraternity party). Thus, it is clear that this necessary research domain for DUI prevention is only in its infancy. The good news is that many grass roots groups, government agencies, enforcement officials, and treatment professionals are available. Unfortunately, the focus of these groups has been on the development and enforcement of ineffective contingencies for punishing the alcohol-impaired driver. Changing the intervention approach of these groups is yet another pressing challenge for the behavior-change professional who wants to make a difference.

ACKNOWLEDGMENTS. The preparation of this document was supported in part by Grant R49 CCR302635-01 from the Centers for Disease Control, Atlanta, Georgia. The author is grateful for the constructive comments of John Edwards, Nason Russ, and Chris Patrick on an earlier draft of this chapter.

References

Aronson, E. (1966). The psychology of insufficient justification: An analysis of some conflicting data. In S. Feldman (Ed.), *Cognitive consistency*. New York: Academic Press.

Aronson, E., & Carlsmith, J. E. (1963). Effect of the severity of threat on the devaluation of forbidden behavior. *Journal of Abnormal and Social Psychology, 66,* 584–588.

Babor, T. F., Mendelson, J. H., Greenberg, I., & Kuchnle, J. (1978). Experimental analysis of the "happy hour": Effects of purchase price on alcohol consumption. *Psychopharmacology, 58,* 35–41.

Babor, T. F., Mendelson, J. H., Uhly, B., & Souza, E. (1980). Drinking patterns in experimental and barroom settings. *Journal of Studies on Alcohol, 41*(7), 634–651.

Bandura, A. (1977). *Social learning theory.* Englewood Cliffs, NJ: Prentice-Hall.

Berger, D. E., & Snortum, J. R. (1985). Alcoholic beverage preferences of drinking-driving violators. *Journal of Studies on Alcohol, 46*(1), 232–239.

Califano, J. A., Jr. (1979). *Healthy people: The surgeon general's report on health promotion and disease prevention.* Washington, DC: U.S. Government Printing Office.

Calvert-Boyanowsky, J., & Boyanowsky, E. O. (1980). *Tavern breath testing as an alcohol countermeasure,* Technical Report. Ottawa, Ontario: Ministry of Transport.

Campbell, R. J., Hunter, W. W., & Stutts, J. C. (1984). The use of economic incentives and education to modify safety belt use behavior of high school students. *Health Education, 15,* 30–33.

Campbell, B. J., Stewart, J. R., & Campbell, F. A. (1987). *1985–1986 experience with belt laws in the United States.* Chapel Hill, NC: UNC Highway Safety Research Center.

Carpenter, J. A. (1962). Effects of alcohol on some psychological processes: A critical review with special reference to automobile driving skill. *Quarterly Journal of Studies on Alcohol, 23,* 274–314.

Cope, J. G., Grossnickle, W. F., & Geller, E.S. (1986). An evaluation of three corporate strategies for safety belt use promotion. *Accident Analysis and Prevention, 18,* 243–251.

Cunliffe, A. P., DeAngelis, F., Foley, C., Lonero, L. P., Pierce, J. A., Siegel, C., Smutylo, T., & Stephen, K. M. (1975, September). *The design and implementation of a seat-belt educational program in Ontario.* Paper presented at the Annual Conference of the Roads and Transportation Association of Canada, Calgary.

Cynecki, J., & Goryl, M. E. (1984). *The incidence and factors associated with child safety seat misuse* (Final Report DOT-HS-806-676). Washington, DC: National Highway Traffic Safety Administration, U.S. Department of Transportation.

Deci, E. L. (1975). *Intrinsic motivation.* New York: Plenum Press.

Deci, E. L., & Ryan, R. M. (1980). The empirical exploration of intrinsic motivational processes. In

L. Berkowitz (Ed.), *Advances in experimental social psychology* (Vol. 13). New York: Academic Press.

Dubowski, K. (1984, June). *Absorption, distribution, and elimination of alcohol: Highway safety aspects.* Paper presented at the meeting of the North American Conference on Alcohol and Highway Safety, Baltimore, MD.

Elman, D., & Killebrew, T. J. (1978). Incentives and seat belt: Changing a resistant behavior through extrinsic motivation. *Journal of Applied Social Psychology, 8,* 72–83.

Federal Register. (1984, July). Federal motor vehicle safety standards: Occupant crash protection, Final Rule, 48 (No. 138). Washington, DC: U.S. Department of Transportation.

Fell, J. C. (1982). Alcohol involvement in traffic crashes. *American Association for Automobile Medicine Quarterly Journal, 4,* 23–42.

Gelfand, D. M., & Hartmann, D. P. (1984). *Child behavior analysis and therapy* (2nd ed). New York: Pergamon Press.

Geller, E.S. (1982a). *Corporate incentives for promoting safety belt use: Rationale, guidelines, and examples.* Washington, DC: U.S. Department of Transportation.

Geller, E. S. (1982b, January). *Development of industry-based strategies for motivating seat-belt usage: Phase II* (Quarterly Report for DOT Contract DTRS5681-C-0032). Blacksburg, VA: Virginia Polytechnic Institute and State University.

Geller, E. S. (1983). Rewarding safety belt usage at an industrial setting: Tests of treatment generality and response maintenance. *Journal of Applied Behavior Analysis, 16,* 189–202.

Geller, E. S. (1984a). A delayed reward strategy for large-scale motivation of safety belt use: A test of long-term impact. *Accident Analysis and Prevention, 16*(5/6), 457–463.

Geller, E. S. (1984b). Motivating safety belt use with incentives: A critical review of the past and a look to the future. *SAE Technical Paper Series* (No. 840326). Warrendale, PA: Society of Automotive Engineers.

Geller, E. S. (1985a). *Community safety belt programs.* Blacksburg, VA: Virginia Polytechnic Institute and State University.

Geller, E. S. (1985b). *Corporate safety belt programs.* Blacksburg, VA: Virginia Polytechnic Institute and State University.

Geller, E. S. (1988). A behavioral science approach to transportation safety. *Bulletin of the New York Academy of Medicine, 65*(7), 632–661.

Geller, E. S., Altomari, M. G., Russ, N. W., & Harwood, M. K. (1985, June). Exploring the drinking/driving behaviors and attitudes of college students. *Resources in Education,* Ms. No. ED252756.

Geller, E. S., & Bigelow, B. E. (1984). Development of corporate incentive programs for motivating safety belt use: A review. *Traffic Safety Evaluation Research Review, 3,* 21–38.

Geller, E. S., Bruff, C.D., & Nimmer, J. G. (1985). "Flash for Life": Community-based prompting for safety belt promotion. *Journal of Applied Behavior Analysis, 18,* 145–159.

Geller, E. S., Casali, J. G., & Johnson, R. P. (1980). Seat-belt usage: A potential target for applied behavior analysis. *Journal of Applied Behavior Analysis, 13,* 669–675.

Geller, E. S., Davis, L., & Spicer, K. (1983). Industry-based rewards to promote seat belt usage: Differential impact on white collar versus blue collar employees. *Journal of Organizational Behavior Management, 5,* 17–29.

Geller, E. S., & Hahn, H.A. (1984). Promoting safety belt use at industrial sites: An effective program for blue collar employees. *Professional Psychology: Research and Practice, 15,* 553–564.

Geller, E. S., Johnson, R. P., & Pelton, S. L. (1982). Community-based interventions for encouraging safety belt use. *American Journal of Community Psychology, 10,* 183–195.

Geller, E. S., & Kalsher, J. J. (1989). *Beer versus mixed-drink consumption at university parties: A time and place for LA beer.* Manuscript submitted for publication.

Geller, E. S., Kalsher, M. J., Rudd, J. R., & Lehman, G. R. (1989). Promoting safety belt use on a university campus: An integration of commitment and incentive strategies. *Journal of Applied Social Psychology, 19,* 3–19.

Geller E. S., & Lehman, G. R. (1988). Drinking-driving intervention strategies: A person-situation-behavior framework. In M. D. Laurence, J. R. Snortum, & F. E. Zimring (Eds.), *The social control of drinking and driving* (pp. 297–320). Chicago: University of Chicago Press.

Geller, E. S., Paterson, L., & Talbott, E. (1982). A behavioral analysis of incentive prompts for motivating safety belt usage. *Journal of Applied Behavior Analysis, 15,* 403–415.

Geller, E. S., Rudd, J. R., Kalsher, M. J., Streff, F. M., & Lehman, G. R. (1987). Employer-based programs to motivate safety belt use: A review of short and long-term effects. *Journal of Safety Research, 18,* 1–17.

Geller, E. S., & Russ, N. W. (1986). Drunk driving prevention: Knowing when to say when. In *Alcohol, accidents, and injuries* (No. P-173). Warrendale, PA: Society of Automotive Engineers.

Geller, E. S., Russ, N. W., & Altomari, M. G. (1986). Naturalistic observations of beer drinking among college students. *Journal of Applied Behavior Analysis, 19,* 391–396.

Geller, E. S., Russ, N. W., & Delphos, W. A. (1987). Does server intervention training make a difference? An empirical field evaluation. *Alcohol, Health and Research World, 11,* 64–69.

Geller, E. S., Winett, R. A., & Everett, P. B. (1982). *Preserving the environment: New strategies for behavior change.* Elmsford, NY: Pergamon Press.

Graham, K. (1984, April). *Determinants of heavy drinking and drinking problems: The contribution of the bar environment.* Paper presented at the Symposium on Public Drinking and Public Policy, Banff, Alberta.

Hanson, D. J., Engs, R. C., & Katter, H. (1985). College students' attitudes toward drinking—1983: Exploring socialization theory. *College Student Journal, 10,* 425–429.

Harris, P. R. (1980). *Promoting health/preventing disease: Objectives for the nation.* Washington, DC: U.S. Government Printing Office.

Harris, P. R. (1981). *Better health for our children: A national strategy.* Washington, DC: U.S. Government Printing Office.

Hartunian, N.S., Smart, C. N., & Thompson, M. S. (1981). *The incidence and economic costs of major health impairments: A comparative analysis of cancer, motor vehicle injuries, coronary heart disease and stroke.* Lexington, MA: Lexington Books.

Harwood, M. K. (1984). *New directions toward increasing awareness of alcohol impairment.* Unpublished senior research paper, Virginia Polytechnic Institute and State University, Blacksburg, VA.

Horne, T. D. (1984, November). Workshop presentation at the Michigan Life Savers Conference, Boyne Mountain, MI.

Horne, T. D., & Terry, T. (1983). *Seat belt sweepstakes—An incentive program.* SAE Technical Paper Series (No. 830474). Warrendale, PA: Society of Automotive Engineers.

Injury in America: A continuing public health problem. (1985). Washington, DC: National Academy Press.

Jessor, R., & Jessor, S. L. (1975). Adolescent development and the onset of drinking: A longitudinal study. *Journal of Studies on Alcohol, 36,* 27–51.

Johnson, D. (1983). *Drunkenness may not be accurately measured by blood-alcohol levels: UCB researchers report* (Public Information Office News). Boulder: University of Colorado.

Johnson, R. P., & Geller, E. S. (1984). Contingent versus noncontingent rewards for promoting seat belt usage. *Journal of Community Psychology, 12,* 113–122.

Kalsher, M. J., & Geller, E. S. (1989). *Beer consumption at university parties: Stimulus control of brand labels.* Manuscript submitted for publication.

Kalsher, M. J., & Geller, E. S. (1988, February). Drug abuse and flight crews: You can make a difference! *Proceedings of the Fifth Annual International Aircraft and Cabin Safety Symposium,* Oakland, CA.

Kalsher, M. J., Geller, E. S., Clarke, S. W., & Lehman, G. R. (in press). Promoting safety belt use on naval bases: A comparison of incentive and disincentive programs. *Journal of Safety Research.*

Kello, J. E., Geller, E. S., Rice, J. C., & Bryant, S. L. (1988). Motivating auto safety belt wearing in industrial settings: From awareness to behavior change. *Journal of Organizational Behavior Management, 9,* 7–21.

Laurence, M. D., Snortum, J. R., & Zimring (Eds.). (1988). *The social control of drinking and driving*, Chicago: University of Chicago Press.

Lawson, D. L., Sleet, D. A., & Amoni, M. (Eds.). (1984). Automobile occupant protection: An issue for health education. *Health Education, 15.*

Lepper, M. (1981). Intrinsic and extrinsic motivation in children: Detrimental effects of superfluous social controls. In W Collins (Ed.), *Aspects of the development of competence: The Minnesota symposium on child psychology, 14*, 155–160.

Lepper, M., Green, D., & Nisbett, R. (1973). Undermining children's intrinsic interest with extrinsic rewards: A test of the overjustification hypothesis. *Journal of Personality and Social Psychology, 28*, 129–137.

Lewin, K. (1958). Group decision and social change. In E. E. Maccoby, T. M. Newcomb, & E. L. Hartley (Eds.), *Readings in social psychology* (pp. 197–211). New York: Holt, Rinehart & Winston.

McGinnis, J. M. (1984). Occupant protection as a priority in national efforts to promote health. *Health Education Quarterly, 11*, 127–131.

Mosher, J. F. (1979). Dram shop liability and the prevention of alcohol-related problems. *Journal of Studies on Alcohol, 40*(9), 773–798.

Mosher, J. R. (1983). Server intervention: A new approach for preventing drinking driving. *Accident Analysis and Prevention, 15*(6), 483–497.

Moskowitz, J. M. (1988). *The primary prevention of alcohol problems: A critical review of the research literature.* Unpublished manuscript, Prevention Research Center, Berkeley, CA.

National Highway Traffic Safety Administration. (1985, September). *The economic costs to society of motor vehicle accidents (1984 update).* Washington, DC: Memorandum, Office of Plans and Policy, National Highway Traffic Safety Administration, U.S. Department of Transportation.

National Highway Traffic Safety Administration. (1986). *Highway safety facts: Monthly fatality report.* Washington, DC: National Center for Statistics and Analysis, U.S. Department of Transportation.

Nimmer, J. G., & Geller, E. S. (1988). Motivating safety belt use at a community hospital: An effective integration of incentive and commitment strategies. *American Journal of Community Psychology, 16*, 381–394.

Oates, J. F. (1976). *Study of self test drivers* (Final Report, DOT-HS-5-01241). Washington, DC: National Highway Traffic Safety Administration.

O'Donnell, M. A. (1985). Research on drinking locations of alcohol-impaired drivers: Implications for present policies. *Journal of Public Health Policy, 6*, 510–525.

O'Neill, B., Williams, A. F., & Dubowski, K. M. (1983). Variability in blood alcohol concentration: Implications for estimating individual results. *Journal of Studies on Alcohol, 44*, 222–230.

Pallak, M. S., Cook, D.A., & Sullivan, J. J. (1980). Commitment and energy conservation. In L. Bickman (Ed.), *Applied social psychology annual* (Vol. 1, pp. 235–253). Beverly Hills, CA: Sage.

Peters, J. E. (1986). Beyond server training: An examination of future issues. *Alcohol, Health and Research World, 10*, 24–27.

Phillips, B. M. (1980, June). *Safety belt education program for employees: An evaluation study.* Opinion Research Corp. (Final Report for Contract DOT-HS-01707). Washington, DC: U.S. Department of Transportation.

Picton, W. R. (1979). An evaluation of a coin-operated self-tester. In I. R. Johnston (Ed.), *Proceedings of the Seventh International Conference on Alcohol, Drugs, and Traffic Safety* (pp. 327–331). Melbourne: Australian Government Publishing Service.

Roberts, M. C. (1987). Public health and health psychology: Two cats of Kilkenny? *Professional Psychology, 18*, 145–149.

Roberts, M. C., Alexander, K., & Knapp, L. (1987). *Motivating children to use seat belts: A program combining rewards and "Flash for Life."* Unpublished manuscript, University of Alabama.

Roberts, M. C., & Brooks, P. H. (Eds.). (1987). Children's injuries: Prevention and public policy. *Journal of Social Issues, 43*(2).

Roberts, M. C., & Fanurik, D. (1986). Rewarding elementary school children for their use of safety belts. *Health Psychology, 5*, 185–196.

Roberts, M. C., Fanurik, D., & Layfield, D. A. (1987). Behavioral approaches to prevention of childhood injuries. *Journal of Social Issues, 43,* 105–118.

Roberts, M. C., Fanurik, D., & Wilson, D. (1988). A community program to reward children's use of seat belts. *American Journal of Community Psychology, 16,* 395–407.

Roberts, M. C., & Layfield, D. A. (1987). Promoting child passenger safety: A comparison of two positive methods. *Journal of Pediatric Psychology, 12,* 257–271.

Roberts, M. C., & Turner, D. S. (1986). Rewarding parents for their children's use of safety seats. *Journal of Pediatric Psychology, 11,* 25–36.

Robertson, L. S. (1975). Safety belt use in automobiles with starter-interlock and buzzer-light reminder systems. *American Journal of Public Health, 65,* 1319–1325.

Robertson, L.S., Kelley, A. B., O'Neill, B., Wixom, C. W., Eiswirth, R. S., & Haddon, W. (1974). A controlled study of the effect of television messages on safety belt use. *American Journal of Public Health, 64,* 1071–1080.

Rogers, R. W. (1984). *Promoting safety belt use among state employees: The effects of prompting, stimulus control and a response-cost intervention.* Unpublished doctoral dissertation, Florida State University, Tallahassee, FL.

Rosenbluth, J., Nathan, P. E., & Lawson, D. M. (1978). Environmental influences on drinking by college students in a college pub: Behavioral observation in the natural environment. *Addictive Behaviors, 3,* 117–121.

Ross, H. L. (1982). *Deterring the drinking driver: Legal policy and social control.* Lexington, MA: D. C. Heath Lexington Books.

Ross, H. L. (1985). Deterring drunken driving: An analysis of current efforts. *Journal of Studies on Alcohol,* Supplement No. 10, 122–128.

Ross, H. L. (1987). Reflections on doing policy-relevant sociology: How to cope with MADD mothers. *American Sociologist, 18,* 173–178.

Rudd, J. R., & Geller, E. S. (1985). A university-based incentive program to increase safety belt use: Toward cost-effective institutionalization. *Journal of Applied Behavior Analysis, 18,* 215–226.

Russ, N. W., & Geller, E. S. (1985, December). Changing the behavior of the drunk driver: Current status and future directions. *Psychological Documents, 15,* 1–30.

Russ, N. W., & Geller, E. S. (1986). Using sobriety tests to increase awareness of alcohol impairment. *Health Education Research: Theory and Practice, 1,* 255–261.

Russ, N. W., & Geller, E. S. (1987). Training bar personnel to prevent drunken driving: A field evaluation. *American Journal of Public Health, 77,* 952–954.

Russ, N. W., & Geller, E. S. (1988). Exploring low alcohol beer consumption among college students: Implications for drunken driving. *Journal of Alcohol and Drug Education, 33,* 1–5.

Shelness, A., & Jewett, J. (1983). Observed misuse of child restraints. In *Proceedings of the 27th Stapp Car Crash Conference: Child Injury and Restraint* (pp. 207–216). Warrendale, PA: Society of Automotive Engineers.

Skinner, B. F. (1938). *The behavior of organisms.* New York: Appleton-Century-Crofts.

Skinner, B. F. (1958). *Science of human behavior.* New York: Macmillan.

Sleet, D. A. (1987). Motor vehicle trauma and safety belt use in the context of public health priorities. *Journal of Trauma, 27,* 695–702.

Sommer, R. (1965). The isolated drinker in the Edmonton beer parlor. *Quarterly Journal of Studies on Alcohol, 26,* 95–110.

Spoonhour, K. A. (1981, September–October). Company snap-it-up campaign achieves 90 percent belt use. *Traffic Safety,* pp. 18–19, 31–32.

Steed, D. K. (1987, November–December). National Highway Traffic Safety Administration. *Proceedings of the 1987 Conference on Injury in America,* U.S. Department of Health and Human Services, Public Health Service, *102,* 667–668.

Steed, D. K. (1988, February). *The administrator.* Washington, DC: National Highway Traffic Safety Administration, U.S. Department of Transportation.

Streff, F. M., & Geller, E. S. (1986). Strategies for motivating safety belt use: The application of applied behavior analysis. *Health Education Research: Theory and Practice, 1,* 47–59.

Stutts, J.C., Hunter, W. W., & Campbell, B. J. (1984). Three studies evaluating the effectiveness of incentives for increasing safety belt use. *Traffic Safety Evaluation Research Review, 3,* 9–20.

Talton, A. (1984). *Increasing safety belt usage through personal commitment: A church-based pledge card program.* Unpublished master's thesis, Virginia Polytechnic Institute and State University, Blacksburg, VA.

Thyer, B. A., & Geller, E. S. (1987). The "buckle-up" dashboard sticker: An effective environmental intervention for safety belt promotion. *Environment and Behavior, 19,* 484–494.

Thyer, B. A., Geller, E. S., William M., & Purcell, S. (1987). Community-based "flashing" to increase safety belt use. *Journal of Experimental Education, 55,* 155–159.

Tolsma, D. D. (1987, November–December). Behavioral aspects of injury. *Proceedings of the 1987 Conference on Injury in America,* U.S. Department of Health and Human Services, Public Health Service, *102,* 605–606.

U.S. DOT. (1979). *A message to my patients* (DOT-HS-804-089). Washington, DC: National Highway Traffic Safety Administration.

von Buseck, C. R., & Geller, E. S. (1984). *The vehicle safety belt reminder: Can refinements increase safety belt use?* Technical Report for General Motors Research Laboratories, Warren, MI.

Wagenaar, A. C. (1983). *Alcohol, young drivers, and traffic accidents.* Lexington, MA: D.C. Heath Lexington Books.

Wagenaar, A. C., Webster, D. W., & Maybee, R. C. (1987). Effects of child restraint laws on traffic fatalities in eleven states. *Journal of Trauma, 27,* 726–731.

Waller, J. A. (1986). State liquor laws as enablers for impaired driving and other impaired behaviors. *American Journal of Public Health, 76,* 787–792.

Waller, J. A. (1987, November–December). An overview of where we are and where we need to be. *Proceedings of the 1987 Conference on Injury in America,* U.S. Department of Health and Human Services, Public Health Service, *102,* 590–591.

Wilson, T., & Lassiter, G. (1982). Increasing intrinsic interest with superfluous extrinsic controls. *Journal of Personality and Social Psychology, 42,* 811–819.

Ziegler, P. (1986, January). Observed safety belt and child safety seat usage at road intersections: 19-city survey results. In *Research Notes.* Washington, DC: Office of Driver and Pedestrian Research, National Highway Traffic Safety Administration, U.S. Department of Transportation.

12

A Two-Factor Model of Energy and Water Conservation

Clive Seligman and Joan E. Finegan

"In the middle of the 20th century, we saw our planet from space for the first time. Historians may eventually find that this vision had a greater impact on thought than did the Copernican revolution of the 16th century, which upset the human self-image by revealing that the Earth is not the center of the universe. From space, we see a small and fragile ball dominated not by human activity and edifice but by a pattern of clouds, oceans, greenery, and soils. Humanity's inability to fit its doings into that pattern is changing planetary systems, fundamentally. Many such changes are accompanied by life-threatening hazards. This new reality, from which there is no escape, must be recognized—and managed." (*Our Common Future: The World Commission on Environment and Development* (WCED, 1987, p. 1).

Introduction

The beautiful opening passage of the report of the WCED, quoted above, makes eloquently clear that the environmental problems we face are not matters of inconvenience but of survival. The WCED report does not offer a new message. Rachel Carson's book *Silent Spring* (1962), the *Global 2000 Report to the President* (U.S. Council on Environmental Quality, 1980), and others have been sounding equally clear warnings of environmental concern. Since the early 1970s, psychologists have researched many environmental resource problems (see review by Stern & Oskamp, 1987). Psychologists were drawn to the issue from a prob-

Clive Seligman • Department of Psychology.   **Joan E. Finegan** • Centre for Administrative and Information Studies, The University of Western Ontario, London, Ontario, Canada N6A 5C2.

lem- or action-oriented approach, and this applied focus has had a guiding influence on the history of psychological research in this field.

Initially the research goals were to show that psychological theories, concepts, and methods were relevant to environmental resource problems. Through manipulations of the types of information or feedback subjects received, and/or incentives or reinforcements provided, various environmental behaviors could be altered, including household energy use, car pooling, littering, and recycling (see Geller, Winett, & Everett, 1982). These early experiments were inspired by the applied behavior analysis perspective, which emphasizes the situational determinants of observable behavior. One important impact of this approach was that the research problem became defined as how to achieve conservation, especially energy conservation. Because of psychologists' natural inclination to study individuals and because of the applied behavior analysts' focus on observable behaviors, conservation was seen as single behaviors that individuals could perform in their own homes or cars—e.g., turning down the thermostat in the winter or driving less. This approach demonstrated successfully that psychological techniques could be applied to environmental problems (e.g., Cone & Hayes, 1980; Geller *et al.* 1982).

Stern and Gardner (1981) made some important comments about the energy conservation research conducted by psychologists. They pointed out that the amount of energy that individuals controlled directly in their homes and in their cars was about one-third of the energy used in the economy. Thus, psychologists were ignoring other sectors of the economy (e.g., commercial and industrial) that use large amounts of energy (but see Oskamp, 1980–1981, for an exception). Indeed, even in the household area, many studies were aimed at reducing air conditioning or lighting, which use only a small amount of energy in that sector. As a result of the focus on individual behavior, psychologists were not investigating possible organizational solutions to the problem, and instead were examining single responses of individuals largely in their homes.

Another important point made by Stern and Gardner was the distinction between energy efficiency and curtailment. Efficiency involves the purchase of more energy-efficient products, such as appliances, insulation, and cars that give more mileage per gallon, and maintenance activities, such as car tune-ups. Thus, consumers can maintain their life-styles at a reduced energy level. Curtailment, however, means giving up some of the benefits of energy-using products in order to reduce energy consumption. Curtailment behaviors, such as turning down the thermostat at night in the winter or car pooling, typically require that consumers do without or use less of some desired commodity. Using public transportation means giving up the convenience and privacy of one's own car; reducing heating and air conditioning consumption can mean being colder in the winter and hotter in the summer than one would like. Interestingly, Stern and Gardner point out that energy curtailment behaviors, which were the targeted behaviors in most of the initial energy conservation research, save significantly less energy than do efficiency actions. Additionally, curtailment activities frequently require doing something on a regular basis, whereas efficiency behaviors are often one-shot purchases of energy-efficient appliances and products.

One implication of the comments by Stern and Gardner was that psychologists had been too concerned with demonstrating that energy conservation could be studied from a psychological framework and too little concerned with the possible impact of the results on the important policy question—namely, how to reduce drastically the nation's energy demand. In time psychologists began to shift their focus to examining how existing large-scale energy conservation programs could be improved.

For example, Yates and Aronson (1983, see also Aronson and Gonzales, this volume) analyzed the home energy audit program of the Residential Conservation Service, which was created by the 1978 U.S. National Energy Conservation Policy Act. The point of the audit was to provide homeowners with tailored advice about how to make their homes more energy-efficient. Yates and Aronson concluded that energy audits would be vastly more successful in boosting participants' interest both in having an audit done and in following the auditors' recommendations if basic social psychological theory about the influence process were incorporated into the audit procedure. Other researchers have made similar arguments about how psychological research could improve various large-scale programs: Geller (1983) discussed implementing communitywide energy conservation strategies; Stern (1986) discussed how models of energy consumption derived from economic theory could be improved; Winkler and Winett (1982) emphasized the fruitfulness of an integrative psychological and economic approach to resource conservation.

Still others examined how evaluation research could improve energy conservation programs. Seligman and Hutton (1981) examined various stages of the evaluation research process (e.g., program development and implementation, randomization and control groups) as applied to a number of energy conservation programs and concluded that rigorous evaluations should be possible. Unfortunately, many of the programs that were undertaken to conserve energy could not be evaluated adequately. Condelli, et al. (1984) criticized the energy conservation programs of the California utilities for, among other reasons, failing to meet acceptable standards in research design, thus making it difficult to gauge the programs' effects. At present, however, the situation seems to be improving, and many recent evaluations have been clearer about the results of various programs (see, for example, Egel, 1987; Hirst, 1987; Kushler, 1989). Increasingly, the information provided by evaluations should lead to improved program effectiveness.

In our reading of the resource conservation literature, one feature struck us as unusual. Reviews of the energy conservation literature were typically organized according to the effects of particular manipulations, such as information, feedback, and incentives. The reviews of several resources (e.g., electricity, water) were generally organized first according to resource and then according to manipulation. Throughout, the impression is given that one resource is conceptually much like another. The assumption seems to be that techniques such as rebates and feedback that enable individuals to save electricity should similarly help them to save water, or gasoline, or whatever. The fact that different resources were discussed under separate subheadings or even chapters seemed to be only an organizational convenience, and not an indicator that there was something psychologically different and interesting about them. This implicit theoretical assumption about the psychological similarity or equivalence among different resources is understandable from an applied behavior perspective with its focus on single behaviors that are controlled by external contingencies. It is also understandable from the policy context outlined above, with its emphasis on aiming at the activity with the highest conservation potential—say, efficiency purchases rather than curtailment behavior. But it seems to us that there are basic psychological differences among the resources that need to be discussed. This discussion should have implications both for a theory of resource use and for the practical purpose of knowing which psychologically based conservation procedures work best with which resources.

In the next section, we will discuss water and energy conservation and provide some support for the notion that factors that are successful in determining consumption for one resource are not necessarily important for another. We then propose a preliminary two-factor model of resource conservation that attempts to show that resource behaviors vary along the dimensions of difficulty to conserve and the public or private nature of the consumption activity. We end the chapter with a discussion of the implications of this model for the techniques used to enhance conservation. We conclude that the underlying psychological nature of the particular resource targeted directs us toward certain conservation strategies and away from others.

Energy and Water Conservation

Energy conservation has received more attention from psychologists than any other resource, and many summaries of this research are available (Baum & Singer, 1981; Cook & Berrenberg, 1981; Geller *et al.*, 1982; *Journal of Consumer Research*, 1981; *Journal of Economic Psychology*, 1983–1984; Morrison & Kempton, 1984; Seligman & Becker, 1981; Stern & Aronson, 1984; Stern & Oskamp, 1987). Water conservation, however, has been studied far less frequently by psychologists (see Perth Water Authority Board, 1986; Syme & Seligman, 1987; Winkler, 1982). In this section, we argue that a psychological procedure used to reduce energy consumption does not necessarily succeed in saving water, or vice versa. To make the comparison between energy and water conservation meaningful it is important to find situations where as many variables as possible are similar in both the energy and water situations. Ideally, of course, we would like to be able to cite studies that applied the exact same conservation strategy to both energy and water conservation in the same setting, but unfortunately we are not aware of any. The best we can do is to limit our discussion to household water and energy usage, where, at least, we can examine the families' use of water and energy in roughly the same circumstances. We will look at the effects of two different variables on energy and water consumption: feedback and subjective norms.

Feedback

Feedback was one of the first variables that psychologists manipulated to attempt to reduce energy (See Geller *et al.,* 1982; Seligman, Becker, & Darley, 1981, for reviews of this literature). In a typical feedback study, homeowners would receive information about their rate of energy consumption every few days. Usually feedback was displayed graphically or in some other written form and posted in a visible place in the house. The feedback compared the household's current use with its consumption in an earlier period. An important feature of the feedback was that it accounted for changes in the weather from one period to the next. Homeowners who received the feedback for a number of weeks would be compared with a control group of homeowners who had not been given feedback. The results of numerous studies have demonstrated that feedback is effective in helping homeowners to conserve approximately 10 to 15% of their energy use. Feedback has also been shown to be effective when it is given only once a month (Hayes & Cone, 1981), or even when residents are asked to monitor and calculate their own feedback (Winett, Neale, & Grier, 1979).

Seligman *et al.* (1981) offered the following explanation of why feedback is an effective conservation procedure. On the assumption that a person is motivated to conserve in the first place, they proposed that feedback can lead to increased conservation efforts by showing that actual conservation is below the level the person wants to achieve. By informing a person of his or her actual level of performance, feedback signals when more effort is needed to reach a desired standard of performance. With greater effort directed toward improving performance, performance often improves. Indeed, the importance of setting a performance goal and the receipt of feedback relevant to that goal have been recognized as basic elements in any self-control process (Kanfer & Karoly, 1972).

The above reasoning was confirmed in a study by Becker (1978). His study examined the joint effects of goal setting and feedback on energy conservation. Homeowners were randomly assigned to one of five conditions. Some families were asked to set an easy goal of reducing their electricity use (largely for air conditioning) by 2%. Others were asked to set a difficult goal of decreasing their consumption by 20%. In each of these conditions, half of the subjects were given feedback about their rate of energy consumption three times a week; the remaining half were not given any feedback. In the final condition, the control households were not asked to set a conservation goal and did not receive feedback.

The results showed that the only experimental condition that differed significantly from the control group was the 20% goal-feedback condition. Of the two groups given the 20% goal, the one receiving feedback used 13% less electricity than the control group, whereas the one not receiving feedback used only 1.3% less. Thus, feedback is effective because it helps individuals to monitor whether they are reaching their conservation goal. Presumably, without feedback, it is easier for people with difficult goals to maintain counterproductive misperceptions about the amount or adequacy of their efforts. Thus, they may put out less effort than they should and consequently perform less well than they can or want to.

We know of only two studies that attempted to decrease water consumption through the use of feedback, and both failed. The first study (reported in Winkler, 1982), conducted in Perth, Australia, compared one group of residents who received a rebate of $1 for each kiloliter of water saved with a group who received only weekly feedback about their water consumption. The rebate households also received the same feedback as did the feedback subjects. Thus, the feedback condition was a control for the implicit feedback information that is revealed by the size of the rebate given to the homeowners. The feedback consisted of information about total consumption used in the previous week and the amount of decrease or increase from the household's baseline average total consumption. The experiment lasted 10 weeks: 4 weeks of baseline measurements, 4 weeks of treatment intervention, and 2 weeks of follow-up. A no-intervention control condition was estimated from total metropolitan consumption. The results showed that neither the rebate nor the feedback significantly influenced total consumption or even outside consumption (e.g., lawn watering).

The second study that examined feedback effects on water consumption was conducted by Geller, Erickson, and Buttram (1983) in Virginia. Their experiment lasted 10 weeks, consisting of a 5-week baseline phase and a 5-week treatment phase. Three interventions were used: educational, feedback, and water devices. The educational manipulation consisted of giving out a handbook that described (a) adverse consequences of wasteful water consumption, (b) the relation between energy and water use, and (c) methods for saving water in the home. In the feedback condition, information was provided daily in writing. Participants were told the gallons of water used in the previous day, percentage increase or decrease from baseline, and percentage of increase or decrease from treatment phase average consumption. Weekly summary graphs were also included. In the third condition, a package of water-saving devices (toilet dam, shower flow control device, faucet aerator, and shut-off shower control) was left for the residents to install. The results showed that only the water-saving devices significantly reduced water consumption. Neither the feedback nor the educational interventions significantly affected water use. It should be noted that the feedback manipulation was designed to be maximally effective in light of successful feedback manipulations used in previous energy conservation studies.

Together these two studies suggest that household water consumption is more difficult to influence than household energy use. Feedback does not lead to a decrease in water consumption, even though it has been very effective in reducing energy consumption. One explanation offered by the authors of both studies is that the cost of water is too low to motivate consumers to conserve. This explanation is certainly plausible, and, indeed, Winkler and Winett (1982) have shown that, even in energy feedback studies, feedback is more effective as the energy costs assume a higher proportion of the family's budget. The cost of a resource, however, is only one reason to conserve. Social influence is another, and it is to this issue that we now turn.

Subjective Norms

One of the most important theories of the determinants of behavior is the theory of reasoned action (Fishbein & Ajzen, 1975). According to the model of Fishbein and Ajzen, behavior that is under volitional control is best predicted by an individual's intention to perform that behavior. The intention to perform a behavior, in turn, can be predicted by two basic perceptions of the individual. The first is the individual's attitude toward performing the behavior (called the attitude toward the act). The second is the individual's view of how those people who are important to that individual regard his or her performance of the behavior (called the subjective norms). Applied to resource conservation, this model suggests that the best predictor of people's intentions to conserve are determined by two variables: individuals' attitudes toward conservation and individuals' perceptions of what other people want them to do regarding conservation.

The model further proposes that individuals' attitudes toward a behavior are determined by their beliefs about the consequences of performing the behavior and by their evaluations of these consequences. The subjective norms held by individuals are influenced by their perceptions of what specific other people think they should do (normative beliefs) and by the individuals' motivations to comply with the advice of these people.

Two studies of household energy and water use have been conducted to test the theory of reasoned action. The first was done by Kantola, Syme, and Campbell (1982) in Perth, Australia, and was concerned with water consumption. The behavioral intention statement used in this study was "I intend to save more water this year than I did last year." The subjective norm measure was "Most people who are important to me think I should save more water this year than I did last year." The attitude toward the act was measured in the usual way by summing subjects' responses to the statement "If I save more water this year than I did last year it will be . . ." on the three scales of good–bad, pleasant–unpleasant, beneficial–harmful. Respondents were asked about the likelihood of several consequences of conserving water. These were as follows: saves money on my water bill, means my lawns and gardens would dry up, results in water price rises, provides a good example to others, helps prevent future water restrictions, and helps prevent water pollution. Each of these consequences was evaluated on a good–bad scale. Normative belief and motivation to comply questions were asked separately about family, friends, and workmates.

The results showed that approximately 21% of the variance in respondents' behavioral intentions to save water were accounted for by attitudes toward conserving and subjective norms. Considering the sample as a whole, it is important to note that subjective norms added significantly to the prediction of behavioral intention, whereas attitude toward the act did not. In other words, one's intention to conserve water seems to be more affected by one's concern about what significant others think than by one's own attitudes toward saving water. When the sample of subjects was partitioned by sex, interest in water conservation, importance of water conservation, and age, only for age did attitude toward conserving make a significant contribution to the regression of behavioral intention, whereas subjective norms was always significant.

The second study to use the theory of reasoned action in a resource conservation context was conducted by Seligman, Hall, and Finegan (1983) in London, Ontario, and focused on household energy used for heating. The behavioral intention measure was "I intend to conserve energy in my home over the next six weeks." The attitude toward the act question was "Conserving energy in my home over the next six weeks would be. . . ." This question was answered on separate scales of good–bad, harmful–beneficial, and wise–foolish. The responses were then summed. The subjective norm item was "Most people who are important to me think I should conserve energy in my home over the next six weeks." The consequences of conserving that were asked about in the study were that it would (1) save money, (2) help solve the energy crisis, (3) be bothersome, (4) make a house more (or less) comfortable, (5) improve (or impair) health, and (6) reduce personal energy waste. The likelihood and goodness or badness of each of these consequences were rated. Normative beliefs were asked about the following referents: government, media personnel, friends, and neighbors, parents, spouses, and utility and energy companies. The respondents' motivation to comply with each of these referents was also measured.

The results showed that 38% of the variance in homeowners' behavioral intentions was explained by their attitudes toward conservation and their subjective norms. Of these two variables, only attitudes toward conservation contributed significantly to the prediction accuracy of the regression equation. Subjective norms did not show a significant relation with behavioral intentions to conserve electricity. This result is, of course, exactly opposite to the results of the previously described water conservation study (Kantola, et al., 1982).

We acknowledge that it is difficult to draw unambiguous conclusions about the causes of effects from two separate studies that differ in several ways. Tentatively, it seems that water conservation is more strongly related to subjective norms than to attitudes toward conservation, whereas energy conservation is more strongly related to attitudes toward conservation than to subjective norms. We realize, of course, that water and energy consumption are not entirely independent. Energy is used to heat water, and, indeed, the hot-water heater is one of the highest users of energy in the home. This fact makes the opposing results of these two studies all the more fascinating.

The differences between household water and energy consumption with regard to feedback, subjective norms, and attitudes may reflect real psychological differences in people's responses to the two resources. Our purpose in this section of the chapter is not to explore the nature of the possible psychological dimensions but to provide empirical evidence that water and energy conservation are not necessarily controlled by the same factors, thereby establishing a need for further analysis. In the next section, we propose a preliminary two-factor model that highlights possible psychological differences between water and energy use. The two factors to be described are (a) the difficulty of doing without the resource or of using less of it, and (b) the private or public nature of the resource consumption activity.

Preliminary Two-Factor Model of Energy and Water Conservation

Many variables have been found to affect the use of one or another resource. So far we have concentrated on feedback, attitudes, and subjective norms. But, as has been implied in passing, previous investigations have also looked at a variety of other factors. These include economic factors (e.g., total and marginal price of resource, rebates and incentives to save), information, prompts, competition, persuasive factors, communication strategies, and thermal comfort. There is probably more than one way that this literature can be conceptualized psychologically. We have chosen to emphasize the two variables described below, because each has been shown to be empirically important and because the model derived from them has heuristic value for us.

Difficulty of Doing Without or of Using Less of a Resource

One variable that seems to be crucial for understanding resource use is the difficulty of doing without the resource or of using less of it. This variable certainly appeals to common sense, because one would assume that using the resource is rewarding for the user, and therefore giving up or using less of the resource means a loss of reward.

Winkler and Winett (1982) have discussed this issue in terms of maximizing theory, which "is based on the assumption that organisms maximize utility, with utility being defined by the organism's choice of 'packages of commodities' or combinations of more than one reinforcer in the face of different opportunities to respond (budgets) and different behavior-consequence relationships" (p. 433). In an energy conservation context, homeowners must choose between maintaining their current consumption level and reducing it to a lower one. There is a penalty associated with either strategy. For example, reduced comfort results from reduced heating, and dollar costs increase with more heating. Homeowners will maximize their utility depending, in part, on the affordability of the resource, sacrificing dollars for comfort when the dollar costs are low and sacrificing comfort for dollars when the dollar costs are high. In either case, Winkler and Winett have shown that the cost of the resource interacts with the homeowners' comfort needs to determine optimal utility and, accordingly, resource consumption. A number of studies have demonstrated that changes in the cost of energy (through rebates or incentives) influence the amount of energy consumed (Geller *et al.*, 1982).

One personal need that has been linked to energy consumption is thermal comfort (see Rohles, 1981). Attitude studies conducted by Seligman and his colleagues (see Seligman, 1986, for a review) have found that the only consistent and statistically significant predictor of household energy consumption across several surveys is comfort. Homeowners who feel that thermal comfort is important to their well-being use more energy than those who place less emphasis on thermal comfort. In other words, the more difficult it is for people to deprive themselves of comfort (whether it is heating in the winter or air conditioning in the summer), the more willing they are to bear the cost of the extra energy to meet their needs.

One additional result of these surveys is that they demonstrate a difference between summer and winter energy use. The results of two of the surveys (Becker, Seligman, Fazio, & Darley, 1981; Seligman, *et al.*, 1979) are shown in Table 1. The table presents the correlations between various attitudinal factors and both winter and summer household consumption. It can be seen that the correlations are higher between attitudes and summer consumption than between attitudes and winter consumption. A multiple regression analysis of summer electricity use revealed that 55% of the variance in summer consumption was accounted for by the attitude predictors. However, a multiple regression analysis of winter natural gas usage found that only 18% of winter consumption was accounted for by the attitudinal variables. In part, the difference in predictability between summer and winter energy use was due to the fact that consumption was twice as large in the summer as in the winter. But this may be because the discretionary use of energy

Table 1. Correlations of Attitude Factors with Household Energy Consumption[a]

	Winter	Summer
Comfort	.28	
Comfort and health		.55
Health	.18	
Optimism/belief in science	.22	
Legitimacy of energy crisis	.15	.25
Individual's role	.14	.34
Family finances	.11	
Perceived savings	.09	.50

[a]Winter correlations are from Becker *et al.* (1981). Summer correlations are from Seligman *et al.* (1979).

for cooling in the summer is much greater than for heating in the winter, at least for northerly climates. Not using air conditioning in the summer is a real alternative; not heating the house in the winter is not.

These results suggest that if comfort is more important for energy use in the winter than in the summer, then it should be more difficult to get people to conserve in the winter than in the summer. There is some support for this hypothesis. For example, Becker, Seligman, and Darley (1979) found that feedback was not significantly effective in reducing winter energy consumption, although it was for summer consumption. Pallak and Cummings (1976) found that a public commitment manipulation resulted in twice as much energy conservation in the summer as in the winter.

In view of the above discussion, we conclude that the consumers' difficulty in doing without a resource or in using less of it is an important determinant of resource use. This appears to be the case whether difficulty is conceived of as intolerance for comfort deprivation, the ability to pay for more of the resource, or an interaction of the two. We now turn to our proposed second crucial variable.

Private and Public Resource Consumption Behaviors

As mentioned earlier in the discussion of the theory of reasoned action, people's concerns for what others think of their behavior is a potent determinant of behavior. The classic work of Sherif (1937) demonstrated that subjects would change their judgments to conform to the judgments of others. Asch (1956) extended this research and showed that even if there was no doubt about the correct answer, a significant number of people would change their answer from a correct one to an incorrect one to conform with the majority. Schachter (1951) has demonstrated that individuals who do not conform to group norms can expect other members of the group to try to dissuade them from their beliefs. If such attempts are unsuccessful, the "deviate" may eventually be expelled from the group. Janis (1982) has shown that the desire to maintain group cohesion may be so strong in some groups that individual members censor themselves to avoid open conflict with the group. The classic findings reported above clearly establish that the power of the group to influence group members is formidable.

We would like to emphasize the well-known finding that conformity pressures are successful to the extent that the targeted behaviors are public—that is, observable to others. In Asch's (1956) studies, for example, conformity was greatly reduced when the subjects could record their answers privately. Social influence is more direct when one's behaviors are visible to others and also when one's responses to the reactions of others are also public. In Kelman's (1974) terms, visible behaviors are susceptible to all three processes of influence: compliance, identification, and internalization. Private behaviors, however, are most likely to be influenced by internalization, possibly identification, but not compliance. Therefore, we have more influence strategies available to affect public behavior than private behavior. Possibly, then, it is easier to change public behaviors. We will now describe two resource-consumption studies that demonstrate this point.

Aronson and O'Leary (1982–1983) were interested in trying to get universtiy atheletes to save water in the shower by encouraging them to turn off the water while they were soaping up. The experimenters found that when students were showering alone, only 6% turned off the water while soaping up. The placement of a large sign in the shower area instructing students to turn off the water during soaping up increased compliance to 19%. When a confederate modeled the proper behavior of turning off the water and soaping up whenever another person entered the shower, compliance increased further to 49%. Finally, when two confederates demonstrated the appropriate behavior in the presence of the subject, 67% of the subjects soaped up with the water turned off.

Pallak and Cummings (1976) examined the effects of public and private commitments to reduce energy usage on actual consumption. After homeowners agreed to participate in an energy conservation study, those in the public commitment group agreed in writing to have the results of the study published, including their names as participants. Homeowners who were assigned to the private commitment condition were treated the same as those in the public condition, except that they were promised that their names would not be revealed. Homeowners in both conditions were informed about energy-saving methods. A control condition consisted of residents who were asked, after the experiment, if their utility records could be looked at.

The results demonstrated the success of the manipulation. The public commitment group, compared with the control condition, reduced their natural gas consumption for winter heating by 12% and their summer air conditioning use by 24%. However, the private commitment condition saved only 3% more natural gas and only 6% more electricity than the control group. Moreover, these results were substantially the same 1 year after the experiment was declared over. It should be noted that no one's name was made public.

The findings of the above two studies show that resource-consumption behavior that is either directly observable by others or is believed to be open to the scrutiny of others is amenable to social influence. This does not mean that private resource-consumption behaviors cannot be altered, but only that it will be more difficult to do so for private than for public behaviors.

Now that we have highlighted two crucial variables to consider in thinking about resource conservation, let us consider where a number of different resource-using behaviors would fall along the dimensions of these two variables.

Crucial Variables and Resource Consumption Activities

Table 2 presents a 2 X 2 matrix formed by crossing the two crucial variables of (a) difficulty of doing without the resource or of using less of it and (b) public and private resource-consumption behaviors. For simplicity, we will discuss only

**Table 2. Crucial Psychological Variables and Resource
Consumption Activities**

	Perceived difficulty of conserving	
	More difficult	Less difficult
Public consumption	Car driving	Outdoor water use
Private consumption	Household heating, indoor water use	Air conditioning

two levels of each variable, although future research may indicate that more are
needed. We have placed a number of different resource-consumption behaviors in
the cells of the matrix in a way that we think is faithful to our description of the
crucial variables and also to the main findings of the resource-conservation literature. Our initial placement of the various resource-consumption behaviors in the
matrix is meant as a point of departure for discussion, and we recognize that our
decisions may be somewhat arbitrary.

Perceived Difficulty of Conserving

We have classified automobile driving, household heating, and indoor water
usage as consumption activities individuals find difficult to deprive themselves of.
Though there are considerable data to show that applied behavior analysis techniques can reduce gasoline consumption (Reichel & Geller, 1981), these techniques are not considered cost-effective. Additionally, many of the continual behaviors that people would have to do to reduce driving or increase fuel efficiency
involve obvious inconveniences. These include organizing car and van pools, with
the accompanying loss of privacy and forced interpersonal contact, inconveniently
scheduled or crowded public transportation, frequent car maintenance activities
(e.g., proper tire inflation and tune-ups), possible increases in travel times, and
so on.

Heating, as already discussed, appears to be more difficult to reduce than air
conditioning. Reduced heating has a direct effect on thermal comfort, and individuals who value their comfort tend to use more energy. Individuals may also find
it inconvenient to wear additional clothing or to change the thermostat setting each
evening and morning.

We do not know of any water conservation study that has been able to get
households to save indoor water through curtailment means. Indoor water use
includes bathing, clothes washing and dishwashing, and toilet flushing. Cowan,
Rose, and Rose (1985) have pointed out the role that the value of cleanliness has
played in influencing resource use. It is likely that our concern with bodily cleanliness has been an impediment to indoor water conservation (although arguably to
many of us, a welcome impediment). Homeowners, in the Geller et al. (1983)

study mentioned earlier, were able to save water only in the condition where water-saving devices were left at the home. The modeling strategy used in the Aronson and O'Leary (1982–1983) shower study is, of course, inapplicable in the home, and in institutional shower rooms it is completely dependent on the presence of appropriate models.

We have placed outdoor water use (lawn and garden watering, car washing) and air conditioning in the "easier to give up" category. Outdoor water use is certainly less crucial to one's life than indoor use. It is easier, for example, to give up washing one's car than oneself. Grass is surprisingly resilient and lawns can go for a long time without water and not suffer serious damage. Moreover, in times of shortages, outdoor watering is usually restricted, so homeowners are somewhat familiar with occasionaly having to save outdoor water. In comparison with heating, air conditioning is relatively easy to give up. Of course, in southern climates, the location of heating and air conditioning in the matrix may have to be reversed, to take into account the greater emphasis on cooling requirements and the reduced need for heating.

Public and Private Consumption Behaviors

These resource-consumption activities can also be looked at in terms of the public and private dimension. We have listed car driving and outdoor water use as public consumption. The size of car we drive is observable to others. Not only does it make a possible statement to others about our status or personality, but it also implies our concern about gasoline consumption. The change from large cars to small cars has been helped by the growing social acceptability of small cars. Instead of indicating primarily low income, compact and subcompact cars are perceived as more appropriate vehicles for our life-style and economy than gas guzzlers. Of course, the price of gasoline is important, and as gasoline prices stablize, it will be interesting to see if big cars regain their earlier popularity. Whichever way it goes, the types of cars other people drive will have an influence on one's purchase.

Outdoor watering is an activity that is observable to others in two ways. The activity is directly observable to others because it takes place outside, and indirectly observable because the effects of watering are clear-cut. One need only look at a homeowner's lawn in the summer to know whether it has been frequently watered. During times of water restrictions, it is more difficult to cheat on using water outside the house than inside.

Private resource consumption includes indoor heating, water uses, and air conditioning. Typically, these consumption activities are not open to scrutiny by others, because they take place inside the house. This is certainly the case for indoor water use. Interestingly, although the size and age of one's house, like the size of one's car, reveals information about us, including an educated estimate of energy use for heating and cooling, there is no comparable term for gas guzzler that is applied to large houses. In our experience, people who are able to buy large houses are considered fortunate rather than wasteful. We would consider household heating to be almost entirely private. Air conditioning, while generally a private affair, may be considered, in part, public, depending on how easy it is to detect whether the air-conditioner is on. A central air-conditioning unit makes a considerable amount of noise and, if located close to the front of the house, may be detected from the street. Window air-conditioners are often more easily noticed. Diamond (personal communication, 1984) has reported that in a study of a town house complex for the elderly, the residents were very aware of their neighbors' air-conditioning use because of the visibility (and audibility) of the window air-conditioners. He cites the case of one resident who used her air-conditioner more frequently than she wanted to and could afford because she did not want her neighbors to think that she was poor.

Implications of the Two-Factor Model for Conservation

As previously discussed, research on resource conservation has been organized around the central question: "How can we get people to conserve resources?" We have argued that a theoretical approach that focuses on the psychological nature of conservation behaviors could generate alternative ways of examining this question and may lead to improved strategies for conservation. In our analysis, we have pointed out that resource-consumption activities may differ on two psychological dimensions: perceived difficulty of doing without (or with less of) the resource and whether the resource consumption activity is open to public observation. If, as we suggest, these variables are important, then we need to examine their implications for different resource-consumption behaviors.

Before we begin to explore some of these implications, however, we should be clear that considerable conservation of energy has already been achieved since the 1973–1974 oil embargo. Savitz (1984) reports that there has been a 20% reduction in household energy consumption since 1970. During 1978–1980, 12 million households said they had added attic or roof insulation (Meyers & Schipper, 1984). In 1980 alone, consumers bought over $3 billion worth of energy conservation equipment and services (*Energy Auditor and Retrofitter*, 1984).

Despite this achievement, energy experts point out that a great deal more energy could be conserved, perhaps doubling the savings (Ross & Williams, 1981; Stobaugh & Yergin, 1979). The gap between possible energy savings and actual energy savings has intrigued psychologists (and others). Two findings are often highlighted. First, very few households take advantage of the free energy audits or conservation services offered by utility companies. Indeed, typically less than 5% of homeowners show any interest in energy audits, and even when grants and rebates are offered for subsequent retrofits this percentage rises only to 7% (Stern, *et al.*, 1986). Second, half of the energy savings made in the buildings sector has derived from curtailment and operational activities, e.g., temperature setbacks

(Savitz, 1984). Thus, there is an apparent failure to take advantage of conservation through available energy-efficient products and services. With regard to energy, the homeowner has been "muddling through," taking the easiest and cheapest route to saving energy, which consists largely of curtailment actions (Simmons, Talbot, & Kaplan, 1984–1985). We will now discuss the implications of the two factors of our model for alternative conservation strategies.

Difficulty of Doing Without or of Using Less of a Resource

Consumption activities that are actually (or perceived to be) difficult to cut back (car driving, household heating, and indoor water use) are not likely to be changed to a great extent if the change involves curtailment activities (that is, activities that require people to do without or with less). Our society has probably already made all the curtailment adjustment it is likely to make for these activities. Further reductions must come from efficiency measures (e.g., better maintenance of equipment, more efficient equipment). Here the role for psychologists is to suggest ways to make clear to the consumer that investments in efficiency are worthwhile. One strategy is economic, to make clear to consumers the actual dollar savings and the payback period. However, Stern (1986; Stern et al., 1986) has argued convincingly that an economic approach to the problem is not enough. Even though people would save money by following efficiency recommendations, people sometimes do not respond as rational economic models would suggest. For example, a psychological variable, the credibility of the source of energy information, has been shown to be important. Craig and McCann (1978) found that pamphlets alleged to have originated from a utility company were less effective than the same pamphlet alleged to have originated from a state regulatory agency (see also Miller & Ford, 1985). A number of other energy researchers have examined different psychological aspects of the problem of how to get consumers to purchase energy-efficient products—e.g., focusing on the information consumers have about energy use and conservation, investigating the ways consumers process information, considering the relative merits of a mass media approach compared with a more personal one, (see Aronson & Gonzales, this volume; Costanzo, Archer, Aronson & Pettigrew, 1986; Darley & Beniger, 1981; Kempton, Harris, Keith, & Weihl, 1985; Seligman, 1985; Stern & Aronson, 1984).

The point is that when people do not want to give up or reduce their resource-consumption activities, because of the obvious benefits they derive from them, a way must be found that allows consumers to satisfy their needs and conserve at the same time. The irony is that for resource-consumption needs, the means (gasoline-efficient automobiles, insulation, shower flow restrictors,) exist to satisfy them and save energy and water at the same time. It is truly a situation where consumers could have their cake and eat it too, but they're not eating.

We turn now to a consideration of those resource-consumption activities that we have classified as *relatively* less difficult to do without or with less (outdoor water use and air conditioning, in more northerly climates). Here a combination of efficiency and curtailment strategies seems optimal. Certainly, more energy-efficient air-conditioners should be encouraged. But, since, as indicated earlier, there is more discretionary use for cooling than for heating, it should be possible to decrease air-conditioning use through curtailment procedures. Some research bears this out. For example, Becker and Seligman (1978) showed that homeowners could reduce their air conditioning by 15% by being made aware when the outside temperature became cool enough for them to turn off the air-conditioner and open the windows. Other psychological curtailment strategies such as feedback have also proven to be effective in decreasing air conditioning (see Geller, *et al.*, 1982)

Outdoor water use should be amenable to psychological curtailment procedures. In a review of the literature on the effects of water conservation (information) campaigns during droughts, Syme and Seligman (1987) concluded that people voluntarily reduce their water consumption by about 15% in response to voluntary conservation campaigns. The Perth domestic water study (Perth Water Authority Board, 1986) indicates that during drought conditions, consumers are aware of voluntary conservation campaigns and make some appropriate long-term behavioral changes—e.g., decreasing their lawn size, increasing the planting of native plants (which require less water), and increasing paved and wood-chip areas. Curtailment procedures, however, may not always be successful. Because the cost of water is very low, there may be no incentive to conserve. Furthermore, it is possible that under certain psychological conditions it may be more difficult to do without the resource. For example, in Australia, the garden is very important and many people are reluctant to give it up (Syme, Thomas & Salerian, 1983). In this case, conservation programs need to pay attention to the attitudes and values people hold and not just concentrate on the products they should buy.

Private and Public Resource-Consumption Behaviors

It is also instructive to examine resource-consumption activities from the perspective of public and private consumption. *Private* consumption is not open to the surveillance of others. This being so, we should expect a change in the household's consumption patterns only when the household members accept the reasons for making the change (i.e., Kelman's, 1974, concept of internalization). However, people may change their *public* consumption activities for a variety of reasons, including compliance and internalization processes, and because through social comparison people may come to have a new definition of what appropriate resource-consumption behaviors are. Although social comparison processes apply to both private and public behaviors, it may be the case that what is private behavior for one is also private behavior for another, and there is, consequently, less opportunity for social comparison of private consumption behaviors than of public ones.

The greater difficulty of getting people to conserve when the behavior is private was demonstrated in a study by Wilk and Wilhite (1984). They were interested in why homeowners were not weatherstipping and caulking their homes. In the sample of homeowners that they studied, about one-third had spent an average of $1,900 on conservation measures such as solar water heaters, wood stoves, and greenhouses, yet they had not weatherstipped their homes. Compared with these other measures, weatherization is relatively cheaper and likely to save between 10 and 20% of their heating and cooling costs, but it is also less visible. One of the reasons given by homeowners for not weatherstipping was that since it was not visible to their neighbors, they could not get the same positive feedback that they received from adding solar collectors.

One way other people influence our private behavior is through instruction. Winett, Leckliter, Chinn, Stahl, and Love (1985) have shown that one viewing of a film in which some energy conservation practices were modeled resulted in a 22% reduction in energy for heating and cooling. The source of the instruction is also important. Darley and Beniger (1981) have argued that when people are considering new products and practices like energy conservation, they are more likely to adopt the innovation if they learn about it from a personal experience with someone who has already tried it. Hearing a testimonial from a trusted neighbor, seeing the energy-conserving product in place, and reading the evidence from the utility bills that it works are likely to be powerful inducements to conservation.

Conclusions

The two-factor model presented here suggests that when considering the development of a conservation strategy, it is useful to consider the targeted conservation behavior in terms of where it falls along the dimensions of difficulty to conserve and public and private consumption. We have argued that difficulty-to-conserve activities are best approached with an efficiency agenda, whereas relatively less difficult-to-conserve consumption behaviors are amenable to curtailment and efficiency procedures. Public consumption activities are susceptible to a variety of social influence pressures, whereas private consumption behaviors are more likely to be affected by internalization processes. Since resource-consumption behaviors are located on both dimensions, conservation strategies that take into account both dimensions are recommended.

ACKNOWLEDGMENT. We would like to thank Geoff Syme for his many helpful suggestions during the preparation of this chapter.

References

Aronson, E., & O'Leary, M. (1982–1983). The relative effectiveness of models and prompts on energy conservation: A field experiment in a shower room. *Journal of Environmental Systems, 12*, 219–224.

Asch, S. E. (1956). Studies of independence and conformity: A minority of one against a unanimous majority. *Psychological Monographs, 70*(9, Whole No. 416.

Baum, A., & Singer, J. E. (Eds.). (1981). *Advances in environmental psychology (Vol. 3): Energy: Psychological perspectives.* Hillsdale, NJ: Erlbaum.

Becker, L. J. (1978). Joint effect of feedback and goal setting on performance: A field study of residential energy conservation. *Journal of Applied Psychology, 63,* 428–433.

Becker, L. J., & Seligman, C. (1978). Reducing air conditioning by signalling it is cool outside. *Personality and Social Psychology Bulletin, 4,* 412–415.

Becker, L. J., Seligman, C., & Darley, J. M. (1979). *Psychological strategies to reduce energy consumption: Project summary report.* Center for Energy and Environmental Studies, Report 90. Princeton, NJ: Princeton University.

Becker, L. J., Seligman, C., Fazio, R. H., & Darley, J. M. (1981). Relating attitudes to residential energy use. *Environment and Behavior, 13,* 590–609.

Carson, R. (1962). *Silent spring.* Boston: Houghton Mifflin.

Condelli, L., Archer, D., Aronson, E., Curbow, B., McLeod, B., Pettigrew, T., White, L., & Yates, S. (1984). Improving utility conservation programs: Outcomes, interventions, and evaluations. *Energy, 9,* 485–495.

Cone, J. D., & Hayes, S. C. (1980). *Environmental problems/behavioral solutions.* Monterey, CA: Brooks/Cole.

Cook, S. W., & Berrenberg, L. J. (1981). Approaches to encouraging conservation behavior: A review and conceptual framework. *Journal of Social Issues, 37,* 73–107.

Costanzo, M., Archer, D., Aronson, E., & Pettigrew, T. (1986). Energy conservation behavior: The difficult path from information to action. *American Psychologist, 41,* 521–528.

Cowan, R. S., Rose, M. H. & Rose, M. S. (1985). Clean homes and large utility bills 1900–1940. In J. Byrne, D. Schulz, & M. B. Sussman (Eds.), *Families and the energy transition.* New York: Haworth.

Craig, C. S., & McCann, J. M. (1978). Assessing communication effects on energy conservation. *Journal of Consumer Research, 5,* 82–88.

Darley, J. M., & Beniger, J. R. (1981). Diffusion of energy-conserving innovations. *Journal of Social Issues, 37,* 150–171.

Egel, K. (1987). Evaluation of an alternative home energy audit program. *Evaluation Review, 11,* 116–130.

Energy Auditor and Retrofitter. (1984). *1.*

Fishbein, M., & Ajzen, I. (1975). *Belief, attitude, intention and behavior: An introduction to theory and research.* Reading, MA: Addison-Wesley.

Geller, E. S. (1983). The energy crisis and behavioral science: A conceptual framework for large-scale intervention. In A. W. Childs & G. B. Melton (Eds.), *Rural psychology.* New York: Plenum Press.

Geller, E. S., Erickson, J. B., & Buttram, B. A. (1983). Attempts to promote residential water conservation with educational, behavioral and engineering strategies. *Population and Environment, 6,* 96–112.

Geller, E. S., Winett, R. A., & Everett, P. B. (1982). *Preserving the environment: New strategies for behavior change.* Elmsford, NY: Pergamon Press.

Hayes, S. C., & Cone, J. D. (1981). Reduction of residential electricity consumption through simple monthly feedback. *Journal of Applied Behavioral Analysis, 14,* 81–88.

Hirst, E. (1987). *Cooperation and community Conservation.* Final Report, Hood River Conservation Project, DOE/BP-11287-18.

Janis, I. (1982). *Groupthink: Psychological studies of policy decisions and fiascoes* (2nd ed.). Boston: Houghton Mifflin.

Journal of Consumer Research. (1981). *8.*

Journal of Economic Psychology. (1983–1984).

Kanfer F. H., & Karoly, P. (1972). Self-control: A behavioristic excursion into the lion's den. *Behavior Therapy, 3,* 398–416.

Kantola, S. J., Syme, G. J., & Campbell, N. A. (1982). The role of individual differences and external variables in a test of the sufficiency of Fishbein's model to explain behavioral intentions to conserve water. *Journal of Applied Social Psychology, 12,* 70–83.

Kelman, H. C. (1974). Further thoughts on the processes of compliance, identification, and internalization. In J. T. Tedeschi (Ed.), *Perspectives on social power* (pp. 125–171). Chicago: Aldine.

Kempton, W., Harris C. K., Keith, J. G., & Weihl, J. S. (1985). Do consumers know "what works" in energy conservation? In J. Byrne, D. A. Schulz, & M. B. Sussman (Eds.), *Families and the energy transition.* New York: Haworth.

Kushler, M. G. (1989). The utilization of evaluation in energy conservation programs: A review and case study. *Journal of Social Issues, 45,* 153–168.

Meyers, S. & Schipper, L. (1984). Energy in American homes: Changes and prospects. In B. M. Morrison & W. Kempton (Eds.), *Families and energy: Coping with uncertainty.* East Lansing, MI: Institute for Family and Child Study, Michigan State University.

Miller, R. D., & Ford, J. M. (1985). Shared savings in the residential market; A public/private partnership for energy conservation. Baltimore: Energy Task Force, Urban Consortium for Technology Initiatives.

Morrison, B. M., & Kempton, W. (1984). *Families and energy: Coping with uncertainly.* East Lansing, MI: Institute for Family and Child Study, Michigan State University.

Oskamp, S. (1980–1981).Energy conservation by industrial and commercial users; Two surveys. *Journal of Environmental Systems, 10,* 201–213.

Our common future: The world commission on environment and development. (1987). Oxford: Oxford University Press.

Pallak, M. S., & Cummings, W. (1976). Commitment and voluntary energy conservation. *Personality and Social Psychology Bulletin, 4,* 27–30.

Perth Water Authority Board. (1986). Perth domestic water study.

Reichel, D. A., & Geller, E. S. (1981). Applications of behavioral analysis for conserving transportation energy. In A. Baum & J. E. Singer (Eds.), *Advances in experimental psychology (Vol. 3): Energy: Psychological perspectives* (pp. 53–92). Hillsdale, NJ: Erlbaum.

Rohles, F. H. (1981). Thermal comfort and strategies for energy conservation. *Journal of Social Issues, 37,* 132–149.

Ross, M. J., & Williams, R. H. (1981). *Our energy: Regaining control.* New York: McGraw-Hill.

Savitz, M. (1984). Ten years out: A problem not a crisis. In B. M. Morrison & W. Kempton, (Eds), *Families and energy: Coping with uncertainty.* East Lansing, MI: Institute for Family and Child Study, Michigan State University.

Schachter, S. (1951). Deviation, rejection and communication. *Journal of Abnormal and Social Psychology, 46,* 190–207.

Seligman, C. (1985). Information and energy conservation. In J. Byrne, D. A. Schulz, & M. B. Sussman (eds.), *Families and the energy transition.* New York: Haworth.

Seligman, C. (1986). Energy consumption, attitudes, and behavior. In M. J. Saks & L. Saxe (Eds.), *Advances in applied social psychology* (Vol. 3, pp. 153–180). Hillsdale, NJ: Erlbaum.

Seligman, C., & Becker, L. J. (Eds.). (1981). Energy conservation. *Journal of Social Issues, 37.*

Seligman, C., Becker, L. J., & Darley, J. M. (1981). Encouraging residential energy conservation through feedback. In A. Baum & J. E. Singer (Eds.), *Advances in environmental psychology (Vol.3): Energy: Psychological perspectives* (pp. 93–113). Hillsdale, NJ: Erlbaum.

Seligman, C., Hall, D., & Finegan, J. E. (1983). Predicting home energy conservation: An application of the Fishbein-Ajzen model. In R. P. Bagozzi & A. M. Tybout (Eds.), *Advances in consumer research* (Vol. 10, pp. 647–651). Ann Arbor MI: Association for consumer Research.

Seligman, C., & Hutton, R. B. (1981). Evaluating energy conservation programs. *Journal of Social Issues, 37*(2), 51–72.

Seligman, C., Kriss, M., Darley, J. M., Fazio, R. H., Becker, L. J., & Pryor, J. B. (1979). Predicting summer energy consumption from homeowners' attitudes. *Journal of Applied Social Psychology, 9,* 70–90.

Sherif, M. (1937). An experimental approach to the study of attitudes. *Sociometry 1,* 90–98.

Simmons, D. A., Talbot, J. F., & Kaplan, R. (1984–1985). Energy in daily activities: Muddling toward conservation. *Journal of Environmental Systems, 14,* 147–155.

Stern, P. C. (1986). Blind spots in policy analysis: What economics doesn't say about energy use. *Journal of Policy Analysis and Management, 5*, 200–227.

Stern, P. C. & Aronson, E. (Eds.). (1984). *Energy use: The human dimension*. San Francisco: Freeman.

Stern, P. C., Aronson, E., Darley, J. M., Hill, D. H., Hirst, E., Kempton, W., & Wilbanks, T. J. (1986). The effectiveness of incentives for residential energy conservation. *Evaluation Review, 10*, 147–176.

Stern, P. C., & Gardener, G. T. (1981). Psychological research and energy policy. *American Psychologist, 36*, 329–342.

Stern P. C. & Oskamp, S. (1987). Managing scarce environmental resources. In D. Stokols & I. Altman (Eds.), *Handbook of environmental psychology* (pp. 1073–1088). New York: Wiley.

Stobaugh, R., & Yergin, D. (Eds.). (1979). *Energy future*. New York: Random House.

Syme, G. J., & Seligman, C. (1987). The planning and evaluation of public information campaigns to encourage water conservation. In *Proceedings of the national workshop on urban demand management* (pp. 608–658). Canberra: AustralianWater Resources Council.

U.S. Council on Environmental Quality and U.S. Department of State. (1980). *The global 2000 report to the president: Entering the twenty-first century*. Washington, DC: U.S. Government Printing Office.

Wilk, R., & Wilhite, H. (1984). Why don't people weatherize their homes?: An ethnographic explanation. In *Proceedings of the 1984 Summer Study: American Council for an Energy Efficient Economy*. Washington, DC: ACEEE.

Winette, R. A., Leckliter, E. M., Chinn, A. E., Stahl, B., & Love, S. Q. (1985). Effects of television modelling on residential energy conservation. *Journal of Applied Behavioral Analysis, 18*, 33–44.

Winett, R. A., Neale, M. S., & Grier, H. C. (1979). Effects of self-monitoring and feedback on residential electricity consumption. *Journal of Applied Behavior Analysis, 12*, 173–184.

Winkler, R. C. (1982). Water conservation. In E. S. Geller, R. A. Winett, & P. B. Everett (Eds.), *Preserving the environment: New strategies for behavioral change*. New York: Pergamon Press.

Winkler, R. C., & Winett, P. B. (1982). Behavioral intervention and resource conservation: A systems approach based on behavioral economics. *American Psychologist, 37*, 421–435.

Yates, S., & Aronson, E. (1983). A social psychological perspective on energy conservation in residential buildings. *American Psychologist, 38*, 435–444.

13

Alternative Social Influence Processes Applied to Energy Conservation

Elliot Aronson and Marti Hope Gonzales

The Arab Oil Embargo of 1973 first brought the energy crisis to the attention of the American public. The severity of the crisis increased throughout the 1970s, peaking in 1979 when a minor but sudden shortfall of fossil fuels made energy consumers acutely aware of the consequences of fluctuating supplies of foreign oil. Gasoline and heating oil prices rose precipitously, consumers hoarded oil products, and there were long lines and even occasional outbreaks of violence at service stations.

The energy crisis also brought home the strategic consequences of our country's energy dependence on the Middle East. Given the fact that the United States relied heavily on oil from OPEC countries, chronic instability in that part of the world represented a potential threat to our economic and military security. Not only was the United States dependent on foreign oil, but our country had agreed to share supplies with its allies in the event of a shortfall. And of course, because our allies were themselves highly dependent on Middle Eastern oil, policymakers realized that any disruption in supply, however brief, would produce global repercussions.

But by 1982 the outward manifestations of the crisis had changed: With a worldwide oversupply of oil, falling crude oil prices (at one point below $10 per barrel), and gasoline prices below $.80 per gallon in many parts of the country, for most Americans, the energy crisis seemed like a distant memory. It was certainly tempting to believe that increased domestic production and energy effi-

Elliot Aronson • Department of Psychology, Stevenson College, University of California, Santa Cruz, California 95064.   **Marti Hope Gonzales** • Department of Psychology, University of Minnesota, Minneapolis, Minnesota 55455.

ciency were no longer national priorities. Indeed, in a public opinion poll, only 7% of respondents identified energy as one of our nation's most pressing problems (Hershey, 1982).

However reassuring a belief in the demise of the energy crisis might seem, such optimism, then and now, is unwarranted. The United States *continues* to import approximately 20% of its petroleum from the Middle East, and agreements to share oil reserves with allies still exist. As James Schlesinger, former Secretary of the Department of Energy, remarked in 1982, "The energy crisis is over until we have our next energy crisis" (Martin, 1982). The involvement of our navy in the protection of tankers in the Persian Gulf in 1988 serves to remind us that any apparent stability in the energy domain is but a temporary respite from a chronic problem. Given finite reserves of fossil fuel in such a volatile part of the world as the Middle East, the "next" energy crisis is inevitable. And although the development of alternative sources of energy (e.g., solar, wind, and fusion power) represents a potential alternative to reliance on imported fossil fuels, continued efforts to promote long-range conservation are an essential component of any responsible national energy policy.

The potential value of such efforts to promote conservation cannot be overstated. Experts widely agree that using currently available technology, the United States could achieve energy savings of 40 to 50% by the year 2000 (Ross & Williams, 1976; Stobaugh & Yergin, 1979). By taking such simple measures as increasing ceiling, wall, and floor insulation, plugging air leaks, and maintaining furnaces properly, the typical American energy consumer could reduce by 50 to 75% the cost of home heating (Williams & Ross, 1980). For example, in one study, Sinden (1978) noted that homes with glazed windows and ceiling and wall insulation used 60% less space-heating fuel than comparable homes in the same geographical area. The energy efficiency of those same homes was increased an additional two-thirds by adding extra caulking and insulation to plug all remaining air leaks. Thus, the technology needed to increase energy efficiency currently exists and is within the financial means of most homeowners. Yet the vast majority of homeowners have not taken advantage of these opportunities.

The public's failure to utilize advancing energy technology is especially puzzling, given efforts on the part of the government to encourage them to do so. One such effort to promote long-range conservation was the Residential Conservation Service Program (RCS) established in 1978 by an act of Congress. The RCS program required major gas and electric utility companies to offer customers a wide variety of conservation services. Among the services mandated were local utilities' provision of information about conservation practices and programs and their costs; lists of contractors, financial institutions, and suppliers providing assistance to homeowners who decide to retrofit their homes; and provision of free or low-cost home energy audits to customers. The latter were designed to provide homeowners with information uniquely tailored to the needs of their individual households. The hope was that this information, coupled with tax incentives, interest-free loans, and similar benefits, would result in a flurry of activity on the part of homeowners to retrofit their homes.

But by the mid-1980s only a small percentage of eligible homeowners had requested audits (U.S. Department of Energy, 1984). Moreover, research has shown that of those homeowners who did request audits, a very small percentage acted upon the recommendations of the auditors (Hirst, Berry, & Soderstrom, 1981). Clearly, this considerable investment of resources on the part of the federal government and local utility companies has not produced the impressive results for which policymakers had hoped. What has gone awry? Why is it that people do not act in their own economic self-interest, and conserve energy? The answer to these questions lies in the assumptions that have traditionally guided attempts to induce people to conserve energy.

Shortcomings of Traditional Economic Assumptions

For most of this century, energy has been viewed as a commodity or a collection of commodities (e.g., coal, electricity, oil, natural gas). Such concepts as "energy supplies," "energy reserves," and "projected energy demand" reflect this view of energy as a product to be bought and sold (Stern & Aronson, 1984). This view of energy as commodity reflects a certain set of beliefs, and shapes national energy policy—policy that to date has been based largely upon an economic theory of the free market. Producers and consumers alike are viewed as participants in economic transactions. Further, this model assumes that participants in these transactions are rational decision makers. For example, it is assumed that producers and consumers first survey available alternatives (e.g., electric vs. natural gas clothes dryers); second, collect and weigh all information relevant to each alternative; third, estimate costs and benefits associated with each potential strategy, and make probability judgments about risks and uncertainties associated with the adoption of any given course of action; and, fourth, select the most cost-effective strategy to maximize utility and minimize cost (Yates & Aronson, 1983).

In light of this view of energy as commodity in the free marketplace, major energy policies have traditionally assumed that rising prices and technological improvements will produce needed shifts in energy consumption (i.e., ultimately, the more efficient use of energy resources). Of course, this argument is not without merits—there is some evidence that rising prices do have the desired impact on energy consumer behavior. After the Arab oil embargo, Peck and Doering (1976) found that following a substantial increase in the cost of liquid petroleum, users of this fuel significantly reduced their consumption after conservation appeals, compared with users of natural gas, who experienced no such rate hike. However, it now seems clear that sole reliance on price increases is not a promising strategy. First, as Yergin (1979) noted, it will take decades for rising prices to reduce consumption enough to alleviate our country's energy problem. Moreover, such free-market-based programs that depend on skyrocketing prices for their effectiveness are economically regressive—hardest on the poor, who are not this country's major energy consumers (Newman & Day, 1975). Finally, human beings are not simple economic machines; rather they are complex creatures with hopes, needs, values, habits, and cognitive styles. Any or all of these personal and situational forces can override formal logical concerns and cause people to endorse and act on preferences that are not, in the most narrow sense, economically rational. We do not wish to imply that human behavior is incoherent or unpredictable, but rather to underscore the fact that behavior is best understood by addressing a multiplicity of coherently related factors—cognitive, personal, and social forces that in addition to economic realities, structure a situation. The failure to attain conservation goals should not be viewed as solely a technological or economic problem. It is a *people* problem, and to make headway in conservation efforts, policymakers and utility companies need to address the "human dimension" of energy use.

Enter Social Psychology

It is precisely for this reason, that we[1] became interested in the energy crisis as a social psychological issue. Several of us had been thinking about the social psychological underpinnings of conservation behavior, decrying the fact that policymakers were failing to take social psychological events into consideration, when an interesting coincidence occurred: A summer conference was organized by the American Council for an Energy Efficient Economy (ACEEE). This group consisted, for the most part, of policy makers, economists, engineers, physicists, architects, and the like—all actively working in the domain of energy conservation. The coincidence rested on the fact that the conference was to be held on the campus of our own university. And, because one of the local physicists knew that our group was interested in energy conservation, we (Dane Archer, Tom Pettigrew, and Elliot Aronson) were invited—as an afterthought.

This conference proved to be something of a watershed for the penetration of social psychology into public policy on energy conservation—for reasons that will become clear in a moment. Initially, most of the policymakers, economists, and physical scientists didn't know what to make of us. They didn't know what we were doing there, or what we could possibly have to offer—so we were asked to simply observe the proceedings and make comments if and when we deemed them appropriate.

---

[1]The word *we* refers to a social psychological research team at the University of California at Santa Cruz. It is led by Dane Archer, Elliot Aronson, and Tom Pettigrew, and includes an ever-changing array of talented graduate students. Over the years, the group has included Suzanne Yates, Beverly McLeod, Barbara Curbow, Larry Condelli, Larry White, Marti Hope Gonzales, Garry Rollison, Mark Costanzo, Scott Coltrane, and others.

What we observed was a collection of very intelligent, talented energy experts, several of whom frankly indicated that they were puzzled by the "irrational" behavior of homeowners. What was even more interesting was that while in theory most of the participants professed to a rather narrow rational economic conception of conservation behavior, they were unwittingly applying "commonsense" notions of social influence in their deliberations about policy. One example will suffice: In the course of a discussion, a policymaker noted with chagrin that most consumers were more interested in installing solar water heaters than insulation—even though solar technology is typically less cost-effective—because (in his words) solar technology is "sexier" than insulation. He suggested that this "irrational" behavior could be remedied by withdrawing tax credits for solarizing unless the homeowner had first done something more useful—such as installing insulation or weatherstripping. At first glance, such a strategy seems to make good common sense—it is akin to telling children they cannot have dessert unless they first eat their vegetables. However, such an approach is social-psychologically naive—and almost certainly counterproductive. Thus, in our comments at the conference, we contrasted this suggested policy with the existing data from social psychological research on the "foot-in-the-door" phenomenon (Freedman & Fraser, 1966). In this experiment, the investigators were far more successful at inducing homeowners to allow an ugly sign promoting safe driving to be placed on their lawn, after they had first "softened them up" by having them sign a petition favoring safe driving. Extrapolating from these results, we suggested that if homeowners were interested in installing solar collectors, they should not be discouraged from doing so, for it is likely that taking that first step would motivate them toward further behaviors that would make their homes still more energy-efficient.

In retrospect, it does not seem that our comments on this and other issues were particularly insightful or profound. Yet they were received with enthusiasm. As it turns out, many of the experts at the conference had been struggling for several months to try to understand the failure of what seemed to be sensible conservation policy; we were able to suggest an array of possible reasons for the failure, and to make some useful suggestions for research and policy. Because of our contributions to the conference, policymakers began to turn to us for advice and consultation. Among other things, our group was asked to consult with the California Public Utilities Commission to evaluate the multi-million-dollar conservation efforts of the state's utility companies, and one of us was asked to chair a National Academy of Sciences committee on behavioral aspects of energy use, which resulted in an influential report (see Stern & Aronson, 1984).

Having experts turn to social psychologists for advice was flattering—at the same time, it presented us with a difficult challenge. While at that time none of us knew a great deal about the specifics of conservation behavior, we did have some promising leads. Over the past several years, our colleagues had done some interesting work researching problems in social cognition that we thought might be of relevance to inform policy in this domain. But at the time of the conference, there was a paucity of research attempting to apply these results directly to the area of energy conservation. Thus, our remarks were primarily speculative. Before we could give firm and reliable advice we felt it would be necessary to test some of these notions in the energy domain. It is to this research that we now turn.

As mentioned above, efforts to promote energy conservation have been based on implicit, if not explicit, theories of persuasion, attitude change, and consumer information-processing strategies. And to "market" conservation, large-scale information campaigns—the most widely used vehicles for promoting conservation—have relied on two vague theories of conservation behavior: the *attitude-behavior model* and the *rational-economic model* (for a detailed discussion of these models and their shortcomings, see Archer, Aronson, & Pettigrew, 1983; Archer *et al.*, 1987; Condelli *et al.*, 1984; Costanzo, Archer, Aronson, & Pettigrew, 1986; White *et al.*, 1984.) Briefly, the attitude-behavior model is based on the assumption that behaviors follow more or less automatically from positive attitudes toward conservation. It is no longer held by most social psychologists (see Ajzen & Fishbein, 1977). The rational-economic model is based on the assumption that consumers will rationally evaluate the financial advantages of energy conservation measures (e.g., tax credits, rebates, long-term monetary savings) and will act in their own economic self-interest.

Social science research has demonstrated that there is rarely a direct, consistent relationship between the attitudes people hold, and their subsequent behaviors (Ajzen & Fishbein, 1977; McGuire, 1985; Olsen, 1981). This tenuous relationship between attitudes and behavior is especially problematic in energy conservation efforts, for behavior change (i.e., conserving energy) is the ultimate goal of information campaigns. For example, regional survey research conducted by our group (Archer *et al.*, 1987) showed that approximately 85% of respondents believed that the energy crisis was serious, and over half believed that the crisis would worsen. Given these attitudes, one might expect that those same concerned respondents would have made efforts to conserve energy. However, there was no clear relationship between respondents' attitudes and their behaviors. Furthermore, respondents who endorsed conservation as the best way to ameliorate the current energy problem were no more likely than others to engage in energy-conserving actions.

Neither are financial incentives and penalties predicted solely on the rational-economic model likely to prove useful. Before consumers can take advantage of economic incentives or avoid penalties, they must first understand the provisions of conservation programs. And consumers often claim to understand conservation incentives more than they really do. In a recent survey of public awareness and understanding of four major conservation programs, the majority of respondents claimed to understand their provisions. However, respondents' claimed familiarity far exceeded the *accurate understanding* when they were asked to provide concrete information about the four programs (Archer *et al.*, 1987). For example, although 72% of respondents claimed familiarity with federal solar tax credits, only 13% actually understood the provisions of that tax incentive, and although 57% claimed to understand the Home Energy Audit Program, just over 1% could demonstrate their understanding of the program's provisions—and our standards for "accuracy" were lenient. The substantial discrepancy between what people *claimed* they knew and what the *really did* know points to the failure of many conservation campaigns to communicate the information so essential for their success.

It would be foolish to conclude from this that attitudes and economics are unimportant mediators of individual behavior in this domain; they are of great importance. But what is needed is a more differentiated model of energy use based on the social psychological processes that guide so much of human behavior.

A Social Psychological Alternative

Such an integration of attitude and economic models has been proposed by Costanzo *et al.*, (1986). As this model (shown in Figure 1) illustrates, the path from information to action is complex—there are many intervening steps between

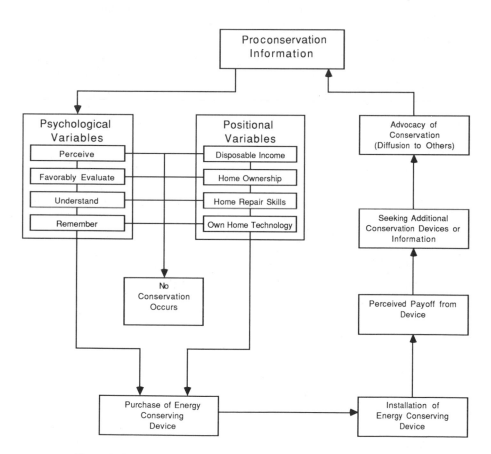

Figure 1. Psychological and social factors in energy-conservation behavior.

exposure to information relevant to energy conservation at one end and actual adoption of energy-conserving devices at the other. For people to conserve energy by adopting such technologies as home insulation or solar heating, a complex series of social influence processes must occur.

The proposed model consists of two interacting sets of factors: *psychological* and *"positional."* The former addresses individual information processing; the latter addresses characteristics of an individual's situation that encourage or inhibit action. In order for any energy conservation information campaign to be successful, a number of psychological and positional factors must first obtain.

Psychological factors include four interdependent but conceptually distinct intrapsychic events that must occur before individuals will adopt an energy-conserving technology. They must take note of information, evaluate it favorably, comprehend the message, and, finally, remember it. These four steps seem rather obvious to the psychologically sophisticated but are often overlooked by organizations that work to promote energy conservation. Of course, even if consumers perceive, favorably evaluate, understand, and remember proconservation information, they must be in the position to adopt conservation technology. For example, if individuals lack a sufficient disposable income, they will not be able to invest in relatively costly conservation devices—such as solar heating—no matter how motivated they are to do so. Thus, there is a complex interplay between psychological and positional factors—the latter support or constrain the behavior of energy users who are psychologically motivated to take action.

Finally, what happens after an energy conservation device is purchased and installed will facilitate or inhibit subsequent energy-conserving behaviors. For example, if after device adoption and installation, people experience a payoff (financial or social), they will likely seek out additional conservation devices or information, and recommend such devices to their friends or acquaintances. Satisfied customers then become for others an additional source of information about the how-to's and benefits of energy conservation strategies—via social diffusion processes to be discussed in more detail later.

Enhancing Psychological Variables

To be effective, a message must be *perceived*. It must capture and hold the attention of the audience. Unfortunately, much energy-use information provided to consumers via government pamphlets or utility bill inserts is presented in a dull and uninteresting way (Stern & Aronson, 1984). The information contained in these pamphlets or inserts is of course valuable, but it often fails to capture the attention of the typical energy consumer.

Research in cognitive social psychology has revealed that people tend to assign disproportionate weight to information that is "vivid"—that is, concrete and personalized (Borgida & Nisbett, 1977; Hamill, Wilson, & Nisbett, 1980). For example, Nisbett, Borgida, Crandall, and Reed (1976) offered the following scenario:

> Let us suppose that you wish to buy a new car and have decided that on the grounds of economy and longevity you want to purchase one of those solid, stalwart, middle-class Swedish cars—either a Volvo or a Saab. As a prudent and sensible buyer, you go to Consumer Reports, which informs you that the consensus of the readership is that the Volvo has the better repair record. Armed with this information, you decide to go and strike a bargain with the Volvo dealer before the week is out. In the interim, however, you go to a cocktail party where you announce this intention to an acquaintance. He reacts with disbelief and alarm: "A Volvo! You've got to be kidding. My brother-in-law had a Volvo. First, that fancy fuel injection computer thing went out. 250 bucks. Next he started having trouble with the rear end. Had to replace it. Then the transmission and the clutch. Finally sold it three years later for junk." (p.129)

If people were rational information-processors, this vivid anecdotal account of another person's misfortunes with his Volvo would be no more influential than a single case from the thousands of cases reported in *Consumer Reports*. However, Nisbett and his colleagues have found that this kind of vivid information exerts a disproportionately powerful influence on people's decision-making processes. To cite a parallel in the energy conservation domain, there is little reason to believe that dull, complicated, impersonal lists of kilowatts or therms saved will successfully capture and hold consumers' attention. Why? Because this format is less vivid than case histories, information tailored to the consumer's present situation, or details transmitted via face-to-face contact.

Yates and Aronson (1983) extrapolated from this body of research in cognitive psychology and provided a number of suggestions for improving the home energy audit. Specifically, information can be made more vivid and personal—more impactful—if auditors use the following methods: (1) Use customers' own utility bills to illustrate points about energy conservation, (2) provide normative information about similar individuals who have saved energy and money by completing retrofits, and (3) provide consumers with case studies of local "superconservers"—people who have reaped exceptional benefits in conserving energy. Of course, home energy audits are already vivid and personal, given face-to-face communications between auditors and customers, but the impact of the information presented can be easily enhanced by incorporating the above suggestions into the audit. In addition, these principles can be used in all information campaigns, including the print and television media.

Cognitive psychologists have also found that the way a communication is "framed" can have a potent effect on the behavior of the perceiver. For example, Kahneman, Slovic, and Tverksy (1982) have shown that people experience stronger reactions at the prospect of *losing* a certain sum of money than at the prospect of gaining the same sum—even though the logical status of the two events is identical. Data collected by Kahneman and Tverksy (1979) also show that individuals are more willing to take a risk to avoid a loss than they are if the goal of the gamble is to secure a positive outcome. The relevance of this phenomenon to the current topic is clear: The typical energy conservation campaign strategy, with its emphasis on savings, may inadvertently be discouraging consumers from changing their energy-related behaviors. It seems reasonable to expect that recommendations framed in terms of energy or money *lost* via inaction rather than in terms of energy or money *gained* or *saved* via action will be more likely to capture consumers' attention, and to motivate them to take recommended actions.

Vivid, impactful information is more likely to be perceived by consumers, but there is no guarantee that this information will be *evaluated positively*. Energy users receive information from a multitude of sources: local, state, and federal governments; electric and gas utility companies; personal acquaintances; and building contractors. All other things being equal, consumers are more likely to rely on sources they perceive to be most credible. Research in social psychology has shown that there is a direct relationship between the credibility of the source of a message, and the effectiveness of that message (Hovland, Janis, & Kelley, 1953; McGuire, 1985). That is, messages attributed to a credible source produce greater attitude change in recipients than do messages attributed to a less credible source (Aronson, Turner, & Carlsmith, 1963).

Credibility is a function of both the perceived expertise and perceived trustworthiness of the source of a message. Because many sources of information about energy conservation are perceived as expert, consumers are more likely to rely on the trustworthiness of these sources in evaluating information. In one study, for example, consumers receiving energy conservation pamphlets allegedly distributed by a state regulatory agency actually used less energy than consumers receiving the same pamphlets allegedly distributed by a local utility company (Craig & McCann, 1978). Moreover, survey research has revealed that utility companies are often viewed as especially untrustworthy (Bruner & Vivian, 1979; Milstein, 1978).

This is especially unfortunate, for utility companies are a common source of information about energy conservation. However, Stern and Aronson (1984) have suggested several alternatives to allay consumer suspicions about the trustworthiness of information sources. For example, low and high credibility sources can form partnerships (e.g., make the resources of utility companies available to nonprofit consumer or community groups); grass roots and existing neighborhood groups can be used to disseminate information; new energy-related organizations—free of conflicts of interest—can be created; and new and existing providers of information can be more strictly regulated.

The rational-economic model views consumers as rational decision-makers who weigh all available information and act to maximize future disposable income. However, determining the cost-effectiveness of a given investment is a complex task—consumers are forced to integrate a myriad of relevant factors. Kempton and his colleagues have shown that consumers often fail to take into account all of the information necessary to make informed energy-use decisions. They have discovered that people are aware of their energy bills and do attempt to conduct some form of cost-benefit analysis before deciding to invest in energy-conserving technology. Unfortunately, consumers tend to use a simplified strategy that—although intuitively appealing—produces systematic errors in prediction (Kempton, Gladhart, & O'Keefe, 1983; Kempton & Montgomery, 1982). For example, when calculating the projected savings likely to result from the installation of home insulation, most homeowners fail to take into account general inflation and rising fuel costs. They thereby underestimate the monetary benefits of such retrofits and fail to take actions that an "expert" economist would recommend.

Thus, it is not surprising that adherents of the rational-economic model are puzzled and frustrated at consumers' apparently "irrational" behavior. In many cases, the amount of information relevant to energy-use decisions is overwhelming. The average consumer often does not understand complex messages addressing energy units, tax incentives, projected utility rate increases, general inflation, pay-back periods, peak usage rates, and so on. Furthermore, an additional source of consumers' apparently irrational decision making lies in the variety of noneconomic factors (e.g., safety, status, comfort, performance, convenience) people often use to make decisions about energy conservation.

Although Costanzo and his colleagues treated *memory* as conceptually distinct from the other psychological factors, they acknowledge that it is difficult to separate memory processes from beliefs and motives. For example, people tend to remember information that is compatible with preexisting attitudes and values (Norman, 1976). However, basic learning theory principles predict that information that is clear, specific, and concrete is remembered best. Moreover, research on energy conservation has shown that vague messages (e.g., "don't be fuelish" or "conserve energy") are significantly less effective than messages containing specific recommendations or relatively simple indices that enable consumers to compare the energy efficiency of various appliances (Ester & Winett, 1982). For example, the miles-per-gallon index of gasoline efficiency (MPG) is a simple, concrete, and memorable way to measure and compare the fuel economy of various automobiles, as is the "R-Value" index used to compare the insulating power of various kinds of wall or ceiling insulation.

The Influence of Positional Determinants

In addition to psychological factors, positional factors are powerful predictors of energy-conserving behaviors. Survey data have identified four positional variables that influence whether or not consumers will adopt energy-conserving technologies: socioeconomic status (SES), home ownership, ownership of home technologies, and the presence of a household member capable of making home repairs (Archer *et al.*, 1987). Not surprisingly, people with *high incomes* are better able to absorb the cost of investments in more expensive energy technologies (e.g., solar devices, home insulation). *Home Ownership* is another straightforward predictor of conservation behaviors. Overall, homeowners tend to be less transient and wealthier than renters. Furthermore, even wealthier and geographically stable renters hesitate to invest in the improvement of someone else's dwelling. Although the remaining two positional predictors are less obvious, they are logically related to consumers' decisions to adopt energy-conserving technologies. *Home technologies* refer to such "hi-tech" consumer products as microwave ovens, personal computers, videocassette recorders, home video games, and hot tubs. The predictive power of this variable is twofold: First, people who own these home technologies are attracted to all forms of technological innovation, including energy-conserving technologies such as solar heating devices. Second, they are more likely than others to spend disposable income on home technologies. Finally, households in which there is a person skilled in making *home repairs*—a handyperson—are able to save on the cost of installation and maintenance of conservation devices. The presence of such a handyperson also renders such devices more comprehensible (see, for example, Darley & Beniger, 1981).

Conservation campaigns that target appeals to households in a position to respond are likely to succeed in inducing consumers to adopt energy conservation technologies. In addition, such campaigns can be designed to circumvent existing positional barriers to technology adoption. For example, free assistance with installation, free maintenance, or financial assistance to low-income households are all means by which providers of information can increase the odds of consumers acting on specific recommendations.

Postadoption Processes

Once a particular conservation device has been adopted and installed, what will be the effect on consumers' future energy-related attitudes and behaviors? Part of the answer to this question lies in research on *information feedback* and *self-justification processes.*

For the most part, energy technologies render the flow of energy in a household *invisible* to its residents. Consumers are therefore unaware of just where their fuel and money go. For most utility customers, the monthly bill is the only aspect of energy use that remains visible, and the bills frequently reflect only total energy usage—for all household appliances, lighting, and, often, water and space heating. This undifferentiated feedback information provided via utility bills makes awareness and understanding of patterns of energy use unlikely. Kempton and Montgomery (1982) provide a vivid analogue to the situation in which utility customers find themselves when they receive their utility bills at the end of the month. They ask people to imagine

> "a [grocery] store without prices on individual items, which presented only one total bill at the cash register. In such a store, the shopper would have to estimate item price by weight or packaging, by experimenting with different purchasing patterns, or by using consumer bulletins based on average prices" (p. 817).

The reader can easily visualize how frustrating it would be under those circumstances to devise an effective cost-cutting strategy. A similar situation holds for homeowners who must rely on the typical utility bill for information on how to best cut energy costs.

Given this state of affairs, it is not surprising that there is widespread misunderstanding of just what a household's biggest energy users are. For example, a Michigan household survey revealed that the typical homeowner erroneously believed that turning off unnecessary lighting would save twice as much money as using less hot water (Kempton, Harris, Keith, & Weihl, 1982). Why? In all probability because the energy used to heat water or to run a refrigerator is "invisible"—those appliances "run themselves"—while the energy used to provide lighting or run a television set is literally visible and under the energy user's control (Stern & Aronson, 1984).

One solution to the invisibility problem is to make patterns of energy use more salient to consumers. Researchers have typically utilized three methods to provide visible feedback on energy use patterns: installing devices that continuously monitor usage and provide digital readouts (e.g., cents per day in energy costs); providing consumers with daily or weekly readings of gas or electric meters; and providing a detailed, itemized list of energy expenditures on the monthly bill. Such feedback has been demonstrated to be effective (Shipee, 1980; Winett & Neale, 1979), especially when consumers (1) set quantifiable goals for reduced consumption, (2) understand the information, (3) receive frequent feedback, and (4) spend a large proportion of the household budget on energy. From the perspective of the current model, such feedback about energy-use patterns serves as a salient reminder to consumers that energy conservation efforts have paid off.

Cognitive dissonance theory predicts that once consumers have invested time, energy, and money to adopt energy technologies, they will be motivated to justify their effort—that is, they will work to rationalize their decision to conserve energy. Dissonance research has shown that once people have made a decision—especially a difficult one—they will focus on the positive aspects of the chosen alternative and devalue the positive aspects of the rejected alternative (Brehm, 1956; Darley & Berscheid, 1967). This self-justification process is most strong when commitment to the decision is costly and irrevocable (Axsom & Cooper, 1980; Knox & Inkster, 1986).

Similarly, once a person has made a small commitment to a given course of action, he or she is likely to make a larger commitment to a similar course of action in the future. In a now classic study, Freedman and Fraser (1966) found that people who agreed to sign a petition favoring safe driving and were subsequently asked to put an ugly sign advertising safe driving on their lawns were more likely to comply than a random sample of people who were not asked to sign the petition first. Similarly, Schwartz (1970) found that over half of his sample of college-students agreed to be on call as bone marrow donors—a highly painful prospect—*after* they had agreed to a series of escalating commitments. In the energy realm, small investments in energy-conserving technologies (e.g., caulking, weatherstripping) often "pave the way" for subsequent—and more costly—energy conservation behaviors (e.g., installing insulation). And as Michael Pallak and his colleagues have discovered, commitment—especially *public* commitment—is a powerful inducement to conserve energy. Pallak and Cummings (1976) found that people who volunteered to conserve energy were far more successful when they were informed that their names and intentions would appear in a newspaper article. Furthermore, people's efforts to conserve continued for at least a year after they were informed that the article would not be published (Pallak, Cook & Sullivan, 1980).

Unfortunately, the very same justification processes that reinforce conservation behaviors can also perpetuate inertia. As Stern and Aronson (1984) have pointed out, people who refuse to take action in response to energy conservation incentives are motivated to justify their decision *not* to act. For example, people who fail to take advantage of tax credits for the installation of solar devices may work to convince themselves—and others—that cloudy days render solar heating ineffective.

A Social Psychological Perspective on the Limits of Mass Media Appeals

As we mentioned previously, expensive mass market media appeals to "sell" conservation have met with mixed success at best. This is due in part to the fact that messages are often too vague, too uninteresting, or too complex for information to be understood, and to the fact that there is a long and complicated path from information to action. There is yet another reason why these efforts often fail to induce people to engage in conservation behaviors.

An advertising approach is premised on a view of energy conservation as a product to be bought and sold. In a vague sense, conservation is a product, but one that differs substantially from other products. Media advertising is most effective when the goal is to increase sales of products already purchased routinely by customers (e.g., toothpaste, detergent, food). An advertising campaign may be successful in converting consumers from one brand to another comparably priced brand, but these small changes in consumer behavior typically involve little expense or effort, and no dramatic alteration of life-style. Once customers are committed to buying a product, there are relatively few obstacles to inducing them to change brand loyalties.

The purchase and installation of an energy conservation device is another proposition. Target behaviors in conservation advertising are not routine, and they are costly in terms of time, effort, and money. It's as if consumers are asked not to switch brands of toothpaste, but to adopt toothbrushing as a brand-new behavior. So while there are few impediments to changing the brand of toothpaste or beer one purchases, there are a variety of obstacles confronting someone planning to adopt an energy-conserving device: lack of previous experience with the new technology, doubts about its proven efficiency, anxiety about the technical demands of installation and maintenance, and a tendency to postpone tasks outside the normal household routine. And although advertising appeals are used to market some new technologies—such as stereo televisions of personal computers—these products, unlike passive solar technology, are recreational or time-saving devices.

We have argued here and elsewhere (Costanzo *et al.*, 1984; Yates & Aronson, 1983) that although mass media advertising can be a useful tool for creating awareness, it is wasteful to invest our efforts and money on conservation strategies with such a low probability of success. Advertising is expensive. For example, it cost a California utility company more to promote an insulation program for low-income families than it would have to actually install the insulation in their homes (Pope, 1982). In addition, no matter how slick, funny, or interesting a media appeal "selling" conservation might be, there are too many obstacles—psychological and structural—that prevent members of the target audience from taking recommended actions.

It is important to note that there are "small-scale" exceptions to the limitations of widespread television advertising. For example, in one experiment, town house and apartment dwellers in Blacksburg, Virginia, viewed videotaped messages about energy-saving behavioral changes. After watching these messages, consumers *did* change energy-related habits and *did* save electricity used to heat and cool their homes (Winett *et al.*, 1982), especially when they were provided frequent feedback on energy consumption. More recently, Winett and his colleagues used a local television cable channel to provide residents of a Virginia subdivision with a 20-minute program about ways to reduce summer cooling bills. As in the previous study, the program was specifically tailored to the target audience—models were similar in age and similarly situated, for example. Moreover, the program was designed to capture and hold attention, and to describe and model desired conservation behaviors, possible obstacles, and solutions vividly and concretely. After seeing the program only once, a significant proportion of viewers adopted many of the conservation strategies modeled in the program, and reduced their energy use by 10% overall (Winett, Leckliter, Chinn, Stahl, & Love, 1985).

The above results hold promise for those who hope to improve the use of television to promote conservation. Commercial television already uses *social marketing* in new program development, *fast-paced formatting* to capture and hold attention during children's programming and many advertisements, and *models* of both prosocial and antisocial behaviors. In current mass market conservation advertising, the crucial "missing " ingredient seems to be the provision of concrete information. Many television advertisements are little more than simple exhortations to "save" energy. Television advertising needs to provide viewers with vivid examples of the "how-to's" of energy efficiency, and with a concrete description of obstacles and ways to circumvent them. Unfortunately, Winett and his colleagues (1985) have noted a number of structural impediments to widespread adoption of these programs by the national television medium.

An alternative approach views energy-conserving technologies not as products to be advertised, bought, and sold but as specific instances of *innovations*—like new medical treatments or agricultural methods.

Promoting Social Diffusion: A Promising Alternative

Social scientists have viewed the adoption of energy-conserving technologies as an instance of *social diffusion,* rather than an instance of attitude change or rational decision-making processes (e.g., Darley & Beniger, 1981). This conceptualization emphasizes the crucial role of social reference groups. That is, compared with nonpersonal sources of information, information transmitted via social diffusion processes has a more powerful impact on behavior. To return to the proposed model in Figure 1, there is every reason to believe that information received through interpersonal channels is more likely to be perceived, favorably evaluated, understood, and remembered than information from such impersonal channels as bill inserts, pamphlets, or television advertising. Moreover, because reference groups are composed of individuals who are similarly situated, receivers of interpersonal communications are in a better position to act on the information.

The decision to invest in energy-conserving technologies can be viewed as a specific case of a decision to adopt an innovation, and innovations typically are diffused via existing social networks. That is, most people decide to adopt an innovation only after its effectiveness has been demonstrated through the positive experiences of friends or acquaintances. What social influence processes are involved in the diffusion of innovations?

Especially in ambiguous situations, people tend evaluate their own behaviors by comparing themselves to similarly situated others (Suls & Miller, 1980). People in the process of making decisions about energy conservation strategies face a host of complicated and ambiguous concerns. For example, energy supplies and costs fluctuate unpredictably, and consumers are confronted with information and recommendations from a multitude of sources that vary in credibility. In the face of this complexity, people will rely heavily on information received from similar others when it comes time to make decisions related to the adoption of energy-conserving technological innovations.

There are a number of reasons why social networks are especially influential sources of information. First, as we mentioned earlier, information received via face-to-face contact is vivid and personal. Second, friends and acquaintances are more likely to be perceived as trustworthy than are impersonal sources, such as utility companies. Thus, because of the nature of information transmitted within social networks, people tend to assign disproportionate weight to interpersonal communications during the decision-making process. Third, social psychological research has long recognized the importance of imitation and modeling as a powerful influence on human behavior. The impact of modeling is greatest when a respected model engages in behavior that results in some form of reinforcement or payoff (Bandura, 1977). In the case of social networks, models are likely to be respected friends or colleagues, and these satisfied energy consumers are likely to make the rewards of their efforts apparent to others. Thus, social diffusion via networks provides not only for the dissemination of information but also for the modeling of desirable behavior.

The potent influence of modeling and imitation has been demonstrated by researchers studying energy-use behavior. Ester and Winett (1982) have shown that modeling energy-conserving behavior is more impactful than presenting information alone. Aronson and O'Leary (1982–1983) also conducted a small demonstration project on the importance of modeling for conservation behaviors. Briefly, they observed shower-taking behaviors in a university athletic field house. Introducing an obtrusive prompt into the men's shower room (a large sign in the middle of the room instructing users to tun off the water while soaping up) resulted in a compliance rate of 19% (compared with 6% in an unprompted control condition). When these researchers employed one student to model the appropriate behavior—turning off the water while soaping up—whenever another student entered the room, the number of people who performed the requested behavior rose to 49%. And when two people simultaneously modeled the proper behavior, compliance rates were higher still—67%.

In other domains, it has been demonstrated that social diffusion processes are preferable to traditional media appeals. For example, Nisbett and his colleagues (1976) cited the U.S. Agricultural Extension project as an illustration of the efficacy of a social diffusion approach. In the 1930s, the federal government attempted to promote the adoption of innovative agricultural equipment and practices. These initial efforts met with little success when pamphlets were used to disseminate information. Subsequent attempts to promote agricultural innovation were more successful when the government established a "demonstration project." Government consultants worked side by side with farmers on selected farms, and these trained farmers served as models for others nearby. When word spread about the positive results of the new program (e.g., an improved harvest), the techniques and equipment spread rapidly, and government efforts to make use of social diffusion processes proved a tremendous success.

Energy researchers Darley and Beniger (1981) have suggested such an approach to promote energy conservation. Government consultants would evaluate a home to determine which specific energy innovations make sense, determine the homeowner's base rate of energy use prior to the installation of those devices, and assist the homeowner with the installation of those simple innovations. Subsequent energy-use patterns would be monitored, and the savings resulting from the retrofits would serve as an inducement for the satisfied customer to undertake additional conservation measures. In addition, the satisfied homeowner would become a vivid, credible, and informative example for friends, colleagues, and acquaintances.

There is additional evidence that interpersonal sources are more potent than media appeals. Leonard-Barton (1981), for example, has found that the best predictor of people's intention to invest in solar devices is the number of friends who currently own such equipment. Moreover, adopters and nonadopters alike cited interpersonal sources of information as the most potent factors influencing their decisions. These results were echoed in our own research at the University of California (Archer *et al.*, 1976). Survey data indicated that the best predictor of solar equipment ownership was a personal (nonmedia) source of information. A vivid illustration of this phenomenon can be found by walking through any middle-class neighborhood. Solar collectors tend to "cluster" throughout the neighborhood—reflecting the social networks of residents who purchase and install solar heating devices. Finally, Darley (1978) found that the adoption of a newly developed clock thermostat diffused through existing social networks.

Thus, research on the social diffusion of advancing technologies has demonstrated the importance of interpersonal influence processes. Although media sources may be effective in generating awareness of technological options, *interpersonal* sources are far more influential in motivating people to adopt a new technology.

Improving the RCS Home Energy Audit Program: A Field Study

Among existing programs, the RCS Home Audit Program was the one that utilized face-to-face communications between energy "experts" and homeowners. Home energy auditors convey information about the benefits of various conservation measures directly to homeowners in their own homes. In a typical "Class A" home energy audit, for example, auditors arrive and inspect customers' homes for the presence of various conservation devices (e.g., caulking, weatherstripping, attic and wall insulation, water heater blankets, and low-flow showerheads). During the hour they spend with customers, auditors measure the dwelling, solicit information about energy-use habits and conservation devices, and provide specific energy conservation recommendations. But, as mentioned early in this article, the home audit program has been a flop—for example, in 1980, less than 6% of all eligible homeowners had requested an audit—and of those, a very small percentage actually followed the recommendations of the auditor (Hirst *et al.*, 1981; U.S. Department of Energy, 1984). If face-to-face communication is the best vehicle for transmitting information, why has the home energy audit program not been more effective?

Although auditors are well trained in assessing the energy efficiency of buildings, previous researchers paid little attention to *how* auditors communicate their findings and recommendations. Our guess, based on limited experience with our own home audits, is that most auditors were not communicating in a highly effective manner. What a golden opportunity for a group of social psychologists! If we were allowed to train auditors to communicate effectively (given the solid principles uncovered in our basic research labs), we could, perhaps, make a significant contribution to the RCS Home Energy Audit program.

But it wasn't easy. In order to train auditors we would need the cooperation of a major utility company. And over the years, our group had been openly critical of some of the programs and evaluation methodology of the major California utilities. Indeed, some of these criticisms were expressed in a formal report (Archer *et al.*, 1983) authorized by the California Public Utilities Commission. Since this commission oversees all the financial dealings of the California utility companies, and hundreds of millions of dollars were involved, it is perhaps understandable that our group was not exactly popular with the utility companies. Specifically, the utility companies were unresponsive to our request to work with them on their conservation campaigns. (We are not using the term *unresponsive* lightly; we could not get a reply to our letters nor were our telephone calls returned!) This proved to be very frustrating.

And then, once again, fate stepped in. One of us (E. A.) was interviewed in *Psychology Today*. In the course of the interview, he discussed his frustration at not being able to do the experiment that was crying to be done, and outlined the hypotheses and procedure. A ranking executive with Pacific Gas & Electric (California's largest utility) happened to read the article, and, thinking the research was important enough to bury old grievances, called and asked us to do the experiment (Gonzales, Aronson, & Costanzo, 1988).

Our first step was to train a sample of PG&E auditors to communicate in ways that we thought would be effective. Many of the principles we employed in the training have been discussed elsewhere in this chapter: information vividness, the personalization of statistical data, inducing commitment, and information framing. The following is a brief description of ways in which these principles were applied in the training procedure.

Vivid Information

Given the fact that the typical energy consumer is not a "rational" and "expert" processor of complex information (e.g., Kempton *et al.*, 1983; Kempton & Montgomery, 1982), there is every reason to believe that the provision of complicated statistical summaries of potential savings, payback periods, and the like, will be ineffective at inducing attitude and behavior change in homeowners. An alternative proposed by Yates and Aronson (1983) would be to use vivid case studies of friends or neighbors who saved more energy—and money—than average: nearby "superconservers." These portraits would include concrete examples of their conservation strategies and of the benefits that followed. Of course, "superconservers" are low-probability cases, but they serve as dramatic examples of actualized conservation potential—and exert a disproportionately powerful effect on the behavior of audit customers.

Research has shown that *language* that conjures up a vivid image is likely to capture and hold people's attention (Nisbett & Ross, 1980). For example, auditors frequently noted the absence of weatherstripping or attic insulation, and recommended their installation. Undoubtedly, some customers would comply; but for most, a small crack does not seem worth attending to—it is simply not compelling cognitive input. Our guess was that far more homeowners would be motivated to act in response to the following vivid description:

> "You know, if you were to add up all the cracks around and under these doors here, you'd have the equivalent of a hole the size of a basketball in your living room wall. Think for a moment about all the heat that would escape from a hole that size. That's why I recommend you install weather-stripping. . . . And your attic totally lacks insulation. We professionals call that a 'naked' attic. It's as if your home is facing winter not just without an overcoat, but without any clothing at all."

Psychologically, cracks around doors may be seen as minor, but a hole the size of a basketball feels disastrous. Similarly, insulation is something people don't often think about—but the idea of being naked in winter forces attention and increases the probability of action.

Of course, statistical summaries should not be entirely neglected. But the impact of these "generic" data can be enhanced if auditors make them personally relevant to the customers' current situation. Rather than leave homeowners with a boring computer summary of conservation strategies and the potential savings associated with them, auditors could be trained to tailor their presentations to customers' individual households—by using customers' own utility bills to illustrate current losses or potential savings, for example.

Commitment

The more *involved* the auditors can get homeowners in the nuts and bolts of the audit, the better. Auditors might ask homeowners to accompany them on their inspection tours, and enlist their aid in taking measurements or reading meters. Customers might even be induced to climb a ladder and peer into an uninsulated attic, bend down and measure cracks around and under doors, or place their hand on an uninsulated water heater. After this investment of time and energy, homeowners will be likely to see themselves as people concerned about, and committed to, energy conservation—assisting the auditor could serve as a foot-in-the-door (Freedman & Fraser, 1966) to more costly energy conservation behaviors. Auditors might also secure a *verbal commitment* from homeowners to make the recommended changes. For example, "When do you think you'll have the weather-stripping completed? . . . I'll give you a call around then, just to see how it's coming along, and to see if you're having any problems." These commitment procedures may seem inconsequential, but they can serve as an additional inducement for homeowners to complete energy-conserving retrofits.

Framing

The communication strategies of auditors with whom we worked did not differ markedly from those employed in the typical conservation campaign—that is, auditors focused their attempts at persuasion on the amount of energy or money homeowners would *save* after completing the recommended home improvements. Auditors might be more successful in motivating homeowners when they frame their recommendations in terms of energy and money *lost* via inertia rather than in terms of energy or money *gained* or *saved* once the retrofits are completed. For example, "It's like having a hole in your pocket" or "until you get the flu fixed, your hard-earned cash is flying right up the chimney."

We made such recommendations in two training workshops with PG&E auditors from four districts within the utility company's California service area. A total of 18 auditors participated in the study—9 in the experimental group and 9 in the control group. There were no systematic demographic or skill differences in the auditors in the two conditions prior to our intervention, nor were there systematic socioeconomic or demographic differences among the customers served by trained and untrained auditors.

Auditor training consisted of two 5-hour workshops 4 months apart, in which the above social psychological concepts and their potential applications to the home energy audit were discussed with the auditors. The primary dependent variable consisted of an excellent set of records—assembled PG&E—of retrofits actually performed. These records reflected the number of customers in each condition who completed applications for participation in the CASHBACK rebate and ZIPLOAN zero-interest loan retrofit finance programs. Because consumers could not apply for these highly beneficial programs until *after* they had completed the work, these records served as an invaluable *behavioral* measure of the success of our intervention.

As can be noted in Table 1, the results are striking. Combining across finance programs, over half again as many experimental as control customers followed through on requests for participation in one or another retrofit finance program (60.9% vs. 39.1%, respectively). The difference is highly significant ($p < .0001$). Moreover, the hit rate in the *control* condition is almost three times higher than the national average—and twice as high as the hit rate in that same group just a

Table 1. Number of Adult Recipients Who Actually Applied for PG&E Finance Programs

Finance program	Experimental group[a]		Control group[a]		
	N	%	N	%	
CASHBACK	75	37.1	44	21.8	$z = 3.383$[b]
ZIPLOAN	48	23.8	35	17.3	$z = 1.599$
CASHBACK or ZIPLOAN	123	60.9	79	39.1	$z = 4.377$[c]

[a]Experimental group $N = 202$, control group $N = 202$.
[b]$p < .001$.
[c]$p < .0001$.

few months earlier. While these differences could be due to one or more of several possibilities, one powerful possibility is that there was some leakage of recommendations from auditors in the experimental condition to those in the control condition—districts from which auditors were selected differed markedly in the opportunities afforded auditors to interact with one another "informally" outside the work setting. Of course, it would be idle to make too much of this; it is simply worth noting that the 60% compliance rate is not only significantly greater than the rate in the control condition, it is gigantic when compared with the national average.

The Rocky Road from Data to Policy

The results can be considered a triumph for social psychology. Here was a successful application of well-established social psychological principles to a complex and difficult area. An expensive program that had been foundering for years was made to work well with a simple and inexpensive addition to the auditor training program. Unfortunately, our sense of triumph was short-lived. For it turned out that although the operation was a great success, the patient died. The ink was hardly dry on our final report to PG&E when the utility began dismantling the home energy audit program! It appears that on the basis of several years of failure, the decision to dismantle the program had been made months earlier at corporate headquarters.

If there is a moral buried in there somewhere, it is this: The inroads of social psychology into public policy are neither wide nor deep. This means that in general, policymakers are not accustomed to thinking of social psychologists when they need help in designing and implementing their programs. Thus, in the present case, by the time the social psychologists entered, the death rattle of the program was already being heard. Is there anything we might do to contribute to the possible widening and deepening of policymakers' awareness of our existence and potential usefulness? Our usual strategy is simply to publish our findings in traditional mainstream journals, sit back, and possibly hope that our "triumphs" eventually will be noticed by people who make policy. But publishing in traditional mainstream journals guarantees, at best, only that our stuff will get read by a few traditional mainstream social psychologists. This is not good enough; although it goes against the grain for most research psychologists, we may need to become more assertive in advertising and targeting our usefulness. If social psychologists are to be effective in informing policy, they must not hesitate to do the additional work of getting their data into the view of people who make decisions. The first step might be as simple as discovering the journals that policymakers read and trying to write for those journals. In this case, we have taken this first step by submitting our findings to a home energy trade journal. We did this with the realization that, while it was PG&E that invited us to do the research, they are not the only game in town. There are other utilities that are still struggling to make the home energy audit program work. Our hope is that by targeting our findings, we not only can have an impact on the effectiveness of energy policy but can also enhance the image policymakers hold of social psychology and its potential usefulness.

ACKNOWLEDGMENT. Research for this paper was underwritten by a grant from California's Universitywide Energy Conservation Research Group. (UERG) to Elliot Aronson.

References

Ajzen, I., & Fishbein, M. (1977). Attitude-behavior relations: A theoretical analysis and review of empirical research. *Psychological Bulletin, 84,* 888–918.

Archer, D., Aronson, E., & Pettigrew, T. F. (1983). *An evaluation of the energy conservation research of California's major utility companies, 1977–1980* (Report to the California Public Utilities Commission). Santa Cruz, CA: University of California, Stevenson College, Energy Conservation Research Group.

Archer, D., Pettigrew T., Costanzo, M., Iritani, B., Walker, I., & White, L. (1987). Energy conservation and public policy: The mediation of individual behavior. In W. Kempton & M. Meiman (Eds.), *Energy efficiency: perspectives on individual behavior.* Washington, D.C: ACEEE.

Aronson, E., & O'Leary, M. (1982–1983). The relative effects of models and prompts on energy conservation. *Journal of Environmental Systems, 12,* 219–224.

Aronson, E., Turner, J. A., & Carlsmith, M. (1963). Communicator credibility and communication discrepancy as determinants of opinion change. *Journal of Abnormal and Social Psychology, 67,* 31–36.

Axsom, D., & Cooper, J. (1980). Reducing weight by reducing dissonance: The role of effort justification in inducing weight loss. In E. Aronson (Ed.), *Readings about the social animal* (3rd ed., pp. 164–177). San Francisco: Freeman.

Bandura, A. (1977). *Social learning theory.* Englewood Cliffs, NJ: Prentice-Hall.

Borgida, E., & Nisbett, R. (1977) The differential impact of abstract vs. concrete information on decision. *Journal of Applied Social Psychology, 7,* 258–271.

Brehm, J. W. (1956). Post decision changes in the desirability of alternatives. *Journal of Abnormal and Social Psychology, 52,* 384–389.

Bruner, R. D., & Vivian, W. E. (1979, July). *Citizen viewpoints on energy policy.* Ann Arbor, MI: University of Michigan, Institute of Public Policy Research.

Condelli, L., Archer, D., Aronson, E., Curbow, B., McLeod, B., Pettigrew, T. F., White, L. W., & Yates, S. (1984). Improving utility conservation programs: Outcomes, interventions, and evaluations. *Energy, 9,* 485–494.

Costanzo, M., Archer, D., Aronson, E., & Pettigrew, T. (1986). Energy conservation behavior: The difficult path from information to action. *American Psychologist, 41.* 521–528.

Craig, C. S., & McCann, J. M. (1978). Assessing communication effects on energy conservation. *Journal of Consumer Research, 5,* 82–88.

Darley, J. (1978). Energy conservation techniques as innovations and their diffusion. *Energy and Buildings, 1,* 339–343.

Darley, J., & Beniger, J. R. (1981). Diffusion of energy-conserving innovations. *Journal of Social Issues, 37(2),* 150–171.

Darley, J., & Berscheid, E. (1967). Increased liking as a result of the anticipation of personal contact. *Human Relations, 20,* 29–40.

Ester, P., & Winett, R. A. (1982). Toward more effective antecedent strategies for environmental programs. *Journal of Environmental Systems, 11,* 201–221.

Freedman, J. & Fraser, S. (1966). Compliance without pressure: The foot-in-the-door technique. *Journal of Personality and Social Psychology, 4,* 195–202.

Gonzales, M. H., Aronson, E., & Costanzo, M. (1988). Using social cognition and persuasion to promote energy conservation: A quasi-experiment. *Journal of Applied Social Psychology, 18,*(12), 1049–1066.

Hamill, R., Wilson, T. D., & Nisbett, R. (1980). Insensitivity to sample bias: Generalizing from a typical case. *Journal of Personality and Social Psychology, 39*(4), 578– 589.

Hershey, R. D., Jr. (1982). The dark side of the oil glut. *New York Times,* March 21.

Hirst, E., Berry, L., & Soderstrom, J. (1981). Review of utility home energy audit programs. *Energy, 6,* 621–630.

Hovland, C., Janis, I., & Kelley, H. (1953). *Communication and persuasion.* New Haven, CT: Yale University Press.

Kahneman, D., Slovic, P., & Tverksy, A. (Eds.). (1982). *Judgment under uncertainty: Heuristics and biases.* Cambridge: Cambridge University Press.

Kahneman, D., & Tversky, A. (1979). A prospect theory: An analysis of decision under risk. *Econometrica, 47,* 263–291.

Kempton, W., Gladhart, P., & O'Keefe, D. (1983). Home insulation: The user's view. In S. A. Goran, D. M. Greason, & J. D. McAllister (Eds.), *Thermal insulation, materials, and systems for energy conservation in the 1980's* (pp. 117–137). Philadelphia: American Society for Testing and Materials.

Kempton, W., Harris, C. K., Keith J. G., & Weihl, J. S. (1982, August). *Do consumers know "what works" in energy conservation?* Paper presented at the meeting of the American Council for an Energy-Efficient Economy, Santa Cruz, CA.

Kempton, W., & Montgomery, L. (1982). Folk quantification of energy. *Energy, 7,* 817–827.

Knox, R., & Inkster, J. (1968). Post decision dissonance at post time. *Journal of Personality and Social Psychology, 8,* 319–323.

Leonard-Barton, D. (1981). The diffusion of active residential solar energy equipment in California. In A. Shama (Ed.), *Marketing solar energy innovations* (pp. 243–257). New York: Praeger.

Martin, D. (1982). Energy shortage eases materially; basic shifts in consumption cited. *New York Times,* March 8, pp. A1, D20.

McGuire, W. J. (1985). Attitudes and attitude change. In G. Lindzey & E. Aronson (Eds.), *Handbook of social psychology* (pp. 223–246). New York: Random House.

Milstein, J. S. (1978, March). *Soft and hard energy paths: What people on the street think* (Unpublished report). Washington, D.C.: U.S. Department of Energy, Office of Conservation and Solar Applications.

Newman, D. K., & Day, D. (1975). *The American energy consumer.* Cambridge MA: Ballinger.

Nisbett, R., Borgida, E., Crandall, R., & Reed, H. (1976). Popular induction: Information is not necessarily informative. In J. S. Carroll & J. W. Payne (Eds.), *Cognition and social behavior* (pp.47–64). Hillsdale, NJ: Erlbaum.

Nisbett, R., & Ross, L. (1980). *Human inference: Strategies and shortcomings of social judgment.* Englewood Cliffs, NJ: Prentice-Hall.

Norman, D. A. (1976). *Memory and attention.* New York: Wiley.

Olsen, M. E. (1981). Consumers' attitudes toward energy conservation. *Journal of Social Issues, 37*(2), 108–131.

Pallak, M. S., Cook, D. A., & Sullivan, J. J. (1980). Commitment and energy conservation. In L. Bickman (Ed.), *Applied social psychology annual* (Vol. 1, pp. 235–254). Beverly Hills, CA: Sage.

Pallak, M. S., & Cummings, W. (1976). Commitment and voluntary energy conservation. *Personality and Social Psychology Bulletin, 2,* 27–30.

Peck, A. E., & Doering, O. C. (1976). Voluntarism and price response: Consumer reactions to the energy shortage. *Bell Journal of Economics, 7,* 287–292.

Pope, E. (1982). PG&E's loans aimed at poor miss the mark. *San Jose Mercury,* December 10, p. 6B.

Ross, M. H., & Williams, R. H. (1976). Energy efficiency: Our most underrated energy resources. *Bulletin of the Atomic Scientists,* November, 30–38.

Schwartz, S. H. (1970). Elicitation of moral obligation and self-sacrificing behavior: An experimental study of volunteering to be a bone marrow donor. *Journal of Personality and Social Psychology, 15,* 283–293.

Shipee, G. (1980). Energy consumption and conservation psychology: A review and conceptual analysis. *Environmental Management, 4,* 297–314.

Sinden, F. W. (1978). A two-thirds reduction in the space heat requirement of a Twin Rivers townhouse. *Energy and Buildings, 1,* 243–260.

Stern, P. C., & Aronson, E. (Eds.). (1984). *Energy use: The human dimension.* New York: Freeman.

Stobaugh, R., & Yergin, D. (Eds.). (1979). *Energy future: Report of the energy project at the Harvard Business School.* New York: Random House.

Suls, J. M., & Miller, R. I. (1980). *Social comparison processes: Theoretical and empirical perspectives.* New York: Wiley.

U.S. Department of Energy. (1984). *Residential conservation service evaluation report* (Hearings before the Committee on Energy and Natural Resources of the United States Senate, Ninety-eighth Congress). Washington, DC: U.S. Government Printing Office.

White, L., Archer, D., Aronson, E., Condelli, L., Curbow, B., McLeod, B., Pettigrew, T., & Yates, S. (1984). Energy conservation research at California's utilities: A meta-evaluation. *Evaluation Review, 8,* 167–186.

Williams, R. H., & Ross, M. H. (1980). Drilling for oil and gas in our houses. *Technology Review, March–April,* 24–36.

Winett, R. A., Hatcher, J. W., Fort, T. R., Leckliter, I. N., Love, S. Q., Riley, A. W., & Fishback, J. F. (1982). The effects of videotape modeling and daily feedback on residential electricity conservation, home temperature and humidity, perceived comfort, and clothing worn: Winter and summer. *Journal of Applied Behavior Analysis, 15,* 381–402.

Winett, R. A., Leckliter, I. N., Chinn, d. E., Stahl, B., & Love, S. Q. (1985). Effects of television modeling on residential energy conservation. *Journal of Applied Behavior Analysis, 18,* 33–44.

Winett, R. A., & Neale, N. S. (1979). Psychological framework for energy conservation in buildings: Strategies, outcomes, directions. *Energy and Buildings, 2,* 101–116.

Yates, S., & Aronson, E. (1983). A social-psychological perspective on energy conservation. *American Psychologist, 38,* 435–444.

Yergin, D. (179). Conservation: The key energy source. In R. Stobaugh & D. Yergin (Eds.), *Energy future: Report of the energy project at the Harvard Business School.* New York: Random House.

14

Public Policy and Applied Social Psychology

Bridging the Gap

Michael S. Pallak

Public policy, social issues, the field of social psychology in general, and the specialized domain of social influence processes particularly can be seen as interrelated in several ways. First, the policies carried out by governments and other major social institutions obviously represent one source of social influence on attitudes and behaviors related to social problems. Indeed, a main purpose of many policies is to cope with the problems of society and, in some cases, even prevent them.

Second, public policy clearly matters to social psychology. From a strictly guild perspective, the field depends upon research and training support that constitute outcomes determined by the processes of public policy. As we have seen during several federal administrations, the extent and thrust of social psychological knowledge may be sharply limited or distorted by policy decisions. Forming a more productive relationship with policymakers thus presents a challenge to applied social psychology.

Third, although its impact may seem rather indirect, social psychology matters to the formation of public policy. Or, at least many of us believe that it ought to. There are few problems facing society that do no include issues of human behavior. As a research, application, and education community, social psychology offers a knowledge base and perspective about human behavior that is a potential national resource for tackling complex human problems at the individual, group, organizational, and societal levels. The contributions in this volume clearly dem-

Michael S. Pallak • American Biodyne Research Corp., South San Francisco, California 94080.

onstrate the usefulness of a social psychological perspective, especially involving processes of social influence, when brought to bear on specific problems.

Finally, social psychological knowledge about influence and related processes may be useful in enhancing the impact of social research on agenda setting and policy making. That is, the establishment of priorities and ways of dealing with them can be seen as a "problem" that may be amenable to social influence attempts. Making such attempts, however, requires an understanding of the policy milieu. It is hoped that the observations and experiences conveyed in this chapter will contribute to that understanding.

Translating Knowledge into Policy

While social psychology continues a strong tradition of theoretical and experimental research, it seems clear that the field has also continued a strong problem-oriented tradition coupled with a concern for application within a broader public arena. For example, about 10 years ago, Bickman (1980) observed that "If social psychologists are going to have the impact that their findings often deserve, then they must reach out beyond their own scientific community to make their findings available. We can expect that as the field of applied social psychology matures, we will move from conducting socially relevant but descriptive research, to the development and implementation of social programs that are designed to impact directly on social problems" (p. 17). It is in this spirit that the present chapter stresses the need to move from research on social processes to the translation of findings and active communication of them to governmental and other policymakers.

In order to bridge from our core efforts in the research arena to social problems and programs, the field of social psychology will need a more consistent and better-developed focus on public policy. Part of the sharper focus would include attention to the process of translating our knowledge base into the culture and milieu of the public policy arena and, simultaneously, into specific programs. Further, as a field, we will need to attend to the effects or outcomes of those programs upon people, and be prepared to play a systematic role in reconfiguring those programs for increased effectiveness.

Translating our knowledge base into forms usable by policymakers first entails recognizing that governmental administrations vary in the priority they place on confronting social problems. Regardless of the world-views of particular national administrations, it seems clear that the mentally ill, the poorly educated, the homeless, and other disadvantaged groups in our society do not simply "go away." Their problems are either passed among different components of society (e.g., from the schools to the juvenile justice system) or passed on to succeeding generations (e.g., abused children become likely child abusers as adults). As a nation, we have not done a very good job in counting or acknowledging the cost of such problems to society as a whole and to society in the future. Furthermore, as the chapters in the present volume suggest, we could do better in reducing those costs if the national agenda placed greater emphasis on problem prevention.

The Policy Process

Regardless of the *goals* of particular national administrations, the public policy *process* involved in seeking to achieve those goals remains similar over time. Ironically, perhaps, from the perspective of an academic-based researcher, the policy-formation process functionally involves the familiar persuasion, attitude change, decision-making, and compromise phenomena that social psychology has delineated substantively. The chapters in this volume demonstrate how fully this delineation has thus far progressed. As a field of study, therefore, we do have some implicit understanding of the public policy process, although the cultures of social psychology and public policy are fundamentally distinct. To the extent that we wish to have our perspective utilized in national discussions in a socially responsible fashion, we need to understand how policymakers see social problems such as health and safety, crime, education, prejudice, and resource conservation, and we need to know how the policy process operates. Indeed, it is a truism attributable to the nature of the policy process that unless we take the lead in bridging the gap between the knowledge base and program application, no one else will.

Developing effectiveness in the public policy arena implies having an understanding of how the players view issues. For example, despite our substantive knowledge (e.g., about persuasion, decision making, bargaining), there are fundamental differences in perspective and orientation between social psychologists as researchers and the world of public policy. In the policy and political world, research is secondary and useful only to the extent that it justifies, fits with, or advances the policymaker's established and continuing agenda of goals. (See, for example, the discussion by Aronson and Gonzales in this volume.)

In contrast, our orientation as researchers is one of "let's see what the research data suggest" and then evolve an agenda accordingly. Public policy is rarely research-driven; rather the agendas and motivations of policymakers determine whether, and which, research may be considered. In short, the policy arena selectively utilizes research that is consistent with a particular agenda in contrast to our orientation toward consideration of data in the process of forming an agenda. Thus, getting to a point of involvement with application to social programs implies more routine interaction with the policy and political process. Our expertise won't be utilized unless we shape or translate that expertise in ways that are seen as consistent with various agendas.

Making effective contact with the public policy arena implies our willingness to become involved with the legislative and executive branches, service delivery programs, and the media in terms of shaping public opinion (cf. Pallak & Kilburg, 1986). Each of these components may be viewed in terms of the agendas, assumptions (implicit and explicit), and perspectives that move the policy process along. Each may be viewed in terms of the opportunities for, and barriers to, the process of translating our knowledge base into effective and socially responsible social service delivery programs.

There are a variety of ways to characterize the public policy process. At the risk of seeming to convey a cynical view, the core agenda across the above three components typically comes down to answering two questions: (1) Who receives public funds? (2) For what goods and services? The "missing question" in public policy is the third question: With what effect and outcome? The missing question represents one avenue for long-term impact by the field of applied social psychology as it raises a concern for evidence demonstrating program effectiveness.

The answers to the first two questions are expressed annually in a series of congressional votes on appropriations amounting to more than a trillion dollars in expenditures (in fact more is involved in "off-budget" accounts, trust funds, and commitments to "out-year" expenditures). The federal budget represents the enactment of compromise among large numbers of often conflicting advocates with agendas and priorities that include future elections, constituency pressures, and perceptions of public opinion. While the size of the federal budget is a little bewildering, it is important to emphasize that the compromise and political process involved are understandable in terms of social psychological processes.

The "missing question" of outcomes or effects of the funds allocated by the policy process rarely surfaces because the answers may threaten a *status quo* or a compromise worked out on the one hand, and, on the other, because the answers may take substantial investments of resources and of time (during which the cast of actors and agendas may have shifted toward other priorities). In order to illustrate the role of governmental priorities in affecting the impact of social science on the policy process, it is enlightening to consider some actions of the recent Reagan administration.

Lessons from the Reagan Onslaught

The First Lesson: Organized Efforts

It has been a pleasure to read the contributions in this volume and in other SPSSI-sponsored volumes on applied social psychology. For the most part, such research would not have been supported under the conditions intended by the Reagan administration in 1981. The "Reagan onslaught" upon the social sciences proved to be a major turning point for many individual psychologists in how they viewed "public policy" involvement. It was also a turning point in how organized psychology operated on our behalf in terms of public policy.

The 1981 budget message stated that "support of the behavioral, social, and economic sciences is being reduced significantly because much of the support of those sciences is considered of relatively lesser importance to the economy than support of the natural sciences" (Executive Office of the President, 1981). The proposed Reagan budget reflected major funding cuts in research support within a large number of federal agencies that had traditionally provided support for psychology. Those budget lines that were not completely zeroed out were sharply reduced and scheduled for further reductions in the following years.

The budget explanation clearly reflected negative attitudes about social science that have never been greatly submerged beneath the surface of public opinion and belief. Recall that several of our colleagues had been singled out to receive "Golden Fleece" awards only a few years earlier. Indeed, my own sense of outrage about the awards coupled with the accurate perception that APA had been ineffectual in meeting the issue, led in part to my decision to join the APA Central Office.

The steps that we took on behalf of the science and the field during my tenure as executive officer included a major expansion and reconfiguration of APA efforts directed toward each of the public policy components noted above. These efforts, detailed elsewhere (cf. Pallak, 1984, 1985; Pallak & Kilburg, 1986; Pallak & VandenBos, 1984), were built upon what we know as a field about social processes, persuasion, and attitude change. By August 1981 the U.S. House of Representatives had voted (272 to 163) to restore substantial proportions of the cuts intended, for example, in the NSF research budget for social science and for psychology.

The House vote was an important strategic as well as tactical outcome for us. For the first time, through our collective efforts, a substantial number of members of the Congress went on public record in providing an extensive array of examples of our contributions to an understanding and amelioration of important problems. It was an important step also in that organized psychology came to realize that routine involvement in public policy was critical for the continued development of the field. Finally, our efforts provided a paradigm for the field in approaching public policy issues and in bridging some of the distance between the research world and the public policy arena.

One of the lessons learned involved a distinction between *ad hoc* efforts on the part of individuals and systematic efforts organized and coordinated across individuals and across years. Individual interactions with policymakers are important. However, the effect of one individual writing a letter (however thoughtful) on an issue is diluted by the thousands of letters on myriad issues handled in even one congressional office or one agency director's office. Just as we look for patterns in our everyday lives, policymakers also look for patterns in expressions of concern about an issue. Thus, expressions and comment by psychologists are effective when representing a consensus of large numbers of individuals or when expressed by large numbers of individuals consistently over time. Individual *ad hoc* efforts alone do not provide continuity of expression and information necessary to develop a pattern of ongoing attention to the particular point of view.

While a number of our colleagues as individuals have been involved in public policy from time to time, it has only been since 1981 that one can point to organized, staffed, well-funded, and well-coordinated mechanisms at the APA. Organized efforts with long-term as well as short-term goals are critical for producing impact. Since the process of change in public policy on any given topic is slow and incremental (and not research-driven), change is produced by consistent efforts and by an organized or institutionalized base that does not shift radically depending upon individuals involved.

Organized efforts are also needed because of other sources of inertia (and resistance to change) inherent in the public policy process. For example, whether at the legislative or the executive (i.e., agency) levels of public policy, line items in an agency budget are relatively constrained from one year to the next. Thus, normally, it is relatively difficult to shift line item funds upward (or downward) within a 1-year or 2-year span. Each agency is constrained within the limits imposed by the next administrative unit above and by specific appropriations. Likewise, normally, new initiatives need relatively long lead times to generate support and approval within an agency and need to be approved and forecast within an overall plan and set of budget goals.

There are exceptions, of course, involving issues that capture public, executive, or congressional attention. Social programs may be enacted or reduced depending upon public opinion, the ideological commitments of dominant players in the policy arena, and the perception of what will or won't be endorsed by the public. For example, the Reagan onslaught upon social science was effective in part because the motivation sprang from an obvious ideological agenda that traditionally has been anti-social science. Similarly, that agenda captured the public's latent negative attitudes. In addition, the Office of Management and the Budget (OMB) took control of the usual budget process and handed down specific line item cuts to the agencies involved. At the same time, we (social science, psychology, social psychology) had never been well organized or visibly involved in public policy issues, nor had we paid much attention to public attitudes about social science. Thus, it was not surprising that the social science community was ill-prepared for the specific budget cuts proposed and sent up to the Congress.

The Second Lesson: "Chipping Away" at Issues

We also learned the strategy of chipping away at issues. "Chipping away" means the patient and repeated articulation of a consistent set of themes or perspectives within both congressional and agency offices. As part of the response to the proposed budget cuts we wrote testimony, lined up witnesses and panels of witnesses, developed new opportunities to testify, developed opportunities to brief congressional members and congressional staff, and systematically explored the agendas of public policy officials. As part of the crisis management process we elicited the core issues of members and their staffs and systematically discussed how social science and social psychology could assist with those issues. We provided a variety of information, expert analysis, and expert advice. We also learned the importance of routine and ongoing interaction and problem-solving assistance and the value of facilitating contact between the congressional office and constituents involved in psychology and social psychological research and application.

The chipping away strategy was an iterative process of talking to policymakers about the problems as seen from their perspective, digesting that information, recasting those perceptions in terms of our knowledge base, and then "translating" back into the policy arena. In parallel we developed contacts both at the agency level(s) and at the legislative level(s), thus enabling fuller understanding of the various facets of problems and often forming an informal channel of information. By developing such a pattern of interaction we were able to play a more proactive role in shaping some initiatives over time.

Such an approach fosters the development of attention and perspective within the policy arena. Our impact increased over time as we became both a credible and a familiar presence in the policy arena. Policymakers, just as we ourselves, are most likely to be influenced by those who are familiar, credible, and sensitive to the policymakers' agendas and interests when providing information, advice, and perspective. Within an organized approach, frequent contact and continuity of themes let us work around several barriers and helped develop support from several otherwise unexpected sources (e.g., Senator William Proxmire was very helpful in tackling issues of training support for psychology within the NIMH).

Having recognized that we (social psychology, psychology) were not major actors in the immediate arena of policy issues within Congress, we developed expertise in understanding the directions and motivations underlying specific issues. In the process we were able to illuminate advantages, disadvantages, and alternative outcomes, and to suggest alternative courses of action. Most important, the cumulative effect resulted in our being consulted in advance regarding developing issues, thus adding substantially to our ability to have impact.

At the risk of redundancy, it is important to realize that each social program budget results, in some fashion, from the representations, pressure, and advocacy of groups that have a stake in that particular line item. While "advocacy" within a research-oriented agency may be less obvious to many of us (at least relative to the publicity surrounding social program advocacy), our discussions with agency staff are just as important in building a base for social science and for social psychology as are the efforts at the congressional level of the policy process. As has been shown in research on the influencing powers of numerical minorities, if we are not present and consistent over time in explaining our perspectives as a field, then the clamor of other interests and other agendas will militate against support for social science and against the inclusion of our perspectives in national discussions. If we do not persist with consistent and credible action, we will not be seen as serious in our efforts (and will be ineffective in bridging the gap) to play a socially responsible role in public policy. This would be ironic in light of our substantive understanding of persuasion, compromise, and other social influence processes.

As a field, organized psychology has made a significant investment in the translation process and should be able to continue an expanded array of efforts.

For example, a number of psychologists serve on various agency review and advisory panels, National Research Council committees, SPSSI committees, division committees, and APA committees that have some focus on public policy. In addition, we have numbers of colleagues who hold career positions within various federal agencies, consulting organizations, and congressional staff groups. In one sense, each of these entities can be viewed at attempting to provide analysis of research as well as evaluation of alternatives for relatively specific problems, such as those considered.in this volume. In particular, each of these institutional groups plays an important role in the longer term in shaping priorities and emphases for funding within agencies (e.g., NSF, NIMH, NIA, NHLBI, NIDA, NIAA) that result in increased opportunity for behavioral science funding and long-term impact. Over time, our collective judgments and advice do enter the policy-related milieu, often a budget and appropriation justifications forwarded by the agency or institute director upward through the executive branch to the Congress.

Similarly, an increased (although small in some absolute sense) number of our colleagues provide formal testimony to congressional committees and subcommittees, as part of the ongoing hearings process. In addition, less formal opportunities are provided by briefings in which colleagues present information to committee members and staff (e.g., departmental chairpersons now routinely visit members of both the House and Senate).

The responses that we provide in this step of the policy process ar important but are often within an implicitly restricted framework of questions and topics. Thus, our efforts are designed to justify, as well as to educate about, small changes in an initiative within an agency budget, or within the purview of a particular subcommittee (e.g., an increase of a few million dollars for research on topic "X" or increased training support in area "Y").

The opportunity to provide testimony (and, even better in terms of the implications, to be asked to provide testimony) plays an important justificatory role, but it alone rarely provides the basis for something new or for major expansions. However, if advice to institutes and congressional testimony don't provide the opportunity to inject sweeping new ideas on the spot, they do provide an important step that helps shape perspectives. For example, a behavioral science perspective has emerged with regard to aging, health, and mental health within agencies that were narowly biomedical in orientation only 10 years ago. Similarly, a behavioral science perspective has become more salient, legitimate, and credible as a result of various reports from the National Academy of Science, the National Research Council, the Institute of Medicine, and the American Psychological Association concerning topics of aging, health, mental health, victims of crime, status of women, and similar subjects.

Each of the functions (translation, testimony), sketched above provide an ongoing source of advice in the form of reasonable scientific consensus regarding problem definition, alternative solutions, and steps to meet the problem. More publicly visible opportunities and crystallized consensus may emerge when Congress directs an agency to provide a report on a specific topic and/or appropriates funds for such an activity by an agency. Various executive branch commissions play a role in highlighting specific topics, and in drawing public attention to these topics. To the extent that an organized presence has been established (e.g., the APA) and actively interacts with the executive branch, we have opportunities to ensure behavioral science expertise and perspective through the presence of specific individuals on those commissions and on the commission staff.

These examples represent components of a process by which the implications of research and a research-oriented perspective may be translated into a form that is usable by key entities in the public policy process. The critical element in "chipping away" involves developing effective mechanisms for translating or bridging between the world of research within social psychology and the world that makes policy and establishes or removes social programs.

Public Policy Themes and Action Plans

The *de factor* strategy of organized effort implies a well-worked-out set of themes that guide our approach to policymakers. The development of a consistent approach to policy issues should involve periodic review and discussion within our field and some attention to whether the perspective discussed with Agency "X" is consistent and/or facilitates approaches with Agency "Y."

In all candor, the field needs to devote some more formal recognition to public policy themes, topics, and approaches. It is rare to see attention devoted to developing or crystallizing advice and perspective about policy issues or about social programs. As a field we should develop specific mechanisms (e.g., within SPSSI) for providing policy-oriented analyses or to ensure that those mechanisms in place (e.g., the APA) do so on an ongoing basis.

It should not be difficult to harness the structures that now exist within the APA or SPSSI to develop a series of targeted "white papers" that focus upon a specific topic. A first step is to find those individuals in the public policy arena with an interest in that issue (e.g., illiteracy, adolescent suicide) and to ask them what information/analysis would be helpful from their perspective(s). In addition to synthesizing the literature in a "state of the art" format (which many policy-related groups do), our white paper efforts can take advantage of our colleagues with public policy experience in crafting the analysis in terms of what is legislatively possible now and in the future.

In order to fulfill some of the hope expressed by Bickman (1980), we need to orient our efforts more toward the end user in the translating process rather than to ourselves, while ensuring the research credibility of the product—an orientation that partly plays the role of policy staff for the legislator or administrator. More important, by coordinating with other groups and by embedding the issue and the analysis/recommendations more directly in the public policy process, we increase the probability that our expertise has impact in a social responsible fashion. Just as the authors of chapters in this volume have applied their knowledge of social influence processes to diverse social issues, so can we as a field apply that same knowledge to the challenge of influencing public policy.

The field could also devote attention to public policy issues that focus on social program development and implementation. To the extent that we are motivated along the liens expressed by Bickman (1980), then we should be prepared to encourage a broader set of activities within our graduate and academic programs. On the one hand, we should include training experiences that include policy-analytic experience (e.g., what alternatives exist regarding mental health services and what are the outcomes of each?) as well policy-related research experience. On the other, we should be willing to encourage faculty to take advantage of 1- or 2-year fellowship opportunities to spend career time in the public policy milieu and to return to the departmental setting. As we expand the number of people with hands-on public policy experience, we enlarge the array of training experiences and intellectual perspectives available to our graduate students and to our colleagues.

Of course, as a field and as a system, we do provide various opportunities for disseminating policy-related and applied research, often in our journals and in our convention meetings. However, recognizing that affecting public policy requires additional steps on a systematic basis, we can also ask whether our research is pulled together in a coherent perspective and translated effectively for use by policymakers. If we as members of various organizations ostensibly with that mission fail to ask that question, who will? Framing the issue of "translation" in this fashion is essentially asking ourselves about the outcomes of our collective efforts and whether our current approaches are effective.

The foregoing is a brief sketch regarding some of the complexities of involvement in public policy. It is not intended to be exhaustive but rather to convey some sense of the flavor and perspective of the process. On the one hand, we need to maintain our commitment to effective social programs, perhaps especially those emphasizing prevention as presented in this volume, by continuing to develop a social science perspective in the policy arena. The latter goal involves a recognition both of the complexities and of the need for organized formal efforts within the field, guided, at least in part, by knowledge of social influence strategies. Similarly, effective public policy involvement also implies an expansion of perspectives and recognition within the field of social psychology that public policy involvement adds to the richness and diversity of the intellectual experience within our training and departmental systems.

References

Bickman, L. (1980). Introduction to the Applied Social Psychology Series. In L. Bickman (Ed.), *Applied social psychology annual (Vol. 1)*. Beverly Hills: Sage.

Executive Office of the President and OMB. (1981, April). *Additional details on budget savings: Fiscal Year 1982 budget revisions*. Washington DC: US Government Printing Office.

Pallak, M. S. (1984). Report of the executive officer, 1983. *American Psychologist, 39*, 591–595.

Pallak, M. S. (1985). Report of the executive officer, 1984. *American Psychologist, 40,* 605–612.

Pallak, M. S., & Kilburg, R. R. (1986). Psychology, public affairs, and public policy. *Amerian Psychologist, 41,* 933–940.

Pallak, M. S., & VandenBos, G. R. (1984). Employment of psychologists in the USA: Responses to the crisis of the 1970s. *Journal of the Norwegian Psychological Association, 21,* 65–73.

Index